New Perspectives on

Microsoft® Windows Vista™

Introductory

June Jamrich Parsons
Dan Oja

Joan & Patrick Carey
Carey Associates

Lisa Ruffolo

THOMSON
COURSE TECHNOLOGY

Australia • Canada • Mexico • Singapore • Spain • United Kingdom • United States

THOMSON

COURSE TECHNOLOGY

New Perspectives on Microsoft Windows Vista—Introductory

is published by Thomson Course Technology.

Acquisitions Editor:
Kristina Matthews

Senior Product Manager:
Kathy Finnegan

Product Manager:
Erik Herman

Associate Product Manager:
Brandi Henson

Editorial Assistant:
Leigh Robbins

Senior Marketing Manager:
Joy Stark

Marketing Coordinator:
Jennifer Hankin

Developmental Editor:
Judy Adamski

Senior Content Project Manager:
Catherine G. DiMassa

Composition:
GEX Publishing Services

Text Designer:
Steve Deschene

Cover Designer:
Elizabeth Paquin

Cover Art:
Bill Brown

Preface

The New Perspectives Series' critical-thinking, problem-solving approach is the ideal way to prepare students to transcend point-and-click skills and take advantage of all that Microsoft Windows Vista has to offer.

In developing the New Perspectives Series for Microsoft Windows Vista, our goal was to create books that give students the software concepts and practical skills they need to succeed beyond the classroom. We've updated our proven case-based pedagogy with more practical content to make learning skills more meaningful to students.

With the New Perspectives Series, students understand *why* they are learning *what* they are learning, and are fully prepared to apply their skills to real-life situations.

"I really love the Margin Tips, which add 'tricks of the trade' to students' skills package. In addition, the Reality Check exercises provide for practical application of students' knowledge."
—Terry Morse Colucci
Institute of Technology, Inc.

About This Book

This book provides a thorough, hands-on introduction to the new Microsoft Windows Vista operating system, and includes the following:

- Complete coverage of Microsoft Windows Vista basics so that students can use the operating system with confidence and ease
- Guidance around the Windows Vista desktop, Start menu, and file system, teaching students how to start Windows, run programs, and organize files
- Exploration of the exciting new features in Windows Vista, including Windows Aero, the Navigation pane and updated Address bar in folder windows, new file and folder views, Windows Sidebar, Windows Calendar, and Windows Meeting Space
- Opportunities for personalizing Windows Vista, navigating the Web, exchanging e-mail, and finding files with the updated Search tools
- Expanded and in-depth coverage of managing computer security with Windows Vista, including Internet Explorer and Windows Mail security features
- New business case scenarios throughout, which provide a rich and realistic context for students to apply the concepts and skills presented

System Requirements

This book assumes a typical installation of Microsoft Windows Vista Ultimate with the Aero color scheme turned on. (Note that most tasks in this text can also be completed using the Windows Vista Home Premium or Business editions). The browser used for any steps that require a browser is Internet Explorer 7.

The New Perspectives Approach

Context
Each tutorial begins with a problem presented in a "real-world" case that is meaningful to students. The case sets the scene to help students understand what they will do in the tutorial.

Hands-on Approach
Each tutorial is divided into manageable sessions that combine reading and hands-on, step-by-step work. Colorful screenshots help guide students through the steps. **Trouble?** tips anticipate common mistakes or problems to help students stay on track and continue with the tutorial.

InSight

InSight Boxes
New for Windows Vista! InSight boxes offer expert advice and best practices to help students better understand how to work with the software. With the information provided in the InSight boxes, students achieve a deeper understanding of the concepts behind the software features and skills.

Tip

Margin Tips
New for Windows Vista! Margin Tips provide helpful hints and shortcuts for more efficient use of the software. The Tips appear in the margin at key points throughout each tutorial, giving students extra information when and where they need it.

Reality Check

Reality Checks
New for Windows Vista! Comprehensive, open-ended Reality Check exercises give students the opportunity to complete practical, real-world tasks, such as managing their files and folders and personalizing the Windows Vista environment.

Review

In New Perspectives, retention is a key component to learning. At the end of each session, a series of Quick Check questions helps students test their understanding of the concepts before moving on. Each tutorial also contains an end-of-tutorial summary and a list of key terms for further reinforcement.

Apply

Assessment
Engaging and challenging Review Assignments and Case Problems have always been a hallmark feature of the New Perspectives Series. Colorful icons and brief descriptions accompany the exercises, making it easy to understand, at a glance, both the goal and level of challenge a particular assignment holds.

Reference Window

Task Reference

Reference
While contextual learning is excellent for retention, there are times when students will want a high-level understanding of how to accomplish a task. Within each tutorial, Reference Windows appear before a set of steps to provide a succinct summary and preview of how to perform a task. In addition, a complete Task Reference at the back of the book provides quick access to information on how to carry out common tasks. Finally, each book includes a combination Glossary/Index to promote easy reference of material.

Our Complete System of Instruction

Coverage To Meet Your Needs

Whether you're looking for just a small amount of coverage or enough to fill a semester-long class, we can provide you with a textbook that meets your needs.

- Brief books typically cover the essential skills in just 2 to 4 tutorials.
- Introductory books build and expand on those skills and contain an average of 5 to 8 tutorials.
- Comprehensive books are great for a full-semester class, and contain 9 to 12+ tutorials.

So if the book you're holding does not provide the right amount of coverage for you, there's probably another offering available. Go to our Web site or contact your Thomson Course Technology sales representative to find out what else we offer.

Student Online Companion

This book has an accompanying online companion Web site designed to enhance learning. This Web site includes:

- Student Data Files
- PowerPoint presentations

CourseCasts – Learning on the Go. Always available...always relevant.

Want to keep up with the latest technology trends relevant to you? Visit our site to find a library of podcasts, CourseCasts, featuring a "CourseCast of the Week," and download them to your mp3 player at http://coursecasts.course.com.

Our fast-paced world is driven by technology. You know because you're an active participant—always on the go, always keeping up with technological trends, and always learning new ways to embrace technology to power your life.

Ken Baldauf, host of CourseCasts, is a faculty member of the Florida State University Computer Science Department where he is responsible for teaching technology classes to thousands of FSU students each year. Ken is an expert in the latest technology trends; he gathers and sorts through the most pertinent news and information for CourseCasts so your students can spend their time enjoying technology, rather than trying to figure it out. Open or close your lecture with a discussion based on the latest CourseCast.

Visit us at http://coursecasts.course.com to learn on the go!

Instructor Resources

We offer more than just a book. We have all the tools you need to enhance your lectures, check students' work, and generate exams in a new, easier-to-use and completely revised package. This book's Instructor's Manual, ExamView testbank, PowerPoint presentations, data files, solution files, figure files, and a sample syllabus are all available on a single CD-ROM or for downloading at www.course.com.

Blackboard

Skills Assessment and Training

SAM 2007 helps bridge the gap between the classroom and the real world by allowing students to train and test on important computer skills in an active, hands-on environment.

SAM 2007's easy-to-use system includes powerful interactive exams, training or projects on critical applications such as Word, Excel, Access, PowerPoint, Outlook, Windows, the Internet, and much more. SAM simulates the application environment, allowing students to demonstrate their knowledge and think through the skills by performing real-world tasks.

Designed to be used with the New Perspectives Series, SAM 2007 includes built-in page references so students can print helpful study guides that match the New Perspectives textbooks used in class. Powerful administrative options allow instructors to schedule exams and assignments, secure tests, and run reports with almost limitless flexibility.

Online Content

Blackboard is the leading distance learning solution provider and class-management platform today. Thomson Course Technology has partnered with Blackboard to bring you premium online content. Content for use with *New Perspectives on Microsoft Windows Vista, Introductory* is available in a Blackboard Course Cartridge and may include topic reviews, case projects, review questions, test banks, practice tests, custom syllabi, and more.

Thomson Course Technology also has solutions for several other learning management systems. Please visit http://www.course.com today to see what's available for this title.

Acknowledgments

I would like to thank the following reviewers for their contributions in the development of this text: Anton Bruckner, Sinclair Community College; Ken McDaniel, Santa Barbara Business College; and Deborah Meyer, St. Louis Community College–Forest Park. Their valuable insights and excellent feedback helped to shape this text, ensuring it will meet the needs of instructors and students both in the classroom and beyond.

Many thanks to everyone on the New Perspectives team for their guidance, insight, and encouragement, including Kristina Matthews, Cathie DiMassa, and Brandi Henson. Special thanks to Kathy Finnegan, whose thoughtfulness and good humor make this book more engaging and useful, and to Judy Adamski, who shepherded this text over many hurdles. I also appreciate the careful work of Susan Whalen, John Freitas, Danielle Shaw, and Nicole Ashton, Manuscript Quality Assurance testers. Additional thanks go to June Parsons, Dan Oja, and Joan and Patrick Carey, on whose previous work this book is based.

–Lisa Ruffolo

Brief Contents

Table of Contents

Tutorial 3 Personalizing Your Windows Environment

Changing Microsoft Windows Vista Desktop Settings . . . .WIN 97

Tutorial 4 Working with the Internet and E-Mail

Tutorial 5 Protecting Your Computer

Tutorial 6 Searching for Information and Collaborating with Others
Finding and Sharing Information ....WIN 267

Objectives

Session 1.1
- Start Windows Vista and tour the desktop
- Explore the Start menu
- Run software programs, switch between them, and close them
- Manipulate windows
- Identify and use the controls in menus, toolbars, and dialog boxes

Session 1.2
- Navigate your computer with Windows Explorer and the Computer window
- Change the view of the items in your computer
- Get help when you need it
- Turn off Windows Vista

Exploring the Basics of Microsoft Windows Vista

Investigating the Windows Vista Operating System

Case | Metro Learning Center

Metro Learning Center is a small but growing training company in Des Moines, Iowa. It offers academic tutoring and supplemental classes to help high school students and others prepare for college and other postsecondary education. In addition to classes that help students prepare for entrance exams, develop study and research skills, and earn high school equivalency diplomas, Metro Learning Center provides general training for using computers productively. Laura Halverson is the director of computer education at Metro, and she coordinates demonstrations and classes on developing computer skills, ranging from basic introductions to computers, Windows, and the Internet, to more advanced topics such as using word-processing programs, designing Web pages, and setting up home networks. Laura recently hired you as a computer trainer, and so far you have taught introductory classes on searching the Internet and exchanging e-mail. Now she asks you to prepare a demonstration on the fundamentals of the Microsoft Windows Vista operating system. She has scheduled demos with a few nonprofit agencies in Des Moines and surrounding communities and offers to help you identify the topics you should cover and the skills you should demonstrate. Overall, she suggests starting with turning on the computer and then explaining how to open and close programs, work with windows and dialog boxes, and navigate the computer. Finally, she wants you to demonstrate ways to turn off Windows Vista.

In this tutorial, you will start Windows Vista and practice some fundamental computer skills. Then, you'll learn how to navigate with the Computer window and Windows Explorer. Finally, you'll use the Windows Vista Help system, and turn off Windows Vista.

Starting Data Files

There are no starting Data Files needed for this tutorial.

Session 1.1

Starting Windows Vista

Laura Halverson begins helping you plan the demonstration by first defining the operating system. She explains that the **operating system** is software that helps the computer perform essential tasks such as displaying information on the computer screen and saving data on disks. (Software refers to the **programs**, or **applications**, that a computer uses to complete tasks.) Your computer uses the **Microsoft Windows Vista** operating system—**Windows Vista** for short. Windows is the name of the operating system, and Vista indicates the version you are using. Microsoft has released many versions of Windows since 1985 and is likely to continue developing new versions.

Much of the software created for the Windows Vista operating system shares the same look and works the same way. This similarity in design means that after you learn how to use one Windows Vista program, such as Microsoft Office Word (a word-processing program), you are well on your way to understanding how to use other Windows Vista programs. Windows Vista allows you to use more than one program at a time, so you can easily switch between your word-processing program and your appointment book program, for example. Windows Vista also makes it easy to access the **Internet**, a worldwide collection of computers connected to one another to enable communication. All in all, Windows Vista makes your computer an effective and easy-to-use productivity tool.

Windows Vista starts automatically when you turn on your computer. After completing some necessary startup tasks, Windows Vista displays a Welcome screen. Depending on the way your computer is set up, the Welcome screen might list only your user name or it might list all the users for the computer. Before you start working with Windows Vista, you must click your user name and perhaps type a password. A **user name** is a unique name that identifies you to Windows Vista, and a **password** is text—often a confidential combination of letters and numbers—that you must enter before you can work with Windows Vista. After selecting your user name, the Windows Vista desktop appears and the Welcome Center window opens, which provides information about your computer and how to set it up according to your preferences.

To begin your demo of Windows Vista, Laura asks you to start Windows Vista.

To start Windows Vista:

▶ **1.** Turn on your computer. After a moment, Windows Vista starts and the Welcome screen appears.

   Trouble? If you are asked to select an operating system, do not take action. Windows Vista should start automatically after a designated number of seconds. If it does not, ask your instructor or technical support person for help.

   Trouble? If this is the first time you have started your computer with Windows Vista, messages might appear on your screen informing you that Windows is setting up components of your computer.

▶ **2.** On the Welcome screen, click your user name and enter your password, if necessary. The Welcome Center window opens on the Windows Vista desktop, as shown in Figure 1-1. Your desktop might look different.

   Trouble? If your user name does not appear in the list of users on the Welcome screen, ask your instructor or technical support person which name you should click.

   Trouble? If you need to enter a user name and a password, type your assigned user name, press the Tab key, type your password, and then click the Continue button or press the Enter key to continue.

   Trouble? If the Welcome Center window does not open and only the desktop appears, continue with Step 3.

Welcome Center window open on the Windows Vista desktop ◄ **Figure 1-1**

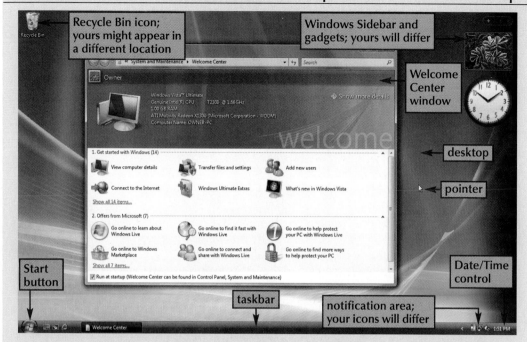

▶ **3.** Look at your desktop and locate the objects labeled in Figure 1-1. The objects on your desktop might differ or appear larger or smaller than those in Figure 1-1, depending on your monitor's settings. Figure 1-2 describes the purpose of each of these objects.

Elements of the Windows Vista desktop ◄ **Figure 1-2**

Element	Description
Icon	A small picture that represents an object available to your computer
Pointer	A small object, such as an arrow, that moves on the screen when you move the mouse
Desktop	Your workplace on the screen
Sidebar and gadgets	A place on the desktop where Windows stows gadgets, which are small, handy programs such as sticky notes and clocks
Date/Time control	An element that shows the current date and time and lets you set the clock
Notification area	An area that displays icons corresponding to services running in the background, such as an Internet connection
Taskbar	A strip that contains buttons to give you quick access to common tools and the programs currently running
Start button	A button that provides access to Windows Vista programs, documents, and information on the Internet
Welcome Center window	A window that lists tasks first-time users can perform to quickly set up their computers

Trouble? If a blank screen or animated design replaces the Windows Vista desktop, your computer might be set to use a **screen saver**, a program that causes a monitor to go blank or to display an animated design after a specified amount of idle time. Press any key or move your mouse to restore the Windows Vista desktop.

The Windows Vista screen uses a **graphical user interface** (**GUI**, pronounced *gooey*), which displays icons that represent items stored on your computer, such as programs and files. A computer **file** is a collection of related information; typical types of files include text documents, spreadsheets, digital pictures, and songs. Your computer represents files with **icons**, which are pictures of familiar objects, such as file folders and documents. Windows Vista gets its name from the rectangular work areas called **windows** that appear on your screen as you work, such as the Welcome Center window shown in Figure 1-3. You will learn more about windows later in this tutorial.

Figure 1-3 ▷ **Welcome Center window**

The user interface in Windows Vista is called **Aero**, and is available in two versions. The Aero experience features a semitransparent glass design that lets you see many objects at the same time, such as two or more overlapping windows. (Aero is available only in the following versions of Windows Vista: Business, Enterprise, Home Premium, and Ultimate.) Aero also offers other features for viewing windows that are demonstrated later in this tutorial. To take advantage of the Aero experience, your computer requires hardware with features designed for enhanced graphics. (The Microsoft Web site at *www.microsoft.com* has detailed information about these requirements.) Otherwise, you can use the basic version of Aero, which provides the same elements as the enhanced experience, including windows and icons, but not the same graphic effects. This book assumes that you are using the Aero experience. If you are using the Basic experience, the images on your screen will vary slightly from the figures, and some features will not be available. (These are noted throughout the book.)

Touring the Windows Vista Desktop

In Windows terminology, the background area displayed on your screen when Windows Vista starts represents a **desktop**—a workspace for projects and the tools that you need to manipulate your projects. When you first start a computer, it uses **default settings**, those preset by the operating system. The default desktop you see after you first install Windows Vista, for example, displays an abstract image that shades from blue to green to yellow. However, Microsoft designed Windows Vista so that you can easily change the appearance of the desktop. You can, for example, change images or add patterns and text to the desktop.

Interacting with the Desktop

To interact with the objects on your desktop, you use a **pointing device**. Pointing devices come in many shapes and sizes. The most common one is called a **mouse**, so this book uses that term. If you are using a different pointing device, such as a trackball or touchpad, substitute that device whenever you see the term *mouse*. Some pointing devices are designed to ensure that your hand won't suffer fatigue while using them. Some are attached directly to your computer, whereas others work like a TV remote control and allow you to access your computer without being plugged into it.

You use a pointing device to move the pointer over objects on the desktop, or to **point** to them. The pointer is usually shaped like an arrow ⍦, although it changes shape depending on the pointer's location on the screen and the tasks you are performing. As you move the mouse on a surface, such as a mouse pad, the pointer on the screen moves in a corresponding direction.

When you point to certain objects, such as the objects on the taskbar, a ScreenTip appears near the object. A **ScreenTip** tells you the purpose or function of the object to which you are pointing.

During your demo, Laura suggests that you acquaint Metro Learning Center clients with the desktop by viewing ScreenTips for a couple of desktop objects.

To view ScreenTips:

▶ **1.** Use the mouse to point to the **Start** button 🪟 on the taskbar. After a few seconds, you see a ScreenTip identifying the button, as shown in Figure 1-4.

Viewing ScreenTips ◀ Figure 1-4

▶ **2.** Point to the time displayed at the right end of the taskbar. A ScreenTip for today's date (or the date to which your computer's calendar is set) appears.

Clicking refers to pressing a mouse button and immediately releasing it. Clicking sends a signal to your computer that you want to perform an action with the object you click. In Windows Vista, you perform most actions with the left mouse button. If you are told to click an object, position the pointer on that object and click the left mouse button, unless instructed otherwise.

When you click the Start button, the Start menu opens. A **menu** is a group or list of commands, and a **menu command** is text that you can click to complete tasks. If a right-pointing arrow follows a menu command, then you can point to the command to open a **submenu**, which is a list of additional choices related to the command.

The **Start menu** provides access to programs, documents, and much more. To explore the Start menu, Laura suggests you click the Start button to open the Start menu.

To open the Start menu:

▶ **1.** Point to the **Start** button 🪟 on the taskbar.

▶ **2.** Click the left mouse button. The Start menu opens. An arrow ▶ points to the All Programs command on the Start menu, indicating that you can view additional choices by navigating to a submenu. See Figure 1-5; your Start menu might show different commands.

Figure 1-5 ▶ **Start menu**

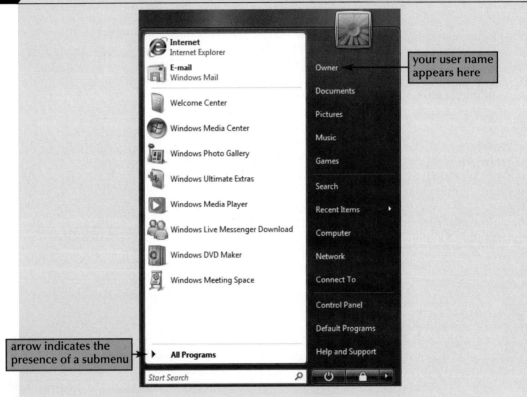

arrow indicates the presence of a submenu

your user name appears here

▶ **3.** Click the **Start** button 🪟 on the taskbar to close the Start menu.

You need to select an object before you can work with it. To **select** an object in Windows Vista, you usually need to point to and then click that object. Windows Vista often shows you that an object is selected by highlighting it, typically by changing the object's color, putting a box around it, or making the object appear to be pushed in.

Depending on your computer's settings, you can select certain objects by pointing to them. To demonstrate selecting a menu command by pointing, Laura suggests that you point to the All Programs command on the Start menu to open the All Programs submenu.

To select a menu command:

▶ **1.** Click the **Start** button 🪟 on the taskbar.

2. Point to **All Programs** on the Start menu. The All Programs command is highlighted to indicate it is selected. After a short pause, the All Programs submenu opens. See Figure 1-6.

All Programs submenu | Figure 1-6

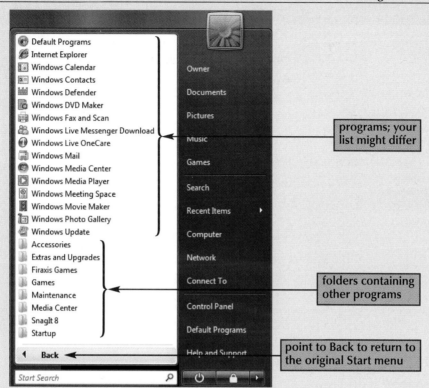

Trouble? If a submenu other than the All Programs submenu opens, you pointed to a different command. Move the mouse so that the pointer points to All Programs.

3. Click the **Start** button 🟢 on the taskbar to close the Start menu. You return to the desktop.

Clicking an object usually selects it; in contrast, you double-click an object to open or start the item associated with it. For example, you can double-click a folder icon to open the folder and see its contents. Or you can double-click a program icon to start the program. **Double-clicking** means to click the left mouse button twice in quick succession.

Laura suggests that you have students practice double-clicking by opening the Recycle Bin. The Recycle Bin holds deleted items such as folders until you remove them permanently.

To view the contents of the Recycle Bin:

1. In the upper-right corner of the Welcome Center window, click the **Close** button ▣ to close the window.

2. Click the desktop background, and then point to the **Recycle Bin** icon on the desktop. After a few moments, a ScreenTip appears that describes the Recycle Bin.

3. Click the left mouse button twice quickly to double-click the **Recycle Bin** icon. The Recycle Bin window opens, as shown in Figure 1-7.

Figure 1-7 ▶ **Contents of the Recycle Bin**

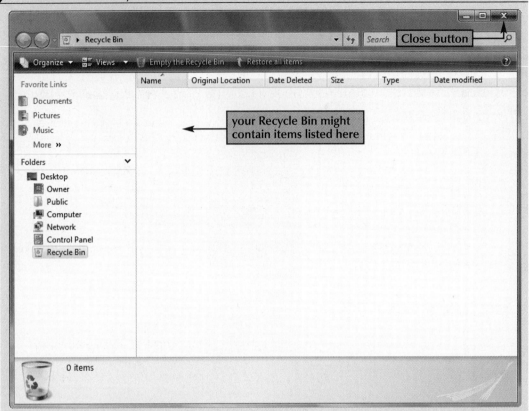

Trouble? If the Recycle Bin window does not open, and you see only the Recycle Bin name highlighted below the icon, you double-clicked too slowly. Double-click the icon again more quickly.

Now you can close the Recycle Bin window.

▶ **4.** Click [✕] in the upper-right corner of the Recycle Bin window.

You'll learn more about opening and closing windows later in this session.

Your mouse has more than one button—in addition to the left button, the mouse has a right button that you can use for performing certain actions in Windows Vista. However, the term *clicking* continues to refer to the left button; clicking an object with the *right* button is called **right-clicking**.

In Windows Vista, right-clicking selects an object and also opens its **shortcut menu**, which lists actions you can take with that object. You can right-click practically any object—the Start button, a desktop icon, the taskbar, and even the desktop itself—to view commands associated with that object. Laura suggests that when you're not sure what to do with an object in Windows Vista, right-click it and examine its shortcut menu. She also reminds you that you clicked the Start button with the left mouse button to open the Start menu. Now you can right-click the Start button to open the shortcut menu for the Start button.

To right-click an object:

▶ **1.** Position the pointer over the **Start** button 🟢 on the taskbar.

▶ **2.** Right-click the **Start** button 🟢 to open its shortcut menu. This menu offers a list of actions you can take with the Start button. See Figure 1-8.

Start button shortcut menu ◀ Figure 1-8

shortcut menu; yours might differ

these commands appear if you are working on a network or a multiuser computer

Trouble? If the shortcut menu does not open and you are using a trackball or a mouse with three buttons or a wheel, make sure you click the button on the far right, not the one in the middle.

Trouble? If your menu looks slightly different from the one in Figure 1-8, it is still the correct Start button shortcut menu. Its commands often vary by computer.

▶ 3. Press the **Esc** key to close the shortcut menu. You return to the desktop.

Now that you've opened the Start menu and its shortcut menu, you're ready to explore the contents of the Start menu.

Exploring the Start Menu

Recall that the Start menu is the central point for accessing programs, documents, and other resources on your computer. The Start menu is organized into two **panes**, which are separate areas of a menu or window. Each pane lists items you can point to or click. See Figure 1-9.

Start menu ◀ Figure 1-9

left pane

right pane

pinned items list

commands for accessing files

most frequently used programs

All Programs command

tools for accessing resources on your computer; yours might differ

Start Search box for finding files and other items on your computer

buttons for logging off and turning off your computer

Tip

To pin a program to the Start menu, right-click the program icon, and then click Pin to Start Menu on the shortcut menu.

The left pane organizes programs for easy access. The area at the top of the left pane is called the **pinned items list**. Pinned items stay on the Start menu until you remove them. By default, Windows Vista lists the Web browser and e-mail program on your computer in the pinned items list. You can pin other items to this list if you like. When you use a program, Windows Vista adds it to the **most frequently used programs list**, which appears below the pinned items list. Windows Vista can list only a certain number of frequently used programs—after that, the programs you have not opened recently are replaced by the programs you used last.

Near the bottom of the left pane is the All Programs command, which you have already used to display the All Programs submenu. The All Programs submenu provides access to the programs currently installed on your computer. You'll use the All Programs submenu shortly to start a program.

The **Start Search box** helps you quickly find anything stored on your computer, including programs, documents, pictures, music, videos, Web pages, and e-mail messages. When you want to use the Start Search box, you open the Start menu and type one or more words related to what you want to find. For example, if you want to find and play the Happy Birthday song, you could type *birthday* in the Start Search box. Windows Vista searches your computer for that song and displays it and any other search results in the left pane of the Start menu where you can click the song to play it.

Tip

Point to an item in the left or right pane of the Start menu to display a Screen-Tip describing the item.

From the right pane of the Start menu, you can access common locations and tools on your computer. For example, the **Documents folder** is your personal folder, a convenient place to store documents and other work. **Computer** is a tool that you use to view, organize, and access the programs, files, and drives on your computer.

From the lower section of the right pane, you can open windows that help you work effectively with Windows Vista, including **Control Panel**, which contains specialized tools that help you change the way Windows Vista looks and behaves, and **Help and Support**, which provides articles, demonstrations, and steps for performing tasks in Windows Vista. (You'll explore Windows Help and Support later in this tutorial.) Finally, you also log off and turn off your computer from the Start menu. When you **log off**, you end your session with Windows Vista but leave the computer turned on.

Now that you've explored the Start menu, you're ready to use it to start a program.

Reference Window | **Starting a Program**

- Click the Start button on the taskbar, and then point to All Programs.
- If necessary, click the folder that contains the program you want to start.
- Click the name of the program you want to start.

or

- Click the name or icon of the program you want to start in the pinned items list or the most frequently used programs list on the Start menu.

Laura mentions that Windows Vista includes an easy-to-use word-processing program called WordPad. Suppose you want to start the WordPad program and use it to write a letter or report. You open Windows Vista programs from the Start menu. Programs are usually located on the All Programs submenu or in one of its folders. As mentioned earlier, a **folder** in Windows Vista is a container that helps to organize the contents of your computer. In the All Programs submenu, a folder contains programs that share a similar purpose. For example, the Accessories folder contains standard useful programs, such as a calculator. WordPad is stored in the Accessories folder because it is a typical accessory you can use for basic word processing.

To start the WordPad program from the Start menu:

▶ **1.** Click the **Start** button 🔘 on the taskbar to open the Start menu.

▶ **2.** Point to **All Programs** to open the All Programs submenu.

▶ **3.** Click **Accessories**. The Accessories folder opens, as shown in Figure 1-10.

Start menu and related submenus ◀ **Figure 1-10**

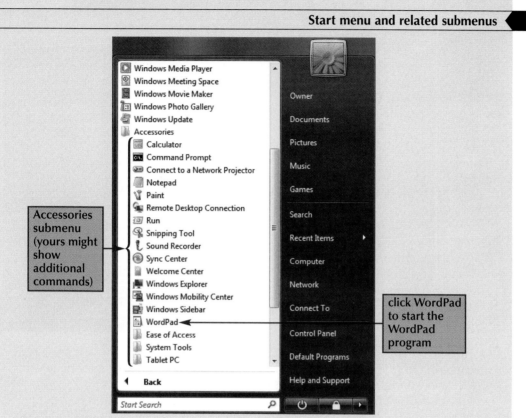

Trouble? If a different menu or folder opens, point to Back to return to the initial Start menu, point to All Programs, and then click Accessories.

▶ **4.** Click **WordPad**. The WordPad program window opens, as shown in Figure 1-11.

Figure 1-11 WordPad program window

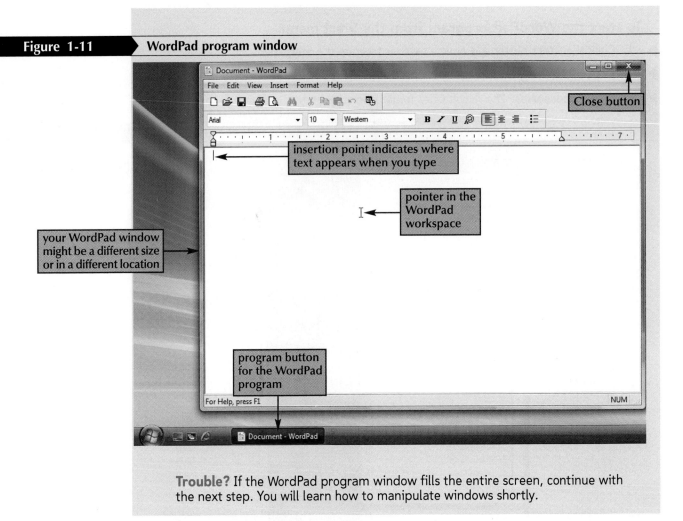

Trouble? If the WordPad program window fills the entire screen, continue with the next step. You will learn how to manipulate windows shortly.

When a program is started, it is said to be open or running. A **program button** appears on the taskbar for each open program. You click a program button to switch between open programs. When you are finished using a program, you can click the Close button located in the upper-right corner of the program window to **exit**, or close, that program.

To exit the WordPad program:

▶ 1. Click the **Close** button ⬛ in the upper-right corner of the WordPad window. The WordPad program closes and you return to the Windows Vista desktop.

Now that you have started one program, you can start another program and run two at the same time.

Running Multiple Programs

One of the most useful features of Windows Vista is its ability to run multiple programs at the same time. This feature, known as **multitasking**, allows you to work on more than one task at a time and to switch quickly between projects. To demonstrate multitasking, Laura suggests that you start WordPad and leave it running while you start Paint, which is a program used to draw, color, and edit digital pictures.

To run WordPad and Paint at the same time:

▶ **1.** Start WordPad again.

▶ **2.** Click the **Start** button 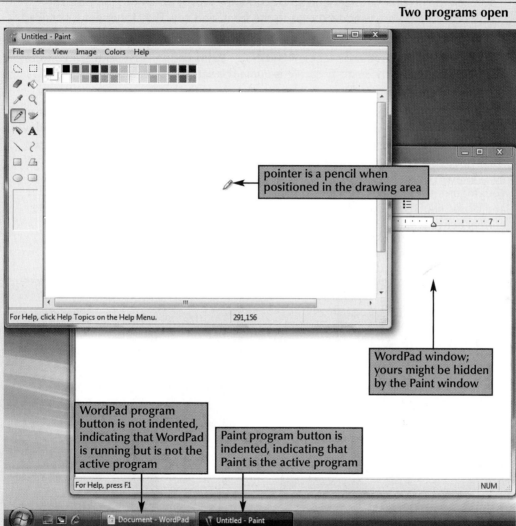 on the taskbar.

▶ **3.** Point to **All Programs**, and then click **Accessories**.

▶ **4.** Click **Paint**. The Paint program window opens, as shown in Figure 1-12. Now two programs are running at the same time.

Two programs open ◀ **Figure 1-12**

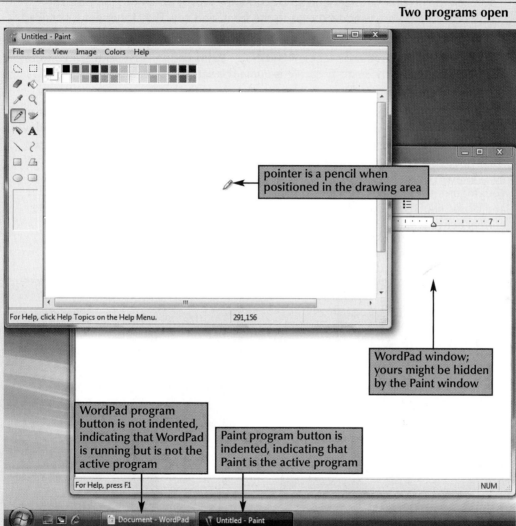

pointer is a pencil when positioned in the drawing area

WordPad window; yours might be hidden by the Paint window

WordPad program button is not indented, indicating that WordPad is running but is not the active program

Paint program button is indented, indicating that Paint is the active program

Trouble? If the Paint program window fills the entire screen, continue with the next set of steps. You will learn how to manipulate windows shortly.

The **active program** is the one you are currently using—Windows Vista applies your next keystroke or command to the active program. Paint is the active program because it is the one in which you are currently working. If two or more program windows overlap, the active window appears in front of the other windows. The program button for the active program is indented on the taskbar. The WordPad program button is still on the taskbar, indicating that WordPad is still running even if you can't see its program window. The taskbar organizes all the open windows so you can quickly make a program active by clicking its taskbar button.

Tip

In the Aero experience, when you point to a program button on the taskbar, a small picture appears that shows you a miniature version of the program window, including its contents.

Switching Between Programs

Because only one program is active at a time, you need to switch between programs if you want to work in one or the other. The easiest way to switch between programs is to use the program buttons on the taskbar.

To switch between WordPad and Paint:

▶ 1. Click the program button labeled **Document - WordPad** on the taskbar. The WordPad program window moves to the front, and now the Document - WordPad button looks pushed in, indicating that WordPad is the active program.

▶ 2. Click the program button labeled **Untitled - Paint** on the taskbar to switch to the Paint program. The Paint program is again the active program.

You can also use the Switch between windows button on the Quick Launch toolbar to switch from one open window to another. When you click the Switch between windows button, Windows activates **Flip 3D**, which displays all your open windows in a rotated stack so you can see the windows from the side, the way you view the spine of a book. See Figure 1-13. To flip through the stack, you press the Tab key or scroll the wheel on your mouse. Clicking any window in the stack makes that window the active program and closes Flip 3D; you click outside the stack to close Flip 3D without changing the current active window.

| Figure 1-13 | Windows Flip 3D |

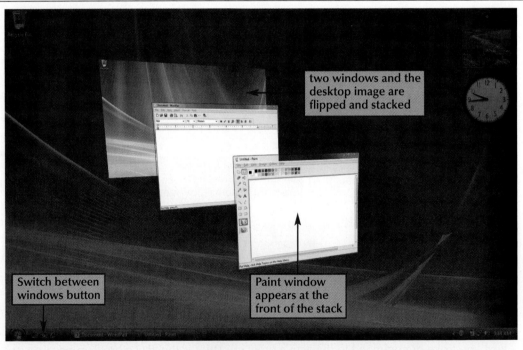

Note that Flip 3D is only available in the Aero experience. If you are using the Basic experience, clicking the Switch between windows button opens a task switcher window that displays a generic icon for each program that is running. See Figure 1-14. You can point to an icon to display information about the program it represents. Clicking an icon makes that program the active program and closes the task switcher window; clicking outside the task switcher window closes it without changing the current active window.

Clicking the Switch between windows button in the Basic experience ◄ **Figure 1-14**

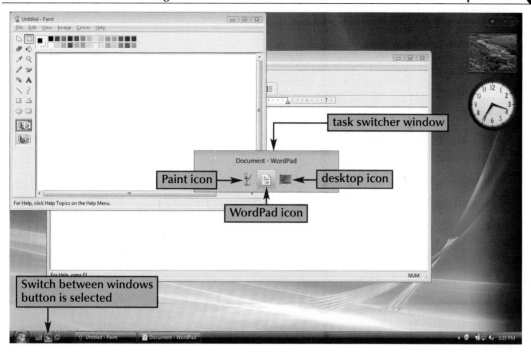

If you like to use keyboard shortcuts and are working in the Aero experience, you can also switch from one window to another using Windows Flip. When you hold down the Alt key and press the Tab key once, Windows Flip displays thumbnails (miniature versions) of your open windows. See Figure 1-15. While continuing to hold down the Alt key, you can press the Tab key to select the thumbnail for the program you want; you release the Alt key to close Windows Flip. (If you are using the Basic experience, the Alt+Tab keyboard shortcut opens the task switcher window shown in Figure 1-14.)

Windows Flip ◄ **Figure 1-15**

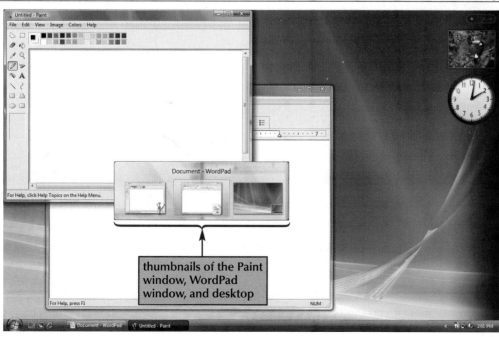

To switch between program windows using Flip 3D:

▶ **1.** Click the **Switch between windows** button 🖾 on the taskbar. Windows arranges the Paint and WordPad windows and the desktop in a stack, with the Paint window at the top of the stack.

Trouble? If the Switch between windows button does not appear on your taskbar, right-click a blank part of the taskbar, point to Toolbars, and then click Quick Launch. Then complete Step 1.

Trouble? If a task switcher window similar to the one shown in Figure 1-14 opens when you click the Switch between windows button, you are not using the Aero experience. Click outside the task switcher window and then read, but do not perform, the remaining steps.

▶ **2.** Press the **Tab** key to flip the WordPad window to the front of the stack. The Paint window moves to the back of the stack.

▶ **3.** Click the **WordPad** program window to turn off Flip 3D and make WordPad the active program.

Flip 3D is especially useful when many windows are open on the desktop, and the one you want to use is hidden by other windows. Flip 3D provides a handy alternative to switching windows from the taskbar, which can get crowded with program buttons.

In addition to using the taskbar and Flip 3D to switch between open programs, you can also close programs from the taskbar.

Closing Programs from the Taskbar

You should always close a program when you are finished using it. Each program uses computer resources, such as memory, so Windows Vista works more efficiently when only the programs you need are open. Laura reminds you that you've already closed an open program using the Close button in the upper-right corner of the program window. You can also close a program, whether active or inactive, by using the shortcut menu associated with the program button on the taskbar.

To close WordPad and Paint using the program button shortcut menus:

▶ **1.** Right-click the **Untitled - Paint** button on the taskbar. The shortcut menu for the Paint program button opens. See Figure 1-16.

Figure 1-16 ▶ **Program button shortcut menu**

shortcut menu opens when you right-click a program button

click to close the selected program

▶ **2.** Click **Close** on the shortcut menu. The Paint program closes, and the program button labeled "Untitled - Paint" no longer appears on the taskbar.

Trouble? If a message appears asking if you want to save changes, click the Don't Save button.

▶ **3.** Right-click the **Document - WordPad** button on the taskbar, and then click **Close** on the shortcut menu. The WordPad program closes, and its program button no longer appears on the taskbar.

Now that you've learned the basics of using the Windows Vista desktop, you're ready to explore other Windows Vista features, including windows and dialog boxes.

Using Windows and Dialog Boxes

When you run a program in Windows Vista, the program appears in a window. Recall that a window is a rectangular area of the screen that contains a program, text, graphics, or data. A window also contains **controls**, which are graphical or textual objects used for manipulating the window and for using the program. Figure 1-17 describes the controls you are likely to see in most windows.

Window controls ◀ Figure 1-17

Control	Description
Menu bar	Contains the titles of menus, such as File, Edit, and Help
Sizing button	Lets you enlarge, shrink, or close a window
Status bar	Displays information or messages about the task you are performing
Title bar	Contains the window title and basic window control buttons
Toolbar	Contains buttons that provide you with shortcuts to common menu commands
Window title	Identifies the program and document contained in the window
Workspace	Includes the part of the window where you manipulate your work—enter text, draw pictures, and set up calculations, for example

Laura mentions that the WordPad program is a good example of a typical window. She suggests that you start WordPad and identify its window controls.

To look at the window controls in WordPad:

▶ **1.** Start WordPad.

▶ **2.** On your screen, identify the controls that are labeled in Figure 1-18.

Figure 1-18	WordPad window controls

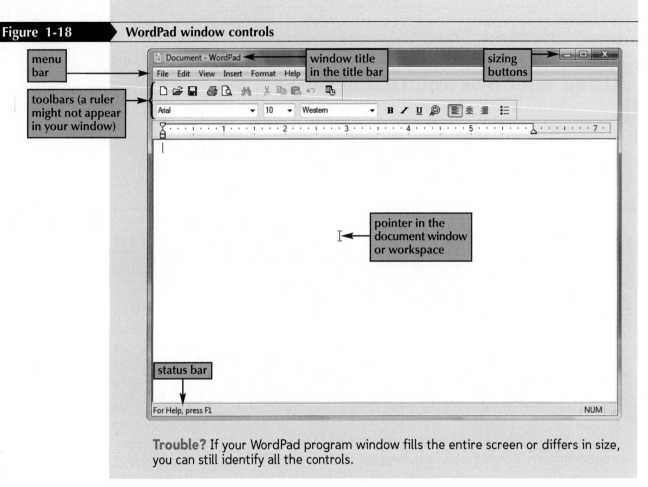

Trouble? If your WordPad program window fills the entire screen or differs in size, you can still identify all the controls.

After you open a window, you can manipulate it by changing its size and position.

Manipulating Windows

In most windows, three buttons appear on the right side of the title bar. The first button is the Minimize button, which hides a window so that only its program button is visible on the taskbar. Depending on the status of the window, the middle button either maximizes the window or restores it to a predefined size. You are already familiar with the last button—the Close button. Figure 1-19 illustrates how these buttons work.

Window buttons ◄ Figure 1-19

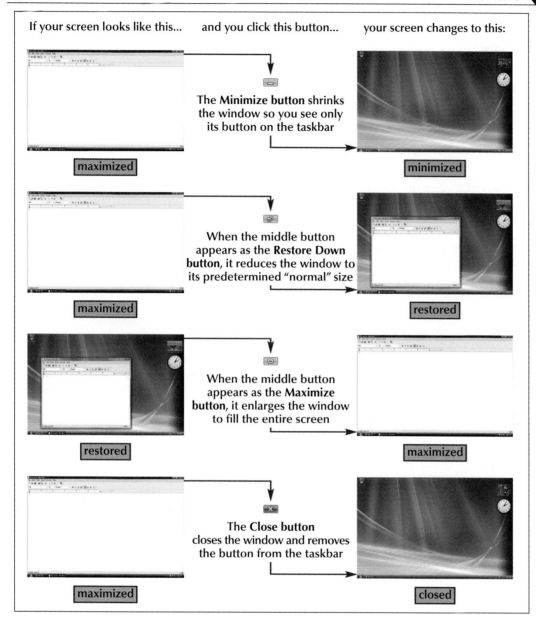

Now that WordPad is open, Laura encourages you to show students how to use its window controls to manipulate the program window. You can use the Minimize button when you want to temporarily hide a window but keep the program running.

To minimize the WordPad window:

▶ **1.** Click the **Minimize** button 🗕 on the WordPad title bar. The WordPad window shrinks so that only the Document - WordPad button on the taskbar is visible.

Trouble? If the WordPad program window closed, you accidentally clicked the Close button. Use the Start button to start WordPad again, and then repeat Step 1. If you accidentally clicked the Maximize or Restore Down button, repeat Step 1.

You can redisplay a minimized window by clicking the program's button on the taskbar. When you redisplay a window, it becomes the active window.

To redisplay the WordPad window:

▶ **1.** Click the **Document - WordPad** button on the taskbar. The WordPad window is redisplayed.

The taskbar button provides another way to switch between a window's minimized and active states.

▶ **2.** Click the **Document - WordPad** button on the taskbar again to minimize the window.

▶ **3.** Click the **Document - WordPad** button once more to redisplay the window.

The Maximize button enlarges a window so that it fills the entire screen. Laura recommends that you work with maximized windows when you want to concentrate on the work you are performing in a single program.

To maximize the WordPad window:

▶ **1.** Click the **Maximize** button 🔲 on the WordPad title bar.

Trouble? If the window is already maximized, it fills the entire screen, and the Maximize button doesn't appear. Instead, you see the Restore Down button. Skip this step.

The Restore Down button reduces the window so that it is smaller than the entire screen. This feature is useful if you want to see more than one window at a time. Also, because the window is smaller, you can move the window to another location on the screen or change the dimensions of the window.

To restore a window:

▶ **1.** Click the **Restore Down** button 🔲 on the WordPad title bar. After a window is restored, the Restore Down button 🔲 changes to the Maximize button 🔲.

You can use the mouse to move a window to a new position on the screen. When you click an object and then press and hold down the mouse button while moving the mouse, you are **dragging** the object. You can move objects on the screen by dragging them to a new location. If you want to move a window, you drag the window by its title bar. You cannot move a maximized window.

To drag the restored WordPad window to a new location:

▶ **1.** Position the mouse pointer on the WordPad title bar.

▶ **2.** Press and hold down the left mouse button, and then move the mouse up or down a little to drag the window. The window moves as you move the mouse.

▶ **3.** Position the window anywhere on the desktop, and then release the left mouse button. The WordPad window stays in the new location.

▶ **4.** Drag the WordPad window to the upper-left corner of the desktop.

You can also use the mouse to change the size of a window. When you point to an edge or corner of a window, the pointer changes to the resize pointer, which is a double-headed arrow, similar to ⤡ . You can use the resize pointer to drag an edge or corner of the window and change the size of the window.

To change the size of the WordPad window:

▶ **1.** Position the pointer over the lower-right corner of the WordPad window. The pointer changes to 🢅. See Figure 1-20.

Preparing to resize a window   **Figure 1-20**

▶ **2.** Press and hold down the mouse button, and then drag the corner down and to the right.

▶ **3.** Release the mouse button. Now the window is larger.

▶ **4.** Practice using the resize pointer to make the WordPad window larger or smaller.

You can also use the resize pointer to drag any of the other three corners of the window to change its size. To change a window's size in any one direction only, drag the left, right, top, or bottom window borders left, right, up, or down.

Selecting Options from a Menu

Many Windows Vista programs use menus to organize the program's features and available functions. The menu bar is typically located at the top of the program window, immediately below the title bar, and shows the names of the menus, such as File, Edit, and Help.

When you click a menu name, the choices for that menu appear below the menu bar. Like choices on the Start menu, these choices are referred to as menu commands. To select a menu command, you click it. For example, the File menu is a standard feature in some Windows Vista programs that contains the commands typically related to working with a file: creating, opening, saving, and printing. Menu commands that are followed by an ellipsis (...) open a dialog box. A **dialog box** is a special kind of window in which you enter or choose settings for how you want to perform a task. For example, you use the Page Setup dialog box to set margins and some printing options.

Tip

If you open a menu, and then decide not to select a command, you can close the menu by clicking its name again or by pressing the Esc key.

Because the Page Setup dialog box contains many typical controls, Laura suggests you use the Page Setup command on the WordPad File menu to open that dialog box.

To select the Page Setup menu command on the File menu:

▶ **1.** Click **File** on the WordPad menu bar to open the File menu. See Figure 1-21.

Figure 1-21	File menu

▶ **2.** Click **Page Setup** to open the Page Setup dialog box.

▶ **3.** After examining the dialog box, click the **Cancel** button to close the Page Setup dialog box.

When you select options in the Page Setup dialog box that you want to retain, you click the OK button instead of the Cancel button.

Not all commands immediately carry out an action—some show submenus or ask you for more information about what you want to do. The menu gives you visual hints about what to expect when you select an item. These hints are sometimes referred to as **menu conventions**. Figure 1-22 shows examples of these menu conventions.

Figure 1-22	Examples of menu conventions

Figure 1-23 describes the Windows Vista menu conventions.

Menu conventions ◀ **Figure 1-23**

Convention	Description
Check mark	Indicates a toggle, or on/off switch (like a light switch), that is either checked (turned on) or not checked (turned off)
Ellipsis	Three dots that indicate you can make additional selections after you select that command. Commands without dots do not require additional choices—they take effect as soon as you click them. If a command is followed by an ellipsis, a dialog box opens so you can enter details about how you want a task carried out.
Triangular arrow	Indicates the presence of a submenu. When you point to a menu option that has a triangular arrow, a submenu appears.
Dimmed command	Command that is not currently available
Keyboard shortcut	Key or combination of keys that you can press to select the menu command without actually opening the menu

Using Toolbars

Many Windows Vista programs include one or more toolbars, which are typically displayed near the top of the program window. A toolbar is a row, column, or block of buttons or icons that gives you one-click access to frequently used menu commands. Just as menu commands are grouped on menus according to task, the buttons on a toolbar are also grouped and organized by task.

Toolbars, Menus, and Ribbons		InSight

Some Windows Vista programs such as Microsoft Office 2007 combine the toolbars and menu bar into a single component called the Ribbon. The Ribbon organizes commands into logical groups that are displayed on a tab. Each tab is designed for a particular activity, such as writing or designing a page. Many buttons on the Ribbon are similar to the buttons on a toolbar—they perform a command with one click. Buttons with arrows work like menus—you click a button to display a menu of related options.

Laura reminds you that Windows Vista programs often display ScreenTips to indicate the name or function of a window component such as a button. She suggests exploring the WordPad toolbar buttons by looking at their ScreenTips.

To determine the names and descriptions of the buttons on the WordPad toolbar:

▶ 1. Position the pointer over the **Print Preview** button on the WordPad toolbar, which is located immediately below the menu bar. After a short pause, the Screen-Tip for the button appears near the button, and a description of the button appears in the status bar at the bottom of the window.

▶ 2. Move the pointer to each of the remaining buttons on the WordPad toolbar to display its name.

You select a toolbar button by clicking it, which performs the button's command. One of the buttons you pointed to on the WordPad toolbar is called the Undo button. Clicking the Undo button reverses the effects of your last action. Laura says you can see how this works by typing some text, and then clicking the Undo button to remove that text.

To use the Undo button on the WordPad toolbar:

▶ **1.** Type your name in the WordPad window.

▶ **2.** Click the **Undo** button 🔄 on the WordPad toolbar. WordPad reverses your last action by removing your name from the WordPad window.

Besides menus and toolbars, windows can contain list boxes and scroll bars, which you'll learn about next.

Using List Boxes and Scroll Bars

As you might guess from the name, a **list box** displays a list of available choices from which you can select one item. In WordPad, the Date and Time dialog box includes a list box that contains formats for displaying the date and time. You can choose a date and time format from the Available formats list box in the Date and Time dialog box. List box controls usually include arrow buttons, a scroll bar, and a scroll box. A scroll bar appears when the list of available options is too long or wide to fit in the list box. You use the arrows and scroll box to move through the complete list.

To practice using a list box and scroll bar, Laura advises you open the Date and Time dialog box in WordPad and select a date format.

To use the list box in the Date and Time dialog box:

▶ **1.** Click the **Date/Time** button 📅 on the WordPad toolbar to open the Date and Time dialog box, which lists the current date in many formats. See Figure 1-24.

Figure 1-24 ▶ **List box**

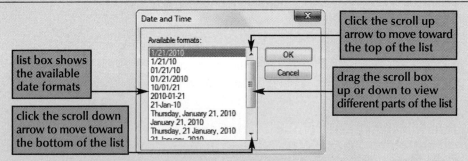

▶ **2.** To scroll down the list, click the **scroll down arrow** button on the scroll bar.

▶ **3.** Drag the **scroll box** to the top of the scroll bar by pointing to the scroll box, pressing and holding down the left mouse button, dragging the scroll box up, and then releasing the left mouse button. The list scrolls back to the beginning.

▶ **4.** Find a date format similar to "January 21, 2010" in the Available formats list box, and then click that date format to select it.

▶ **5.** Click the **OK** button to close the Date and Time dialog box. The current date is inserted into your document in the format you selected.

A list box is helpful because it includes only those options that are appropriate for your current task. For example, you can select only dates and times in the available formats from the list box in the Date and Time dialog box—no matter which format you choose, WordPad recognizes it. Sometimes a list might not include every possible option, so you can type the option you want to select. In this case, the list box includes an arrow on its right side. You can click the list arrow to view options and then either select one of the options or type appropriate text.

Buttons can also have arrows. The arrow indicates that the button has more than one option. Rather than crowding the window with a lot of buttons, one for each possible option, including an arrow on a button organizes its options logically and compactly into a list. Toolbars often include list boxes and buttons with arrows. For example, the Font Size button list box on the WordPad toolbar includes an arrow. To select an option other than the one shown in the list box or on the button, you click the arrow, and then click the option that you want to use.

Laura suggests you select a different font size using the arrow on the Font Size button list box.

To select a new font size from the Font Size button list box:

▶ **1.** Click the **Font Size button arrow** `10 ▾` on the WordPad toolbar.

▶ **2.** Click **18**. The Font Size list closes, and the font size you selected appears in the list box.

▶ **3.** Type a few characters to test the new font size.

▶ **4.** Click the **Font Size button arrow** `10 ▾` on the WordPad toolbar again.

▶ **5.** Click **12**.

▶ **6.** Type a few characters to test this type size. The text appears in 12-point text.

Dialog boxes also contain scroll bars and list boxes. You'll examine a typical dialog box next.

Working with Dialog Boxes

Recall that when you select a menu command or item followed by an ellipsis (...), a dialog box opens that allows you to provide more information about how a program should carry out a task. Some dialog boxes organize different kinds of information into groups. For example, the Print dialog box in Figure 1-25 includes the Select Printer and Page Range groups. Within these groups, you usually find tabs, option buttons, check boxes, and other controls that the program uses to collect information about how you want it to perform a task. Figure 1-25 displays examples of common dialog box controls.

Figure 1-25	Examples of dialog box controls

click a tab to view a group of controls whose functions are related

option buttons appear in groups; you click one option button in a group, and a dot indicates your selection

click in the text box and then type an entry

click a check box to turn an option off (not checked) or on (checked); you can select more than one check box in a group

click the up or down arrow to increase or decrease the number in the box

Laura says a good way to learn how dialog box controls work is to open a typical Windows Vista dialog box in WordPad, such as the Options dialog box. You use this dialog box to determine how text fits in the WordPad window and which toolbars appear. You'll remove the check mark from a check box and select an option button, and then see how these settings affect the WordPad window. Note that by default the status bar appears at the bottom of the WordPad window and that the ruler uses inches.

To work with a typical Windows Vista dialog box:

▶ **1.** Click **View** on the WordPad menu bar, and then click **Options**. The Options dialog box opens, by default, to the Rich Text tab.

   Trouble? If the Options dialog box does not display the Rich Text options, click the Rich Text tab.

▶ **2.** Click the **Status bar** check box to remove the check mark.

▶ **3.** Click the **Options** tab to select the measurement units that the WordPad ruler uses.

▶ **4.** Click the **Centimeters** option button.

▶ **5.** Click the **OK** button. WordPad accepts your changes and closes the Options dialog box.

Examine the WordPad window and note that the ruler now uses centimeters instead of inches, and the status bar no longer appears at the bottom of the window. You can use the Options dialog box again to restore the WordPad window to its original condition.

To restore the WordPad window:

▶ **1.** Click **View** on the WordPad menu bar, and then click **Options**. The Options dialog box opens.

▶ **2.** On the Rich Text tab, click the **Status bar** check box to insert a check mark.

▶ **3.** Click the **Options** tab, and then click the **Inches** option button.

> **4.** Click the **OK** button. The WordPad window now includes a status bar and a ruler that uses inches as its measurement unit.
>
> **5.** Click the **Close** button ❎ on the WordPad title bar to close WordPad.
>
> **6.** When you see the message "Do you want to save changes to Document?" click the **Don't Save** button.

Tip

You can also close a program window by clicking File on the menu bar, and then clicking Close or Exit.

In this session, you started Windows Vista and toured the desktop, learning how to interact with the items on the desktop and on the Start menu. You also started two Windows programs, manipulated windows, and learned how to select options from a menu, toolbar, and dialog box.

Session 1.1 Quick Check | Review

1. What does the operating system do for your computer?
2. A(n) _____ is a group or list of commands.
3. Name two ways to change the size of a window.
4. In Windows Vista, right-clicking selects an object and opens its

   _____ .
5. How can you access the programs listed on the All Programs submenu?
6. True or False. When you're not sure what to do with an object in Windows Vista, it's a good idea to right-click the object and examine its shortcut menu.
7. Even if you can't see an open program on your desktop, the program might be running. How can you tell if a program is running?
8. Why should you close a program when you are finished using it?

Session 1.2

Exploring Your Computer

To discover the contents and resources on your computer, you explore, or navigate, it. **Navigating** means moving from one location to another on your computer, such as from one file or folder to another. Windows Vista provides two ways to navigate, view, and work with the contents and resources on your computer—Computer and Windows Explorer.

Navigating with the Computer Window

When you use Computer, a window opens showing your computer, its storage devices, and other objects. The icons for these objects appear in the right pane of the Computer window. The Computer window also has a left pane, called the Navigation pane, which shows icons and links to other resources. As shown in Figure 1-26, this window also contains a toolbar with buttons that let you perform common tasks, and a Details pane at the bottom of the window that displays the characteristics of an object you select in the Computer window.

Figure 1-26   Relationship between your computer and the Computer window

Each storage device you can access on your computer is associated with a letter. If you have an older computer, it might have one or more 3.5-inch disk drives; the first one is drive A and the second is drive B. The first hard drive is usually drive C. (If you add other hard drives, they are usually drives D, E, and so on.) If you have a CD or DVD drive or plug a USB flash drive into a USB port, it usually has the next available letter in the alphabetic sequence. If you can access hard drives located on other computers in a network, those drives sometimes (although not always) have letters associated with them as well. Naming conventions for network drives vary. In the example shown in Figure 1-26, the network drive has the drive letter D.

You can use Computer to keep track of where your files are stored and to organize your files. In this session, you will explore the contents of your hard disk, which is assumed to be drive C. If you use a different drive on your computer, such as drive E, substitute its letter for *C* throughout this session.

Laura Halverson, the director of Metro Learning Center, is helping you plan a demonstration of the basics of Windows Vista. She wants you to start this session by opening the Computer window and exploring the contents of your computer.

To explore the contents of your computer using Computer:

▶ **1.** If you took a break after the previous session, make sure that your computer is on and Windows Vista is running.

▶ **2.** Click the **Start** button 🏁 on the taskbar, and then click **Computer**. The Computer window opens. See Figure 1-27. Your window might look different.

Computer window | Figure 1-27

3. In the Navigation pane, click the **Music** folder. A window opens showing the contents of that folder. See Figure 1-28.

| Figure 1-28 | Contents of the Music folder |

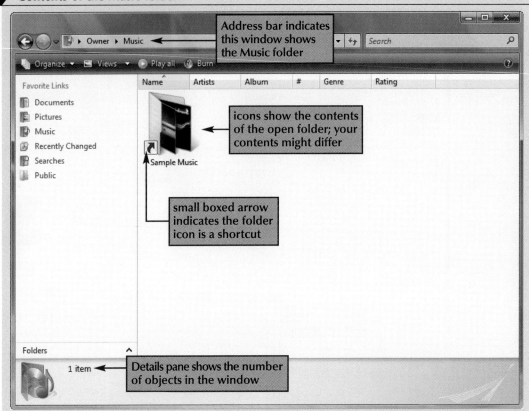

The Music folder is a convenient location for storing your music files. Many digital music players use this location by default when you rip, download, play, and burn music. Note that in Figure 1-28, the Sample Music icon represents a **shortcut**, a special type of file that serves as a direct link to another location that your computer can access, such as a folder, document, program, Windows tool, or Web site.

Trouble? If your window looks different from Figure 1-28, you can still perform the rest of the steps. For example, your window might contain a different number of folders and files.

▶ 4. Double-click the **Sample Music** icon to open the Sample Music folder. The right pane of the window shows the contents of the folder you double-clicked. You can learn more about the contents of a folder by selecting one or more of its files.

▶ 5. Click the first file listed in the Sample Music folder to select it. See Figure 1-29.

Viewing files in a folder ◄ **Figure 1-29**

As you open folders and navigate with the Computer window, the contents of the toolbar change so that they are appropriate for your current task—in Figure 1-29, the toolbar lists actions to take with the selected music file, such as Play all and Burn.

Laura mentions that you can change the appearance of most windows to suit your preferences. You'll change the view of the Computer window next so you can see the file icons more clearly.

Changing the View

Windows Vista provides at least six ways to view the contents of a folder—Extra Large Icons, Large Icons, Medium Icons, Small Icons, List, Details, and Tiles. The default view is Details view, which displays a small icon and lists details about each file. The icon provides a visual cue to the type of file. Although only Details view lists all file details, such as the file size and the date it was modified, you can see these details in any other view by pointing to an icon to display a ScreenTip.

Selecting a View | InSight

The view you select depends on your preferences and needs. When you display files in one of the large icon views, the icon displays a preview of the file's content. The preview images are big and easy to see, though the window can show fewer files. When you display files using smaller icons, the window can show more files but the preview images are not as easy to see.

Reference Window | **Changing the Icon View**

- In a folder window, click the Views button arrow on the toolbar, and then click a view.

or
- To cycle through the views listed on the Views menu, click the Views button more than once.

or
- Click the Views button arrow on the toolbar, and then drag the slider.

To practice switching from one view to another, Laura says you can display the contents of the Sample Music folder in Large Icons view. To do so, you'll use the Views button on the toolbar.

To view files in Large Icons view:

▶ **1.** In the Sample Music folder window, click the **Views button arrow** on the toolbar. See Figure 1-30.

Trouble? If you click the Views button instead of the arrow, you cycle through the views. Click the Views button arrow, and then continue with Step 2.

Figure 1-30 ▶ **Preparing to change views**

Tip

To change the appearance of the icons using the Views button, you can also drag the Views slider to select an icon size or set a size somewhere between the predefined views.

▶ **2.** Click **Large Icons**. The window shows the same files, but with larger icons than in Details view.

▶ **3.** Click the **Views button arrow** on the toolbar, and then click **Details** to return to Details view.

No matter which view you use, you can sort the file list by filename or other detail, such as size, type, or date. If you're viewing music files, you can sort by details such as artist or album title, and if you're viewing picture files, you can sort by details such as date taken or size. Sorting helps you find a particular file in a long file listing. For example, suppose you want to listen to a song by a certain artist, but can't remember the song title. You can sort the music file list in alphabetic order by artist to find the song you want.

To sort the music file list by artist:

▶ **1.** Click the **Artists** button at the top of the list of files. The up-pointing arrow on the Artists button indicates that the files are sorted in ascending (A–Z) alphabetic order by artist name.

▶ **2.** Click the **Artists** button again. The down-pointing arrow on the Artists button indicates that the sort order is reversed, with the artists listed in descending (Z–A) alphabetic order.

▶ **3.** Click the **Close** button ⬛ to close the Sample Music window.

Now Laura says you can compare Computer to Windows Explorer, another navigation tool.

Navigating with Windows Explorer

Like Computer, Windows Explorer also lets you easily navigate the resources on your computer. Most of the techniques you use with the Computer window apply to Windows Explorer—and vice versa. Both let you display and work with files and folders. By default, however, Windows Explorer also lets you see the hierarchy of all the folders on your computer. Viewing this hierarchy makes it easier to navigate your computer, especially if it contains many files and folders.

Laura suggests that during your Windows Vista demo, you compare navigation tools by using Windows Explorer to open the same folders you opened in the Computer window. As with other Windows Vista programs, you start Windows Explorer using the Start menu.

To start Windows Explorer:

▶ **1.** Click the **Start** button 🟢 on the taskbar, point to **All Programs**, click **Accessories**, and then click **Windows Explorer**. The Windows Explorer window opens, as shown in Figure 1-31. By default, when you start Windows Explorer from the All Programs submenu, the Documents folder opens. The Address bar shows the name of the open folder.

Figure 1-31 ▶ Windows Explorer window

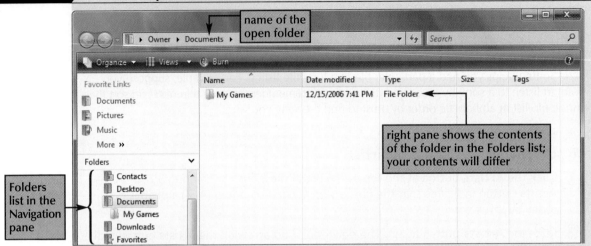

Trouble? If your Windows Explorer window looks slightly different from the one displayed in Figure 1-31, the configuration of your computer probably differs from the computer used to take this picture. Continue with Step 2.

▶ **2.** If the Windows Explorer window is not maximized, click the **Maximize** button on the Windows Explorer title bar.

Windows Explorer has the same tools and features you used in the Computer window: the Navigation pane, toolbar, Details pane, and file list in the right pane. However, the default Navigation pane in Windows Explorer includes a Folders list, which displays the folders on your computer. In the Folders list, you can click any folder to navigate directly to it.

The Folders list organizes your files and folders based on their location in the hierarchy of objects on your computer. Initially, the Folders list shows the main objects you can access from your desktop, including the Documents folder. If your desktop contains other folders or objects, those are displayed as well. The right pane of the Windows Explorer window displays the contents of the object selected in the Folders list. When you point to the Folders list, triangles appear next to some icons. An open triangle ▷ indicates that a folder contains other folders that are not currently displayed in the Folders list. Click the triangle to open the folder and display its subfolders. A filled triangle ◢ indicates the folder is open, and its subfolders are listed below the folder name. To display the contents of a folder or object in the right pane of Windows Explorer, click the name of the folder or object.

InSight	**Navigating with Windows Explorer and the Computer Window**

Navigating with Windows Explorer usually involves clicking triangles in the Folders list to open objects and find the folder you want, and then clicking that folder to display its contents in the right pane. In contrast, navigating with the Computer window usually involves double-clicking folders in the right pane to open them and find the file you want. In general, it's easier to navigate your computer using the Folder list because it shows the hierarchy of folders on your computer.

To compare Windows Explorer to the Computer window, Laura suggests that you open the same folder you opened before using the Computer window.

To open a folder:

▶ **1.** Click the **Music** folder in the Folders list. The contents of the Music folder appear in the right pane of the Windows Explorer window, and the folder you opened is selected in the left pane.

Trouble? If the Music folder does not appear in the Folders list, click the open triangle icon next to your personal folder (the one with your name).

▶ **2.** In the right pane, double-click **Sample Music**. The same music files you displayed earlier appear in the window.

▶ **3.** Click the **Close** button [X] on the title bar to close the window.

Before completing your demonstration, Laura says it is always a good idea to show people how to get help when they need it.

Getting Help

Windows Vista Help and Support provides on-screen information about the program you are using. Help for the Windows Vista operating system is available by clicking the Start button and then clicking Help and Support on the Start menu.

When you start Help for Windows Vista, the Windows Help and Support window opens, which gives you access to Help files stored on your computer as well as Help information stored on the Microsoft Web site. If you are not connected to the Web, you have access to only the Help files stored on your computer.

Laura suggests that you start Windows Vista Help, and then explore the information provided in the Windows Help and Support window.

Tip
For Help with a program such as WordPad, first start the program, and then click Help on the program's menu bar.

To start Windows Vista Help:

▶ **1.** Click the **Start** 🟦 button on the taskbar.

▶ **2.** Click **Help and Support**. The home page of Windows Help and Support opens. See Figure 1-32. The contents of the home page differ depending on whether you are connected to the Internet.

Tip
You can also start Windows Vista Help and Support from the Computer window or Windows Explorer by clicking the Help button (a circled question mark) on the toolbar.

Figure 1-32   **Windows Help and Support window**

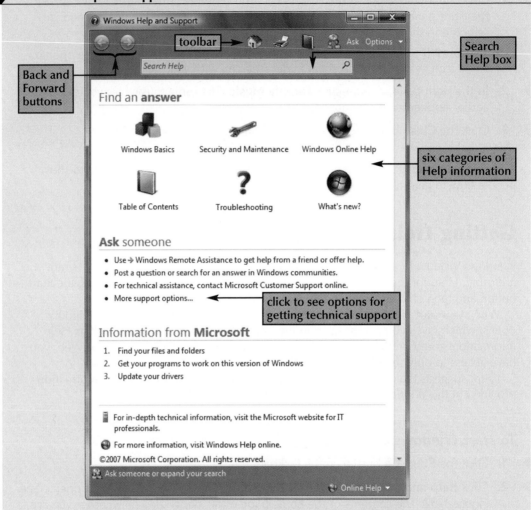

Trouble? If the Help and Support window does not display the page you see in Figure 1-32, click the Home icon on the toolbar at the top of the window to view Help contents.

The home page in Windows Help and Support organizes the vast amount of help and support information into six categories: Windows Basics, Security and Maintenance, Windows Online Help, Table of Contents, Troubleshooting, and What's new? The Windows Basics topics are designed for novice Windows users, and What's new? is for users who are familiar with earlier versions but who are new to Windows Vista. You are more likely to use Windows Online Help and the Table of Contents when you are more experienced and are looking for an answer to a particular question. (You need an Internet connection to use Windows Online Help.) Security and Maintenance provides articles about keeping your computer and Windows Vista in top condition, and Troubleshooting guides you step by step through procedures to help you solve problems.

To view the topics in a category, you click a category icon in the Find an answer section of the Windows Help and Support home page. Click a topic to open an article providing detailed information about that topic or instructions for performing a task. You can also use the toolbar to navigate Windows Help and Support. For example, click the

Home button to return to the Windows Help and Support home page. In addition to buttons providing quick access to pages in Windows Help and Support, the toolbar contains two other navigation buttons—the Back button and the Forward button. You use these buttons to navigate the pages you've already opened. Use the Back button to return to the previous page you viewed. After you do, you activate the Forward button, which you can click to go to the next page of those you've opened.

If you can't find the topic you want listed in any of the Help categories, the word that you are using for a feature or topic might be different from the word that Windows Vista uses. You can use the Search Help box to search for all keywords contained in the Help pages, not just the topic titles. In the Search Help box, you can type any word or phrase, click the Search Help button, and Windows Vista lists all the Help topics that contain that word or phrase.

Viewing Windows Basics Topics

Windows Vista Help and Support includes instructions on using Help itself. You can learn how to find a Help topic by using the Windows Basics category on the Windows Help and Support home page.

To view Windows Basics topics:

▶ 1. Click **Windows Basics**. A list of topics related to using Windows Vista appears in the Windows Help and Support window.

▶ 2. Scroll down to the "Help and support" heading, and then click **Getting help**. An article explaining how to get help appears, with the headings in the article listed in the "In this article" section.

▶ 3. Click **Getting help with dialog boxes and windows**. The Windows Help and Support window scrolls to that heading in the article.

▶ 4. Click the **Back** button on the toolbar. You return to the previous page you visited, which is the Windows Basics: all topics page. The Forward button is now active.

You can access the full complement of Help pages by using the Table of Contents.

Selecting a Topic from the Table of Contents

The Table of Contents logically organizes all of the topics in Windows Help and Support into books and pages. In the Table of Contents, you click a book to display the titles of its pages. Click a page to get help about a particular topic. For example, you can use the Table of Contents to learn more about files and folders.

To find a Help topic using the Table of Contents:

▶ 1. Click the **Help and Support home** button 🔘 on the Windows Help and Support toolbar.

▶ 2. Click **Table of Contents** on the home page. A list of books appears in the Windows Help and Support window.

▶ 3. Click **Files and folders** to display the list of pages included in the Files and folders book.

▶ 4. Click the topic **Working with files and folders**. The page you selected opens in the Windows Help and Support window.

▶ **5.** In the first line below the "What are files and folders" heading, click the word **file**, which is green by default. A tip shows the definition of *file*.

▶ **6.** Click a blank area of the Windows Help and Support window to close the tip.

Another Help tool is the Search Help box, a popular way to find answers to your Windows Vista questions.

Searching the Help Pages

If you can't find the topic you need by using Windows Basics or the Table of Contents, or if you want to quickly find Help pages related to a particular topic, you can use the Search Help box. Laura provides a typical example. Suppose you want to know how to exit Windows Vista, but you don't know if Windows refers to this as exiting, quitting, closing, or shutting down. You can search the Help pages to find just the right topic.

To search the Help pages for information on exiting Windows Vista:

▶ **1.** Click in the Search Help box. A blinking insertion point appears.

▶ **2.** Type **shutdown** and then click the **Search Help** button 🔍. A list of Help pages containing the word *shutdown* appears in the Windows Help and Support window. See Figure 1-33.

Figure 1-33 **Search Help results**

▶ **3.** Click the **Turning off your computer properly** topic. The article appears in the Windows Help and Support window.

If this article did not answer your question, you could click the **Ask someone or expand your search** link at the bottom of the Windows Help and Support window. Doing so opens a page listing other ways to get Help information.

▶ **4.** Click the **Close** button ❎ on the title bar to close the Windows Help and Support window.

If you are connected to the Internet, you can use Windows Online Help to find up-to-date information about Windows Vista on the Microsoft Web site. From the Help and Support home page, you can also contact Microsoft support or get in touch with other users of Windows Vista.

Now that you know how Windows Vista Help works, Laura reminds you to use it when you need to perform a new task or when you forget how to complete a procedure.

Turning Off Windows Vista

When you're finished working in Windows Vista, you should always turn it off properly. Doing so saves energy, preserves your data and settings, and makes sure your computer starts quickly the next time you use it.

You can turn off Windows Vista using a Lock button command or the Power button at the bottom of the Start menu. If your computer provides a Sleep option, you can click the Power button to put your computer to sleep. Windows saves your work, and then turns down the power to your monitor and computer. A light on the outside of your computer case blinks or turns yellow to indicate that the computer is sleeping. Because Windows saves your work, you do not need to close your programs or files before putting your computer to sleep. To wake your desktop computer, you press any key or move the mouse. To wake a notebook computer, you might need to press the hardware power button on your computer case instead. The screen looks exactly as it did when you turned off your computer.

If your computer does not provide a Sleep option or you otherwise need to shut down your computer, you can click the arrow next to the Lock button and then select a turn off command such as Shut Down or Restart. You sometimes need to shut down or restart your computer after installing new programs or hardware. Unlike putting your computer to sleep, shutting down closes all open programs, along with Windows itself, and then turns off your display and computer completely. Because shutting down doesn't save your work, you must save your files first.

Instead of using the Sleep, Shut Down, or Restart command, your school might prefer that you select the Log Off command on the Lock button menu. This command logs you off of Windows Vista but leaves the computer turned on, allowing another user to log on without restarting the computer. Check with your instructor or technical support person for the preferred method at your lab.

Log Off or Turn Off? | InSight

If more than one person uses your computer, you should generally log off Windows rather than turning off the computer. That way, the computer is ready for someone else to use. In either case, it's a good idea to log off (or shut down) when you're finished working to prevent an unauthorized person from accessing and changing your work.

In addition to the Shut Down, Restart, and Log Off commands, your Lock button menu might include the Standby and Cancel commands. You choose Standby when you want to put your computer into an idle state in which it consumes less power, but is still available for immediate use. Choose Cancel if you do not want to end your Windows session, but want to return to your previous task.

Laura suggests that you compare putting your computer to sleep and shutting down Windows Vista.

To turn off Windows Vista:

▶ **1.** Click the **Start** button 🪟 on the taskbar and then point to the **Power** button ⏻ .

▶ **2.** If the Power button is yellow, click the **Power** button ⏻ . Windows Vista saves your work, and then puts the computer to sleep. Wait a few moments, and then press any key or move the mouse. (If you are using a notebook computer, you might need to press the hardware power button, usually located on your computer case.)

Trouble? If your Power button is not yellow or does not look like the Power button in Step 1, skip to Step 3.

▶ **3.** Click the **Start** button 🪟 on the taskbar and then point to the arrow next to the Lock button 🔒 .

▶ **4.** Click **Shut Down**. Windows Vista turns off the computer.

Trouble? If you are supposed to log off rather than shut down, click Log Off instead and follow your school's logoff procedures.

In this session you learned how to start and close programs and how to use multiple programs at the same time. You learned how to work with windows and the controls they provide. Finally, you learned how to get help when you need it and how to turn off Windows Vista. With Laura's help, you should feel comfortable with the basics of Windows Vista and well prepared to demonstrate the fundamentals of using this operating system.

Review | **Session 1.2 Quick Check**

1. The _____ command on the Start menu provides access to your computer, its storage devices, and other objects.

2. Explain how to open a folder in the Folders list and display its subfolders.

3. When you navigate from the Computer window displaying the drives on your computer to the Sample Music folder, what happens to the toolbar in the Computer window?

4. How can you decide which view to use to display file and folder icons in the Computer window or Windows Explorer?

5. In the Windows Explorer window, what appears in the right pane when you click a folder icon in the left pane?

6. In Windows Help and Support, the _____ page organizes a vast amount of help and support information into six categories.

7. How can you quickly find Help pages related to a particular topic in the Windows Help and Support window?

8. Instead of using the Shut Down command on the Lock button menu, you can end your session with Windows Vista by clicking the _____ _____ at the bottom of the Start menu.

Review | **Tutorial Summary**

In this tutorial, you learned the basics of Windows Vista. You toured the desktop and learned how to open objects on the desktop. You explored the Start menu and opened its submenus and folders. You started programs from the Start menu, and then switched between multiple programs. You worked with windows by manipulating them. You selected options from a menu and buttons on a toolbar. You also examined typical dialog boxes and their controls. Then you explored using the Computer window and Windows Explorer, learned how to get help when you need it, and finally compared options for turning off Windows Vista.

Key Terms

active program
Aero
application
click
Computer
control
Control Panel
default settings
desktop
dialog box
Documents folder
double-click
drag
exit
file
Flip 3D
folder
graphical user
    interface (GUI)

Help and Support
icon
Internet
list box
log off
menu
menu command
menu convention
Microsoft Windows Vista
most frequently used
    programs list
mouse
multitask
navigate
operating system
pane
password
pinned items list

point
pointing device
program
program button
right-click
screen saver
ScreenTip
select
shortcut
shortcut menu
Start menu
Start Search box
submenu
user name
window
Windows Vista

Practice | Review Assignments

Practice the skills you learned in the tutorial.

There are no Data Files needed for the Review Assignments.

The day before your first Windows Vista demonstration for Metro Learning Center clients, Laura Halverson offers to observe your tour of the operating system and help you fine-tune your demo. You'll start working on the Windows Vista desktop, with no windows opened or minimized. Complete the following steps, recording your answers to any questions according to your instructor's preferences:

1. Start Windows Vista and log on, if necessary.
2. Use the mouse to point to each object on your desktop. Record the names and descriptions of each object as they appear in the tips.
3. Click the Start button. How many menu items or commands are on the Start menu?
4. Start WordPad. How many program buttons are now on the taskbar? (Don't count toolbar buttons or items in the notification area.)
5. Start Paint and maximize the Paint window. How many programs are running now?
6. Switch to WordPad. What are two visual clues that tell you that WordPad is the active program?
7. Close WordPad, and then restore the Paint window.
8. Open the Recycle Bin window. Record the number of items it contains.
9. Drag the Recycle Bin window so that you can see both it and the Paint window.
10. Close the Paint window from the taskbar.
11. Click the Organize button on the toolbar in the Recycle Bin window. Write down the commands on the menu. Point to Layout, and then click Menu Bar to display the menu bar.
12. Use any menu on the Recycle Bin menu bar to open a dialog box. What steps did you perform? What dialog box did you open? What do you think this dialog box is used for? Click Cancel to close the dialog box.
13. Click the Organize button on the toolbar, point to Layout, and then click Menu Bar to close the menu bar. Close the Recycle Bin window.
14. Open the Computer window, maximize it, and then open the Public folder in the Navigation pane. (*Hint*: If the Folders list is open, click the Folders button to close the list so you can see all of the folders in the Navigation pane.)
15. Open any folder in the Public folder that interests you. List the name and contents of that folder.
16. Close all open windows.
17. Start Windows Explorer. Use the Folders list in the Navigation pane to navigate to the same folder you opened in Step 15. What steps did you perform?
18. Change the view of the icons in the right pane of the Windows Explorer window. What view did you select? Describe the icons in the Windows Explorer window.
19. Close the Windows Explorer window.
20. Open Windows Help and Support.
21. Use the What's new? topics to learn something new about the Windows Vista desktop. What did you learn? How did you find this topic?
22. Use the Table of Contents to find information about the topic of mobile PCs, an enhanced feature in Windows Vista. How many topics are listed? What is their primary subject matter?
23. Use the Search Help box to find information about the topic of mobile PCs. How many topics are listed?
24. Close Help, and then close any other open windows.

25. Turn off Windows Vista by using the Sleep command, shutting down, or logging off.

26. Submit your answers to the preceding questions to your instructor, either in printed or electronic form, as requested.

| Apply | **Case Problem 1** |

Use the skills you learned in the tutorial to explore the contents of a computer for a client of At Your Service.

There are no Data Files needed for this Case Problem.

At Your Service   At Your Service is a small business with three locations in Boulder, Colorado, that provides troubleshooting and repair services for desktop and notebook personal computers. Roy Farwell, the manager of the west side branch, has hired you to do on-site troubleshooting and repair. You are preparing for a visit to a client who is new to Windows Vista and wants to determine the contents of his computer, including sample media files and related programs already provided in folders or menus. Complete the following steps:

1. Start Windows Vista and log on, if necessary.
2. From the Start menu, open the Computer window.
3. List the names of the drives on the computer.
4. Click the Documents link in the Navigation pane. Does the Documents folder contain any subfolders? If so, what are the names of the subfolders? If your Documents folder does not contain subfolders, click the Pictures and Music links in the Navigation pane and identify the contents of one of those folders.
5. Display the Folders list in the Computer window. (*Hint:* Click the Folders button near the bottom of the Navigation pane.) Where is the Documents folder located in the folder structure of your computer?
6. Open the Pictures folder, and then open a folder containing images, if necessary. View the files as Extra Large Icons.
7. Navigate to a folder that contains graphics, music, or other media files, such as videos or recorded TV. Point to a file to open the ScreenTip. What type of file did you select? What details are provided in the ScreenTip?
8. Close the Computer window, and then start Windows Explorer. In the Folders list, navigate to the Public folder.
9. Open the Public Pictures folder in the Public folder. Describe the contents of this folder. (If you cannot access the Public Pictures folder, return to the Pictures folder.) Open a subfolder, and then double-click a file icon. Describe what happens.
10. Close all open windows, and then use the Start menu to open a program that you could use with picture files. What program did you start?
11. Open Windows Help and Support, and then find and read topics that explain how to use a program you started in a previous step.
12. Close all open windows.
13. Submit your answers to the preceding questions to your instructor, either in printed or electronic form, as requested.

Apply	**Case Problem 2**

Use the skills you learned in the tutorial to work with Windows Vista installed on a computer for a garden center.

There are no Data Files needed for this Case Problem.

Dover Landscapes After earning a degree in horticulture and working as a master gardener and landscape designer in Dover, Delaware, Liz Borowski started a garden center specializing in native plants and environmental designs. So that she can concentrate on landscape designs and marketing, she hired you to help her perform office tasks as her business grows. She asks you to start by teaching her the basics of using her computer, which runs Windows Vista. She especially wants to know which programs are installed on her computer and what they do. Complete the following steps:

1. Open the Start menu and write down the programs on the pinned items list.
2. Start one of the programs on the pinned items list and then describe what it does. Close the program.
3. Open the Start menu and write down the programs on the most frequently used programs list.
4. Start one of the programs on the most frequently used programs list and then describe what it does. Close the program.
5. Open the Accessories folder on the All Programs submenu, and examine the list of programs in the Accessories folder and its subfolders.
6. Use Windows Help and Support to research one of the programs you examined in the previous step, such as Calculator or Notepad. Determine the purpose of the program and how to perform a task using that program.
7. Use the Search Help box in Windows Help and Support to list all the Help topics related to the program you researched in the previous step.

⊕ **EXPLORE**   8. Start the program you researched. Click Help on the program's menu bar (or click the Help button) and then click each command on the Help menu to explore the Help topics. Compare these topics to the ones included in the Windows Help and Support window.

⊕ **EXPLORE**   9. Open and read a Help topic in the program. Find a similar topic in Windows Help and Support, and then read that topic. Compare the topics, if they are different, to determine when you would be likely to use Windows Help and Support, and when you'd use the program's Help.

10. Close all open windows.
11. Submit the results of the preceding steps to your instructor, either in printed or electronic form, as requested.

Challenge	**Case Problem 3**

Extend what you've learned to customize the Windows Explorer window for a financial consultant.

There are no Data Files needed for this Case Problem.

Vernon Taylor Moe Vernon and Brett Taylor recently started their own small firm called Vernon Taylor in Bloomington, Indiana, which analyzes the finances of Bloomington businesses and recommends ways to plan for growth and success. Most of these businesses want to provide employee benefits while increasing revenues and profits. Brett Taylor uses his Windows Vista computer to write reports, study and compare data, and communicate with clients. He typically uses the Windows Explorer window to work with his files, but suspects he is not taking full advantage of its features. As his new assistant, he asks you show him around the Windows Explorer window and demonstrate how to customize its appearance. Complete the following steps:

1. Start Windows Explorer. Click the Organize button on the Windows Explorer toolbar, and write down any commands that seem related to changing the appearance of the window.

⊕ EXPLORE

2. Select a command that lays out the Windows Explorer window so that it displays a single pane for viewing files. Then restore the window to its original condition.

3. Navigate to a folder containing graphic files, such as the Pictures folder. Double-click the Sample Pictures folder to open it. (If your computer does not contain a Sample Pictures folder, open any folder that displays pictures.) Display the icons using Large Icons view.

4. Change the view to Details view. Describe the differences between Large Icons and Details view.

⊕ EXPLORE

5. Click the Slide Show button on the toolbar. Describe what happens, and then press the Esc key.

6. With the Details pane open, click a picture file. Describe the contents of the Details pane.

⊕ EXPLORE

7. Repeatedly click the Views button to cycle from one view to another. Describe the changes in the window.

8. Display the window in Details view.

⊕ EXPLORE

9. Close the Folders list. (*Hint*: Click the Folders button.) On the Organize button menu, click Folder and Search Options to open the Folder Options dialog box. Select the option that uses Windows classic folders, and then click the OK button. Describe the changes in the Sample Pictures window.

⊕ EXPLORE

10. Open the Folder Options dialog box again, click the Restore Defaults button, and then click the OK button.

11. Open the Windows Help and Support window and search for information about folder options. Find a topic explaining how to show or hide file extensions for known file types. Record your findings.

12. Close all open windows.

13. Submit the results of the preceding steps to your instructor, either in printed or electronic form, as requested.

Research	**Case Problem 4**

Work with the skills you've learned, and use the Internet, to provide information to an academic tour company.

There are no Data Files needed for this Case Problem.

Go and Learn Tours   Years after spending their college junior year abroad in Salzburg, Austria, Rebecca Springer and Betsy Modine decided to start a travel service for people who wanted to learn about the history, art, literature, and music of Austria. Betsy spends most of the year in Washington, D.C., marketing the business and enrolling travelers on a Go and Learn tour. Rebecca works part-time in the Washington, D.C., office and often travels to Salzburg to organize the local lecturers. Both use laptop computers running Windows Vista to run their business when they are on the move. They have hired you as a consultant to help them use and maintain their computers. For your first task, Betsy asks you to help her research wireless networks. She wants to set up a wireless network in the Go and Learn office so that she and Rebecca can easily connect to the Internet wherever they are working. You suggest starting with Windows Help and Support, and then expanding to the Internet to search for the latest information. Complete the following steps:

1. In Windows Help and Support, find information about the hardware Betsy and Rebecca need to set up a wireless network.

2. On the Windows Help and Support home page, use the Windows Online Help link to visit the Microsoft Web site containing Windows Vista information.

3. Use the Search text box on the Microsoft Web site to search for information about setting up a wireless network.

4. Choose a topic that describes how to set up a wireless network for a home or small office, and then read the topic thoroughly.

5. Write one to two pages for Betsy and Rebecca explaining what they need to set up a wireless network and the steps they should perform.

6. Submit the results of the preceding steps to your instructor, either in printed or electronic form, as requested.

Assess | **SAM Assessment and Training**

If you have a SAM user profile, you may have access to hands-on instruction, practice, and assessment of the skills covered in this tutorial. Log in to your SAM account (**http://sam2007.course.com**) to launch any assigned training activities or exams that relate to the skills covered in this tutorial.

Review | **Quick Check Answers**

Session 1.1

1. The operating system is software that helps the computer perform essential tasks such as displaying information on the computer screen and saving data on disks.
2. menu
3. Drag a border or corner of the window or restore or maximize the window.
4. shortcut menu
5. Click the Start button, and then point to the All Programs command.
6. true
7. Its button appears on the taskbar.
8. to conserve computer resources such as memory

Session 1.2

1. Computer
2. Point to the Folders list, and then click an open triangle next to a folder.
3. Some buttons change to let you perform tasks appropriate for music files, such as Play All and Burn.
4. The view you select depends on your preferences and needs. In large icon views, icons are big and easy to see, though the window can show only a few files. Small icon views display more files, but the icons are not as easy to see.
5. the contents of the folder you clicked
6. home
7. Use the Search Help box.
8. Power button

Ending Data Files

There are no ending Data Files needed for this tutorial.

Objectives

Session 2.1
- Develop file management strategies
- Plan the organization of your files and folders
- Explore files and folders
- Find files quickly

Session 2.2
- Create folders
- Select files and folders
- Name, copy, move, and delete files
- Work with new files

Session 2.3
- Sort, group, and stack files
- Set the appearance of a folder window
- Compress and extract files
- Copy files to removable media

Organizing Your Files

Managing Files and Folders in Windows Vista

Case | Azalea Inn

The Azalea Inn is a hotel in a historic mansion in Mobile, Alabama, owned by Andrew and Marilynne Ambrose. The Azalea Inn hosts travelers visiting Mobile, and it is a popular site for wedding parties and receptions, especially when the azaleas are in bloom. The Azalea Inn holds a ball during Mobile's Azalea Festival, an annual spring event. Andrew, the marketing manager, has worked hard to position the Azalea Inn at the center of the Azalea Festival. Andrew and Marilynne hired you to assist with marketing, particularly in using computer tools to track repeat customers and measure the success of marketing campaigns. Before you begin, Andrew asks you to organize the files on his new computer. Although he has only a few files, he wants to use a logical organization to help him find his work as he stores more files and folders on his new computer.

In this tutorial, you'll work with Andrew to devise a strategy for managing files. You'll learn how Windows Vista organizes files and folders, and you'll examine Windows Vista file management tools. You'll create folders and organize files within them. You'll also use techniques to display the information you need in folder windows, and explore options for working with compressed files.

Starting Data Files

Tutorial.02 →

Tutorial
Azalea Inn.jpg
Brochure.rtf
Flyer.rtf
Logo.bmp
Marketing Budget.txt
Pink Azalea.jpg
Purple Azalea.jpg
Rate List.mht

Review
Alabama.jpg
Business Plan.rtf
Event Form.xls
Letterhead.bmp
Mobile.jpg
Schedule.rtf

Case1
Bing Cherry.jpg
Buffet.jpg
Class Descriptions.rtf
Fruit Bowl.jpg
Image for Ad.bmp

Case1
Ingredients.txt
Menu-Fall.rtf
Menu-Spring.rtf
Menu-Summer.rtf
Menu-Winter.rtf

Case2
Hanson-BreakEven.xls
Hanson-Commissions.xls
Hanson-General Ledger.xls
Hanson-Tax Reminders.txt

Case2
Moore-BreakEven.xls
Moore-Expenses.xls
Moore-General Ledger.xls
Moore-TaxReminders.txt

Case4
Checklist.txt
Contacts.mdb
Customer Satisfaction.mht
Milestones.ppt
Staff Training.ppt

Session 2.1

Getting Prepared to Manage Your Files

Knowing how to save, locate, and organize computer files makes you more productive when you are working with a computer. Recall that a file, often referred to as a **document**, is a collection of data that has a name and is stored on a computer. After you create a file, you can open it, edit its contents, print it, and save it again—usually with the same program you used to create it. You organize files by storing them in folders, which are containers for your files. You need to organize files and folders so that you can find them easily and work efficiently.

A file cabinet is a common metaphor for computer file organization. A computer is like a file cabinet that has two or more drawers—each drawer is a storage device, or **disk**. Each disk contains folders that hold documents, or files. To make it easy to retrieve files, you arrange them logically into folders. For example, one folder might contain financial data, another might contain your creative work, and another could contain information you're collecting for an upcoming vacation.

A computer can store folders and files on different types of disks, ranging from removable media—such as **USB drives** (also called USB flash drives), **compact discs (CDs)**, and **3.5-inch disks**—to **hard disks**, or fixed disks, which are permanently stored on a computer. Hard disks are the most popular type of computer storage because they can contain many gigabytes of data, millions of times more data than a 3.5-inch disk, and are economical.

To have your computer access a removable disk, you must insert the disk into a **drive**, which is a computer device that can retrieve and sometimes record data on a disk. See Figure 2-1. A hard disk is already contained in a drive, so you don't need to insert it each time you use the computer.

| Figure 2-1 | Computer drives and disks |

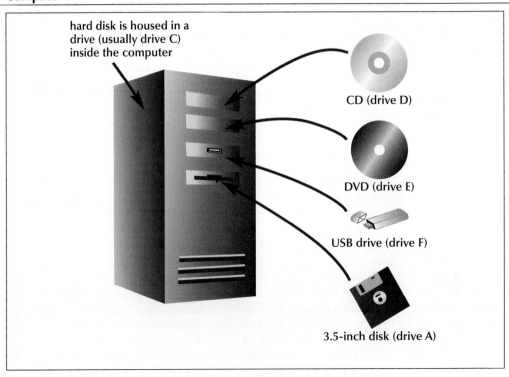

hard disk is housed in a
drive (usually drive C)
inside the computer

CD (drive D)

DVD (drive E)

USB drive (drive F)

3.5-inch disk (drive A)

A computer distinguishes one drive from another by assigning each a drive letter. Recall from Tutorial 1 that if your computer has a 3.5-inch disk drive, it is drive A. The hard disk is usually assigned to drive C. The remaining drives can have any other letters, but are usually assigned in the order that the drives were installed on the computer—so your USB drive might be drive D or drive F.

Understanding the Need for Organizing Files and Folders

Windows Vista stores thousands of files in many folders on the hard disk of your computer. These are system files that Windows Vista needs to display the desktop, use drives, and perform other operating system tasks. To ensure system stability and to find files quickly, Windows organizes the folders and files in a hierarchy, or **file system**. At the top of the hierarchy, Windows stores folders and important files that it needs when you turn on the computer. This location is called the **root directory** and is usually drive C (the hard disk). The term *root* refers to another popular metaphor for visualizing a file system—an upside-down tree, which reflects the file hierarchy that Windows uses. In Figure 2-2, the tree trunk corresponds to the root directory, the branches to the folders, and the leaves to the files.

Windows file hierarchy | Figure 2-2

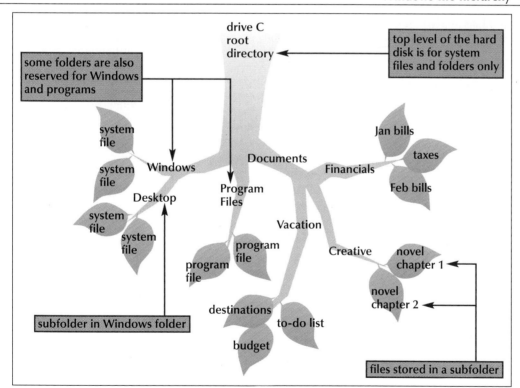

Note that some folders contain other folders. An effectively organized computer contains a few folders in the root directory, and those folders contain other folders, also called **subfolders**.

The root directory, or top level, of the hard disk is for system files and folders only—you should not store your own work here because it could interfere with Windows or a program. (If you are working in a computer lab, you might not be allowed to access the root directory.)

Do not delete or move any files or folders from the root directory of the hard disk; doing so could mean that you can't run or start the computer. In fact, you should not reorganize or change any folder that contains installed software because Windows Vista expects to find the files for specific programs within certain folders; if you reorganize or change these folders, Windows Vista can't locate and start the programs stored in that folder. Likewise, you should not make changes to the folder (usually named Windows) that contains the Windows Vista operating system.

Because the top level of the hard disk is off-limits for your files—the ones that you create, open, and save on the hard disk—you must store your files in subfolders. If you are working on your own computer, you should store your files within the Documents folder. If you are working in a computer lab, you will probably use a different location that your instructor specifies. If you simply store all your files in one folder, however, you will soon have trouble finding the files you want. Instead, you should create folders within a main folder to separate files in a way that makes sense for you.

Even if you store most of your files on removable media, such as USB drives, you still need to organize those files into folders and subfolders. Before you start creating folders, whether on a hard disk or removable disk, you should plan the organization you will use.

Developing Strategies for Organizing Files and Folders

The type of disk you use to store files determines how you organize those files. Figure 2-3 shows how you could organize your files on a hard disk if you were taking a full semester of business classes. To duplicate this organization, you would open the main folder for your documents, create four folders—one each for the Basic Accounting, Computer Concepts, Management Skills II, and Professional Writing courses—and then store the writing assignments you complete in the Professional Writing folder.

If you store your files on removable media, such as a USB drive or rewritable CD, you can use a simpler organization because you do not have to account for system files. In general, the larger the medium, the more levels of folders you should use because large media can store more files and, therefore, need better organization. For example, if you were organizing your files on a 128-MB USB drive, you could create folders in the top level of the USB drive for each general category of documents you store—one each for Courses, Creative, Financials, and Vacation. The Courses folder could then include one folder for each course, and each of those folders could contain the appropriate files.

Organizing folders and files on a hard disk ◄ **Figure 2-3**

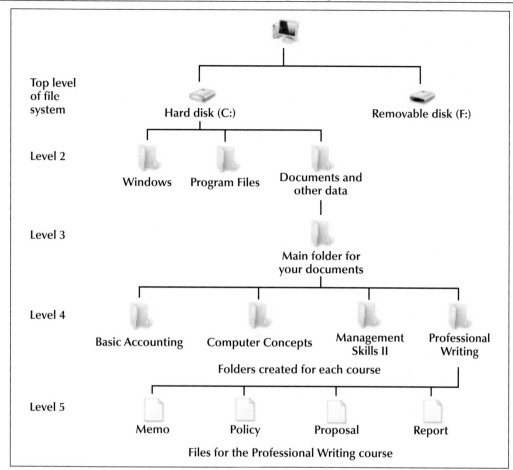

Top level of file system

Hard disk (C:)   Removable disk (F:)

Level 2

Windows   Program Files   Documents and other data

Level 3

Main folder for your documents

Level 4

Basic Accounting   Computer Concepts   Management Skills II   Professional Writing

Folders created for each course

Level 5

Memo   Policy   Proposal   Report

Files for the Professional Writing course

If your computer has a 3.5-inch disk drive, you could also organize these files on 1.44-MB 3.5-inch disks. Because the storage capacity of a 3.5-inch disk is much less than that of a USB drive, you would probably use one 3.5-inch disk for your courses, another for creative work, and so on. If you had to create large documents for your courses, you could use one 3.5-inch disk for each course.

If you work on two computers, such as one computer at an office or school and another computer at home, you can duplicate the folders you use on both computers to simplify transferring files from one computer to another. For example, if you have four folders in your Documents folder on your work computer, you would create these same four folders on your removable medium as well as in the Documents folder of your home computer. If you change a file on the hard disk of your home computer, you can copy the most recent version of the file to the corresponding folder on your removable medium so that it is available when you are at work. You also then have a **backup**, or duplicate copy, of important files that you need.

Planning Your Organization

Now that you've explored the basics of organizing files on a computer, you can plan the organization of your files for this book by recording your answers to the following questions:

1. How do you obtain the files for this book (on a USB drive from your instructor, for example)? _____

2. On what drive do you store your files for this book (drive A, C, D, for example)? _____

3. Do you use a particular folder on this drive? If so, which folder do you use? _____

4. Is this folder contained within another folder? If so, what is the name of that main folder? _____

5. On what type of disk do you save your files for this book (hard disk, USB drive, CD, or network drive, for example)? _____

If you cannot answer all of these questions, ask your instructor for help.

Exploring Files and Folders

As mentioned in Tutorial 1, Windows Vista provides two tools for exploring the files and folders on your computer—Windows Explorer and Computer. Both display the contents of your computer, using icons to represent drives, folders, and files. However, by default, each presents a slightly different view of your computer. Windows Explorer shows the files, folders, and drives on your computer, making it easy to navigate, or move from one location to another within the file hierarchy. Computer shows the drives on your computer and makes it easy to perform system tasks, such as viewing system information. Most of the time, you use one of these tools to open a folder window that displays the files and subfolders in a folder.

InSight	**Using Folder Windows**

The term *folder window* refers to any window that displays the contents of a folder, including the Computer, Windows Explorer, and Recycle Bin windows, and the Save As and Open dialog boxes (which you'll examine later in this tutorial). In all of these windows, you can use the same techniques to display folders and their contents, navigate your computer, and filter, sort, group, and stack files. Instead of distinguishing between Computer and Windows Explorer, think of managing your files in a folder window.

The Windows Explorer and Computer windows are divided into two sections, called panes. The left pane is the Navigation pane, and contains a **Favorite Links list**, which can provide quick access to the folders you use often. (You'll work with the Favorite Links list later in the tutorial.) The right pane lists the contents of your folders and other locations. If you select a folder in the Navigation pane, the contents of that folder appear in the right pane. In addition to the Favorite Links list, the Navigation pane can display a Folders list, which shows the hierarchy of the folders and other locations on your computer.

If the Folders list showed all the folders on your computer at once, it could be a very long list. Instead, you open drives and folders only when you want to see what they contain. If a folder contains undisplayed subfolders, an expand icon ▷ appears to the left of the folder icon. (The same is true for drives.) To view the folders contained in an object, you click the expand icon. A collapse icon ◢ then appears next to the folder icon; click the collapse icon to hide the folder's subfolders. To view the files contained in a folder, you click the folder icon, and the files appear in the right pane. See Figure 2-4.

Tip

To display or hide the Folders list in a folder window, click the Folders bar in the Navigation pane.

Viewing files in Windows Explorer   Figure 2-4

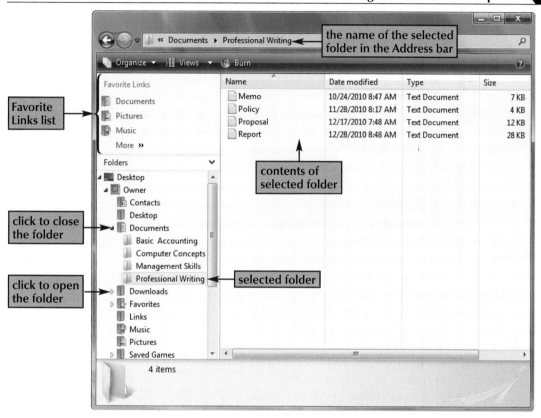

Using the Folders list helps you navigate your computer and orients you to your current location. As you move, copy, delete, and perform other tasks with the files and folders in the right pane of a folder window, you can refer to the Folders list to see how your changes affect the overall organization.

Both Windows Explorer and Computer let you view, organize, and access the drives, folders, and files on your computer. In addition to using the Folders list, you can navigate your computer in other ways:

• **Opening drives and folders in the right pane**: To view the contents of a drive or folder, double-click the drive or folder icon in the right pane of the folder window. For example, to view the contents of the Professional Writing folder shown in Figure 2-5, you can double-click the Professional Writing icon in the right pane.

Figure 2-5 | **Viewing folders in Windows Explorer**

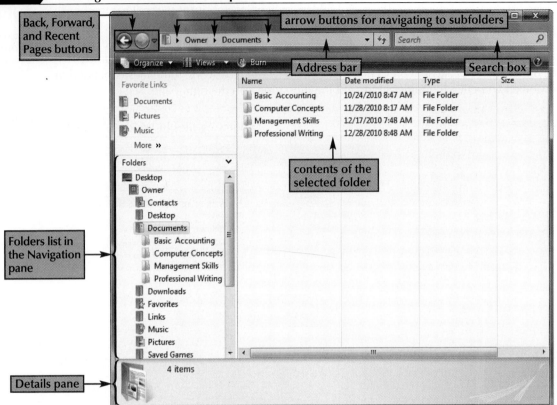

- **Using the Address bar**: You can use the Address bar to navigate to a different folder. The Address bar displays your current folder as a series of locations separated by arrows. Click a folder name, such as "Owner" in Figure 2-5, or an arrow button to navigate to a different location. You'll explore these controls later in the tutorial.
- **Clicking the Back, Forward, and Recent Pages buttons**: Use the Back, Forward, and Recent Pages buttons to navigate to other folders you have already opened. After you use the Address bar to change folders, for example, you can use the Back button to return to the original folder. As with the Address bar arrow button, you can click the Recent Pages button to navigate to a location you've visited recently.
- **Using the Search box**: To find a file or folder stored in the current folder or its subfolders, type a word or phrase in the Search box. The search begins as soon as you start typing. Windows finds files based on text in the filename, text within the file, and other characteristics of the file, such as tags (descriptive words or phrases you add to your files) or the author. For example, if you're looking for a document named September Income, you can type *Sept* in the Search box. Windows searches the current folder and its subfolders, and then displays any file whose filename contains a word starting with *Sept,* including the September Income document.

These navigation controls are available in Windows Explorer, Computer, and other folder windows, including many dialog boxes. In fact, all of these folder windows share common tools. By default, when you first open Computer, it shows all the drives available on your computer, whereas Windows Explorer shows the folders on your computer. However, by changing a single setting, you can make the two windows interchangeable. If you open the Folders list in Computer, you have the same setup as Windows Explorer. Likewise, if you close the Folders list in the Windows Explorer window, you have the same setup as in the Computer window.

Andrew is accustomed to starting Windows Explorer when he wants to manage his files. You'll use Windows Explorer to manage files in the rest of this tutorial.

Using Windows Explorer

Windows Vista provides a personal folder for your subfolders and files. Your personal folder is labeled with the name you use to log on to the computer, such as *Andrew*. Your personal folder contains folders that most users open frequently, such as Pictures, Music, and Favorites. Your personal folder also contains a **Documents folder**, which is designed to store your data files—the memos, reports, spreadsheets, presentations, and other files that you create, edit, and manipulate in a program. Although the Pictures folder is designed to store graphics and the Music folder is designed to store music files, you can store graphics, music, or any other type of file in the Documents folder, especially if doing so makes it easier to find these files when you need them. If you are working in a computer lab, you might not be able to access the Documents folder, or you might be able to store files there only temporarily because that folder is emptied every night. Instead, you might permanently store your Data Files on removable media or in a different folder on your computer or network.

When you start Windows Explorer, it opens to the Documents folder by default. If you can't access the Documents folder, the screens you see as you perform the following steps will differ. However, you can still perform the steps accurately.

To examine the organization of your computer using Windows Explorer:

▶ **1.** Click the **Start** button 🪟 on the taskbar, point to **All Programs**, click **Accessories**, and then click **Windows Explorer**. The Windows Explorer window opens.

▶ **2.** Scroll the Folder list, if necessary, and then click the **expand** icon ▷ next to the Computer icon. The drives on your computer appear under the Computer icon, as shown in Figure 2-6. The contents of your computer will differ.

Figure 2-6 ▶ **Viewing the contents of your computer**

3. Click the **expand** icon ▷ next to the Local Disk (C:) icon. The contents of your hard disk appear under the Local Disk (C:) icon.

   Trouble? If you do not have permission to access drive C, skip Step 3 and read but do not perform the remaining steps.

   Documents is still the selected folder. To view the contents of an object in the right pane, you can click the object's icon in the Folders list.

4. Click **Public** in the Folders list. Its contents appear in the right pane. Public is a built-in Windows Vista folder that contains folders any user can access on this computer.

You've already mastered the basics of navigating your computer with Windows Explorer. You click expand icons in the Folders list until you find the folder that you want. Then, you click the folder icon in the Folders list to view the files it contains, which are displayed in the right pane.

Navigating to Your Data Files

To navigate to the files you want, it helps to know the **file path**, a notation that indicates a file's location on your computer. The file path leads you through the folder and file organization to your file. For example, the Logo file is stored in the Tutorial subfolder of the Tutorial.02 folder. If you are working on a USB drive, for example, the path to this file might be as follows:

   F:\Tutorial.02\Tutorial\Logo.bmp

This path has four parts, with each part separated by a backslash (\ ):

- **F**: The drive name; for example, drive F might be the name for the USB drive. If this file were stored on the primary hard disk, the drive name would be C.
- **Tutorial.02**: The top-level folder on drive F
- **Tutorial**: A subfolder in the Tutorial.02 folder
- **Logo.bmp**: The full filename with the file extension

If someone tells you to find the file F:\Tutorial.02\Tutorial\Logo.bmp, you know you must navigate to your USB drive, open the Tutorial.02 folder, and then open the Tutorial folder to find the Logo file. Windows Explorer and Computer can display the full file path in their Address bars so you can keep track of your current location as you navigate.

You can use Windows Explorer to navigate to the Data Files you need for the rest of this tutorial. Refer to the information you provided in the "Planning Your Organization" section and note the drive on your system that contains your Data Files. In the following steps, that drive is assumed to be Removable Disk (F:), a USB drive. If necessary, substitute the appropriate drive on your system when you perform the steps.

> **Tip**
>
> To display the file path in a folder window, click to the right of the text in the Address bar.

To navigate to your Data Files:

▶ 1. Make sure your computer can access your Data Files for this tutorial. For example, if you are using a USB drive, insert the drive into the USB port.

 Trouble? If you don't have the starting Data Files, you need to get them before you can proceed. Your instructor will either give you the Data Files or ask you to obtain them from a specified location (such as a network drive). In either case, make a backup copy of your Data Files before you start using them so you will have the original files available in case you need to start over. If you have any questions about the Data Files, see your instructor or technical support person for assistance.

▶ 2. In the Windows Explorer window, click the **expand** icon ▷ next to the drive containing your Data Files, such as Removable Disk (F:). A list of the folders on that drive appears.

▶ 3. If the list of folders does not include the Tutorial.02 folder, continue clicking the **expand** icon ▷ to navigate to the folder that contains the Tutorial.02 folder.

▶ 4. Click the **expand** icon ▷ next to the Tutorial.02 folder to expand the folder, and then click the **Tutorial.02** folder. Its contents appear in the Folders list and in the right pane of the Windows Explorer window. The Tutorial.02 folder contains the Case1, Case2, Case4, Review, and Tutorial folders, as shown in Figure 2-7. (Because Case Problem 3 does not require any files, the Tutorial.02 folder does not include a Case3 folder.) The other folders on your system might vary.

Figure 2-7 | Navigating to the Tutorial.02 folder

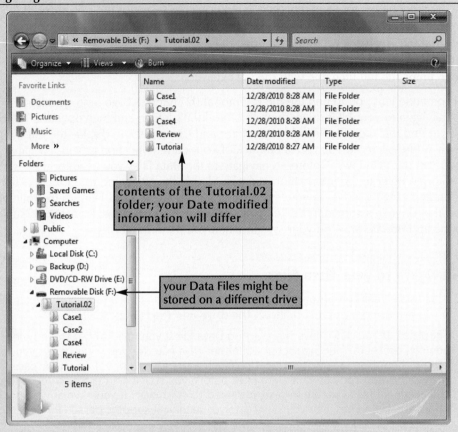

▶ **5.** In the left pane, click the **Tutorial** folder. The files it contains appear in the right pane. You want to view them as medium icons.

▶ **6.** Click the **Views button arrow** on the toolbar, and then click **Medium Icons**. The files appear in Medium Icons view in the Windows Explorer window. See Figure 2-8.

Files in the Tutorial folder in Medium Icons view ◂ Figure 2-8

Because the icons used to identify types of files depend on the programs installed on your computer, the icons that appear in your window might be different from the ones shown in Figure 2-8.

Although you changed the view of the files in the Tutorial folder to Medium Icons view, other folders continue to display files in the default Details view unless you change the view.

Next, you can navigate with the Address bar to compare using that technique to using the Folders list.

Navigating with the Address Bar

Recall that the Address bar, located at the top of every folder window, displays your current folder as a series of locations separated by arrows. For example, in Figure 2-9, the Address bar shows the Tutorial.02 and Tutorial folders separated by an arrow, indicating that Tutorial is the current folder and it's stored in the Tutorial.02 folder. If a chevron button « appears, you can click it to list the folders and drives containing the locations displayed in the Address bar. In Figure 2-9, the first item in this list is Removable Disk (F:), which contains the Tutorial.02 folder. The next item in this list is Computer, which contains Removable Disk (F:). This list also includes locations at higher levels in the folder hierarchy of your computer, such as Computer and Recycle Bin.

To change your location, you can click or type a folder name in the Address bar. For example, you can click Tutorial.02 to navigate to that folder. You can also type the path to the folder you want or type the name of a standard, built-in Windows folder, such as Documents, Favorites, Music, or Pictures.

Figure 2-9 ▸ **Navigating with the Address bar**

After you've navigated to a location by any method, you can click the Back, Forward, and Recent Pages buttons to revisit folders you've already opened. For example, if you navigate first to drive F:, then to the Tutorial.02 folder, and then to the Tutorial folder, you can click the Back button to open your previous location, the Tutorial.02 folder. When you do, the Forward button becomes active. You can then click the Forward button to again open the next location in your sequence, the Tutorial folder. To navigate to any recent location, click the Recent Pages button, and then click a location in the list.

Tip

To navigate to a subfolder of a folder that appears in the Address bar, click the arrow to the right of that folder name, and then click the subfolder you want.

To navigate using the Address bar and Back button:

1. In the folder window displaying the contents of your Tutorial folder, click the **chevron** button ⟪ on the Address bar, and then click the drive containing your Data Files, such as Removable Disk (F:), in the list. The window displays the contents of the drive containing your Data Files.

   Trouble? If the drive containing your Data Files is not listed in the chevron button menu, click Computer.

2. Click the **arrow** button ▶ to the right of Computer, and then click **Local Disk (C:)**.

   Trouble? If Local Disk (C:) does not appear in the list of drives on your computer, click any other drive.

3. Click the **Back** button ◄ on the Address bar one or more times to return to the drive containing your Data Files.

4. Click the **Recent Pages** button ▾ to display a list of locations you visited, and then click **Tutorial.02**. The subfolders in your Tutorial.02 folder appear in the right pane.

Leave the Windows Explorer window open so that you can work with other file and folder tools.

Using the Search Box to Find Files

After you use a computer awhile, you're likely to have many hundreds of files stored in various folders. If you know where you stored a file, it's easy to find it—you can use any navigation technique you like to navigate to that location and then scan the file list to find the file. Often, however, finding a file is more time consuming than that. You know that you stored a file somewhere in a standard folder such as Documents or Music, but finding the file might mean opening dozens of folders and scanning many long file lists. To save time, you can use the Search box to find your file quickly.

The **Search box** appears next to the Address bar in any folder window. To find a file in the current folder or any of its subfolders, you start typing text associated with the file. This search text can be part of the filename, text in the file, tags (keywords you associate with a file), or other file properties. By default, Windows searches for files by examining the filenames and contents of the files displayed in the folder window, including files in any subfolders. If it finds a file whose filename contains a word starting with the search text you specify, it displays that file in the folder window. For example, you can use the search text *inn* to find files named Azalea Inn and Innsbruck Plans. Windows also looks for files that contain a word starting with your search text. If it finds one, it displays that file in the folder window. For example, using *inn* as the search text also finds files containing words such as inning, inner, and innovate.

Andrew asks you to find a digital photo of azaleas. He knows he gave you at least one photo of an azalea along with the other files he wants you to organize. You can find this file by starting to type *azalea* in the Search box.

To use the Search box to find a file:

▶ **1.** In the folder window displaying the contents of your Tutorial.02 folder, click in the Search box.

▶ **2.** Type **a** and then pause. Windows Vista examines the names and the contents of the files in the Tutorial.02 folder and its subfolders, searching for a file whose filename or contents includes a word starting with *a*. Many files in the Tutorial.02 folder meet this criterion. You can continue typing to narrow the selection.

▶ **3.** Type **za** so that the search text is now *aza*. Only eight files have filenames or contents that include a word beginning with *aza*. See Figure 2-10.

Searching for a file ◀ Figure 2-10

Trouble? If only three files appear in the search results, click the Search in File Contents link in the right pane to search the file contents in addition to filenames.

▶ **4.** Click each file and view the information in the Details pane, which displays a thumbnail of the file contents and the file properties, such as the filename, file type, and other details.

Three of the files you found using *aza* as the search text have filenames that contain words starting with *aza*: Azalea Inn, Pink Azalea, and Purple Azalea. Five of the files you found contain text that match your criterion. By examining the file contents and properties in the Details pane, you found two photos of azaleas for Andrew—the Pink Azalea file and the Purple Azalea file.

In this session, you examined why you need to organize files and folders and began to plan your organization. You also navigated your computer using Windows Explorer and learned how to navigate to your Data Files using the Folders list and the Address bar. Finally, you used the Search box to find files quickly based on their filenames and contents.

| Review | | **Session 2.1 Quick Check** |

1. What is the term for a collection of data that has a name and is stored on a disk or other storage medium?
2. The letter *C* is typically used for the _____ drive of a computer.
3. What are the two tools that Windows Vista provides for exploring the files and folders on your computer?
4. True or False. One way to find files using the Search box is to type text contained in the file itself.
5. What is the notation you can use to indicate a file's location on your computer?
6. Describe three ways to navigate your computer in a folder window.
7. True or False. Your Documents folder is labeled with the name you use to log on to the computer.
8. The _____ , which is located at the top of every folder window, displays your current location as a series of links separated by arrows.

Session 2.2

Managing Files and Folders

After you devise a plan for storing your files, you are ready to get organized by creating folders that will hold your files. You can do so using Computer or Windows Explorer. For this tutorial, you'll create folders in the Tutorial folder. When you are working on your own computer, you will usually create folders within the Documents folder and other standard folders, such as Music and Pictures.

Examine the files shown in Figure 2-8 again and determine which files seem to belong together. Azalea Inn, Logo, Pink Azalea, and Purple Azalea are all graphics files that the inn uses for marketing and sales. The Brochure and Flyer files were created for a special promotion the inn ran during the spring Azalea Festival. The other files are for general inn management.

One way to organize these files is to create three folders—one for graphics, one for the Azalea Festival, and another for the management files. When you create a folder, you give it a name, preferably one that describes its contents. A folder name can have up to 255 characters. Any character is allowed, except / \ : * ? " < > or |. Considering these conventions, you could create three folders as follows:

- **Marketing Graphics folder**: Azalea Inn, Logo, Pink Azalea, and Purple Azalea files
- **Festival folder**: Brochure and Flyer files
- **Management folder**: Rate List and Marketing Budget files

Before creating the folders, you show your plan to Andrew. You point out that instead of creating a folder for the graphics files, he could store them in the Pictures folder that Windows provides for photos, clip art, drawings, and other graphics. But Andrew wants to keep these marketing graphic files separate from any other files. He also thinks storing them in a subfolder along with the Festival and Management subfolders will make it easier to find his marketing files later.

Guidelines for Creating Folders | InSight

Keep the following guidelines in mind as you create folders:

- **Keep folder names short and familiar**: Long folder names can be more difficult to display in their entirety in folder windows, so use names that are short but clear. Choose names that will be meaningful later, such as project names or course numbers.
- **Develop standards for naming folders**: Use a consistent naming scheme that is clear to you, such as one that uses a project name as the name of the main folder, and includes step numbers in each subfolder name, such as 01Plan, 02Approvals, 03Prelim, and so on.
- **Create subfolders to organize files**: If a file listing in a folder window is so long that you must scroll the window, consider organizing those files into subfolders.

Andrew asks you to create the three new folders. After that, you'll move his files to the appropriate folder.

Creating Folders

You've already seen folder icons in the windows you've examined. Now, you'll create folders within the Tutorial folder using the Windows Explorer toolbar.

Creating a Folder in a Folder Window | Reference Window

- In the Folders list, click the drive or folder in which you want to create a folder.
- Click Organize on the toolbar, and then click New Folder.
- Type a name for the folder, and then press the Enter key.

or

- Right-click a folder in the Folders list or right-click a blank area in the folder window, point to New, and then click Folder.
- Type a name for the folder, and then press the Enter key.

Now you can create three folders in your Tutorial folder as you planned—the Marketing Graphics, Festival, and Management folders.

To create folders using Windows Explorer:

▶ 1. If necessary, start Windows Explorer, and then navigate to the **Tutorial** folder included with your Data Files. Click the **Tutorial** folder in the left pane and change to **Medium Icons** view, if necessary.

▶ 2. Click the **Organize** button on the toolbar, and then click **New Folder**. A folder icon with the label "New Folder" appears in the right pane. See Figure 2-11.

| Figure 2-11 | Creating a folder in the Tutorial folder |

Trouble? If the "New Folder" name is not selected, right-click the new folder, click Rename, and then continue with Step 3.

Windows uses "New Folder" as a placeholder, and selects the text so that you can replace it with the name you want.

▶ 3. Type **Marketing Graphics** as the folder name, and then press the **Enter** key. The new folder is named "Marketing Graphics" and is the selected item in the right pane.

You are ready to create a second folder. This time, you'll use a shortcut menu to create a folder.

▶ 4. Right-click a blank area in the right pane, point to **New** on the shortcut menu, and then click **Folder**. A folder icon with the label "New Folder" appears in the right pane with the "New Folder" text selected.

▶ 5. Type **Festival** as the name of the new folder, and then press the **Enter** key.

▶ 6. Using the toolbar or the shortcut menu, create a folder named **Management**. The Tutorial folder now contains three new subfolders.

Now that you've created three folders, you're ready to organize your files by moving them into the appropriate folders.

Moving and Copying Files and Folders

If you want to place a file into a folder from another location, you can either move the file or copy it. **Moving** a file removes it from its current location and places it in a new location you specify. **Copying** also places the file in a new location you specify, but does not remove it from its current location. Windows Vista provides several techniques for moving and copying files. The same principles apply to folders—you can move and copy folders using a variety of methods.

Moving a File or Folder in a Folder Window | Reference Window

- Right-click and drag the file or folder you want to move to the destination folder.
- Click Move Here on the shortcut menu.

or

- Right-click the file or folder you want to move, and then click Cut on the shortcut menu.
- Navigate to and right-click the destination folder, and then click Paste on the shortcut menu.

Andrew suggests that you move some files from the Tutorial folder to the appropriate subfolders. You'll start by moving the Marketing Budget file to the Management folder.

To move a file using the right mouse button:

1. Point to the **Marketing Budget** file in the right pane, and then press and hold the *right* mouse button.

2. With the right mouse button still pressed down, drag the **Marketing Budget** file to the **Management** folder. When the "Move to Management" ScreenTip appears, release the button. A shortcut menu opens.

3. With the left mouse button, click **Move Here** on the shortcut menu. The Marketing Budget file is removed from the main Tutorial folder and stored in the Management subfolder.

   Trouble? If you release the mouse button before you've dragged the Marketing Budget file all the way to the Management folder and before seeing the "Move to Management" ScreenTip, press the Esc key to close the shortcut menu, and then repeat Steps 1 through 3.

4. In the right pane, double-click the **Management** folder. The Marketing Budget file is in the Management folder.

5. Click the **Back** button ⊙ on the Address bar to return to the **Tutorial** folder. The Tutorial folder no longer contains the Marketing Budget file.

The advantage of moving a file or folder by dragging with the right mouse button is that you can efficiently complete your work with one action. However, this technique requires polished mouse skills so that you can drag the file comfortably. Another way to move files and folders is to use the **Clipboard**, a temporary storage area for files and information that you have copied or moved from one place and plan to use somewhere else. You can select a file and use the Cut or Copy commands to temporarily store the file on the Clipboard, and then use the Paste command to insert the file elsewhere. Although using the Clipboard takes more steps, some users find it easier than dragging with the right mouse button.

You'll move the Brochure file to the Festival folder next by using the Clipboard.

To move files using the Clipboard:

▶ **1.** Right-click the **Brochure** file, and then click **Cut** on the shortcut menu. Although the file icon is still displayed in the folder window, Windows Vista removes the Brochure file from the Tutorial folder and stores it on the Clipboard.

▶ **2.** In the Folders list, right-click the **Festival** folder, and then click **Paste** on the shortcut menu. Windows Vista pastes the Brochure file from the Clipboard to the Festival folder. The Brochure file icon no longer appears in the folder window.

▶ **3.** In the Folders list, click the **Festival** folder to view its contents in the right pane. The Festival folder now contains the Brochure file. See Figure 2-12.

Figure 2-12	Moving a file

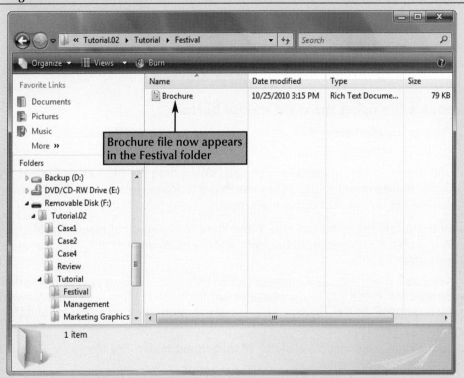

You'll move the Flyer file from the Tutorial folder to the Festival folder.

▶ **4.** Click the **Back** button on the Address bar to return to the Tutorial folder, right-click the **Flyer** file in the folder window, and then click **Cut** on the shortcut menu.

▶ **5.** Right-click the **Festival** folder, and then click **Paste** on the shortcut menu.

▶ **6.** Click the **Forward** button on the Address bar to return to the Festival folder. The Festival folder now contains the Brochure and Flyer files.

One way to save steps when moving or copying multiple files or folders is to select all the files and folders you want to move or copy, and then work them as a group. You'll see how to do that next.

Tip

To use keyboard shortcuts to move files, click the file you want to move, press Ctrl+X to cut the file, navigate to a new location, and then press Ctrl+V to paste the file.

Selecting Files and Folders

You can select multiple files or folders using any of several techniques, so you can use the most convenient method for your current task. First, you open the folder that contains the files or folders you want to select. Then select the files or folders using any one of the following methods:

- To select files or folders that are listed together in a window, click the first item, hold down the Shift key, and then click the last item.
- To select files or folders that are listed together in a window without using the keyboard, drag the pointer to create a selection box around all the items you want to include.
- To select files or folders that are not listed together, hold down the Ctrl key, and then click each item you want to select.
- To select all of the files or folders, click Organize on the toolbar, and then click Select All.
- To clear the selection of an item in a selected group, hold down the Ctrl key, and then click each item you want to remove from the selection.
- To clear the entire selection, click a blank area of the window.

Copying Files and Folders

When you copy a file or folder, you make a duplicate of the original item. You can copy a file or folder using techniques similar to the ones you use when moving.

Copying a File or Folder in a Folder Window | Reference Window

- Right-click and drag the file or folder you want to move to the destination folder.
- Click Copy Here on the shortcut menu.
or
- Right-click the file or folder you want to copy, and then click Copy on the shortcut menu.
- Navigate to and right-click the destination folder, and then click the Paste on the shortcut menu.

You'll copy the four graphics files from the Tutorial folder to the Marketing Graphics folder now.

To copy files using the Clipboard:

1. Return to the Tutorial folder window, and then click the **Azalea Inn** file.
2. Hold down the **Ctrl** key, click the **Logo** file, click the **Pink Azalea** file, click the **Purple Azalea** file, and then release the **Ctrl** key. Four files are selected in the Tutorial folder window.
3. Right-click a selected file, and then click **Copy** on the shortcut menu. Windows Vista copies the files to the Clipboard.
4. Right-click the **Marketing Graphics** folder, and then click **Paste** on the shortcut menu. Windows copies the four files to the Marketing Graphics folder.

Now that you have copied files using the Copy and Paste commands, you can use the right-drag technique to copy the Rate List file to the Management folder. As with moving files, to right-drag a file, you point to the file, hold down the right mouse button, and then drag the file to a new location. When you release the mouse button, however, you click Copy Here (instead of Move Here) on the shortcut menu to copy the file.

To copy a file:

▶ **1.** Right-drag the **Rate List** file from the Tutorial folder to the Management folder.

▶ **2.** Release the mouse button, and then click **Copy Here** on the shortcut menu.

When you move or copy a folder, you move or copy all the files contained in the folder. You'll practice moving and copying folders in the Case Problems at the end of this tutorial.

There is a third way to copy or move a file or folder. You can drag the file or folder (using the left mouse button) to another location. Whether the file or folder is copied or moved depends on where you drag it. A ScreenTip appears when you drag a file to a new location—the ScreenTip indicates what happens when you release the mouse button. Figure 2-13 summarizes how to copy and move files and folders by dragging.

Figure 2-13	▶	Dragging to move and copy files

Drag a File or Folder:	To:
Into a folder on the same drive	Move the file or folder to the destination folder
Into a folder on a different drive	Copy the file or folder to the destination folder

Although the copy and move techniques listed in Figure 2-13 are common ways to copy and move files and folders, be sure you can anticipate what happens when you drag a file or folder.

Naming and Renaming Files

As you work with files, pay attention to **filenames**—they provide important information about the file, including its contents and purpose. A filename such as Car Sales.docx has three parts:

- **Main part of the filename**: The name you provide when you create a file, and the name you associate with a file
- **Dot**: The period (.) that separates the main part of the filename from the file extension
- **File extension**: Usually three or four characters that follow the dot in the filename

The main part of a filename can have up to 255 characters—this gives you plenty of room to name your file accurately enough so that you'll know the contents of the file just by looking at the filename. You can use spaces and certain punctuation symbols in your filenames. Like folder names, however, filenames cannot contain the symbols \ / ? : * " < > or | because these characters have special meaning in Windows Vista.

A filename might display an **extension**—three or more characters following a dot—that identifies the file's type and indicates the program in which the file was created. For example, in the filename Car Sales.docx, the extension *docx* identifies the file as one created by Microsoft Office Word 2007, a word-processing program. You might also have a file called Car Sales.xlsx—the *xlsx* extension identifies the file as one created in Microsoft Office Excel 2007, a spreadsheet program. Though the main parts of these filenames are identical, their extensions distinguish them as different files. The filename extension also helps Windows identify what program should open the file. For example, the .txt extension in a file named Agenda.txt indicates that it is a text file and can be opened by programs associated with that extension, such as WordPad, Notepad, and Microsoft Word. You usually do not need to add extensions to your filenames because the program that you use to create the file adds the file extension automatically. Also, although Windows Vista keeps track of extensions, not all computers are set to display them.

Be sure to give your files and folders meaningful names that will help you remember their purpose and contents. You can easily rename a file or folder by using the Rename command on the file's shortcut menu.

Guidelines for Naming Files		InSight

The following are best practices for naming your files:

- **Use common names**: Avoid cryptic names that might make sense now, but could provide confusion later, such as nonstandard abbreviations or imprecise names like Stuff08.
- **Don't change the file extension**: Do not change the file extension when renaming a file. If you do, Windows might not be able to find a program that can open it.
- **Find a comfortable balance between too short and too long**: Use filenames that are long enough to be meaningful, but short enough to be read easily on the screen.

Andrew notes that the Brochure file in the Festival folder could contain the information for any brochure. He recommends that you rename that file to give it a more descriptive filename. The Brochure file was originally created to store text specifically for the Azalea Festival brochure, so you'll rename the file Azalea Festival Brochure. As you do, you can use the Recent Pages button, which appears next to the Forward button on the Address bar. You can click the Recent Pages button to display a list of folders you've opened recently. Click a folder name in the Recent Pages list to select that folder in the Folders list and display its contents in the right pane.

To rename the Brochure file:

▶ 1. Click the **Recent Pages** ▼ button on the Address bar, and then click **Festival**. The contents of the Festival folder appear in the right pane.

▶ 2. Right-click the **Brochure** file, and then click **Rename** on the shortcut menu. The filename is highlighted and a box appears around it.

▶ 3. Type **Azalea Festival Brochure**, and then press the **Enter** key. The file now appears with the new name.

   Trouble? If you make a mistake while typing and you haven't pressed the Enter key yet, press the Backspace key until you delete the mistake, and then complete Step 3. If you've already pressed the Enter key, repeat Steps 2 and 3 to rename the file again.

   Trouble? If your computer is set to display file extensions, a message might appear asking if you are sure you want to change the file extension. Click the No button, right-click the Brochure file, click Rename on the shortcut menu, type "Azalea Festival Brochure.rtf", and then press the Enter key.

All the files that originally appeared in the Tutorial folder are now stored in appropriate subfolders. You can streamline the organization of the Tutorial folder by deleting the duplicate files you no longer need.

Deleting Files and Folders

You should periodically delete files and folders you no longer need so that your main folders and disks don't get cluttered. In a folder window, you delete a file or folder by deleting its icon. When you delete a file from a hard disk, Windows Vista removes the file from the folder, but stores the file contents in the Recycle Bin. The **Recycle Bin** is an area on your hard disk that holds deleted files until you remove them permanently; an icon on

Tip

To retrieve a deleted file from the hard disk, double-click the Recycle Bin, right-click the file you want to retrieve, and then click Restore.

the desktop allows you easy access to the Recycle Bin. When you delete a folder from the hard disk, the folder and all of its files are stored in the Recycle Bin. If you change your mind and want to retrieve a file deleted from your hard disk, you can use the Recycle Bin to recover it and return it to its original location. However, after you empty the Recycle Bin, you can no longer recover the files it contained.

When you delete a file from removable media, such as a USB drive, it does not go into the Recycle Bin. Instead, it is deleted as soon as its icon disappears, and you cannot recover it.

Andrew reminds you that because you copied the Azalea Inn, Logo, Pink Azalea, Purple Azalea, and Rate List files to the subfolders in the Tutorial folder, you can safely delete the original files. As is true for moving, copying, and renaming files and folders, you can delete a file or folder in many ways, including using a shortcut menu or selecting one or more files and then pressing the Delete key.

To delete files in the Tutorial folder:

▶ **1.** Use any technique you've learned to navigate to and open the **Tutorial** folder.

▶ **2.** Click **Azalea Inn**, hold down the **Shift** key, click **Rate List** (the last file in the file list), and then release the **Shift** key. All the files in the Tutorial folder are now selected. None of the subfolders should be selected.

▶ **3.** Right-click the selected files, and then click **Delete** on the shortcut menu. Windows Vista asks if you're sure you want to delete these files.

▶ **4.** Click the **Yes** button.

So far, you've worked with files using Windows Explorer and Computer, but you haven't viewed any of their contents. To view file contents, you open the file. When you double-click a file in Windows Explorer or Computer, Windows Vista starts the appropriate program and opens the file. You'll have a chance to try these techniques in the next section.

Working with New Files

The most common way to add files to a drive or folder is to create new files when you use a program. For example, you can create a text document in a word-processing program, a drawing in a graphics program, or a movie file in a video-editing program. When you are finished with a file, you must save it if you want to use the file again. To work with the file again, you open the file in an appropriate program; you can usually tell which programs can open a file by examining the filename extension or file icon.

Before you continue working with Andrew's files, you decide to create a to-do list to summarize your remaining tasks. You'll create the to-do list file, save it, close it, and then reopen it to add some items to the list.

Creating a File

You create a file by starting a program and then saving the file in a folder on your computer. Some programs create a file when you open the program. When you open WordPad, for example, it starts with a blank page. This represents an empty (and unsaved) file. You start typing and, when you are finished, you save your work using the Save As dialog box, where you can select a location for the file and enter a filename that identifies the contents. By default, most programs save files in common folders such as Documents, Pictures, and Music, which makes it easy to find the files again later.

The to-do list you want to create is a simple text document, so you can create this file using Notepad, the basic text-editing program that Windows Vista provides.

To create a Notepad file:

► **1.** Start Notepad by clicking the **Start** button 🌀 on the taskbar, pointing to **All Programs**, clicking **Accessories**, and then clicking **Notepad**. The Notepad program window opens. See Figure 2-14.

Creating a file ◄ **Figure 2-14**

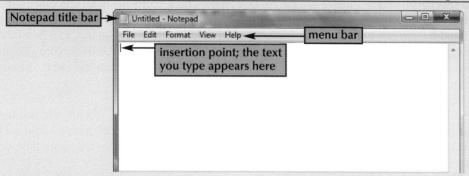

► **2.** Type the following text in the Notepad window, pressing the **Enter** key at the end of each line, including the last line:

To Do for Andrew's Files

1. Arrange files in a folder window.

2. Show and hide file extensions.

3. Compress and extract files.

The Notepad title bar indicates that the name of this file is "Untitled." To give it a more descriptive name, preserve the contents, and store the file where you can find it later, you must save the file.

Saving a File

As you are creating a file, you should save it frequently so you don't lose your work. When you save a new file, you use the Save As dialog box to specify a filename and a location for the file. When you open a file you've already created, you can usually click a toolbar button to save the file with the same name and location. If you want to save the file with a different name or in a different location, however, you use the Save As dialog box again to specify the new name or location. You can create a folder for the new file at the same time you save the file.

As a special type of folder window, the Save As dialog box can contain the same elements as all folder windows, such as an Address bar, Search box, Navigation pane, and right pane displaying folders and files. To display all of these navigation tools, you click the Browse Folders button to expand the Save As dialog box. Then you can specify the file location, for example, using the same navigation techniques and tools that are available in all folder windows. In addition, the Save As dialog box always includes a File name text box where you specify a filename, a Save as type list box where you select a file type, and other controls for saving a file. If the expanded Save As dialog box covers too much of your document or desktop, you can click the Hide Folders button to collapse the dialog box so it hides the Navigation pane, right pane, and toolbar. You can still navigate with the Back, Forward, and Recent Pages buttons, the Address bar, and the Search box, and you can still use the controls for saving a file, but you conserve screen space.

Now that you've created a to-do list, you need to save it. The best name for this document is probably "To-Do List." However, none of the folders you've already created for Andrew seems appropriate for this file. It belongs in a separate folder with a name such as "Daily Documents." You can create the Daily Documents folder at the same time you save the to-do list file.

To save the Notepad file:

▶ **1.** In the Notepad window, click **File** on the menu bar, and then click **Save As**. The Save As dialog box opens.

▶ **2.** If the Navigation pane does not appear in the Save As dialog box, click the **Browse Folders** button. If necessary, also click the **Folders** button to display the Folders list. See Figure 2-15.

Figure 2-15	Saving a new file

by default, the Save As dialog box saves text files in the Documents folder

Folders button

use the Folders list or the Address bar to navigate to a different location for saving the file

Hide Folders button collapses the dialog box so it takes up less space

type the name for the file

By default, Notepad saves files in the Documents folder. You want to create a folder in the Tutorial folder for this document.

▶ **3.** Use any technique you've learned to navigate to the **Tutorial** folder in the Save As dialog box.

▶ **4.** Click the **New Folder** button on the toolbar. A new folder appears in the Tutorial folder, with the "New Folder" name highlighted and ready for you to replace.

▶ **5.** Type **Daily Documents** as the name of the new folder, and then press the **Enter** key. The Daily Documents folder opens. Now you are ready to specify a filename and save the to-do list file in the Daily Documents folder.

▶ **6.** Click in the **File name** text box, and then type **To-Do List**. Notepad automatically provides a .txt extension to this filename.

▶ **7.** Click the **Save** button. Notepad saves the To-Do List file in the Daily Documents folder. The new filename now appears in the Notepad title bar.

▶ **8.** Click the **Close** button ❎ to close Notepad.

Next, you can open the file to add another item to the to-do list.

Opening a File

If you want to open a file in a running program, you use the Open dialog box, which is a folder window with additional controls for opening a file, similar to the Save As dialog box. You usually click an Open button on a toolbar or you click File on the menu bar and then click Open to access the Open dialog box, which you use to navigate to the file you want, select the file, and click the Open button. If the program you want to use is not running, you can open a file by double-clicking it in a folder window. The file usually opens in the program that you used to create or edit it. If it's a text file with a .txt extension, for example, it opens in a text editor, such as Notepad. If it's a text file with a .docx extension, it opens in the Microsoft Word 2007 word-processing program.

Not all documents work this way. Double-clicking a digital picture file usually opens a picture viewer program, which displays the picture. To actually edit the picture, you need to use a graphics editor program. When you need to specify a program to open a file, you can right-click the file, point to Open With on the shortcut menu, and then click the name of the program that you want to use.

Tip

To select the default program for opening a particular type of file, right-click the file, point to Open With on the shortcut menu, and then click Choose Default Program. Click a program, and then click the OK button.

To open and edit the To-Do List file:

▶ **1.** In the right pane of the Tutorial folder window, double-click the **Daily Documents** folder.

▶ **2.** Double-click the **To-Do List** file. Notepad starts and opens the To-Do List file.

   Trouble? If a program other than Notepad starts, such as WordPad, click the Close button to close the program, right-click the To-Do List file, point to Open With, and then click Notepad.

▶ **3.** Press **Ctrl+End** to move the insertion point to the end of the document, and then type **4. Review how to customize folder windows.**

   Because you want to save this file using the same name and location, you can use the Save command on the File menu to save your work this time.

▶ **4.** Click **File** on the menu bar, and then click **Save**. Notepad saves the To-Do List file without opening the Save As dialog box because Notepad uses the same name and location as the last time you saved the file.

As long as Notepad is still open, you can create another simple text file that describes the graphics in the Marketing Graphics folder.

To create and save another file:

▶ **1.** Click **File** on the menu bar, and then click **New** to open a new, blank document.

▶ **2.** Type the following text in the Notepad window, pressing the **Enter** key at the end of each line:

Marketing Graphics files:

Azalea Inn: Photo of the inn

Logo: Copy of the inn's logo for stationery and ads

Pink Azalea: Photo of pink azaleas

Purple Azalea: Photo of a purple azalea

▶ **3.** Click **File** on the menu bar, and then click **Save**. The Save As dialog box opens.

▶ **4.** Navigate to the **Marketing Graphics** folder.

▶ **5.** Click in the File name text box, and then type **Graphic Descriptions**.

▶ **6.** Click the **Save** button. Notepad saves the Graphic Descriptions file in the Marketing Graphics folder.

▶ **7.** Click the **Close** button [X] to close Notepad.

In this session, you managed files and folders by creating folders and then selecting, moving, and copying files. You also renamed and deleted files according to your organization plan, and then created a file, saved it in a new folder, and opened and edited the file.

Review | **Session 2.2 Quick Check**

---

1. _____ a file removes it from its current location and places it in a new location you specify.
2. True or False. The advantage of moving a file or folder by dragging with the right mouse button is that you can efficiently complete your work with one action.
3. Describe two ways to select files that are listed together in a window.
4. When you drag a file into a folder on the same hard disk, are you moving or copying the file to the destination folder?
5. What does a filename extension indicate about a file?
6. True or False. You should periodically delete files and folders you no longer need so that your main folders and disks don't get cluttered.
7. The _____ is an area on your hard disk that holds deleted files until you remove them permanently.
8. When you first create a file, what must you do if you want to use the file again?

Session 2.3

Refining Your Organization

Your main tasks when managing files are to formulate a logical plan for organizing your files, create the folders you need to store the files, and then move and copy your existing files into those folders. As you create files using programs, save them in an appropriate folder and use filenames that help you identify the file contents. Performing these basic management tasks helps you keep track of your files so you can easily find information when you need it.

To refine your organization, you can fine-tune the view of your files and folders in a folder window. Changing the view can often help you find files and identify those that share common features, such as two versions of the same file. One way to change the view is to sort your files. **Sorting** files and folders means to list them in a particular order, such as alphabetically by name or type or chronologically by their modification date. You can also **filter** the contents of a folder to display only files and folders with certain characteristics, such as all those you modified yesterday. In short, sorting reorganizes all of the files and folders in a list, while filtering displays only those files and folders that share a characteristic you specify. Both actions change your view of the files and folders, not the items themselves.

Windows Vista provides two other ways to change the view of your files and folders—stacking and grouping. When you **stack** files, you arrange all of the files in the list into piles, called stacks. If you stack by type, for example, Windows displays Microsoft Word documents in one stack and photo files with a .jpg extension in another stack. If you want to view only the Word documents, open the appropriate stack. Unlike a stack, which hides the files it contains behind an icon, a **group** displays a sequential list of all the files in a folder, grouped according to a file detail. When you group your files by type, for example, Windows separates the files into several groups, with each group displaying all the files of the same type.

You want to show Andrew these four ways to change the view of his files so he can choose one that makes the most sense for him or his current task.

Sorting and Filtering Files

To sort or filter the files listed in a folder window, you use the column headings in the right pane of the window. To sort files by type, for example, click the Type column heading. You can sort files in ascending order (A to Z, zero to nine, or earliest to latest date) or descending order (Z to A, nine to zero, or latest to earliest date). To switch the order, click the column heading again. Sorting is often an effective way to find a file or folder in a relatively short file list. By default, Windows Vista sorts the contents of a folder in ascending alphabetic order by filename, so a file named April Budget appears at the top of the list, and a file named Winter Expenses appears at the end. You can change the sort criterion to list files according to any other file characteristic.

If you are working with a longer file list, filtering the list might help you find the file you want. To filter the contents of a folder, you click the arrow to the right of a column heading, and then click a file property such as a filename, date created or modified, author, or file type, and Windows displays only files and folders with those properties. For example, if you want to list only music files by a particular artist, you can filter by that artist's name.

All of the views, including Extra Large Icons and Large Icons, provide column headings corresponding to file details, so you can sort and filter in any view. However, only Details view lists all the file details in these columns—the other views list only some details and provide the others in the Details pane or in the ScreenTip that appears when you point to an icon. This means Details view is usually the most effective one for sorting and filtering.

> **Tip**
>
> To sort by a file detail that does not appear as a column heading, right-click any column heading and then select a file detail; the column heading appears in the folder window so you can sort by that detail.

To sort and filter the files in the Marketing Graphics folder:

▶ **1.** Navigate to the **Marketing Graphics** folder in the Tutorial folder.

▶ **2.** Click the **Views button arrow** on the toolbar, and then click **Details**.

▶ **3.** Click the **Size** column heading to sort the files in descending order according to file size. An indented sort arrow appears at the top of the Size column heading. The sort arrow points down to indicate the column is sorted in descending order.

Trouble? If the Size column does not appear in your folder window, right-click any column heading and then click Size. Then complete Step 3.

▶ 4. Click the **Size** column heading again to reverse the sort order. The sort arrow now points up, indicating the column is sorted in ascending order.

▶ 5. Right-click any **column heading** to display a list of file details. Details with a check mark are displayed in the folder window. If Tags is listed with a check mark, click **Tags** to remove this column from the folder window.

▶ 6. Right-click any **column heading** again, and if Rating is listed with a check mark, click **Rating** to remove this column from the folder window. If Date taken is also listed with a check mark, repeat this step to remove the **Date taken** column.

▶ 7. If the Date modified column heading does not appear in your folder window, right-click any **column heading**, and then click **Date modified** to display this column. Your folder window should now display only the Name, Size, and Date modified columns.

Trouble? If your folder window contains columns other than Name, Size, and Date modified, right-click any column heading, and then click the name of the column you want to remove from the folder window.

▶ 8. Click the **Date modified** column heading to sort the files chronologically by the date they were modified. See Figure 2-16.

| Figure 2-16 | Sorting files by date modified |

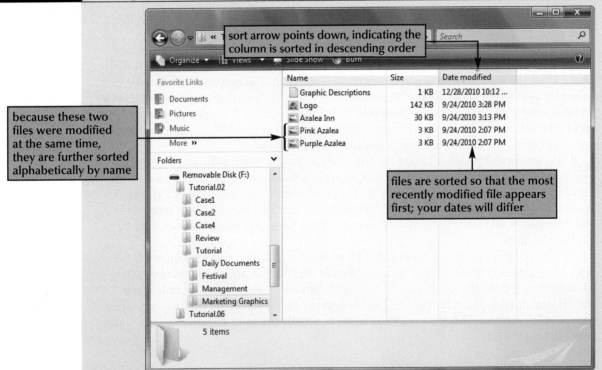

To compare sorting and filtering, you can filter the files by their modified date to display only the files you modified today.

▶ 9. Point to the **Date modified** column heading, and then click its arrow button to display a list of filtering, grouping, and stacking options.

▶ 10. Click the **Today** check box to select today's date. The folder window displays only the Graphic Descriptions file. See Figure 2-17.

Trouble? If you modified the Graphic Descriptions file on a different date, click that date on the calendar.

Trouble? If you clicked Today rather than the check box, repeat Steps 9 and 10 to select today's date.

Filtering to display files modified today

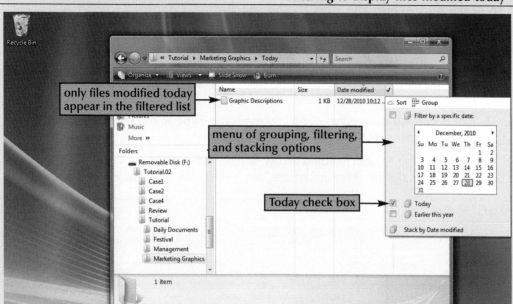

Note that you can filter by two or more properties by selecting the corresponding check boxes.

▶ **11.** Click a blank area of the window to close the list. A check mark appears next to the Date modified column heading to indicate the file list is filtered by a Date modified detail.

Next, you can stack and group the files in the Marketing Graphics folder and compare these views to the ones displayed when you sorted and filtered the files.

Stacking and Grouping Files

Stacking and grouping are similar ways to change your view of files and folders, and are especially effective when working with long file lists. You can stack or group files according to any file detail currently displayed in the folder window. To stack files by author, for example, click the Authors column heading list arrow, and then click Stack by Authors. Windows arranges the contents of the folder into stacks, one for each author, such as one for files you wrote and another for files your colleague wrote. Only stack icons appear for each group of files, not the files themselves. To view the files you wrote, double-click the stack with your name.

To group files, you click a column heading list arrow, and then click Group. When you group files by author, for example, Windows divides the folder window into sections, with one section listing files you wrote and another section for files your colleague wrote. Stacking and grouping files have similar results—the only difference is that stacking hides the files behind a stack icon, while grouping displays the files in different sections in the folder window.

Before stacking or grouping files, you must remove any filters you are using in the folder window. If you don't, you'll rearrange only the files that appear in the filtered list. After removing the filter, you'll stack and then group the files in the Marketing Graphics folder by type.

To stack and group the files in the Marketing Graphics folder:

▶ 1. In the Marketing Graphics folder window, click the **check mark** on the Date modified column heading, and then click the **Today** check box (or the **Filter by a specific date** check box if you selected a date on the calendar earlier) to clear the check box. Click a blank area of the folder window. The complete list of Marketing Graphics files appears in the window.

▶ 2. Right-click any **column heading**, and then click **Type** to display that column in the folder window.

▶ 3. Click the **Type column heading arrow**, and then click **Stack by Type**. Windows hides the files and displays three stack icons, one for each file type. See Figure 2-18.

| Figure 2-18 | Stacking files |

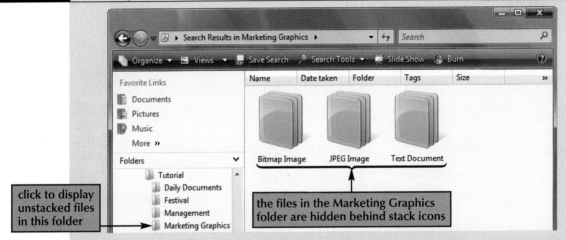

click to display unstacked files in this folder

the files in the Marketing Graphics folder are hidden behind stack icons

▶ 4. Double-click the **JPEG Image** stack icon. (JPEG is a typical file type for photographs.) Windows displays the three JPEG files in the stack.

▶ 5. Click **Marketing Graphics** in the Folders list to show the unstacked files in that folder.

▶ 6. Click the **Type column heading arrow**, and then click **Group**. Windows arranges all five files in the Marketing Graphics folder into three groups, one for each file type. See Figure 2-19.

Grouping files ◄ **Figure 2-19**

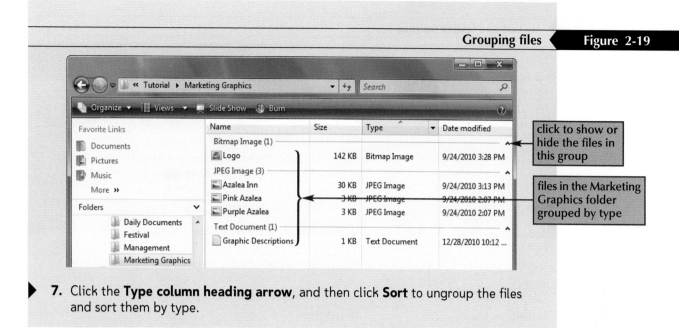

click to show or hide the files in this group

files in the Marketing Graphics folder grouped by type

▶ **7.** Click the **Type column heading arrow**, and then click **Sort** to ungroup the files and sort them by type.

After showing Andrew how to sort, filter, stack, and group files in a folder window, he mentions that he might want to hide or show elements of the folder window itself, such as the Navigation pane or the Details pane. You'll show him how to customize the folder window elements next.

Customizing a Folder Window

You can change the way your folder windows look and work to suit your needs. For example, you can hide the Details pane or the Navigation pane to devote more space to file lists. To do so, you use the Layout command and the Folder and Search Options command on a folder window's Organize button. The Layout command lists the panes you can display in a folder window. When you select the Folder and Search Options command, the Folder Options dialog box opens, where you can select settings that change the behavior and appearance of the folder window. Figure 2-20 summarizes the ways you can customize the appearance of a folder window. Note that the Folder and Search Options command is not available for the Save As and Open dialog boxes.

Figure 2-20 | **Layout and folder options**

Layout Options	
Option	**Description**
Menu Bar	Hide or show the menu bar in this window only.
Search Pane	Display buttons for conducting a search (not available in the Save As and Open dialog boxes).
Details Pane or Preview Pane	Hide or show the Details pane when you are viewing folder contents or the Preview pane when you select one or more items.
Navigation Pane	Hide or show the Navigation pane.

Folder Options Dialog Box Setting	
Settings on the General Tab	**Description**
Use Windows classic folders	Turn off the Navigation pane, Preview pane, and toolbar in all folders. (To turn the panes back on, click Show preview and filters.)
Restore Defaults	Restore the original settings for your folders.
Settings on the View Tab	**Description**
Always show icons, never thumbnails	Always show static icons of files and never show thumbnail previews of files. Use this setting if the thumbnail previews are slowing down your computer.
Show hidden files and folders	Display files and folders marked as hidden. Use this setting if you need to work with files that are usually hidden from view, such as user files that have been marked as hidden.
Display simple folder view in Navigation pane	Display folders with lines that connect folders and subfolders.
Hide extensions for known file types	Show or hide extensions as a part of filenames.
Restore Defaults	Restore the original settings on the View tab.

You'll show Andrew how to change the layouts in a folder window, and then how to customize the appearance of the folder contents. Finally, you'll demonstrate how to add items and make other changes to the Navigation pane.

Changing the Layout of a Folder Window

You can change the layout of a folder window by showing or hiding one or more of the following elements: the Navigation pane, Preview pane, Details pane, and menu bar. Recall that the Navigation pane appears on the left side of a folder window and lets you change the view to other folders. You can click an item in the Favorite Links list in the Navigation pane to open a built-in Windows folder, such as the Documents folder. If you often go to the same folder, you can also drag that folder to the Favorite Links list to make it one of your favorite locations. The Details pane appears at the bottom of a folder window and displays details about the folder and its contents. The Preview pane appears at the right side of a folder window and displays the contents of many kinds of files; if you select an e-mail message, text file, or picture, for example, you can see its contents in the Preview pane without opening the file in a program. Figure 2-21 shows a folder window with all the panes open.

Folder window displaying the Navigation, Details, and Preview panes ◄ Figure 2-21

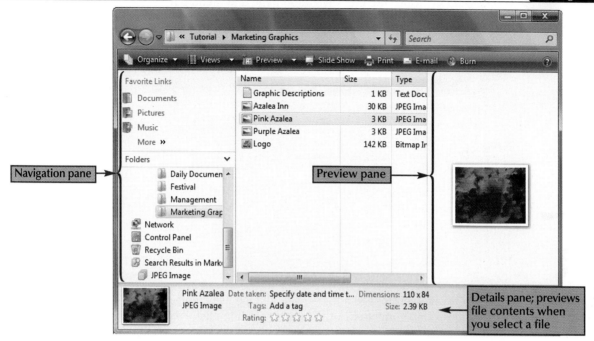

You have also used the toolbar to perform many tasks, particularly to change the appearance of your files and folders. If you used previous versions of Windows, such as Windows XP, you probably performed many of these same tasks using a menu bar. As in programs, Windows Vista folder windows can display a menu bar that shows the names of the menus, such as File, Edit, and Help. The folder window menu bar in Windows Vista is hidden by default because you can use the toolbar or the shortcut menu that opens when you right-click a file or folder to perform the tasks associated with the menu bar commands.

Andrew is accustomed to the folder windows in Windows XP, so he asks you to display the menu bar and hide the Details pane. The Marketing Graphics folder window should currently be open in Details view, with files sorted according to type.

To change the layout of a folder window:

▶ **1.** Click **Organize** on the toolbar, point to **Layout**, and then click **Details Pane** to close the Details pane.

▶ **2.** Click **Organize** on the toolbar, point to **Layout**, and then click **Menu Bar** to display the menu bar in folder windows. See Figure 2-22.

Figure 2-22 ▶ **Folder window displaying the Navigation pane and menu bar**

Another way to customize a folder is to change its type. If you store mostly pictures in a folder, for example, right-click the folder, and then click Properties on the shortcut menu. In the folder's Properties dialog box, click the Customize tab, click the Use this folder as a template arrow button, and then click a folder type, such as Pictures and Videos. That folder window then includes features, such as toolbar buttons, designed for working with pictures and videos.

Customizing the File List

Recall that although Windows Vista refers to a file extension to identify a file's type, file extensions are not displayed by default in a folder window. Windows hides the extensions to make filenames easier to read, especially for long filenames. If you prefer to display file extensions, you can show them in all the folder windows.

Another type of file not displayed by default in a folder window is a hidden file. A **hidden file** is not listed in a folder window, though it is actually stored in that folder. Windows hides many types of files, including temporary files it creates before you save a document. It hides these files so that you do not become confused by temporary filenames, which are similar to the names of the files you store on your computer. You can also use a file's Properties dialog box to hide files. Keep in mind that hidden files still take up space on your disk. Windows Vista also hides system files by default, which are those the operating system needs to work properly. You should keep these files hidden unless a reliable expert, such as a technical support professional, instructs you to display them. You use the Folder Options dialog box to show and hide filename extensions, hidden files, and system files.

You can change folder settings in the Marketing Graphics window to show the file-name extensions in all windows.

To show filename extensions:

▶ 1. Click the **Organize** button on the toolbar, and then click **Folder and Search Options** to open the Folder Options dialog box.

▶ 2. Click the **View** tab. See Figure 2-23. The settings on the View tab of your Folder Options dialog box might differ.

Folder Options dialog box ◄ **Figure 2-23**

3. In the Advanced settings section, click the **Hide extensions for known file types** check box to clear the box and display file extensions.

   Trouble? If the Hide extensions for known file types check box is already cleared, skip Step 3.

4. Click the **OK** button. The Marketing Graphics folder window should look similar to Figure 2-24.

Folder window showing file extensions ◄ **Figure 2-24**

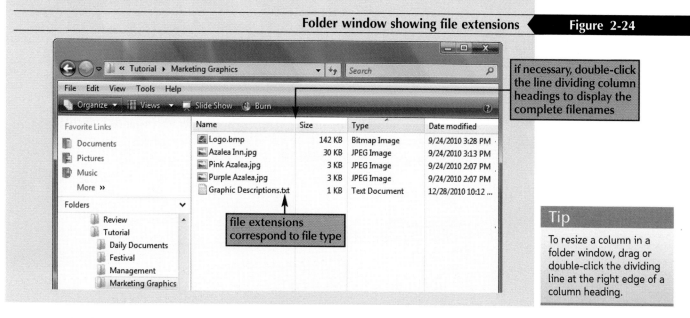

Tip

To resize a column in a folder window, drag or double-click the dividing line at the right edge of a column heading.

Now the file list in the Marketing Graphics folder window includes file extensions. Next, you can customize the Navigation pane by changing its appearance and adding a folder to the Favorite Links list.

Customizing the Navigation Pane

You can customize the Navigation pane by moving the links in the Favorite Links list and by adding, renaming, and removing items in the list. First, you'll add the Daily Documents folder to the Favorites Links list so you can access it quickly. Then you'll move and rename this link to distinguish it from the Documents link. When you rename an item in the Favorites Link list, you rename the link only, not the actual file or folder. Later, when you restore the settings on your computer, you'll delete this link.

To customize the Navigation pane:

▶ **1.** Use any navigation method you've learned to display the folders in the Tutorial folder.

▶ **2.** Click the **Folders** button in the Navigation pane to close the Folders list.

▶ **3.** Drag the **Daily Documents** folder from the Tutorial folder to the end of the Favorite Links list in the Navigation pane. When an insertion line appears at the end of the list, release the mouse button to insert a new link named Daily Documents. See Figure 2-25.

| Figure 2-25 | Daily Documents folder as a link in the Favorite Links list |

▶ **4.** In the Favorite Links list, drag the **Daily Documents** folder to the top of the list.

▶ **5.** Right-click the **Daily Documents** link in the Favorite Links list, and then click **Rename** on the shortcut menu. The Rename dialog box opens.

▶ **6.** Type **Daily Projects** as the new name of this link, and then click the **OK** button. The link is renamed, but the Daily Documents folder in the Tutorial folder still has its original name. See Figure 2-26.

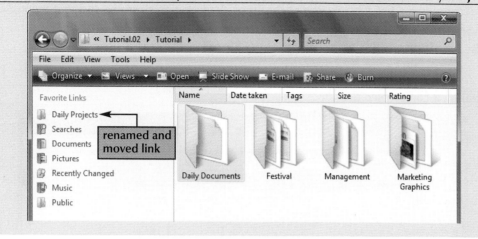

Now that you've refined your file organization and customized the folder window, you are ready to show Andrew two final tasks—compressing and extracting files.

Working with Compressed Files

If you transfer files from one location to another, such as from your hard disk to a removable disk or vice versa, or from one computer to another via e-mail, you can store the files in a **compressed (zipped) folder** so that they take up less disk space. You can then transfer the files more quickly. When you create a compressed folder using Windows Vista's compression tool, a zipper appears on the folder icon.

You compress a folder so that the files it contains use less space on the disk. Compare two folders—a folder named Pictures that contains about 8.6 MB of files and a compressed folder containing the same files, but requiring only 6.5 MB of disk space. In this case, the compressed files use about 25 percent less disk space than the uncompressed files.

You can create a compressed folder using the Send To Compressed (zipped) Folder command on the shortcut menu of one or more selected files or folders. Then, you can compress additional files or folders by dragging them into the compressed folder. You can open files directly from a compressed folder, although you cannot modify the file. To edit and save a compressed file, you must extract it first. When you **extract** a file, you create an uncompressed copy of the file in a folder you specify. The original file remains in the compressed folder.

If a different compression program has been installed on your computer, such as WinZip or PKZIP, the Send To Compressed (zipped) Folder command might not appear on the shortcut menu. Instead, it might be replaced by the name of your compression program. In this case, refer to your compression program's Help system for instructions on working with compressed files.

Andrew suggests you compress the files and folders in the Tutorial folder so that you can more quickly transfer them to another location.

To compress the folders and files in the Tutorial folder:

▶ **1.** In the Navigation pane, click the **Folders** button to open the Folders list again.

▶ **2.** Select all the folders in the Tutorial folder, right-click the selected folders, point to **Send To**, and then click **Compressed (zipped) Folder**. After a few moments, a new compressed folder with a zipper icon appears in the Tutorial window.

Trouble? If the Send To Compressed (zipped) Folder command does not appear on the shortcut menu, a different compression program is probably installed on your computer. Click a blank area of the Tutorial window to close the shortcut menu, and then read but do not perform the remaining steps.

▶ 3. Type **Zipped Files**, and then press the **Enter** key to rename the compressed folder. See Figure 2-27.

Figure 2-27 | Creating a compressed file

compressed file is renamed

You open a compressed folder by double-clicking it. You can then move and copy files and folders in a compressed folder, although you cannot rename them. When you extract files, Windows Vista uncompresses and copies them to a location that you specify, preserving the files in their folders as appropriate.

InSight | **Understanding Compressed File Types**

Some types of files, such as JPEG picture files (those with a .jpg or .jpeg file extension), are already highly compressed. If you compress JPEG pictures into a folder, the total size of the compressed folder is about the same as the collection of pictures uncompressed. However, if you are transferring the files from one computer to another, such as by e-mail, it's still a good idea to store the compressed files in a zip folder to keep them together.

To extract the compressed files:

▶ 1. Right-click the **Zipped Files.zip** compressed folder, and then click **Extract All** on the shortcut menu. The Extract Compressed (zipped) Folders Wizard starts and opens the Select a Destination and Extract Files dialog box.

Trouble? If you are using a different compression program, the Extract All command might not appear on the shortcut menu. Read but do not perform the remaining steps.

▶ **2.** Press the **End** key to deselect the path in the text box, press the **Backspace** key as many times as necessary to delete "Zipped Files," and then type **Extracted**. The final three parts of the path in the text box should be "\Tutorial. 02\Tutorial\Extracted." See Figure 2-28.

Extracting files from a compressed file ◀ Figure 2-28

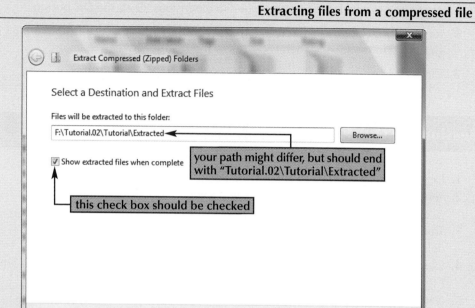

▶ **3.** Make sure the Show extracted files when complete check box is checked, and then click the **Extract** button. Windows extracts the files, and then opens the Extracted folder, showing the Daily Documents, Festival, Management, and Marketing Graphics folders.

▶ **4.** Open each folder to make sure it contains the files you worked with in this tutorial.

▶ **5.** Close the Extracted folder window.

You tell Andrew that you have finished organizing the files on his Windows Vista computer. Before you end your Windows Vista session, however, you should restore your computer to its original settings.

Restoring Your Settings

If you are working in a computer lab or a computer other than your own, complete the steps in this section to restore the original settings on your computer.

To restore your settings:

▶ **1.** In the Tutorial folder window, click the **Organize** button on the toolbar, point to **Layout**, and then click **Details Pane** to display the Details pane in the folder window.

▶ **2.** Click the **Organize** button on the toolbar, point to **Layout**, and then click **Menu Bar** to hide the menu bar.

3. Click the **Organize** button on the toolbar, and then click **Folder and Search Options** to open the Folder Options dialog box.

4. Click the **View** tab.

5. In the Advanced settings section, click the **Hide extensions for known file types** check box to check the box and hide file extensions. Click the **OK** button.

6. Right-click the **Daily Projects** link in the Navigation pane, click **Remove Link** on the shortcut menu, and then click **Yes** in the Delete File dialog box.

7. Close all open windows.

Review | Session 2.3 Quick Check

1. Explain the difference between sorting and filtering files.
2. You sort, filter, stack, and group files in a folder window using the _____ _____ , which correspond to file details.
3. True or False. Renaming or deleting a link in the Favorite Links list renames or deletes the corresponding folder in the file list.
4. Explain what happens in a folder window when you click the arrow on the Date Created column and then click today's date.
5. Name two ways that you can change the layout of a folder window.
6. True or False. By default, Windows hides file extensions in a folder window to make the filenames easier to read.
7. Under what circumstances would you store files in a compressed folder?
8. When you _____ a file, you create an uncompressed copy of the file and folder in a folder you specify.

Review | Tutorial Summary

In this tutorial, you examined the Windows Vista file organization, noting that you need to organize files and folders to work efficiently. You learned about typical file management strategies, whether you are working on a hard disk or a removable disk. Then, you applied these strategies to organizing files and folders by creating folders, moving and copying files, and renaming and deleting files. You also learned how to copy files to a compressed (zipped) folder and then extract files from a compressed folder.

Key Terms

3.5-inch disk	drive	hidden file
backup	extension	move
Clipboard	extract	Recycle Bin
compact disc (CD)	Favorite Links list	root directory
compressed (zipped) folder	file path	Search box
copy	file system	sort
disk	filename	stack
document	filter	subfolder
Documents folder	group	USB drive
	hard disk	

Practice	**Review Assignments**

Practice the skills you learned in the tutorial.

For a list of Data Files in the Review folder, see page 47.

Andrew has saved a few files from his old computer on a removable disk. He gives you these files in a single, unorganized folder, and asks you to organize them logically into subfolders. Before you do, devise a plan for managing the files, and then create the subfolders you need. Also rename, copy, move, and delete files, and perform other management tasks to make it easy for Andrew to work with these files and folders. Complete the following steps, recording your answers to any questions in the spaces provided:

1. Use Computer or Windows Explorer to navigate to and open the Tutorial.02\Review folder provided with your Data Files.
2. Examine the six files in the Review folder included with your Data Files, and then answer the following questions:
   - How will you organize these files? _____
   _____
   - What folders will you create? _____
   _____
   - Which files will you store in these folders? _____
   _____
3. In the Review folder, create three folders: Financial, Planning, and Travel.
4. Move the **Business Plan** and **Event Form** files from the Review folder to the Financial folder. Move the **Alabama**, **Letterhead**, and **Mobile** files to the Travel folder. Move the **Schedule** file to the Planning folder.
5. Copy the **Letterhead** file in the Travel folder to the Planning folder.
6. Rename the **Event Form** file in the Financial folder to **Promotional Events**. Rename the **Mobile** file in the Travel folder to **Historic Mobile**.
7. Return to the Review folder and use the Search box to find a file containing the text *Executive Summary*. Rename this file **Business Plan Form**.
8. Create a Notepad file that includes the following text:
   Agenda for Board Meeting
   7 p.m. Welcome and introductions
9. Save the Notepad file as **Agenda** in the Planning folder. Close the Notepad window.
10. Navigate to the Planning folder, open the **Agenda** file, and then add the following agenda item:
    7:15 Review business plan
11. Save the **Agenda** file with the same name and in the same location. Open a new document, and then type the following text:
    Financial Contact List
    Corgan, Richard (Banker) 555-4187
12. Save the file as **Contact List** in the Financial folder. Close Notepad.
13. Navigate to the Financial folder and make sure the Date modified column is displayed in the folder window. (*Hint*: Right-click a column heading, and then click the Date modified if you need to display this column.) Sort the files by Date modified. How many files appear in the folder window? Filter the files by today's date (or the date you created the two text files). How many files appear in the folder window?
14. Remove the filter, and then stack the files by type.
15. Navigate to the Travel folder, and then display file extensions in the folder window. Group the files by size.

16. Change the layout of the folder window by hiding the Details pane.

17. Display the Review folder, and then add the Travel folder to the top of the Favorite Links list in the Navigation pane. Rename the link **Travel Info**.

18. Click the Travel Info link, and then press the Alt+Print Screen keys to capture an image of the folder window. Start Paint, and then press the Ctrl+V keys to paste this image in a file. Save this file as **Review** in the Tutorial.02\Review folder provided with your Data Files. Close Paint.

19. Restore your computer's settings by displaying the Details pane, hiding file extensions in the folder window, and removing the Travel Info link from the Favorite Links list in the Navigation pane.

20. Create a compressed (zipped) folder in the Review folder named **Zipped Review Files** that contains all the files and folders in the Review folder.

21. Extract the contents of the Zipped Review Files folder to a new folder named **Extracted** in the Review folder. (*Hint*: The file path will end with "\Tutorial.02\Review\Extracted.")

22. Close all open windows.

23. Submit the results of the preceding steps to your instructor, either in printed or electronic form, as requested.

| Apply | | Case Problem 1 |

Use the skills you learned in the tutorial to manage files and folders for a catering service.

For a list of Data Files in the Case1 folder, see page 47.

Rossini Catering   Sharon Rossini owns Rossini Catering in Providence, Rhode Island, and provides catering services to businesses and others for conferences, weddings, and other events. Specializing in authentic regional Italian dishes, Sharon's clientele has expanded as word of her innovative menus has spread throughout Providence. She recently started offering cooking classes and was surprised to discover that her class on fruit plates was among the most popular. Knowing you are multitalented, Sharon hired you to help her design new classes and manage other parts of her growing business, including maintaining electronic business files and communications. Your first task is to organize the files on her new Windows Vista computer. Complete the following steps:

1. In the Tutorial.02\Case1 folder provided with your Data Files, create three folders: **Classes**, **Fruit Pictures**, and **Menus**.

2. Move the **Menu-Fall**, **Menu-Spring**, **Menu-Summer**, and **Menu-Winter** files from the Case1 folder to the Menus folder.

3. Rename the four files in the Menus folder to remove "Menu-" from each name.

4. Move the three JPEG files from the Case1 folder to the Fruit Pictures folder.

5. Copy the remaining three files to the Classes folder. Also copy the **Ingredients** and **Class Descriptions** files to the Menus folder.

6. Delete the **Class Descriptions**, **Ingredients**, and **Image for Ad** files from the Case1 folder.

7. Open the Recycle Bin folder by double-clicking the Recycle Bin icon on the desktop, and then complete the following steps:
   a. Sort the contents of the Recycle Bin by filename in descending order.
   b. Filter the files by their deletion date to display only the files you deleted today. (*Hint*: If you deleted files from the Case1 folder on a different date, click that date on the calendar.)
   c. Do the Class Descriptions, Ingredients, and Image for Ad files appear in the Recycle Bin folder? Explain why or why not.
   d. Remove the filter, and then close the Recycle Bin window.

8. Make a copy of the Fruit Pictures folder in the Case1 folder. The name of the duplicate folder appears as "Fruit Pictures - Copy". Rename the Fruit Pictures - Copy folder as **Ad Photos**.

9. Locate and move the **Image for Ad** file to the Ad Photos folder. Rename this file **Green Grapes**.

10. Find a file in the Case1 subfolders that contains the text **Fruit plate**. Copy this file to the Classes folder and rename it **Sample Menu**.

11. Send one copy of each graphic file from the Ad Photos folder to a new compressed folder named **Illustrations** in the Case1 folder.

12. Close all open windows.

13. Submit the results of the preceding steps to your instructor, either in printed or electronic form, as requested.

Apply	**Case Problem 2**

Use the skills you learned in the tutorial to manage files and folders for an accounting firm.

For a list of Data Files in the Case2 folder, see page 47.

Lincoln Small Business Accountants   Jack Takamoto is the vice president of Lincoln Small Business Accountants, a firm in Lincoln, Nebraska, that provides accounting services to local small businesses. You work as Jack's assistant and devote part of your time to organizing client files. Jack recently upgraded to Windows Vista and asks you to examine the folder structure and file system on his computer, and then begin organizing the files for two clients. Complete the following steps:

⊕ E X P L O R E

1. Start Windows Explorer and then click each link in the Favorite Links list on the Navigation pane to open each folder. (*Hint*: Click the More button to display links hidden by the Folder list.) Describe the contents of each folder in the Favorite Links list.

2. Open the Pictures folder and open a subfolder, if necessary, to display two or more picture files. Change the view to Extra Large Icons. Stack the files by Name. (*Hint*: Click the arrow button on the Name column, and then click Stack by Name.) Press the Alt+Print Screen keys to capture an image of the folder window. Start Paint, and then press the Ctrl+V keys to paste this image in a file. Save the file as **Case2Step2** in the Tutorial.02\Case2 folder provided with your Data Files. Close Paint, and then close the folder window displaying stacked picture files.

3. Examine the files in the Tutorial.02\Case2 folder provided with your Data Files. Based on the filenames and the descriptions displayed in the Details pane, devise an organization plan for the files.

4. In the Tutorial.02\Case2 folder, create the folders you need according to your plan.

5. Move the files from the Case2 folder to the subfolders you created. When you finish, the Case2 folder should contain at least two subfolders and the Case2Step2 file.

6. Rename the files in each subfolder so that they are shorter but still clearly reflect their contents.

7. Search for a file that contains *refund* in the contents.

8. Open the text document you found, and then add the following note at the end of the file: **Client expects a tax refund this year.** Save and close the file.

9. Open the window for one of the subfolders you created. Display the menu bar in the folder window.

⊕ EXPLORE 10. Click View on the menu bar and then click Tiles to change the view of the folder window. Press the Alt+Print Screen keys to capture an image of the folder window, and then save the image as **Case2Step10** in the Tutorial.02\Case2 folder provided with your Data Files. Close Paint.

⊕ EXPLORE 11. Send all the spreadsheet files (that is, all but the text documents) in the Case2 sub-folders to a new compressed folder named **Spreadsheets** in the Case2 folder. (*Hint*: After you create the compressed folder, drag spreadsheet files from other subfolders to the new compressed folder.)

12. Restore your computer by hiding the menu bar in the folder window.

13. Close all open windows.

14. Submit the results of the preceding steps to your instructor, either in printed or electronic form, as requested.

Challenge | Case Problem 3

Extend what you've learned to discover other methods of managing files for a home healthcare organization.

There are no Data Files needed for this Case Problem.

MedFirst Hospital Home Health Services Anders Guillickson is the director of the MedFirst Hospital Home Health services (MHHH) in Nashville, Tennessee. The company's mission is to connect licensed practical nurses with people who need health care at home, usually as part of their recovery from surgery. Anders has a dedicated staff of nurses who are just starting to use Windows Vista notebook computers to record the details of their home visits. Anders hires you as a part-time trainer to teach the nurses how to use their computers efficiently. They report that their major problem is finding files that they have saved on their hard disks. Anders asks you to prepare a lesson on how to find files in Windows Vista. Complete the following:

⊕ EXPLORE 1. Windows Vista Help and Support includes topics that explain how to search for files on a disk without looking through all the folders. Click the Start button and then click Help and Support to open Windows Help and Support. Use one of the following methods to locate topics on searching for files.
  • On the Home page, click Table of Contents. On the Contents page, click Files and folders, then Finding and organizing, then Finding files and folders, and then click the Find a file or folder topic.
  • In the Search Help box, type **searching for files**, and then click the Search Help button. Click Find a file or folder.

⊕ EXPLORE 2. Click the Show all link to show the complete contents of the Find a file or folder topic. Read the topic and click any See also links that provide information about finding files and folders to provide the following information:
  a. Identify three ways to search for files.
  b. If you do not know the entire name of a file, how can you find the file?
  c. Explain how you can save a search so you can use it again.

⊕ EXPLORE 3. Use Windows Vista Help and Support to locate topics about organizing and finding files using properties and tags.

4. Write a short description of one procedure for finding files and folders that was not covered in the tutorial.

5. Submit the results of the preceding steps to your instructor, either in printed or electronic form, as requested.

| Research | | Case Problem 4 |

Work with the skills you've learned, and use the Internet, to organize the files for an architectural design firm.

For a list of Data Files in the Case4 folder, see page 47.

Green Building Arts Green Building Arts is an architectural design firm in St. Paul, Minnesota, known for designing environmentally responsible buildings. They have been at the forefront of creating healthier and more resource-efficient models of construction, renovation, and maintenance. Maggie O'Donnell is the operations manager for Green Building Arts, and you assist her in setting up systems so that the architects can work effectively. Maggie has recently installed Windows Vista on the firm's desktop and note-book computers. She has a collection of files she can't open with any program installed on her Windows Vista computer. You offer to help her identify the file types and organize the files. Complete the following:

1. Examine the files in the Tutorial.02\Case4 folder provided with your Data Files. Use the Folder Options dialog box to display the file extensions for these files. List the file extensions not already discussed in this tutorial.

⊕ EXPLORE

2. Use your favorite search engine to find information about each file type you listed in Step 1. For example, search for MDB files to learn what type of program can open files with an .mdb extension.

3. Based on what you learned about the file types, sketch an organization for these files. Then create the subfolders you need in the Case4 folder.

4. Move the files from the Case4 folder to the subfolders you created.

5. Open the **Checklist** file in Notepad, read the contents, and then close Notepad. Based on the contents of the Checklist file, move it to a different folder, if necessary.

⊕ EXPLORE

6. Right-click the **Checklist** file, and then click Open With. Select a program other than Notepad to use to open the file. Type your name at the beginning of the file, click File on the menu bar, and then click Save As. Use the Save As dialog box to save the file as a different type, such as .rtf or .doc, but using the same location. (*Hint*: Click the Save as type arrow and then click a file type.) Close the program window.

7. Double-click any other file in a Case4 subfolder and describe what happens.

⊕ EXPLORE

8. If a program did not start when you double-clicked the file in Step 6, right-click the file, and then click Open With. Select a program that Windows Vista suggests. Describe what happens.

9. Double-click another file in a Case4 subfolder and describe what happens. Be sure to choose a file other than the one you chose for Step 7.

10. Close all open windows.

11. Submit the results of the preceding steps to your instructor, either in printed or elec-tronic form, as requested.

Review | **Quick Check Answers**

Session 2.1

1. file
2. hard; hard disk
3. Windows Explorer and Computer
4. True
5. file path
6. Folders list; Address bar; Back, Forward, and Recent Pages buttons; Search box; opening folders in the right pane of a folder window
7. False
8. Address bar

Session 2.2

1. moving
2. True
3. Click the first item, hold down the Shift key, and then click the last item. Click an item, hold down the Ctrl key, and then click the rest of the items. You can also drag the pointer to create a selection box around all the items you want to include.
4. moving
5. The extension identifies the file's type and indicates the program in which the file was created.
6. True
7. Recycle Bin
8. save the file

Session 2.3

1. Sorting reorganizes all of the files and folders in a list, whereas filtering displays only those files and folders that share a characteristic you specify. Both actions change your view of the files and folders, not the items themselves.
2. column headings
3. False
4. Only the files and folders created today appear in the filtered list.
5. by showing or hiding the Navigation pane, Details pane, Preview pane, or menu bar
6. True
7. If you transfer files from a hard disk to a removable disk or from one computer to another via e-mail, you can compress the files so that they take up less disk space and transfer more quickly.
8. extract

Ending Data Files

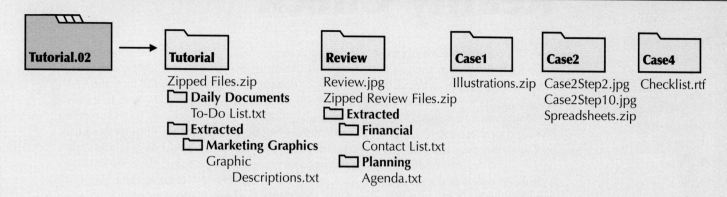

Tutorial.02 → Tutorial

Tutorial
Zipped Files.zip
📁 **Daily Documents**
   To-Do List.txt
📁 **Extracted**
   📁 **Marketing Graphics**
      Graphic
         Descriptions.txt

Review
Review.jpg
Zipped Review Files.zip
📁 **Extracted**
📁 **Financial**
   Contact List.txt
📁 **Planning**
   Agenda.txt

Case1
Illustrations.zip

Case2
Case2Step2.jpg
Case2Step10.jpg
Spreadsheets.zip

Case4
Checklist.rtf

Reality Check

Even if you are familiar with some features of Windows Vista or regularly use your computer for certain tasks, such as accessing Web sites or exchanging e-mail, take some time to explore the basics of Windows Vista on your computer. Then organize the files and folders you use for course work or for other projects on your own computer. Be sure to follow the guidelines you learned for developing an organization strategy, creating folders, naming files, and moving, copying, deleting, and compressing files. As you work through this Reality Check exercise, you will first record settings on your computer. To do so, you can capture and save images of the desktop and windows you open by pressing Alt+Print Screen to capture an image of the screen, and then saving the image in a WordPad or Paint file. You can print these images for references if you experience problems with your computer later or want to restore these settings. Complete the following tasks:

1. Start Windows Vista and log on, if necessary.
2. In case you ever need to restore your computer, you should now capture and save images of your current desktop, the Start menu, the Computer window showing the drives on your computer, and your Documents folder.
3. Start Windows Explorer and open a folder in the Documents folder that you are likely to use often. Make sure the Folders list in the Navigation pane shows the location of this folder on your computer. Capture and save an image of this window.
4. To get acquainted with programs that are included with Windows Vista, start at least two accessory programs that are new to you. Open the File menu in each program, and then capture and save the image of each window.
5. Using the toolbar or menu bar in the new programs, find a dialog box in each program that you are likely to use. Capture and save images of the dialog boxes.
6. Use Windows Help and Support to find information about a feature or technique covered in this tutorial. Choose a topic that you want to know more about. Capture and save an image of the Windows Help and Support window displaying information about this topic.
7. Use a program such as Word or Notepad to create a plan for organizing your files. List the types of files you work with, and then determine whether you want to store them on your hard disk or on removable media. Describe the folders and subfolders you will use to manage these files. If you choose a hard disk as your storage medium, make sure you plan to store your work files and folders in a subfolder of the Documents folder.
8. Use both Windows Explorer and Computer to navigate to your files. Determine which tool you prefer for managing files, if you have a preference.
9. Create the main folders you want to use for your files. Then create the subfolders you will use.
10. Move and copy files to the appropriate folders according to your plan, and rename and delete files as necessary.
11. Create a backup copy of your work files by creating a compressed file and then copying the compressed file to a removable medium, such as a USB flash drive.
12. Submit your finished plan to your instructor, either in printed or electronic form, as requested.

Personalizing Your Windows Environment

Changing Microsoft Windows Vista Desktop Settings

Case | Ptolemy Cartography

Ptolemy Cartography is a small business in Charlottesville, Virginia, that specializes in creating historical maps of American locations. Holly Devore started Ptolemy Cartography with Sarah Liner about two years ago. Since then, the business has continued to grow, with Sarah traveling often to meet with potential clients and conduct on-site research and Holly running operations in Charlottesville.

You have been working for Ptolemy Cartography as the office manager for a few months, providing general assistance to Holly, Sarah, and the staff, including the cartographers, project managers, and interns. The company uses computers to research historical documents online, create and illustrate maps, manage company finances, and communicate with clients and each other. Holly recently upgraded the office computers to Windows Vista. She's heard that Windows Vista makes it easy to change settings to suit the needs of her business. She asks you to customize the company's computers so that everyone can access important files and computer resources. She also wants the desktop to reflect the Ptolemy Cartography corporate image. Holly suggests that you start by personalizing her Windows Vista computer, and then apply the changes to the other office computers.

In this tutorial you add and change Windows Vista tools and icons on the desktop, including shortcuts to folders and devices. You'll also work with Control Panel to change settings and personalize the desktop. Finally, you'll modify the taskbar and customize the Start menu.

Starting Data Files

Tutorial.03 → **Tutorial** **Review** **Case1** **Case2** **Case3** **Case4**

Tutorial	Review	Case1	Case2	Case3	Case4
Haleakala.jpg	Charleston.jpg	DaVinci	Beaux Arts.jpg	Bald Island.jpg	(none)
Hawaii District 1.gif	Explorers.jpg	Tank.jpg	Colonial.jpg	Bar Island.jpg	
Hawaii District 2.gif	James River.jpg	Last Supper.jpg	For Sale.jpg	Birch Grass.jpg	
Hawaii Facts.txt	NF Facts.txt	Mona Lisa.jpg	Schoolhouse.jpg	Bridge.jpg	
Hawaiian Islands.gif	NF Map.gif	Polyhedra.bmp	Syracuse Facts.txt	Cad Summit.jpg	
Maui.jpg	NF Outline.gif	Vasari.txt	Victorian.jpg	Driving Directions.txt	
Navigation.bmp	North America.gif	Vitruvian Man.jpg		Peregrine.jpg	
Volcano.jpg	US 1800.jpg				

Session 3.1

Accessing Common Tools on the Desktop

As you know, when you start Windows Vista, the large area you see on your screen is called the desktop. When you first install Windows Vista, the desktop displays at least a background image, Recycle Bin icon, taskbar, Windows Sidebar, and the Welcome Center window by default. See Figure 3-1. Your desktop might include different icons or windows.

Figure 3-1   **Default Windows Vista desktop**

Because the desktop provides your first view of the computer and its contents, it should contain the items you want to access when you start your computer. Depending on how you work, these items might include tools such as Windows Explorer or Computer, programs and devices you use often, and the Documents folder. **Desktop icons** are the most visual and easiest way to access these resources. Figure 3-2 shows the types of icons you can include on the desktop and the objects they represent.

Types of desktop icons | Figure 3-2

Icon	Description
	User's folder desktop icon
	Network desktop icon
	Computer desktop icon
	Control Panel desktop icon
	Recycle Bin desktop icon (full and empty)
	Printer shortcut icon
	Drive shortcut icon
	Folder shortcut icon
	Document shortcut icon

You are already familiar with some icons on your desktop that represent useful Windows tools, such as the Recycle Bin. As Figure 3-2 shows, you can place additional icons on the desktop that represent objects you want to access quickly and frequently, such as other Windows tools, printers, drives, programs, and documents. Windows provides desktop icons for frequently used tools, such as the Recycle Bin, Computer, and your Documents folder. You can add or remove these icons according to your work preferences. Besides these built-in desktop icons, you can use **shortcuts**, which are icons that provide quick ways to start a program or open a file, folder, or other object without having to find its permanent location on your computer. Shortcut icons include a small arrow in the lower-left corner, a reminder that the icon points to an item that is stored elsewhere on the computer. If you double-click a shortcut, its associated file, folder, device, or program opens. When you delete a shortcut icon, you delete only the shortcut—the file or resource it represents remains in its original location. You typically create shortcuts on the desktop (or elsewhere, such as in a folder or on the taskbar) to locations, files, and devices that you use often.

Shortcut icons can simplify tasks you perform regularly. For example, you can create a shortcut icon to a USB flash drive, and then drag files to the shortcut icon to copy them to the flash drive. If you create a shortcut icon for your printer, you can print a file by dragging it to the printer's shortcut icon. You also can create a shortcut icon for a program you use often, and then double-click the icon to start the program. Many programs provide a shortcut icon on the desktop when you install the program.

Sarah Linder is in Hawaii this week meeting with the tourism board and gathering data to create historic maps of the islands. This gives Holly time to work with you to customize her computer so she can work more efficiently. She wants you to start by adding icons to the desktop for system tools she uses often. You'll also explore Windows Sidebar and show her how to change it to suit her preferences and work style. Then you'll show her how to create shortcut icons on the desktop, including those for a USB flash drive, folder, and printer.

Adding Icons to the Desktop

Windows provides five standard desktop icons that can be displayed on the desktop. Besides the Recycle Bin, you can include the Computer icon on the desktop to provide easy access to the Computer window, which you can use to navigate the drives and folders on your computer. If you display the desktop icon for your personal folder (that is, the folder containing the current user's files), you can quickly find and open the folders containing your documents. Display the Network icon to access a window that lists the connections, shared computers, and other resources on your network. You can also add the Control Panel icon to the desktop. Control Panel contains specialized tools you use to change the way Windows looks and behaves. You'll work with Control Panel later in this tutorial.

Reference Window | **Displaying Standard Desktop Icons**

- Right-click an empty area of the desktop, and then click Personalize on the shortcut menu.
- In the left pane of the Personalization window, click Change desktop icons.
- In the Desktop Icon Settings dialog box, click to select a check box for each icon you want to add to the desktop.
- Click the OK button.

Holly mentions that the Windows tools she uses most frequently are her personal folder, Computer, and Control Panel. You'll add these icons to Holly's desktop. Make sure your computer is turned on and displaying the Windows desktop before you perform the following steps.

To display standard desktop icons:

▶ **1.** Close the Welcome Center window, if necessary.

▶ **2.** Right-click the **desktop**, and then click **Personalize** on the shortcut menu. The Personalization window opens, listing tasks you can perform to personalize Windows Vista.

▶ **3.** In the left pane, click **Change desktop icons**. The Desktop Icon Settings dialog box opens. See Figure 3-3.

| Figure 3-3 | ▶ | Desktop Icon Settings dialog box |

Trouble? If the settings in your Desktop Icon Settings dialog box differ from those in Figure 3-3, note the current options, and change them so they match those in Figure 3-3.

▶ **4.** Click the **Computer**, **User's Files**, and **Control Panel** check boxes.

The Recycle Bin check box is already selected, indicating that Windows is displaying the Recycle Bin icon on the desktop. Note that the Recycle Bin icon has two appearances, one when it is empty, and another when it contains deleted items.

> **5.** Click the **OK** button. The icons for your personal folder and for Computer and Control Panel appear on the desktop.

> **6.** Click the **Close** button X to close the Personalization window.

Now that you've added desktop icons for Holly, you can customize their appearance to suit her preferences.

Changing the Appearance of Desktop Icons

You can change the size and appearance of desktop icons depending on how you like to work. For example, Windows displays desktop icons at a medium size by default. If you have only a few icons on your desktop or prefer working with large icons, you can resize the desktop icons so they are larger. On the other hand, if you are familiar with previous versions of Windows or use many icons on your desktop, you might prefer Classic icons, which are smaller than the default size.

If you like a clean, uncluttered desktop, you can hide all of your desktop icons and show them only when you need to use one. Hiding the icons doesn't delete them—it only hides them until you show them again. You can also change the standard arrangement of the icons on the desktop. By default, Windows lists the icons in columns along the left side of your desktop, and aligns the icons to an invisible grid so that they are evenly spaced on the desktop. You can change this arrangement to match your preferences, such as arranging the icons on the right or along the top of the desktop.

Besides personalizing the size and arrangement of the desktop icons, you can change the icon images. For example, the Computer icon shows an image of a desktop computer. If you work on a notebook or tablet computer, you might want to change this image.

Holly asks you to show her the desktop with large and Classic icons to see if she wants to use those sizes. She also wants to know how to move the icons on the desktop and then hide them for privacy when interns use her computer. You can perform all of these tasks using the View command on the desktop shortcut menu.

To change the size and location of desktop icons:

> **1.** Right-click the **desktop**, point to **View** on the shortcut menu, and then click **Large Icons**. The icons on the desktop now appear in a larger size.

> **2.** Right-click the **desktop**, point to **View** on the shortcut menu, and then click **Classic Icons**. The icons appear in their smallest size.

> Next, you'll show Holly how to move the desktop icons so they no longer are aligned along the left side of the desktop.

> **3.** Right-click the **desktop**, point to **View** on the shortcut menu, and then click **Auto Arrange** to remove the check mark. When the Auto Arrange command is unchecked, you can move the icons anywhere on the desktop.

> **Trouble?** If the Auto Arrange command is not checked, skip Step 3.

> **4.** Drag the **Computer** icon to the right of the Recycle Bin icon. Note that Windows aligns the Computer icon to a grid, maintaining a standard amount of space between the two icons. See Figure 3-4.

Figure 3-4 ▶ **Arranging icons on the desktop**

▶ **5.** Right-click the **desktop**, point to **View** on the shortcut menu, and then click **Align to Grid** to clear the check mark. When the Align to Grid command is unchecked, you can change the icons so they are no longer aligned to each other.

    Trouble? If the Align to Grid command is not checked, skip Step 5.

▶ **6.** Drag the **Computer** icon closer to the Recycle Bin icon.

    Finally, you can use the View command on the desktop shortcut menu to hide and then show the desktop icons.

▶ **7.** Right-click the **desktop**, point to **View** on the shortcut menu, and then click **Show Desktop Icons** to remove the check mark. When Show Desktop Icons is unchecked, Windows hides the icons so only the desktop appears on your screen.

▶ **8.** Right-click the **desktop**, point to **View** on the shortcut menu, and then click **Show Desktop Icons**. A check mark appears next to the command, indicating that Windows is displaying the icons on the desktop.

    Because she works on a notebook computer, Holly likes the idea of changing the image for the Computer icon on the desktop. To do so, you use the Personalization window, which you opened earlier to select the Windows icons to display on the desktop.

To change the image of the Computer icon:

▶ **1.** Right-click the **desktop**, and then click **Personalize** on the shortcut menu. The Personalization window opens.

▶ **2.** In the left pane, click **Change desktop icons**. The Desktop Icon Settings dialog box opens.

▶ **3.** In the list of desktop icons, click the **Computer** icon, and then click the **Change Icon** button. The Change Icon dialog box opens and highlights the current image. See Figure 3-5. Note the icon currently used for Computer so you can restore it later.

Change Icon dialog box ◀ **Figure 3-5**

current Computer icon

scroll to find the notebook computer icon

▶ **4.** Scroll the list of images to the right, and then click the **notebook computer** image, which is in the top row and three columns to the right of the current image.

Trouble? If the notebook computer image does not appear in your Change Icon dialog box, click any other suitable image.

▶ **5.** Click the **OK** button to close the Change Icon dialog box, and then click the **OK** button to close the Desktop Icon Settings dialog box. The Computer icon on the desktop now appears as a notebook computer.

▶ **6.** Close the Personalization window.

The standard Windows desktop icons provide quick access to common Windows tools. You can also personalize another feature to save time when you're performing common tasks—the Windows Sidebar.

Using the Windows Sidebar

Windows Sidebar is a long vertical bar displayed by default on the right side of your desktop. It contains miniprograms called **gadgets**, which offer information at a glance and are similar to tools you might keep on your physical desk, such as a pad of sticky notes, an address book, or a calendar. Windows provides a collection of built-in gadgets, which are described in Figure 3-6.

Figure 3-6 ▶ **Windows Sidebar gadgets**

Gadget	Use to:
Calendar	Display the current date and browse a monthly calendar.
Clock	Display the time in your time zone or any other around the world.
Contacts	Keep track of contact information, including e-mail addresses and phone numbers.
CPU Meter	Gauge system performance.
Currency	Convert from one currency to another.
Feed Headlines	Track news headlines, sports scores, and entertainment information.
Notes	Jot down notes and reminders.
Picture Puzzle	Move the pieces of the puzzle to create an image.
Slide Show	Show a continuous slide show of pictures on your computer.
Stocks	Track your favorite stocks.
Weather	Check the weather in cities around the world.

At least two of these gadgets appear on the Sidebar by default: the Clock and the Slide Show. Besides using the Clock gadget to show the current time for your time zone, you can show one or more additional clocks to display the current time for other time zones around the world. In the Slide Show gadget, you can display any pictures stored on your computer, set the speed for playing the show, and change the transition effect between pictures. The Calendar and the Feed Headlines gadgets are two other popular gadgets. The Calendar shows the current date by default and a monthly view when you click it. The Feed Headlines gadget lists frequently updated headlines so you can keep up with the news from your desktop. The headlines are supplied by a Web site that publishes a **feed**, which is online content that is updated often.

InSight | **Understanding Feeds**

A feed, or Really Simple Syndication (RSS) feed, is Web site content that is frequently updated, such as news or Web logs (more commonly called *blogs*). A feed often has the same content as the information provided on a Web site, but it can be delivered directly to your desktop, where you can use the Feed Headlines Sidebar gadget to display the changing content. If you want to keep with news, sports scores, or other frequently updated information, use Internet Explorer to subscribe to a feed on a Web site. Then keep the Feed Headlines gadget open on your desktop so you can view the changing information at a glance.

Holly wants to display a second Clock gadget in the Sidebar and set it to Hawaii time so she can call Sarah at appropriate times while she's visiting the islands. When Sarah returns from Hawaii, Holly can change the second clock to a different time zone or remove it.

To add a second Clock gadget to the Sidebar:

▶ 1. Click the **Add Gadgets** button ➕ at the top of the Sidebar. The gadget gallery opens, showing the gadgets that are currently installed on your computer. Any of these gadgets can be added to the Sidebar. See Figure 3-7.

Gadget gallery ◀ **Figure 3-7**

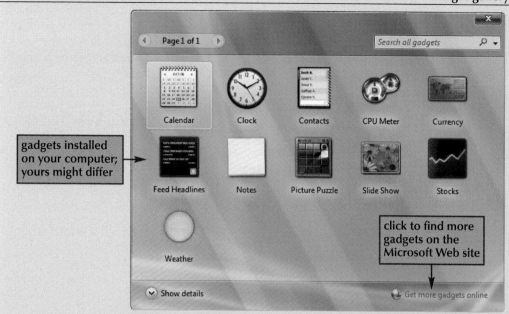

gadgets installed on your computer; yours might differ →

click to find more gadgets on the Microsoft Web site

Trouble? If the Sidebar is not open, click the Start button on the taskbar, point to All Programs, click Accessories, and then click Windows Sidebar.

▶ **2.** Double-click the **Clock** gadget. A second clock opens in the Sidebar. See Figure 3-8.

Buttons on the Clock gadget ◀ **Figure 3-8**

Add Gadgets button

second clock added to the Sidebar

original clock

▶ **3.** Close the gadget gallery.

Next, you'll show Holly how to customize the second Clock gadget to display Hawaiian time.

Customizing the Windows Sidebar

You can customize many of the Sidebar gadgets to suit your preferences, including the Clock, the Slide Show, Notes, Picture Puzzle, Stocks, and Weather. For example, you can select the pictures you want to display in the Slide Show and choose a color for the Notes pad. In addition, you can customize the Sidebar itself by hiding it, keeping it on top of other windows, and adding, removing, and detaching gadgets.

First, you will customize the second Clock gadget to display the current time in Hawaii and then change its appearance to distinguish it easily from the original clock. You will also name the second clock so you can tell at a glance that it displays Hawaiian time.

To customize the second Clock gadget:

▶   **1.** Point to the new **Clock** gadget at the top of the Sidebar, and then click the **Options** button ![icon]. The Clock dialog box opens. See Figure 3-9.

Figure 3-9   ▶   **Clock dialog box**

▶   **2.** Click the **Next** button ⊙ until you select clock image 6 of 8.

▶   **3.** Click in the **Clock name** text box, and then type **Hawaii** as the name of the clock.

▶   **4.** Click the **Time zone** arrow, and then click **(GMT–10:00) Hawaii**.

▶   **5.** Click the **OK** button. The new Clock gadget now has a new appearance, name, and time.

Because the Windows Sidebar is designed to keep handy tools at your fingertips, you can customize it in many ways to fit your work style. One way to personalize the Sidebar is to keep it on top of other windows, so it always appears on the desktop. In that case, when you maximize a window, it widens only as far as the left edge of the Sidebar, and the maximized window and the Sidebar appear side by side.

Holly expects to use the Sidebar regularly. Because she has a wide monitor on her notebook computer, she plans to keep the Sidebar on top of other windows when she finds herself using gadgets often.

Tip

Because of the desktop space Sidebar requires, you should keep the Sidebar on top of other windows only if you're using a large monitor or multiple monitors.

To keep the Sidebar on top of other windows:

1. Right-click a blank spot on the Sidebar, and then click **Properties** on the shortcut menu. The Windows Sidebar Properties dialog box opens.

2. Click the **Sidebar is always on top of other windows** check box.

3. Click the **OK** button. Windows will show the Sidebar even if you maximize other windows or open them so that they overlap the Sidebar.

4. Double-click the **Computer** icon on your desktop, and then click the **Maximize** button to maximize the window. The Computer window expands only as far as the Sidebar. See Figure 3-10.

Maximized window with Sidebar set to stay on top of other windows ◄ **Figure 3-10**

Computer window expands only to the edge of the Sidebar

5. Close the Computer window.

Finally, Holly asks you to remove the Slide Show gadget from the Sidebar because she does not plan to use it right now. If your Sidebar does not display the Slide Show gadget, read but do not perform the following step.

Tip

To move a gadget, right-click it, click Detach from Sidebar on the shortcut menu, and then drag the gadget to a different spot on the desktop.

To remove a gadget from the Sidebar:

▶ 1. Point to the **Slide Show** gadget, and then click the **Close** button ❌.

Trouble? If a dialog box opens asking if you want to close this gadget, click the Close Gadget button.

So far, you've explored how to personalize your desktop by displaying Windows desktop icons and gadgets you use often. These are standard tools that Windows provides to simplify or enhance your computer work. However, other items you access often include documents, folders, and drives, and are different from the items other users access often. In addition, the folders you use frequently one week might differ from those you'll use frequently next week. To personalize your desktop to provide quick access to these items, you can create and use shortcuts.

Using Shortcuts

You can create shortcuts to access drives, documents, files, Web pages, programs, or other computer resources such as a printer. For example, you can easily open a document from the desktop by creating a shortcut icon for the document. A shortcut icon for a document works much the same way as a document icon does in a folder window—you can double-click the shortcut icon to open the document in the appropriate program. However, a shortcut icon is only a link to the actual document. If you move the icon, for example, you move only the shortcut, not the document itself. One advantage of using shortcut icons is that if your desktop becomes cluttered, you can delete the shortcut icons without affecting the original documents.

You can also create shortcut icons for the folders, drives, and devices on your computer. This way, you can access your local hard disk, for example, directly from the desktop, instead of having to open Windows Explorer or Computer and then navigate to the hard disk.

Windows Vista provides several ways of creating shortcuts. For example, you can right-click an object and choose Create Shortcut on the shortcut menu. Figure 3-11 summarizes the techniques you can use to create shortcuts. The one you choose is a matter of personal preference.

Figure 3-11 ▶ **Methods for creating shortcuts**

Method	Description
Drag (for drives and devices only)	To create a drive shortcut on the desktop, use Computer or Windows Explorer to locate the drive icon, and then drag the icon to the desktop. For locations other than the desktop, hold down the Alt key as you drag.
Right-drag	Use Computer or Windows Explorer to locate and select an icon, hold down the right mouse button, and drag to a new location. Release the mouse button and click Create Shortcuts Here on the shortcut menu.
Right-click, Create Shortcut	Use Computer or Windows Explorer to locate an icon, right-click the icon, click Create Shortcut on the shortcut menu, and then drag the shortcut icon to a new location.
Right-click, Send To	To create a shortcut on the desktop, use Computer or Windows Explorer to locate an icon, right-click the icon, point to Send To, and then click Desktop (create shortcut).

Next, you'll create a shortcut to a USB flash drive. You could use any technique listed in Figure 3-11, but you'll use the drag method because it involves the fewest steps.

Creating a Shortcut to a Drive

To create a shortcut to a drive, you can open the Computer or Windows Explorer window, and then drag the drive icon from the window to the desktop. Windows Vista creates a shortcut icon that looks like a drive icon with a shortcut arrow, and includes an appropriate label, such as "Removable Disk (F) – Shortcut." Note that if you drag a document icon from a folder window to the desktop, you move the actual document from its original location to the desktop. However, you cannot move a drive, program, or other computer resource—its location is fixed during installation—so when you drag a drive icon to the desktop, you automatically create a shortcut.

When you create a shortcut to a USB flash drive, you can insert the drive in a USB port, and then double-click the shortcut to view your Data Files, or you can move or copy documents to the drive without having to start Windows Explorer or open the Computer window.

Holly regularly copies image files from her computer to a USB flash drive, and wants to use a shortcut to simplify the task. You'll show her how to create a shortcut on her desktop to a USB flash drive.

The Steps in this tutorial assume that your Data Files are stored on Removable Disk (F:), a USB drive. If necessary substitute the appropriate drive on your system when you perform the steps.

To create a shortcut to a USB flash drive:

▶ 1. If necessary, insert the USB flash drive containing your Data Files into a USB port on your computer.

   Trouble? If you don't have the starting Data Files, you need to get them before you can proceed. Your instructor will either give you the Data Files or ask you to obtain them from a specified location (such as network drive). In either case, make a backup copy of your Data Files before you start using them so you will have the orginal files available in case you need to start over. If you have any questions about the Data Files, see your instructor or technical support person for assistance.

   Trouble? If you do not have a USB flash drive, insert a different type of removable disk, such as a Zip disk, but not a CD, into the appropriate drive.

▶ 2. Double-click the **Computer** icon on the desktop. Resize the Computer window so you can see the icons along the left side of the desktop. You need to see both the desktop icons and the Computer window to drag effectively.

▶ 3. Point to the **Removable Disk (F:)** icon, press and hold the left mouse button and then drag the **Removable Disk (F:)** icon from the Computer window into an empty area of the desktop. (Your flash drive might have a different name or be associated with a different drive letter—substitute that name or drive letter for the remaining steps.)

▶ 4. Release the mouse button. A shortcut labeled "Removable Disk (F) – Shortcut" now appears on the desktop. (Yours might be in a different location.) See Figure 3-12.

Figure 3-12 ▶ **Shortcut to a removable disk**

Trouble? If you dragged with the right mouse button instead of the left, a shortcut menu appears when you release the mouse button. Click Create Shortcuts Here to add the Removable Disk (F) – Shortcut to the desktop.

▶ 5. Point to the **Removable Disk (F) – Shortcut** icon to view its ScreenTip, which indicates the permanent location of the drive on your computer.

Holly received a few files from Sarah containing map images. She can use the shortcut on the desktop to copy the files from the USB flash drive to a new folder for Hawaiian maps.

To use the removable disk shortcut:

▶ 1. In the Navigation pane of the Computer window, click **Pictures** to open the Pictures folder.

▶ 2. Click the **Organize** button on the toolbar, and then click **New Folder** to create a new folder in the Pictures folder.

▶ 3. Type **Hawaii Maps** as the name of the new folder, and then press the **Enter** key.

▶ 4. Double-click the **Hawaii Maps** folder to open it.

▶ 5. Double-click the **Removable Disk (F) – Shortcut** icon on the desktop. A new window opens showing the contents of the USB flash drive.

▶ 6. Open the **Tutorial.03** folder and then the **Tutorial** folder.

▶ 7. Select all of the files in the Tutorial folder, and then drag them to the right pane of the **Hawaii Maps** folder window. All eight files appear in the Hawaii Maps folder.

▶ 8. Close the Hawaii Maps folder window.

Using a shortcut to a drive saves a few steps when you transfer files from one computer to another. If you regularly use certain folders and documents, you can save even more time by creating shortcuts to those items. In fact, Holly expects to receive more documents from Sarah while she's working in Hawaii, and she plans to store those in the Hawaii Maps folder. In addition, Holly plans to use the Hawaii Facts file as a template for creating basic maps of the islands. You'll show her how to create a shortcut to the Hawaii Maps folder and the Hawaii Facts file to save her time.

Creating Shortcuts to Folders and Documents

Creating shortcuts to folders and documents is similar to creating shortcuts to drives—with one crucial difference. Instead of dragging a drive icon from a window to the desktop, you right-drag the folder or document icon to the desktop. (That is, you press and hold the right mouse button as you drag.) Recall that you cannot move a drive by dragging its icon from a window to another location; because the drive's location is fixed during installation, dragging a drive icon to the desktop automatically creates a shortcut. However, if you drag a folder or document icon from Computer to the desktop, you move the folder or document from its original location to the desktop.

You'll show Holly how to create a shortcut to the Hawaii Maps folder using the right-drag method. Then you'll create a shortcut to the Hawaii Facts document using a different method—the Send To menu. When you right-click a file or folder and point to Send To on the shortcut menu, Windows displays a list of the drives and other locations on your computer, including the desktop. If you send an item to the desktop in this way, you create a shortcut to that file or folder.

To create a shortcut to a folder:

1. In the Tutorial folder window, click **Pictures** in the Navigation pane to display the contents of the Pictures folder, including the Hawaii Maps folder. Resize the window as necessary to see both the Hawaii Maps folder icon in the window and the icons on the left side of the desktop.

2. Point to the **Hawaii Maps** folder, press and hold the right mouse button, and then drag the **Hawaii Maps** folder icon from the Pictures window onto the desktop, and then release the mouse button. A shortcut menu appears listing the tasks you can perform with this document. Recall that you can use the shortcut menu to copy or move a document as well as create a shortcut to it.

3. Click **Create Shortcuts Here**. An icon labeled "Hawaii Maps – Shortcut" appears on the desktop.

4. Point to the **Hawaii Maps - Shortcut** icon to display the ScreenTip, which indicates the location of the original folder. See Figure 3-13.

Figure 3-13 Creating a shortcut to the Hawaii Maps folder

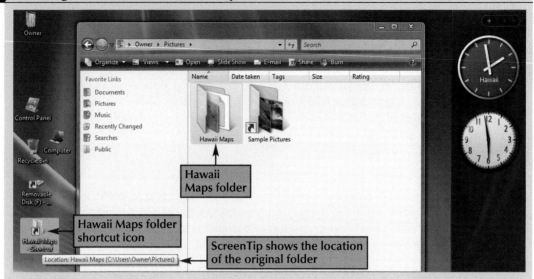

▶ **5.** Close the Pictures window.

Now you can test the folder shortcut and create another shortcut on the desktop, this time to the Hawaii Facts document.

To test the folder shortcut and create a shortcut to a document:

▶ **1.** Double-click the **Hawaii Maps-Shortcut** icon on the desktop. A window opens displaying the contents of the Hawaii Maps folder. Resize the window as necessary to see the contents of the Hawaii Maps folder and a blank area on the left side of the desktop.

▶ **2.** Right-click the **Hawaii Facts** document in the Hawaii Maps window, and then point to **Send To**. The Send To menu opens. See Figure 3-14.

Creating a shortcut using the Send To menu | Figure 3-14

3. Click **Desktop (create shortcut)**. An icon labeled "Hawaii Facts - Shortcut" appears on the desktop.

4. Double-click the **Hawaii Facts - Shortcut** icon on the desktop to open this document in Notepad.

5. Close all open windows.

You now have three shortcuts on the desktop that provide efficient ways to open the Hawaii Maps folder, the Hawaii Facts document, and a USB flash drive. Next, you want to add a printer shortcut to the desktop so that Holly can easily print documents without starting a program.

Creating a Shortcut to a Printer

You can create a printer shortcut in much the same way you created a shortcut for the USB flash drive: by locating the printer device icon in the Printers window, and then dragging the icon onto your desktop. You also can use the other techniques listed in Figure 3-11 to create a shortcut to a printer on the desktop. To open the Printers window, you can use the Start Search text box on the Start menu. (Recall that you can find programs and files on your system by using this text box.) After you create a printer shortcut icon, you can print a document by dragging its icon to the printer shortcut icon on the desktop.

Holly often prints documents to use as a reference when she's working on a map. Instead of starting WordPad or another program, opening the Print dialog box, selecting print settings, and then clicking OK, she can print by dragging a document to a printer shortcut icon. You'll show her how to create a printer shortcut using the Create Shortcut command.

To create a printer shortcut:

▶ **1.** Click the **Start** button 🚩 on the taskbar, and then type **Printers** in the Start Search text box. When the Printers icon appears in the left pane of the Start menu, click **Printers**. The Printers window opens. If necessary, resize the window so you can see both the window and the desktop.

▶ **2.** Right-click the icon for the default printer (the one with the default icon ⊘) to select it.

▶ **3.** Click **Create Shortcut** on the shortcut menu. Windows creates a shortcut to the default printer on the desktop. Because printer names are often long, you can rename the shortcut icon so it's easier to read.

▶ **4.** Right-click the **printer shortcut icon** you just created on the desktop, and then click **Rename** on the shortcut menu.

▶ **5.** Type **Office Printer** as the name of the printer shortcut icon, and then press the **Enter** key. See Figure 3-15.

Figure 3-15 ▶ **Creating a shortcut to a printer**

▶ **6.** Close the Printers window.

Now you can show Holly how to print the Hawaii Facts document using the Office Printer and Hawaii Facts – Shortcut icons. Make sure your default printer is installed, attached to your computer, and turned on before you perform the following steps.

To print the Hawaii Facts document using the printer shortcut icon:

▶ 1. Using the left mouse button, drag the **Hawaii Facts - Shortcut** icon to the **Office Printer** icon on the desktop.

When you release the mouse button, Windows Vista opens the Hawaii Facts document in Notepad or another text-editing program, prints the document, and then closes Notepad.

Now that your desktop contains a variety of icons, including standard desktop icons and shortcuts, you can arrange the icons so they are easy to access.

Organizing Icons on the Desktop

By default, Windows displays the Recycle Bin icon in the upper-left corner of the desktop. When you add other desktop icons to the desktop, Windows lists them above the Recycle Bin. When you add custom shortcut icons, such as the Hawaii Facts - Shortcut icon, Windows lists them below the Recycle Bin in the order that you add them to the desktop. You can change this order by selecting a sort option to list the shortcut icons by name, size, type, or date modified. These sort options are similar to the ones you use when sorting files and folders in a folder window. Sorting by name organizes the icons in alphabetical order by the icon name. Sorting by size organizes them according to the size of their source files (unless the icon is a shortcut to a program—then Windows uses the size of the shortcut itself). Sort by type when you want to keep shortcuts to files of the same type, such as text documents, next to each other on the desktop. Sort by date modified to arrange the icons according to the date you modified the shortcuts.

Before you organize the icons on the desktop, restore the original Auto Arrange and Align to Grid settings. Then you can sort the shortcut icons by name to make them easy to find.

To restore the desktop settings and sort the icons:

▶ 1. Right-click the **desktop**, point to **View** on the shortcut menu, and then click **Auto Arrange** to select that option.

▶ 2. Right-click the **desktop**, point to **View** on the shortcut menu, and then click **Align to Grid** to select that option.

▶ 3. Right-click the **desktop**, point to **Sort By** on the shortcut menu, and then click **Name** to select that option. The shortcut icons are organized on the desktop in alphabetical order. See Figure 3-16.

Figure 3-16	Desktop icons sorted by name

Finally, you can delete a shortcut icon to verify that doing so does not affect its associated device, drive, folder, or document.

Deleting Shortcut Icons

If you delete a document icon in a folder window, you also delete the document. If you delete a shortcut icon, however, you don't delete the document itself, because it is stored elsewhere. You delete only the shortcut that links to the document. The same is true for other types of shortcuts, including those to folders, drives, and devices. You can verify this by deleting the Hawaii Facts – Shortcut icon on the desktop when the Hawaii Maps folder is open.

To delete a shortcut:

▶ **1.** Double-click the **Hawaii Maps – Shortcut** icon on your desktop. Arrange the Hawaii Maps window so that it doesn't overlap the Hawaii Facts - Shortcut icon on the desktop.

▶ **2.** Click the **Hawaii Facts – Shortcut** icon on the desktop, and then press the **Delete** key.

▶ **3.** Click the **Yes** button if you are asked if you are sure you want to send these items to the Recycle Bin.

▶ **4.** Verify that the Hawaii Facts document is still stored in the Hawaii Maps folder, and then close the folder window.

Because you selected Auto Arrange and Align to Grid using the View command on the desktop shortcut menu, Windows rearranges the icons so they remain in a single column and are aligned to one another on the desktop.

So far, you have learned how to access the tools you need from the desktop by displaying system icons and customizing the Windows Sidebar and gadgets. You have also learned how to create desktop shortcuts to a drive, folder, document, and printer, and then organize all the icons on your desktop. Next, you'll learn how to work with Control Panel to continue to customize the desktop and personalize your Windows experience.

Session 3.1 Quick Check | Review

1. To change the size of the icons on the desktop, you can use the _____ command on the desktop shortcut menu.
2. When you delete a shortcut icon, what happens to the file or resource it represents?
3. Describe the two appearances the Recycle Bin icon can have on your desktop.
4. Name three gadgets you can display in the Sidebar.
5. True or False. Although you can customize the Sidebar gadgets, you cannot customize the Sidebar itself.
6. Name three ways you can create a shortcut to the USB flash drive on your desktop.

Session 3.2

Using Control Panel

You've worked with the Windows Sidebar and with standard desktop and shortcut icons to personalize your desktop. You can also personalize other parts of Windows Vista using Control Panel. **Control Panel** is a window that contains specialized tools you use to change the way Windows Vista looks and behaves. Some of these tools help you adjust settings that make your computer more fun to use. For example, use the Personalize tool to select a desktop background image or the sounds Windows plays to signal events such as Windows shutting down or the Recycle Bin emptying. You can also use the Personalize tool to change the **theme**, which is a background plus a set of sounds, icons, and other elements. Other Control Panel tools help you set up Windows so that your computer is easier to use. For example, you can change display settings so that the desktop, icons, and windows are sharp and clear, and you can change mouse settings to switch the default buttons if you are left-handed.

All of the Control Panel tools provide access to dialog boxes that let you select or change the **properties**, or characteristics, of an object. Recall that you already used the Windows Sidebar Properties dialog box to change one of the Sidebar's properties (to keep the Sidebar on top of other windows).

If you added the Control Panel icon to the desktop, you can open Control Panel by double-clicking that icon. Otherwise, you open Control Panel from the Start menu.

To open Control Panel:

▶ **1.** Double-click the **Control Panel** icon on your desktop. The Control Panel window opens. See Figure 3-17. Your Control Panel window might differ.

Figure 3-17 ▶ Control Panel

Trouble? If your desktop does not display a Control Panel icon, click the Start button on the taskbar, and then click Control Panel.

Trouble? If a message appears indicating that the Control Panel is not available, you might be in a computer lab with limited customization access. Ask your instructor or technical support person for options.

By default, the Control Panel window shows tasks in the right pane and related links in the left pane. This default view is called Category View, which groups similar tools into categories. See Figure 3-18.

Control Panel categories ◄ Figure 3-18

Control Panel Category	Description
System and Maintenance	Schedule maintenance checks, increase the space on your hard disk, or configure energy-saving settings.
Security	Maintain Windows security settings and keep Windows up to date.
Network and Internet	Set Internet options, view network status, and set up file sharing and perform other network tasks.
Hardware and Sound	Change the sound scheme or individual sounds on your computer, configure the settings for your sound devices, and change the settings for your printer, keyboard, mouse, camera, and other hardware.
Programs	Install and uninstall programs and Windows features, set options for default settings and programs, and work with Windows programs, such as Sidebar.
Mobile PC	Change battery settings and adjust other common mobility settings for a laptop computer.
User Accounts and Family Safety	Change user account settings, passwords, and associated pictures.
Appearance and Personalization	Change the appearance of desktop items, apply a theme or screen saver, or customize the Start menu and taskbar.
Clock, Language, and Region	Change the date, time, and time zone, the language you use on your computer, and the format for numbers, currencies, dates, and times.
Ease of Access	Change computer settings for vision, hearing, and mobility.
Additional Options	Optional category that covers software other than built-in Windows software.

To open a category and see its related tools, you click the appropriate link. For example, you can open the Appearance and Personalization window to change the desktop background or to set a theme.

To open the Appearance and Personalization category:

▶ 1. In the right pane of Control Panel, click **Appearance and Personalization**. The Appearance and Personalization window opens, showing the tasks and tools related to personalizing your computer's appearance. See Figure 3-19.

Figure 3-19 ▶ **Appearance and personalization options in Control Panel**

The Appearance and Personalization window, like the other Control Panel category windows, lists tasks and tools in the right pane and links to other Control Panel tools in the left pane. To change the desktop background, for example, you click the appropriate task in the right pane. The Desktop Background window opens so you can select a new desktop background and set other background options.

Holly wants her office computers to reflect the company image of Ptolemy Cartography. She'd like the desktop itself to be more appealing to her and her employees. You will work with the desktop properties to change the desktop background and other elements.

Changing the Desktop

In Windows Vista, you can think of all the parts of your computer—the operating system, the programs, and the documents—as individual objects. For example, the desktop, task-bar, drives, programs, and documents are all objects. Each object has properties that you can examine and usually change to suit your needs and preferences. The desktop has many properties, including the image it displays and its font. You can change the proper-ties of an object using the Properties command on its shortcut menu or by using Control Panel. In this session, you will use Control Panel to change desktop properties.

Changing the Desktop Background | Reference Window

- Open the Control Panel window and switch to Category View, if necessary.
- Click Change desktop background in the Appearance and Personalization category.
- Select an image in the Desktop Background window or click the Picture Location arrow or the Browse button to select images stored in a different location.
- Select a positioning option, if necessary.
- Click the OK button.

Changing Your Desktop's Background

You can change the desktop background, or its **wallpaper**, to display one of the images that Windows Vista provides, or you can select your own graphic to use as wallpaper. When you change the background, you are not placing a new object on the desktop; you are only changing its appearance. You can also determine how you want to position the picture—resized to fit the screen, tiled (repeated across the screen), or centered on the screen. If you center the wallpaper on the screen, you can select a color to frame the background image.

Holly wants the staff computers in the Ptolemy Cartography offices to share a company look. You and Holly decide to examine the desktop backgrounds that Windows Vista provides to see if one is suitable.

To change the desktop background:

▶ **1.** In the Appearance and Personalization window, click **Change desktop background** in the Personalization category. The Desktop Background window opens. See Figure 3-20. Your Desktop Background window might differ.

Desktop Background window ◀ **Figure 3-20**

> **2.** Scroll the wallpapers as necessary, and then click the **palm tree branch** image in the Vistas category. (The ScreenTip indicates this image is named img19.) Windows displays the image you selected on the desktop.
>
> **3.** Click the **OK** button.

After examining the desktop, Holly doesn't think the palm tree image is right for her company after all—Ptolemy Cartography specializes in historical maps of the United States, and the desktop should illustrate that somehow. She mentions that she has an image file of historical maps that she has used in marketing materials. That image might be right for the desktop background.

You'll show Holly how to display her graphic as the desktop background. First, however, you'll close the Windows Sidebar so you can continue to experiment with desktop wallpapers.

To use a graphic image as a desktop background:

> **1.** Right-click the **Sidebar**, and then click **Close Sidebar**.
>
> **2.** In the Appearance and Personalization window, click **Change desktop background** to open the Desktop Background window again.
>
> **3.** Click the **Browse** button to open the Browse dialog box.
>
> **4.** Navigate to the **Hawaii Maps** folder in the Pictures folder, and then double-click the **Navigation** image file. The Navigation image appears in the Desktop Background window and on the desktop.
>
> **5.** Minimize the Desktop Background window. See Figure 3-21.

Figure 3-21 | **Navigation image as the desktop background**

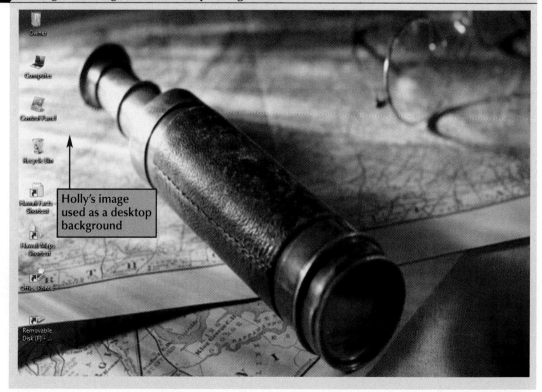

Holly's image used as a desktop background

Holly thinks the Navigation image is perfect for the standard wallpaper for Ptolemy Cartography, though the image is too large. You suggest centering the wallpaper image and selecting a coordinating color to frame the image.

To reposition wallpaper and select a desktop color:

▶ **1.** Restore the Desktop Background window.

▶ **2.** In the How should this picture be positioned? section, click the **Center** option button (point to the positioning images to display their names).

▶ **3.** Minimize the Desktop Background window to verify that Windows centered the Navigation wallpaper on the desktop, and then restore the Desktop Background window.

▶ **4.** Click **Change background color**. The Color dialog box opens.

▶ **5.** In the Basic colors, click the **brown square** in the fifth row, second column. Then click the **OK** button.

▶ **6.** Minimize the Desktop Background window. Windows displays the Navigation image in the center of the desktop with a brown frame. See Figure 3-22.

Navigation image positioned in the center of the window ◀ Figure 3-22

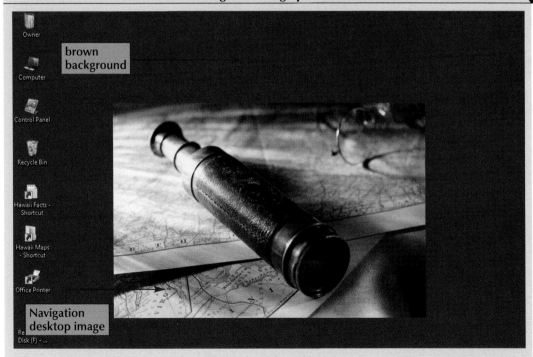

Holly likes the Navigation wallpaper but comments that the colors of the taskbar and desktop icons are not coordinated with that wallpaper. She also wants to change the font of the desktop icon labels to match the font Ptolemy Cartography uses in its marketing materials, which is Palatino. You'll show her how to change the window colors and the font of the desktop elements.

Changing the Appearance of Desktop Elements

Besides changing the desktop background, you can use the Window Color and Appearance tool in Control Panel to set the color of windows, the Start menu, and the taskbar. To set the color of a broader range of Windows elements, such as buttons, ScreenTips, and the background of program windows, you can specify a **color scheme**, which is a set of colors you apply to Windows elements. Windows Vista includes a collection of color schemes. The default color scheme for most Windows editions is Windows Aero (light blue with glassy effects); for other editions, the color scheme is Windows Basic (also light blue, but without the glassy effects). If you select a color for the windows, Start menu, and taskbar using the Window Color and Appearance tool, Windows integrates this color into the color scheme. For example, if you select graphite as the color and are using the Windows Aero color scheme, title bars shade from black to transparent.

You can also use the Window Color and Appearance tool to change the properties of the text for Windows elements, including icons, window title bars, and buttons. For example, you can increase the size or change the font of the text for desktop icons.

To change the window colors and icon font:

▶ **1.** Click the **Desktop Background** button on the taskbar to restore the Desktop Background window, and then click the **Back** button ⬅ to return to the Appearance and Personalization window.

▶ **2.** Click **Personalization** to open the Personalization window. You can perform the rest of your changes in this session from this window.

▶ **3.** Click **Window Color and Appearance**. The Window Color and Appearance window opens. See Figure 3-23.

Figure 3-23 ▶ **Window Color and Appearance window**

Trouble? If you are not using the Aero experience, the Appearance Settings dialog box opens instead of the Windows Colors and Appearance window. Skip Steps 4 and 5. The color of your window elements will differ from those shown in the figures.

▶ **4.** Click **Orange**. The title bar and border change to orange, which coordinates with Holly's Navigation wallpaper.

Now you want to change the font for the desktop icon labels.

▶ **5.** Click **Open classic appearance properties for more color options**. The Appearance Settings dialog box opens. This dialog box lists the color schemes you can use on your computer.

▶ **6.** Click the **Advanced** button. The Advanced Appearance dialog box opens. See Figure 3-24.

Advanced Appearance dialog box | Figure 3-24

7. Click the **Item** arrow, and then click **Icon**. The controls for selecting font properties become active.

8. Click the **Font** arrow, and then click **Palatino Linotype**.

9. Click the **OK** button to close the Advanced Appearance dialog box.

10. Click the **OK** button to close the Appearance Settings dialog box and apply your changes to the desktop, and then minimize the Personalization window. See Figure 3-25.

Figure 3-25   **Personalized desktop**

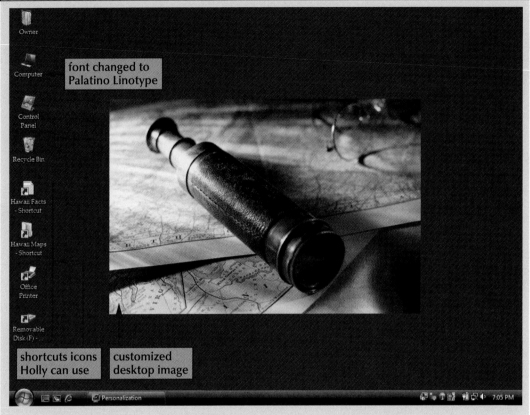

The desktop is now personalized for Holly. It displays the Navigation wallpaper, orange window elements, and Palatino icon labels.

Using Themes

Now that you have changed the desktop, you can save the settings as a theme. Recall that a theme is a collection of customized elements, such as colors and graphics, that you apply to your desktop. If you save your current settings as a theme, you can apply all the changes—the Navigation wallpaper, orange window elements, and Palatino icon labels—at the same time, without selecting the individual settings again. You can save the desktop settings you created for Holly as a theme called Ptolemy.

To save the desktop settings as a theme:

1. Restore the Personalization window, and then click **Theme**. The Theme Settings dialog box opens. See Figure 3-26.

Theme Settings dialog box ◄ **Figure 3-26**

click to select a different theme

preview of the selected theme

current desktop background image and color

2. Click the **Theme** arrow to view the themes you can use on your computer. By default, the themes include at least a Windows Vista and a Windows Classic theme. Your computer might also have themes that correspond to some wallpaper backgrounds in the Desktop Background window.

3. Click **My Current Theme**. The My Current Theme option includes all the appearance and personalization properties currently set for Windows.

4. Click the **Save As** button.

5. In the Save As dialog box, click the **Browse Folders** button, and then navigate to the **Hawaii Maps** folder in your Pictures folder. In the File name text box, type **Ptolemy** as the name of this theme.

6. Click the **Save** button. The Ptolemy theme now appears in the Theme list.

7. Click the **OK** button to close the Theme Settings dialog box.

Now that you've saved the Ptolemy theme, you can personalize another element of the Windows environment—the screen saver.

Activating a Screen Saver

A **screen saver** blanks the screen or displays a moving design whenever you haven't worked with the computer for a specified period of time. Screen savers are entertaining and handy for hiding your data from the eyes of others if you step away from your computer. When a screen saver is on, you restore your desktop by moving your mouse or pressing a key. Windows Vista comes with several screen savers. Some show an animated design and others play a slide show of the pictures stored on your computer.

You can select how long you want the computer to sit idle before the screen saver starts. Most users find settings between 3 and 10 minutes to be the most convenient. You can change this using the options on the Screen Saver Settings dialog box.

InSight | **Using a Screen Saver for Security**

To enhance the security of your computer and prevent unauthorized people from accessing your files, take advantage of a security setting available in the Screen Saver Settings dialog box. If you select the On resume, require logon screen check box in this dialog box, you can dismiss a screen saver and return to your desktop only after you enter the password you use to log on to Windows Vista.

Holly wants to examine the screen savers that Windows provides and then choose the most appropriate one for her company.

To activate a screen saver:

▶ **1.** In the Personalization window, click **Screen Saver**. The Screen Saver Settings dialog box opens. See Figure 3-27. Note the name of the current screen saver so you can restore it later.

Figure 3-27 ▶ **Screen Saver Settings dialog box**

preview of the selected screen saver

click to select a different screen saver

change the settings for some screen savers

▶ **2.** Click the **Screen saver** arrow to display the screen savers installed on your computer.

▶ **3.** Click **Windows Energy**. The animated screen saver plays in the Preview window.

Holly likes that screen saver, but it's not appropriate for her desktop theme. You suggest the Photos screen saver, which plays a slide show of the pictures and videos stored in the Pictures folder, by default. You can change this to any location on the computer, including the Hawaii Maps folder.

▶ **4.** Click the **Screen saver** arrow, and then click **Photos**. The preview window plays a slide show of the graphic files stored in the Pictures folder.

▶ **5.** Click the **Settings** button to open the Photos Screen Saver Settings dialog box. You use this dialog box to specify which files to include in the slide show and other settings, such as the slide show speed.

▶ **6.** Click the **Browse** button. The Browse For Folder dialog box opens.

▶ **7.** Click the **Hawaii Maps** folder in the Pictures folder, and then click the **OK** button.

▶ **8.** Click the **Save** button to close the Photos Screen Saver Settings dialog box. The pictures in the Hawaii Maps folder appear in the Preview window.

▶ **9.** Click the **OK** button to close the Screen Saver Settings dialog box.

After your computer is idle for a few minutes, the screen saver will start, playing a slide show of the maps.

Now that you have worked with the properties for the desktop background, theme, and screen saver, you're ready to explore the display properties that affect the computer monitor itself. The Display Settings dialog box lets you change the sharpness of the images on the desktop and the number of colors your monitor displays.

Changing Display Settings

Use the Display Settings dialog box to control the display settings for your monitor, such as the size of the desktop and whether to use more than one monitor. Windows chooses the best display settings, including screen resolution, refresh rate (also called monitor flicker), and color, based on your particular monitor. The settings you can change depend on your monitor type, so some options in your Display Settings dialog box might be dimmed, indicating they do not apply. Generally, however, you can set the screen resolution and color quality. **Screen resolution** refers to the clarity of the text and images on your screen. At higher resolutions, items appear sharper and smaller, so more items fit on the screen. At lower resolutions, fewer items fit on the screen, but they are larger and easier to see. At very low resolutions, however, images might have jagged edges. The color quality is determined by the number of colors the monitor can assign to a single **pixel**, short for *picture element*, the smallest part of an image on a computer monitor. Computer monitors display images by drawing thousands of pixels in columns and rows, and the more colors each pixel can display, the higher the color quality and the richer the image. Setting your monitor to its highest color quality enhances your Windows experience, though it might slow the performance of your computer.

Selecting the Best Display Settings for Your Monitor | InSight

Display settings vary depending on whether you have an LCD or CRT monitor. (Notebooks and other devices with flat screens often use LCD monitors, while desktop computers sometimes have CRT monitors, which use tubes similar to those in a television.) LCD monitors display vivid color, so use at least a 32-bit color setting. The recommended resolution for a CRT monitor depends on its size. For a 15-inch monitor, use 1024 x 768; for a 17-inch to 19-inch monitor, use 1280 x 1024; and for a 20-inch or larger monitor, use 1600 x 1200.

Changing the Size of the Desktop Area

The Display Settings dialog box has a Resolution slider bar that lets you change the size of the desktop area. You can drag the slider bar to increase or decrease the resolution, or sharpness, of the image. The resolution is measured horizontally and vertically in pixels. If you select a low resolution, such as 800 x 600, the desktop can display fewer objects, but the objects look bigger. If you select a high resolution, such as 1280 x 800 or 1600 x 1200, the desktop can display more objects, though they look smaller.

To change the screen resolution:

▶ **1.** In the Personalization window, click **Display Settings** to open the Display Settings dialog box. Close the Personalization window, and then note the original setting in the Screen resolution area so you can restore it later. See Figure 3-28.

Figure 3-28 | Display Settings dialog box

shows relative size of the desktop

drag to change the screen resolution

click to change the color settings

▶ **2.** To select the 1280 by 800 resolution, if it is not already selected, drag the **Resolution** slider to that setting. The preview area shows the relative size of the new resolution.

Trouble? If your monitor does not display a 1280 by 800 resolution, choose a different resolution, such as 1280 by 720 or 1280 by 768.

▶ **3.** To select the 1024 by 768 resolution, if possible, drag the **Resolution** slider to that setting.

▶ **4.** Return the slider to its original setting. Leave the Display Settings dialog box open.

While changing the screen resolution increases or decreases the sharpness of the images, the number of colors your monitor displays determines how realistic the images look. However, the higher the resolution and color setting, the more resources your monitor needs; the best settings for your computer balance sharpness and color quality with computer resources.

Changing the Colors Setting

You can also use the Display Settings dialog box to change the Colors setting, which specifies the number of colors available to your computer to create shading and other realistic effects. Holly's computers use Highest (32 bit) color, which includes millions of colors.

To view the color settings:

▶ 1. Click the **Colors** arrow to display the list of color settings available to your monitor. Most contemporary monitors allow at least a Medium (16 bit) setting, which displays up to 835,000 colors.

▶ 2. Click **Highest (32 bit)**. Depending on your monitor, your screen can now display up to 16 million colors, which allows realistic shading and gradation.

    Trouble? If Highest (32 bit) doesn't appear in your Colors list, skip Step 2.

▶ 3. Click the **Cancel** button to close the Display Settings dialog box without accepting any changes.

You used Control Panel and its tools to change the properties of Holly's desktop, including the background and the appearance of desktop elements, such as windows and icons. You also changed the window colors, saved Holly's color scheme as a theme, activated a screen saver, and experimented with the display settings. You and Holly can now change the desktops of other computers in her office so they all reflect the corporate image of Ptolemy Cartography.

Session 3.2 Quick Check | Review

1. True or False. A theme is a background image plus a set of sounds, icons, and other elements.
2. What is the purpose of Control Panel?
3. Windows Vista includes a collection of _____ , which are sets of colors you apply to Windows elements.
4. Why might you use a screen saver?
5. What does it mean to say that a monitor's resolution is 1024 x 768?
6. At _____ screen resolutions, items appear sharper and smaller, so more items fit on the screen.
   a. low
   b. high
   c. 32-bit
   d. 16-bit

Session 3.3

Modifying the Taskbar

As you know from previous tutorials, the bar that contains the Start button and appears by default at the bottom of the desktop is the **taskbar**. The taskbar is divided into four sections. You are already familiar with the Start button, which you click to open the Start menu. By default, the taskbar also displays the **Quick Launch toolbar**, which contains buttons you can click to start programs you use often. The middle section of the taskbar displays program buttons, which you click to manipulate windows. The far-right section of the taskbar is the **notification area**, which shows the current time, program icons, and system status information. Figure 3-29 shows the taskbar with these default sections.

Figure 3-29 | **Default taskbar sections**

Start
button

Quick
Launch
toolbar

grouped
taskbar
buttons

notification
area

Tip

To close all the windows in a taskbar group, right-click the group's taskbar button, and then click Close Group.

Figure 3-29 shows the taskbar buttons organized into groups. As you open additional windows, taskbar buttons shrink to accommodate new buttons. When the taskbar becomes crowded, Windows groups the buttons for the same program into a single button. In Figure 3-29, for example, five folder windows are grouped on the Windows Explorer button, which shows the name of the group (Windows Explorer) and the number of items in the group (5). To display a menu of the windows in the group, you click the taskbar button. To activate a window, you click its name in the menu.

Recall that if you are using Windows Aero and you point to a taskbar button, Windows displays a preview of the corresponding window. The preview is designed to help you identify a window by more than the title alone. If a window is playing a video or animation, it also plays in the preview. When you point to a grouped taskbar button, a stack of previews appears, with only the top preview visible.

You can personalize the taskbar to suit your preferences. For example, you can change its size and position or hide it altogether. In addition, you can display toolbars on the taskbar. These toolbars can contain buttons for the icons on your desktop, for programs you use often, and for Web pages to which you want quick access. Including toolbars on the taskbar makes it easy to navigate your computer and open programs, documents, and Web pages without minimizing windows or closing dialog boxes that might be open on the desktop.

InSight | **Monitoring the Notication Area**

The icons in the notification area of the taskbar let you access some computer settings, such as the system time, and communicate the status of programs running in the background. Background programs are those programs that Windows runs to provide a service, such as an Internet connection. If you suspect trouble with a program running in the background, click the Show hidden icons button on the taskbar to display all the icons in the notification area. Then point to an icon to display its status or name. For example, point to the network icon to determine whether your computer is connected to a network. Sometimes an icon displays a notification, or small pop-up window, to notify you about a change in status, such as when you add a new hardware device to your computer. Read the notification to find out whether you need to respond or correct a problem.

So far you've shown Holly how to work with many properties of the Windows Vista desktop. Now you can personalize two other parts of the Windows Vista desktop: the taskbar and the Start menu. You'll start by showing her how to work with the taskbar.

Moving and Resizing the Taskbar

When you first install Windows Vista, the taskbar is locked in its position at the bottom of the desktop. That way, as you learn your way around Windows, you always have access to the Start menu so you can start programs and shut down Windows. Before you can move or resize the taskbar, however, you must unlock it. You can do so by right-clicking the taskbar to open its shortcut menu, and then clicking the Lock the Taskbar command. This command is listed with a check mark by default to indicate that it is selected, so clicking it again removes the check mark, indicating the taskbar is no longer locked.

When Holly is working with graphics programs, she occasionally drags objects onto the taskbar by accident. You'll show her how to move the taskbar to the top of the desktop, where it's out of her way. First, however, you need to unlock the taskbar.

Moving and Resizing the Taskbar | Reference Window

- Make sure the taskbar is unlocked. To do so, right-click any blank spot on the taskbar, and then click Lock the Taskbar on the shortcut menu to remove the check mark.
- To move the taskbar, click a blank spot on the taskbar, hold down the left mouse button, and drag the taskbar to a new location (the top, bottom, left, or right edge of the desktop).
- To resize the taskbar, point to a taskbar border until a resize pointer appears, and then drag the border to a different height or width.

To move the taskbar:

1. Right-click a blank spot on the taskbar, and then, if necessary, click **Lock the Taskbar** on the shortcut menu to uncheck this command.

   Trouble? If the Lock the Taskbar command is already unchecked, skip Step 1.

2. Drag the taskbar to the top of the desktop. See Figure 3-30. Notice that the icons on the desktop moved down slightly to make room for the newly positioned taskbar.

> **Tip**
> You can also select commands on the taskbar shortcut menu that let you cascade windows, stack them, or show them side by side.

Moving the taskbar to the top of the desktop ◀ Figure 3-30

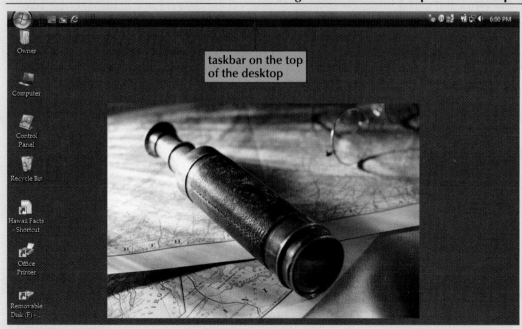

3. Drag the taskbar back down to the bottom of the desktop.

Holly has also noticed that when she has several programs running simultaneously, the icons for those programs fill up the notification area. She often refers to these icons, and wants to display them without sacrificing space for her taskbar buttons. You'll show her how to solve that problem by increasing the size of the taskbar.

To increase the size of the taskbar:

▶ **1.** Point to the upper edge of the taskbar until the pointer changes to $\updownarrow$.

▶ **2.** Drag up to increase the height of the taskbar. See Figure 3-31.

| Figure 3-31 | ▶ | Resizing the taskbar |

taskbar is twice as high

▶ **3.** Drag the upper border of the taskbar to return it to its original height.

Resizing the taskbar is one way to change its appearance. You also can change other taskbar properties, such as those that determine when the taskbar appears.

Setting Taskbar Appearance Properties

In addition to resizing and relocating the taskbar, you can set taskbar appearance properties using the Taskbar and Start Menu Properties dialog box, which you open from a shortcut menu or Control Panel. Using this dialog box, you can increase the amount of screen space available for your program windows by hiding the taskbar. In this case, the taskbar is not closed, removed, or minimized, but hidden either under the border of the desktop or under the program windows open on the desktop. It still remains active and accessible—you can point to the area of your screen where the taskbar would be located to redisplay the taskbar.

By default, the taskbar appears on top of windows on the desktop, but you can change this setting in the Taskbar and Start Menu Properties dialog box so that program windows and dialog boxes cover the taskbar when necessary. You can also use the Taskbar and Start Menu Properties dialog box to determine whether to show the Quick Launch toolbar on the taskbar, group similar taskbar buttons, and show window previews in the Aero experience.

You'll show Holly how to increase the amount of screen space by hiding the taskbar and by letting windows cover the taskbar.

To set taskbar appearance properties:

▶ **1.** Right-click a blank area on the taskbar, and then click **Properties** on the shortcut menu. The Taskbar and Start Menu Properties dialog box opens. See Figure 3-32.

Taskbar and Start Menu Properties dialog box ◄ **Figure 3-32**

taskbar settings

this setting is available only if you are using the Aero experience

Note the options currently selected in this dialog box so you can restore them later.

▶ **2.** Click to select the **Auto-hide the taskbar** check box, and then click the **Apply** button. Windows hides the taskbar.

Trouble? If the Auto-hide the taskbar check box is already selected, skip Step 2.

▶ **3.** Point to the bottom of the desktop to redisplay the taskbar.

▶ **4.** In the Taskbar and Start Menu Properties dialog box, click the **Auto-hide the taskbar** check box to remove the check mark, and then click the **Apply** button. The taskbar appears in its default position at the bottom of the desktop.

▶ **5.** Click the **Keep the taskbar on top of other windows** check box to remove the check mark, and then click the **Apply** button.

Trouble? If the Keep the taskbar on top of other windows check box does not contain a check mark, skip Step 5.

▶ **6.** Drag the Taskbar and Start Menu Properties dialog box to your taskbar. When you release the mouse button, the dialog box overlaps the taskbar.

▶ **7.** Restore the options in this dialog box to their original state, and then click the **OK** button to close the dialog box.

The taskbar shortcut menu also includes options relating to toolbars, which you'll work with next.

Working with Taskbar Toolbars

One way to customize the taskbar is to use it to display toolbars. By default, it displays the Quick Launch toolbar, which contains icons for starting Internet Explorer, switching windows, and showing the desktop. Figure 3-33 describes the toolbars you can include on the taskbar. Your taskbar might be able to display additional toolbars.

Figure 3-33 ▷ **Taskbar toolbars**

Taskbar Toolbar	Description
Address	Use to open any Web page you specify. Open the Address bar by double-clicking it.
Windows Media Player	Use to display controls for playing music and other media, including Play, Stop, and Pause buttons.
Links	Use to access links to product information on the Web and add Web links by dragging them to the toolbar. Open the Links toolbar by clicking the double chevron (>>).
Desktop	Use to access items on your desktop, such as the Recycle Bin and Computer, from the taskbar. Open the Desktop toolbar by clicking the double chevron (>>).
Quick Launch	Use to access icons you can click to quickly open programs, show the desktop, or perform other tasks.
New	Create a custom taskbar toolbar to store shortcuts to folders, documents, or other objects you use often.

The New taskbar toolbar is a custom toolbar you can create to store shortcuts to folders, documents or other objects you use often. In fact, you can move all the shortcut icons you created from the desktop to a custom taskbar toolbar. You can also add program icons to the Quick Launch toolbar, such as those for your e-mail or other programs you use often.

Customizing the Quick Launch Toolbar

You can customize the Quick Launch toolbar by adding program icons to it. To do so, you locate the program you want on the Start menu or on the desktop, and then drag its icon to the Quick Launch toolbar, where you create a shortcut to the program. By default, the Quick Launch toolbar can display only three icons so it doesn't take up too much of the taskbar. If the toolbar contains more than three icons, Windows hides the additional icons. However, you can resize the Quick Launch toolbar to show all of its icons or easily display the hidden icons even if you don't resize the toolbar. You customize the Quick Launch toolbar by working directly with it on the taskbar.

Holly often uses the Windows Photo Gallery program to view pictures of maps and other images. You'll show her how to add that program to the Quick Launch toolbar.

To customize the Quick Launch toolbar:

▷ **1.** Click the **Start** button ⊕ on the taskbar, and then point to **All Programs**. The Windows Photo Gallery program appears in the All Programs menu.

Trouble? If the Windows Photo Gallery program does not appear in the All Programs menu, point to Back or click the Accessories folder to find the program.

▷ **2.** Drag **Windows Photo Gallery** from the Start menu to a blank area on the Quick Launch toolbar until an insertion line appears. See Figure 3-34.

Adding a program to the Quick Launch toolbar   ◀   Figure 3-34

Windows Photo Gallery command on the Start menu

Windows Photo Gallery icon

insertion line on the Quick Launch toolbar

▶ **3.** Release the mouse button to add a shortcut icon to the Quick Launch toolbar. Depending on where you dragged the program icon, the shortcut to the Windows Photo Gallery program might be hidden.

▶ **4.** Click the **expand** button » on the Quick Launch toolbar to display the hidden icons.

▶ **5.** Click a blank area of the desktop, and then point to the **toolbar-sizing handle** ▓ **on the Quick Launch toolbar.**

▶ **6.** When the pointer changes to ⟺, drag the handle to the right to widen the Quick Launch toolbar so it shows all of its icons.

Quick Launch might be the only taskbar toolbar you need. However, you can add other toolbars to the taskbar to facilitate your work.

Adding Toolbars to the Taskbar

You can include several toolbars on the taskbar in addition to the Quick Launch toolbar. You can add these toolbars using the Toolbars tab on the Taskbar and Start Menu Properties dialog box or by using the taskbar's shortcut menu.

Holly often has several programs running at once, filling up the screen and hiding the desktop. She understands the benefit of placing icons on the desktop, but wants to access those desktop icons without having to minimize all of her open windows. You suggest that she place a Desktop toolbar on her taskbar, which contains all the icons on the desktop, though it displays only its name, Desktop, by default. Like the Quick Launch toolbar, the Desktop toolbar includes an expand button that you can click to display all of the icons that appear on the desktop. You can also resize the Desktop toolbar, though it typically takes up a lot of room on the taskbar. You'll show Holly how to add the Desktop toolbar to the taskbar, and then use it to open her personal folder, which is one of the icons on her desktop.

To display the Desktop toolbar:

▶ 1. Right-click a blank area of the taskbar, point to **Toolbars** on the shortcut menu, and then click **Desktop**. The Desktop toolbar appears on the taskbar. See Figure 3-35.

Figure 3-35 ▶ **Displaying the Desktop toolbar**

Tip

To change the date or time on your computer, click the time display in the notification area, and then click Change date and time settings.

modified Quick Launch toolbar

click to display all the icons on the Desktop toolbar

▶ 2. Click the **expand** button on the Desktop toolbar to display a menu of its icons.

▶ 3. Click a blank area on the desktop to close the menu, point to the left border of the Desktop toolbar until the pointer changes to ⟺, and then drag left until you see your user folder, such as Owner.

▶ 4. Click **your user folder** icon on the Desktop toolbar menu to open this folder, and then close the folder window.

Holly likes having the icon for her personal folder on the Desktop toolbar, but wants to see more icons on it. She wants the toolbar to look more like the Quick Launch toolbar, with no names next to the icon and no title displayed for the toolbar. You can modify the toolbar's appearance by changing its properties.

Modifying the Appearance of a Taskbar Toolbar

You can modify the appearance of a taskbar toolbar by showing or hiding its title and by showing or hiding the text labels for each icon. On the taskbar shortcut menu, these commands are checked by default. To hide the title and text labels, you uncheck both commands. You'll modify the Desktop toolbar by hiding its title and text labels.

To modify the appearance of the Desktop toolbar:

▶ 1. Right-click a blank area in the Desktop toolbar, and then click **Show Text** on the shortcut menu to uncheck this command.

Trouble? If the Show Text command does not appear on the shortcut menu, you probably right-clicked one of the buttons on the Desktop toolbar. Be sure to click a blank area on the toolbar.

Trouble? If the Show Text command does not appear with a check mark on the shortcut menu, skip Step 1.

▶ 2. Right-click a blank area in the Desktop toolbar again and click **Show Title** on the shortcut menu to uncheck this command.

Trouble? If the Show Title command does not appear with a check mark on the shortcut menu, skip Step 2.

Figure 3-36 displays the final appearance of the toolbar. Note that each item on the desktop is matched by an item in the toolbar and that the icons are small, like those on the Quick Launch toolbar.

Modified Desktop toolbar | Figure 3-36

drag to resize a taskbar toolbar

Desktop toolbar displaying only icons

Now Holly can access all the items on her desktop without minimizing open windows.

Creating a Custom Toolbar

If the standard taskbar toolbars that Windows Vista provides do not meet your needs, you can create your own taskbar toolbar. For example, if you often work with documents contained in folders in the Documents folder, you could add each folder to a custom toolbar so you can access those documents quickly. To create a custom toolbar, you use the New Toolbar command on the taskbar shortcut menu.

Creating a Custom Taskbar Toolbar | Reference Window

- To create a custom toolbar, right-click a blank area of the taskbar, point to Toolbars, and then click New Toolbar.
- In the New Toolbar – Choose a folder window, click the folder or object you want to turn into a toolbar, and then click the Select Folder button.

Holly experiments with the Desktop toolbar, and notices that when she clicks the Computer icon on the Desktop toolbar it opens the Computer window. Holly asks you to create a taskbar toolbar displaying the icons in the Computer window so she can access her computer's drives easily.

To create a toolbar for Computer window icons:

▶ 1. Right-click a blank area on the taskbar, point to **Toolbars**, and then click **New Toolbar** on the shortcut menu. The New Toolbar – Choose a folder window opens, showing the hierarchy of objects on your computer, which is familiar to you from your work with Computer and Windows Explorer.

▶ 2. Click **Computer** in the Navigation pane of the New Toolbar – Choose a folder window, and then click the **Select Folder** button. The Computer toolbar appears on the taskbar.

▶ 3. To modify the appearance of the Computer toolbar, right-click a blank spot on the Computer toolbar and click **Show Text** on the shortcut menu to remove the check mark.

▶ 4. Right-click a blank spot on the Computer toolbar again and click **Show Title** on the shortcut menu. See Figure 3-37.

Figure 3-37   Toolbars on the taskbar

Having seen how to create and modify toolbars on the taskbar, now you can turn to the other major element you can open from the taskbar—the Start menu.

Customizing the Start Menu

Most of the items on the Start menu are created for you by Windows Vista or by the various programs you install. However, you also can determine the content and appearance of your Start menu, removing items you don't use and adding those you do. In addition, Windows Vista personalizes the left pane of the Start menu as you work to show the programs you use most frequently. You can organize the Start menu and control its appearance to use it most effectively.

Controlling the Appearance of the Start Menu

Recall that the picture associated with the current user appears at the top of the Start menu. When you point to commands in the right pane of the Start menu, this picture changes. For example, when you point to the Documents command, the picture shows an image of a folder containing documents. Although you can't change the images associated with commands, you can change the user picture to personalize the Start menu.

You'll select a user picture for Holly that fits the appearance of her desktop.

To change the user picture on the Start menu:

▶ **1.** Click the **Start** button 🌀 on the taskbar, and then click the **user picture** at the top of the right pane. The User Accounts window opens. See Figure 3-38.

User Accounts window Figure 3-38

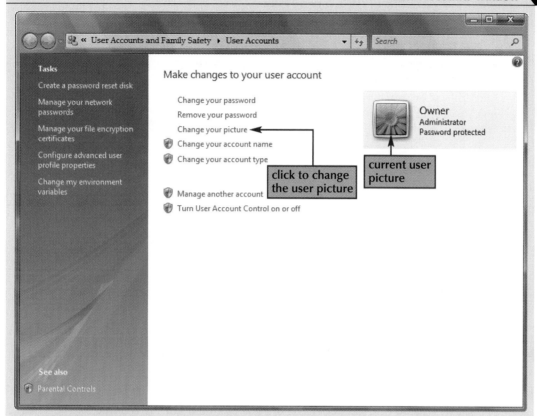

▶ **2.** Click the **Start** button**Change your picture**. The Change Your Picture window opens, displaying a collection of pictures you can use on the Welcome screen and Start menu.

▶ **3.** Click the image of the **bass clef**, which is the first picture in the collection.

▶ **4.** Click the **Change Picture** button.

▶ **5.** Click the **Start** button 🔘 again to verify the new user picture, and then point to the commands in the right pane to see the picture change to reflect the current command.

▶ **6.** Click the **Start** button 🔘 to close the Start menu.

▶ **7.** Close the User Accounts window.

Another feature of the Start menu you can control is whether the menu displays small or large icons. The default is to use large icons, but you can fit more commands on the Start menu by changing this to the smaller icon style. Because the Start button is considered part of the taskbar, you change settings for the Start menu using the same dialog box you used earlier to control the appearance of the taskbar.

To change the size of the icons on the Start menu:

▶ **1.** Right-click the **Start** button 🔘 on the taskbar, and then click **Properties** on the shortcut menu. The Taskbar and Start Menu Properties dialog box opens to the Start Menu tab.

▶ **2.** Click the **Customize** button. The Customize Start Menu dialog box opens. See Figure 3-39.

| Figure 3-39 | Customize Start Menu dialog box |

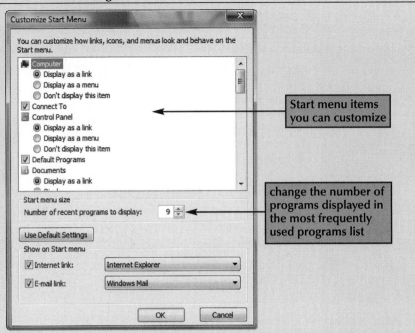

Start menu items you can customize

change the number of programs displayed in the most frequently used programs list

▶ **3.** Scroll the list of items you can customize. At the bottom of the list, click the **Use large icons** check box to remove the check mark.

▶ **4.** Click the **OK** button and then click the **Apply** button. The Taskbar and Start Menu Properties dialog box stays open. Before you open the Start menu to view the small icons, you can drag this dialog box out of the way.

▶ **5.** Drag the Taskbar and Start Menu Properties dialog box to the right side of the desktop.

▶ **6.** Click the **Start** button ⊕, view your changes, and then click the **Start** button ⊕ again to close the menu.

Now that you have plenty of room on the Start menu, you can learn how to add items to it.

Pinning an Item to the Start Menu

Recall that the upper-left area of the Start menu is the pinned items list, which contains shortcuts to programs you use often. By default, the Internet Explorer and Windows Mail shortcuts appear in the pinned items list. Below the pinned items is the most frequently used programs list. As you open programs, Windows Vista adds their shortcuts to this area. For example, if you use Paint often, Windows Vista adds a Paint shortcut to the most frequently used programs list on the Start menu. The items on the right of the Start menu open dialog boxes or submenus. See Figure 3-40.

Typical Start menu ◀ Figure 3-40

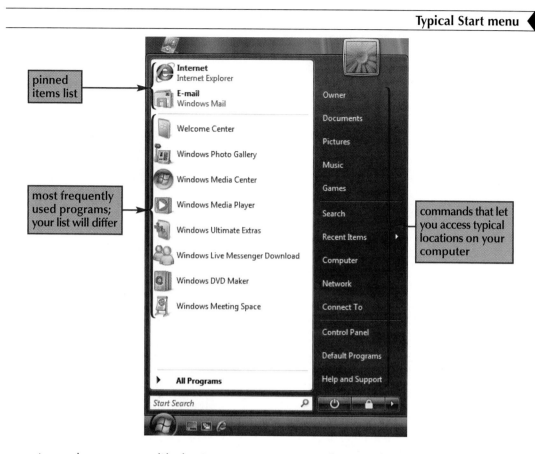

pinned items list

most frequently used programs; your list will differ

commands that let you access typical locations on your computer

A popular way to modify the Start menu is to pin and unpin programs. You can also move the program icons in the pinned items list to change their order. In addition, you can add and remove commands from the right pane of the Start menu. For example, you can remove the Recent Items command to keep your work private.

Holly has become accustomed to using Windows Explorer to navigate her computer. Instead of clicking the Start button on the taskbar, pointing to All Programs, clicking the Accessories folder, and then clicking Windows Explorer, you can pin the Windows Explorer icon to the Start menu for easy access.

To pin Windows Explorer to the Start menu:

▶ **1.** Click the **Start** button 🪟 on the taskbar, point to **All Programs**, and then click the **Accessories** folder.

▶ **2.** Right-click **Windows Explorer**, and then click **Pin to Start Menu** on the short-cut menu.

▶ **3.** Point to **Back** on the Start menu to verify that Windows Explorer is now pinned to the top of the Start menu. See Figure 3-41.

Tip

To add a folder shortcut to the Start menu, drag the folder from a window to the Start button.

Figure 3-41   Windows Explorer pinned to the Start menu

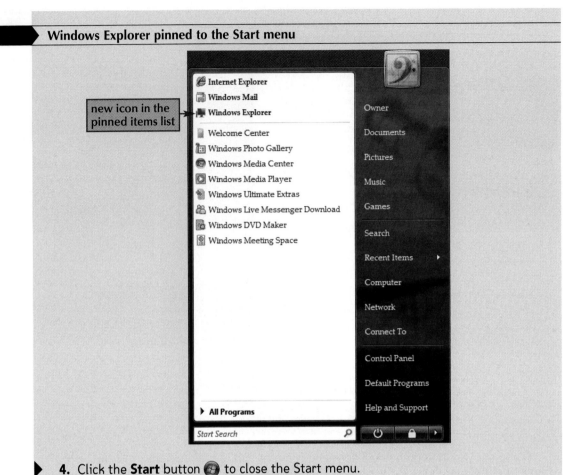

new icon in the pinned items list

4. Click the **Start** button to close the Start menu.

Besides adding programs to the pinned items list, you can add commands to the right pane of the Start menu.

Adding Commands to the Right Pane of the Start Menu

You can add or remove items—such as Computer, Control Panel, and Pictures—that appear on the right side of the Start menu. You can also change some items so that they appear as links or menus.

Holly wants to see how she could use the Start menu to access the Printers folder, which displays all the printers she can use from her computer. Besides the default printer, she also uses a color printer and plotter when creating maps. She asks you to add the Printers command to the Start menu.

To add the Printers command to the Start menu:

▶ **1.** With the Taskbar and Start Menu Properties dialog box still open on the desktop, click the **Customize** button. The Customize Start Menu dialog box opens.

   Trouble? If the Taskbar and Start Menu Properties dialog box is not open on your desktop, right-click the Start button on the taskbar, and then click Properties.

▶ **2.** Scroll the Start menu items, and then click the **Printers** check box.

▶ **3.** Click the **OK** button, and then click the **Apply** button.

▶ **4.** Click the **Start** button 🏁 on the taskbar to verify that the Printers command is now displayed in the right pane.

Holly can now open the Printers folder by clicking the Printers command on the Start menu.

Selecting Start Menu Settings

The Customize Start Menu dialog box lists options and settings for your Start menu. For example, you can display a command on the Start menu as a link or as a submenu. If you display a command as a link, you click it to open the appropriate dialog box or window. For example, the Computer command appears on the Start menu as a link by default—you click Computer to open its window. If you display a command as a submenu, you point to the command until a submenu appears, and then you click a command on the submenu. Instead of a link, you can display the Computer command as a submenu. When you point to Computer, a submenu appears listing the contents of the Computer window, including your local hard disk. Figure 3-42 describes the settings you can select for your Start menu.

Figure 3-42   Start menu settings

Start Menu	Description
Computer	Display this item as a link you click to open the Computer window, as a submenu that lists the contents of Computer, or don't display this item.
Connect To	Display an item that lets you select a network to which you can connect.
Control Panel	Display this item as a link you click to open Control Panel, as a submenu that lists individual tools or categories in Control Panel, or don't display this item.
Default Programs	Display an item that lets you choose the default programs you use for Web browsing, e-mail, playing music, and other activities.
Documents	Display this item as a link you click to open the Documents folder, as a submenu that lists the contents of Documents, or don't display this item.
Enable context menus and dragging and dropping	When you move items on the Start menu, display menus as you drag that indicate the actions you can take.
Favorites menu	Display this item to list your favorite Web sites, files, and folders.
Games	Display this item as a link you click to open the Games folder, as a submenu that lists the contents of the Games folder, or don't display this item.
Help	Display this item to open the Help and Support window.
Highlight newly installed programs	Before you start a newly installed program for the first time, highlight the program name.
Music	Display this item as a link you click to open the Music folder, as a submenu that lists the contents of Music, or don't display this item.
Network	Display this item to open the Network window.
Open submenus when I pause on them with the mouse pointer	Instead of clicking to open a submenu, open the submenu when you point to an item and pause.
Personal folder	Display this item as a link you click to open your personal folder, as a submenu that lists the contents of your personal folder, or don't display this item.
Pictures	Display this item as a link you click to open the Pictures folder window, as a submenu that lists the contents of Pictures, or don't display this item.
Printers	Display this item to open the Printers window.
Run command	Display the Run command to open the Run dialog box.
Search	Display this item to open a Search Results window where you can search the contents of your computer.
Search communications	When searching your computer, have Windows search e-mail and other types of electronic communications.
Search favorites and history	When searching your computer, have Windows search your Web browsing history and the Web sites designated as favorites.
Search files	When searching, have Windows skip searching files, search the index of files on your computer, or search only the current user's files.
Search programs	When searching your computer, search for installed programs.
Sort All Programs menu by name	Display the folders and programs on the All Programs menu in alphabetic order by name.
System administrative tools	Display this item on the All Programs menu, on the All Programs menu and the Start menu, or don't display this item.
Use large icons	Display large program icons on the Start menu.

Holly wants to display the Computer item as a submenu so she has another easy way to access her USB flash drive. The Computer submenu will then contain a shortcut icon that she can click to quickly open her USB flash drive.

To change the Computer command on the Start Menu to display a submenu:

▶ **1.** With the Taskbar and Start Menu Properties dialog box open on the desktop, click the **Customize** button. The Customize Start Menu dialog box opens.

▶ **2.** Click the **Display as a menu** option button under the Computer icon.

▶ **3.** Click the **OK** button, and then click the **Apply** button. Now you can test the Computer submenu on the Start menu.

▶ **4.** Click the **Start** button 🔵 on the taskbar, and then point to **Computer**. The icons in the Computer window appear in the submenu. See Figure 3-43.

New Computer submenu on the Start menu ◀ Figure 3-43

▶ **5.** Click **Removable Disk (F:)** or other item on the Computer submenu. The contents of this drive appear in the Computer window.

▶ **6.** Close all open windows and dialog boxes.

Now that you've finished personalizing the Windows Vista environment on Holly's computer, you should restore the computer to its original settings.

Restoring Your Settings

If you are working in a computer lab or a computer other than your own, complete the steps in this section to restore the original settings on your computer.

To restore your settings:

▶ 1. Right-click the **desktop**, click **Personalize** on the shortcut menu.

▶ 2. Click **Change desktop icons**. Click check boxes to restore the original settings. By default, only the Recycle Bin appears on the desktop.

▶ 3. In the list of desktop icons, click **Computer**, and then click the **Restore Default** button. Click the **OK** button to close the Change Icon dialog box, and then click the **OK** button to close the Desktop Icon Settings dialog box. Minimize the Personalization window.

▶ 4. Right-click the **desktop**, point to **View** on the shortcut menu, and then click **Medium Icons**.

▶ 5. Click a **shortcut icon** on the desktop, hold down the **Ctrl** key, and then click all the other **shortcut icons** you created in this tutorial. Press the **Delete** key to delete the shortcuts, and then click the **Yes** button, if necessary.

▶ 6. Navigate to the **Hawaii Maps** folder in the Pictures folder, and then move it to the **Tutorial.03\Tutorial** folder provided with your Data Files. Delete the original files in the Tutorial.03\Tutorial folder, which should now contain only the Hawaii Maps folder. Close all folder windows.

▶ 7. Open the Sidebar. (Click the **Windows Sidebar** icon 🗔 in the notification area of the taskbar.) Right-click the **Sidebar**, click **Properties** on the shortcut menu, click the **Sidebar is always on top of other windows** check box, and then click the **OK** button. Remove the Hawaii clock from the Sidebar and redisplay the **Slide Show** gadget.

▶ 8. In the Personalization window, click **Theme**. Click the **Theme** arrow, and then click **Windows Vista**. Click the **OK** button to close the Theme Settings dialog box.

▶ 9. In the Personalization window, click **Desktop Background**. Click the **Location** arrow, click **Windows Wallpapers**, scroll to the Vistas category, if necessary, and then click the image that originally appeared on your desktop. By default, this is img24 in the Vistas category. Click the **Fit to Screen** option button, and then click the **OK** button.

   Trouble? If img24 does not appear in the Desktop Background window, click the Browse button, and then double-click img24.

▶ 10. In the Personalization window, click **Window Color and Appearance**, and then click **Default**.

   Trouble? If you are not using the Aero experience, the Appearance Settings dialog box opens when you click Window Color and Appearance. Click Windows Vista Basic in the Color scheme list.

▶ 11. If you are using the Aero experience, click **Open classic appearance properties for more color options**. In the Appearance Settings dialog box, click the **Advanced** button, click the **Item** arrow, and then click **Icon**. Click the **Font** arrow, click **Segoe UI**, click the **OK** button to close the Advanced Appearance dialog box, and then click the **OK** button to close the Appearance Settings dialog box.

▶ 12. In the Personalization window, click **Screen Saver**. Click the **Screen saver** arrow, and then click the original screen saver, which is **Windows Logo** by default. Click the **OK** button to close the Screen Saver Settings dialog box.

▶ **13.** On the Quick Launch toolbar, right-click the **Windows Photo Gallery** icon, click **Delete**, and then click the **Yes** button. Resize the **Quick Launch** toolbar to display only three icons.

▶ **14.** Right-click a blank area of the taskbar, point to **Toolbars**, and then click **Desktop** to remove this toolbar from the taskbar. Do the same to remove the **Computer** toolbar from the taskbar.

▶ **15.** Right-click the taskbar, and then click **Lock the Taskbar** on the shortcut menu.

▶ **16.** Click the **Start** button 🔘 on the taskbar, click the **user picture**, click **Change your picture**, click the original user picture, and then click the **Change Picture** button. Close the User Accounts window.

▶ **17.** Right-click the **Start** button 🔘 , click **Properties**, click the **Customize** button, click the **Use large icons** check box to select it, click the **Printers** check box to remove the check mark, click the **Display as a link** option button under the Computer icon, click the **OK** button to close the Customize Start Menu dialog box, and then click the **OK** button to close the Taskbar and Start Menu Properties dialog box.

▶ **18.** Click the **Start** button 🔘 , right-click **Windows Explorer**, click **Unpin from Start menu**, and then click the **Start** button 🔘 again to close the menu.

▶ **19.** Close all open windows.

Session 3.3 Quick Check | Review

1. Before you can move or resize the taskbar, you must make sure the _____ _____ _____ command on the task bar shortcut menu is not selected.
2. After you hide the taskbar, explain how you can redisplay it.
3. True or False. Only Windows Vista can set the user picture that appears on the Start menu—you cannot change it.
4. On the Start menu, the Internet Explorer and Windows Mail shortcuts appear in the _____ _____ _____ by default.
5. You can display a Start menu command as a link. Identify the other way you can display a command on the Start menu.
6. Identify the four main sections of the taskbar.

Tutorial Summary | Review

In this tutorial, you added icons to the desktop, and then customized and arranged those icons. You also explored the Windows Sidebar and its gadgets by customizing the Sidebar and adding and removing gadgets. You used Control Panel to personalize the desktop by changing the desktop background, setting the appearance of desktop elements, and applying a visual theme. You also selected a different screen saver and changed the display settings. To personalize the taskbar, you moved and resized the taskbar, set its appearance properties, and added toolbars to the taskbar. You also customized the Start menu by changing its appearance, pinning programs to the menu, and adding and changing commands.

Key Terms

color scheme	notification area	screen saver
Control Panel	pixel	shortcut
desktop icon	property	taskbar
feed	Quick Launch toolbar	theme
gadget	screen resolution	wallpaper

Practice	**Review Assignments**

Practice the skills you learned in the tutorial.

For a list of Data Files in the Review folder, see page 97.

You already worked with Holly's notebook computer to personalize its Windows environment. Ptolemy Cartography keeps a computer in its conference area for any employee or intern to use when they need one. Holly asks you to customize that computer so it is appropriate for the company. Holly is also preparing a map of Newfoundland, and wants to store current Newfoundland maps and historical map images on that computer for her employees to use as models. As you perform the following steps, note the original settings of the desktop and other items so you can restore them later. Complete the following steps:

1. Change the desktop icon settings on your computer to display the Computer and Control Panel icons in addition to the default Recycle Bin icon. Change the image for the Computer icon so that it displays any other appropriate image. Close all open windows.
2. Change the size of the desktop icons to display the icons in their smallest size.
3. Customize the Windows Sidebar to display two clocks. One clock should display the time in your time zone. Set the other clock to display the time in the Atlantic Time zone. Select clock 4 of 8, and name it Atlantic.
4. Insert the USB flash drive or other removable media containing your Data Files in the appropriate drive, and then create a shortcut to this drive on the desktop. Name the shortcut Removable Disk Shortcut.
5. Use the Removable Disk Shortcut to move the files from the Tutorial.03\Review folder to a new folder named Historical Maps in your Pictures folder.
6. On the desktop, create a shortcut to the Historical Maps folder. Then create a shortcut to the **NF Facts** text document. Test the shortcut by double-clicking the NF Facts shortcut to start Notepad and open the document.
7. Sort the desktop icons by size so that the Computer icon is the last icon in the list.
8. Change the desktop wallpaper to display any image in the Historical Maps folder.
9. Change the icon font to MS UI Gothic.
10. Save the current desktop settings as a theme named Historical, and store the theme in the Historical Maps folder.
11. Change the screen saver to play a slide show of the images in the Historical Maps folder.
12. Increase the height of the taskbar so it is about twice as high as its current setting.
13. Add the Paint icon to the Quick Launch toolbar. If necessary, modify the Quick Launch toolbar so that it displays all of its icons.
14. Change the appearance of the Start menu so that it displays small icons.
15. Change the user picture on the Start menu so it displays chess pieces.
16. Pin WordPad to the Start menu, and then change the Documents command from a link to a menu. Close all open windows.
17. Open the Start menu, and then press the Print Screen key to capture an image of your desktop with the Start menu open. Open Paint, and then press Ctrl+V to paste the image in a Paint file. Save the file as **ReviewDesktopXY**, where XY are your initials, in the Tutorial.03\Review folder provided with your Data Files.
18. Use the shortcuts on your desktop to move the Historical Maps folder from the Pictures folder on your hard disk to the Tutorial.03\Review folder provided with your Data Files. Close Paint.

19. Restore the settings on your computer. Restore the image of the Computer icon, and then display the original set of icons on the desktop. Change the size of the desktop icons to Medium, and change the font back to Segoe UI. Restore the Windows Sidebar to its original appearance. Delete the shortcut icons on the desktop. Restore the desktop wallpaper and the screen saver to their original images. Resize the taskbar to its original size, and return the Quick Launch toolbar to its default state. Lock the taskbar. Change the user picture to display the original image. Remove WordPad from the pinned items list, change the Documents command from a submenu to a link, and use large icons on the Start menu.
20. Close any open windows.
21. Submit the results of the preceding steps to your instructor, either in printed or electronic form, as requested.

| Apply | **Case Problem 1** |

Use the skills you learned in the tutorial to set up Windows for an engineering firm.

For a list of Data Files in the Case1 folder, see page 97.

Da Vinci Engineering When Hank Van Hise started his own engineering firm in Columbus, Ohio, he named it after Leonardo da Vinci, one of his engineering heroes. Da Vinci Engineering is an environmental engineering firm that participates in public works projects such as building dams and bridges while minimizing their effect on the environment. When he is not on site, Hank manages 15 employees in an office in downtown Columbus. He has hired you to help him run the office. Because he just installed Windows Vista on the office computers, he asks you to personalize the desktop on his computer. As you perform the following steps, note the original settings of the desktop and other items so you can restore them later. Complete the following steps:

1. Change the desktop icon settings on your computer to display the Computer, User's Files, and Control Panel icons. Change the image for the User's Files icon so that it displays any other appropriate image.
2. Change the size of the desktop icons to display the icons in their largest size.
3. Open the Windows Sidebar, if necessary, and then customize it to display the Notes gadget.
4. Insert the USB flash drive or other removable media containing your Data Files in the appropriate drive, and then create a shortcut to this drive on the desktop. Name the shortcut Removable Disk Shortcut.
5. Use the Removable Disk Shortcut to move the files in the Tutorial.03\Case1 folder to a new folder named Leonardo in your Documents folder.
6. On the desktop, create a shortcut to the Leonardo folder. Then create a shortcut to the **Vasari** text document, an account of the life of Leonardo da Vinci by one of his contemporaries. Test the shortcut by double-clicking the Vasari shortcut to start Notepad and open the document.
7. Create shortcuts to two other files in the Leonardo folder.
8. Sort the desktop icons by type.
9. If you are using Windows Aero, change the color of the window title bars and borders to Graphite.
10. Open the Screen Saver Settings dialog box and select the Ribbons screen saver. Move the dialog box to the middle of the desktop. Minimize any other open windows.
11. Increase the height of the taskbar so it is about twice as high as its current setting.
12. Add the WordPad icon to the Quick Launch toolbar.
13. Change the user picture on the Start menu so it displays a robot.

14. Pin the Windows Photo Gallery program to the Start menu, and then remove the Pictures item from the Start menu.

15. Open the Start menu, and then press the Print Screen key to capture an image of your desktop with the Start menu open. Open Paint, and then press Ctrl+V to paste the image in a Paint file. Save the file as **Case1DesktopXY**, where XY are your initials, in the Tutorial.03\Case1 folder provided with your Data Files.

16. Move the Leonardo folder to the Tutorial\Case1 folder.

17. Restore the settings on your computer. Restore the image of the User's Files icon, and then display the original set of icons on the desktop. Change the size of the desktop icons to Medium. Sort the icons by name. Delete the shortcut icons on the desktop. Restore the Windows Sidebar to its original appearance. Restore the windows to their default color and the screen saver to its original image. Return the Quick Launch toolbar to its default state, and resize the taskbar to its original size. Lock the taskbar. Change the user picture to display the original image. Remove Windows Photo Gallery from the pinned items list, and then return the Pictures item to the Start menu.

18. Close any open windows.

19. Submit the results of the preceding steps to your instructor, either in printed or electronic form, as requested.

Apply	**Case Problem 2**

Use the skills you learned in the tutorial to personalize the Windows environment for a small real estate office.

For a list of Data Files in the Case2 folder, see page 97.

B&B Realty   Ed Bolton and Kevin Bestmuller own B&B Realty in Syracuse, New York, and concentrate on home sales and appraisals. One way they distinguish their business from other realty agencies is by providing computers in their downtown office and inviting people to browse real estate listings, learn about architectural styles, and find local businesses that can help them prepare a house for sale or restore a fixer-upper. Some of this information is stored on the office computers, and some, such as the Multiple Listings Service, is on the Web. You are the office manager and work with the agents and clients to use B&B Realty resources. After installing Windows Vista on all the office computers, Ed asks you to personalize the desktop so it reflects the B&B company image. As you perform the following steps, note the original settings of the desktop and other items so you can restore them later. Complete the following steps:

1. Change the desktop icon settings on your computer to display the Network and Control Panel icons in addition to the default Recycle Bin icon. Change the image for the Network icon so that it displays any other appropriate image.

2. Change the size of the desktop icons to display the icons in their smallest size.

3. Open the Windows Sidebar, if necessary, and then close all gadgets except the Clock. Add the Calendar and Contacts gadgets to the sidebar.

4. Insert the USB flash drive or other removable media containing your Data Files in the appropriate drive, and then create a shortcut to this drive on the desktop. Name the shortcut Removable Disk Shortcut.

5. Use the Removable Disk Shortcut to move the files in the Tutorial.03\Case2 folder to a new folder named Houses in the Documents folder.

6. On the desktop, create a shortcut to the Houses folder. Then create a shortcut to the **Syracuse Facts** text document. Test the shortcut by double-clicking the Syracuse Facts shortcut to start Notepad and open the document.

⊕ EXPLORE   7. Create a shortcut to WordPad on the desktop. (*Hint*: Right-click WordPad on the Start menu, point to Send To, and then click Desktop (create shortcut).

8. Create a shortcut to your printer on the desktop.

9. Arrange all of the desktop icons in a row along the top of the desktop. (*Hint*: Turn off the Auto Arrange option on the desktop shortcut menu before moving the icons.)

10. Change the desktop wallpaper to display any image in the Houses folder. Tile the image on the desktop.

11. Change the color of the window title bars and borders to teal.

12. Save the current desktop settings as a theme named B&B, and store the theme in the Houses folder.

13. Change the screen saver to Windows Energy.

14. Auto-hide the taskbar.

15. Display the Desktop toolbar on the taskbar. Add the Paint icon to the Quick Launch toolbar. Modify the Quick Launch toolbar so that it displays all of its icons.

16. Remove the Connect To item from the Start menu.

17. Close all open windows.

⊕EXPLORE 18. Open the Start menu, and then press the Print Screen key to capture an image of your desktop with the Start menu open. Open Paint, and then press Ctrl+V to paste the image in a Paint document. Save the document as **Case2DesktopXY**, where XY are your initials, in the Tutorial.03\Case2 folder provided with your Data Files. Click File on the Paint menu bar, click Page Setup, click the Landscape option button, and change the value in the Adjust to text box to 45. Click the OK button, and then close Paint.

19. Use the printer shortcut on the desktop to print the **Case2DesktopXY** document.

20. Use the shortcuts on your desktop to move the Houses folder from the Documents folder on your hard disk to the Tutorial.03\Case2 folder provided with your Data Files.

21. Restore the settings on your computer. Restore the image of the Network icon, and then display the original set of icons on the desktop. Change the size of the desktop icons to Medium, and move them into a column on the left side of the desktop. Auto-arrange the icons. Restore the Windows Sidebar to its original appearance. Delete the shortcut icons on the desktop. Restore the desktop background and screen saver to their original images. Restore the taskbar to its default state. Restore the Start menu to its original condition.

22. Close any open windows.

23. Submit the results of the preceding steps to your instructor, either in printed or electronic form, as requested.

Challenge | **Case Problem 3**

Extend what you've learned to discover other ways to customize Windows for a nature conservancy.

For a list of Data Files in the Case3 folder, see page 97.

Acadia Nature Conservancy Ellie Larsen is the director of the Acadia Nature Conservancy in Augusta, Maine. The mission of the organization is to protect the most ecologically important lands and waters in Maine. Ellie organizes projects to study and preserve the natural history and diversity of Maine's plants, animals, and natural habitats. Because of your earlier work for the Acadia Nature Conservancy as a dedicated volunteer, Ellie hired you as a project assistant. Ellie recently upgraded to Windows Vista, and she asks you to customize her computer. As you perform the following steps, note the original settings of the desktop and other items so you can restore them later. Complete the following steps:

1. Change the desktop icon settings on your computer to display all of the built-in desktop icons. Change the image for the Computer icon so that it displays any other appropriate image.

2. Insert the USB flash drive or other removable media containing your Data Files in the appropriate drive, and then create a shortcut to this drive on the desktop. Name the shortcut Removable Disk Shortcut.

3. Use the Removable Disk Shortcut to move the files in the Tutorial.03\Case3 folder to a new folder named Nature in the Pictures folder.

4. On the desktop, create a shortcut to the Nature folder. Then create a shortcut to the **Driving Directions** text document. Test the shortcut by double-clicking the Driving Directions shortcut to start Notepad and open the document. Close all open windows.

⊕ **EXPLORE**   5. On the desktop, create a shortcut to the Windows Photo Gallery program. (*Hint:* Right-drag the Windows Photo Gallery program icon from the Start menu to the desktop, and then click Create Shortcuts Here on the shortcut menu.) Use the Windows Photo Gallery shortcut to start the program and view the photos stored on your computer. Resize the Windows Photo Gallery window to display three columns of images, and then drag the window to the middle of the desktop.

⊕ **EXPLORE**   6. Open the Windows Sidebar, if necessary, and make sure it displays only the Slide Show and Clock gadgets. Right-click the Slide Show gadget, and then click Options to open the Slide Show dialog box. Click the Folder arrow, and then click Pictures to play a slide show of the images in the Pictures folder and its subfolders. (Make sure the Include subfolders check box is selected.) Click the Shuffle pictures check box, and then click the OK button.

⊕ **EXPLORE**   7. Add the Picture Puzzle gadget to the Sidebar. Right-click the Picture Puzzle gadget, and then click Options to open the Picture Puzzle dialog box. Display image 10 of 11 in the Picture Puzzle, and then close the Picture Puzzle dialog box.

8. Change the desktop background image to img21.jpg in the Vistas category.

9. If you are using the Aero experience, change the color of the window title bars and borders to frost.

10. Save the current desktop settings as a theme named Acadia, and store the theme in the Nature folder.

⊕ **EXPLORE**   11. Open the Customize Start Menu dialog box, and then change the Number of recent programs to display setting to 4. Click the OK button on all open windows except for the Windows Photo Gallery window.

12. Open the Start menu, and then press the Print Screen key to capture an image of your desktop with the Start menu open. Open Paint, and then press Ctrl+V to paste the image in a Paint file. Save the file as **Case3DesktopXY**, where XY are your initials, in the Tutorial.03\Case3 folder provided with your Data Files.

13. Use the shortcuts on your desktop to move the Nature folder from the Pictures folder on your hard disk to the Tutorial.03\Case3 folder provided with your Data Files.

14. Restore the settings on your computer, and then close all open windows.

15. Submit the results of the preceding steps to your instructor, either in printed or electronic form, as requested.

| Create | | **Case Problem 4** |

Using Figure 3-44 as a guide, personalize the desktop for a Caribbean marina developer.

There are no Data Files needed for this Case Problem.

Island Marinas   After sailing to the Cayman Islands one winter, John Chang settled in Miami, Florida, and started Island Marinas, a company that consults with the municipal governments on Caribbean islands to help them build and maintain marinas. John hired you to manage the Miami office while he travels, and you recently upgraded to Windows Vista. After working with a client in the Bahamas, John shows you a screenshot of that client's desktop. See Figure 3-44. He thinks this desktop would be appropriate for the Island Marinas computers, and asks you to re-create it on your computers.

Figure 3-44

To create this Windows environment, complete the following:

1. Select the following Windows Vista settings:
   - Img19.jpg desktop background
   - Blue window and appearance color
   - Aurora screen saver
   - Sidebar open with a Clock gadget showing image 4 of 8 and the second hand displayed and with the Picture Puzzle gadget displaying image 8 of 11
   - Computer, Control Panel, and Recycle Bin desktop icons, with the Computer icon image showing a handheld computer
2. Open the Screen Saver Settings dialog box.
3. Capture an image of the desktop, and then save the image in a Paint file named **Case4DesktopXY**, where XY are your initials, in the Tutorial.03\Case4 folder provided with your Data Files.
4. Restore the original settings, and then close all open windows.
5. Submit the results of the preceding steps to your instructor, either in printed or electronic form, as requested.

Review | **Quick Check Answers**

Session 3.1

1. View
2. The file or resource it represents remains in its original location.
3. The Recycle Bin icon has two appearances, one when it is empty, and another when it contains deleted items.
4. The Clock, Slide Show, and Feed Headlines are three gadgets that can appear on the Sidebar by default. You can also display gadgets such as sticky notes, a calendar, and an address book.
5. false
6. 1) Drag the USB flash drive icon from the Computer or Windows Explorer window to the desktop; 2) Right-drag the USB flash drive icon from the Computer or Windows Explorer window to the desktop, and then click Create Shortcuts here; 3) Right-click the USB flash drive icon in the Computer or Windows Explorer window, point to Send To, and then click Desktop (create shortcut).

Session 3.2

1. true
2. You can use Control Panel to change the way Windows looks and behaves.
3. color schemes
4. Screen savers are entertaining and offer security by hiding your data from others.
5. The monitor displays 1024 pixels across and 768 pixels down.
6. b

Session 3.3

1. Lock the taskbar
2. Point to the area of your screen where the taskbar is usually located, which is at the bottom of the desktop by default.
3. false
4. pinned items list
5. as a menu
6. Start button, Quick Launch toolbar, middle area for taskbar buttons, and notification area

Ending Data Files

Tutorial.03 →

Tutorial
📁 Hawaii Maps
Ptolemy.Theme

Review
📁 Historical Maps
Historical.Theme
ReviewDesktop*XY*.jpg

Case1
📁 Leonardo
Case1Desktop*XY*.jpg

Case2
📁 Houses
B&B.Theme
Case2Desktop*XY*.jpg

Case3
📁 Nature
Acadia.Theme
Case3Desktop*XY*.jpg

Case4
Case4Desktop*XY*.jpg

Objectives

Working with the Internet and E-Mail

Communicating with Others

Case | Entrée Tours

David Sanchez started Entrée Tours in Fort Collins, Colorado, to run bus and van tours in states west of the Mississippi River for low-mobility travelers. David's clients include people who ride in wheelchairs or otherwise need assistance to visit scenic destinations in Colorado and other Rocky Mountain states. The state of Colorado is especially well equipped to provide accessible travel, and David has so far focused on conducting tours to one of the many adaptive skiing and snowboarding programs available at Colorado resorts. He has formed productive partnerships with van operators and businesses that rent scooters and other wheeled forms of personal transportation.

Recently, David hired you as a travel planner to help him expand his business. In addition to Entrée Tours' popular ski and snowboard vacations, David wants to expand to offer sightseeing, birdwatching, and wilderness trips. One of your main tasks is to research western destinations that are suitable for Entrée Tours and find information that states and businesses provide for adaptive travelers. You regularly use Microsoft Internet Explorer to gather this information on the Web. You also use Windows Mail to exchange e-mail with Entrée Tours' contacts and clients. David asks you to get him up to speed in using these programs.

In this tutorial, you'll explore how the Internet and the Web work, and use Internet Explorer to visit and organize Web pages. You'll also examine e-mail technology and use Windows Mail to send, receive, and reply to e-mail messages. You'll use two programs that work with Windows Mail to help you manage your contacts and schedule.

Starting Data Files

Tutorial.04	→	Tutorial	Review	Case1	Case2	Case3	Case4
		Colorado Itinerary.rtf	Washington Itinerary.rtf	(none)	(none)	(none)	(none)

Exploring the Internet and the World Wide Web

When you connect two or more computers to exchange information and resources, they form a **network**. You can connect networks to each other to share information across a wide area. The worldwide, publicly accessible collection of networks is called the **Internet**, and it consists of millions of computers linked to networks all over the world. The Internet lets you access and exchange information using services such as electronic mail (e-mail), online newsgroups, file transfer, and the linked documents of the **World Wide Web**, better known as the **Web**. See Figure 4-1.

Figure 4-1	Connecting computers to the Internet

As Figure 4-1 shows, the Web is a service that the Internet provides. Whereas the Internet is a collection of networks connected by communication media such as fiber-optic cables and wireless connections, the Web is a collection of documents connected by hyperlinks. A **hyperlink** (or **link**) is text, a graphic, or combination of both in a Web document that targets another part of the document or a different document altogether. You click the link to display the targeted information. For example, in Figure 4-2, you can click links on the first Library of Congress Web document to display related information.

Web page with links to Web pages containing additional information ◀ Figure 4-2

Each hyperlinked text document—or hypertext document—on the Web is called a **Web page** and is stored on an Internet computer called a **Web server**. A **Web site** is a collection of Web pages that have a common theme or focus, such as all the pages containing information about the Library of Congress, a bookseller and its products, or a local literacy foundation. The Web is appealing because it generally displays up-to-date information in a colorful, lively format that can use sound and animation.

When you want to find information on the Web, you can use a Web directory or a search engine. A **Web directory** is a Web page that organizes links to Web sites in topical categories, such as technology or recreation. Yahoo! is a well-known Web directory. **Search engines** are Web sites that conduct searches to retrieve Web pages. To work with a search engine, you enter a word or expression as the search criterion. The search engine lists links to Web pages that fit your criterion. Popular general search engines include Google and Ask.com.

Using Web Browsers

To access documents on the Web, you need a **browser**—a program that locates, retrieves, and displays Web pages. Your browser allows you to visit Web sites around the world; interact with Web pages by clicking links; view multimedia documents; transfer files, images, and sounds to and from your computer; conduct searches for specific topics; and run programs on other computers. The browser included with Windows Vista is called Internet Explorer.

When you attempt to view a Web page, your browser locates and retrieves the document from the Web server and displays its contents on your computer. The server stores the Web page in one location, and browsers anywhere in the world can view it.

For your browser to access the Web, you must have an Internet connection. In a university setting, your connection might come from your campus network. If you are working on a home computer, you have a few options for connecting to the Internet. You might use your phone line and computer modem to establish a **dial-up connection**. More likely, you are using a **broadband connection**, a high-capacity, high-speed medium for connecting to the Internet. Popular broadband technologies include a **digital subscriber line (DSL)**, which is a high-speed connection through your telephone lines, and **digital cable**, which uses a cable modem attached to cable television lines. A **wireless connection** uses infrared light or radio-frequency signals to communicate with devices that are physically connected to a network or the Internet. Home connections also require an account with an **Internet service provider (ISP)**, a company that sells Internet access. The ISP provides instructions for connecting your computer to one of its servers, which is connected to the Internet. You can then use your browser to visit Web sites and access other Internet services.

Getting Started with Microsoft Internet Explorer

Microsoft Internet Explorer, the Web browser that comes with Windows Vista, lets you communicate, access, and share information on the Web. When you start Internet Explorer, it opens to your **home page**, the Web page a browser is set to open by default. The default home page for Internet Explorer is the MSN Web page, a Microsoft Web site with links to information and services. Your computer manufacturer or school might have set up a different home page.

Your first step in showing David how to research travel destinations is to start Internet Explorer.

To start Internet Explorer:

Tip
You can also start Internet Explorer by clicking its icon on the Quick Launch toolbar.

▶ **1.** Click the **Start** button 🟦 on the taskbar, and then click **Internet Explorer**.

Trouble If a Dial-up Connection dialog box opens, enter your user name and password, and then click the Connect button. If you do not know your user name or password, ask your instructor or technical support person for help; you must have an Internet connection to complete the steps in this tutorial.

▶ **2.** If necessary, click the **Maximize** button 🔲 to maximize the Internet Explorer window. Figure 4-3 shows the MSN main page in the Internet Explorer window. You might have a different home page.

Internet Explorer window | Figure 4-3

Figure 4-3 shows the following elements of the Internet Explorer window.

- **Title bar**: Shows the name of the open Web page and includes the resizing buttons
- **Toolbar**: Contains buttons you can click to perform common tasks, such as moving to the next or previous page and printing a Web page
- **Address bar**: Shows the address of the Web page; you can also type an address here.
- **Web page area**: Shows the current Web page
- **Status bar**: Shows information about the browser's actions; for example, indicates that a page is loading or is done loading
- **Live Search box**: Provides a way to search for Web pages
- **Home button**: Click to open the Web page specified as the home page for your browser.
- **Tab**: Each Web page you open can appear on a tab, letting you switch from one Web page to another.
- **URL**: Uniform resource locator; the address of the Web page you want to visit

Now you're ready to use Internet Explorer to open and view a Web page.

Opening a Page on the Web

To find a particular Web page among the billions stored on Web servers, your browser needs to know the **uniform resource locator (URL)** of the Web page. URLs are like addresses—they indicate the location of a Web page. A URL can consist of the following four parts, which are also shown in Figure 4-4:

- Protocol to use when transferring the Web page
- Address of the Web server storing the page
- Pathname of the folder containing the page
- Filename of the Web page

Figure 4-4 ▶ **Parts of a URL**

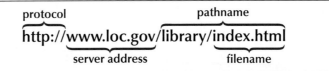

The URL for most Web pages starts with *http*, which stands for **Hypertext Transfer Protocol**, the most common way to transfer information around the Web. (A **protocol** is a standardized procedure used by computers to exchange information.) When the URL for a Web page starts with *http://*, the Web browser uses Hypertext Transfer Protocol to retrieve the page.

The server address indicates the location of the Web server storing the Web page. In *www.loc.gov*, the *www* indicates that the server is a Web server, *loc* is the name the Library of Congress chose for this Web site, and *.gov* means that a government entity runs the Web server. Other common types of Web servers in the United States are .com (commercial), .net (network server providers or resources), .org (not-for-profit organizations), and .edu (educational institutions). The server address in a URL corresponds to an Internet Protocol (IP) address, which identifies every computer on the Internet. An **IP address** is a unique number that consists of four sets of numbers from 0 to 255 separated by periods, or dots, as in 216.35.148.4. An IP address identifies each server or computer connected to the Internet. Although computers can use IP addresses easily, they are difficult for people to remember, so domain names were created. A **domain name** identifies one or more IP addresses, such as loc.gov in Figure 4-4. URLs use the domain name in the server address part of an address to identify a particular Web site.

In addition, each file stored on Web servers has a unique pathname, just like files stored on a disk. The pathname in a URL includes the names of the folders containing the file, the filename, and its extension. The filename extension for Web pages is usually *html*, or just *htm*. In Figure 4-4, the pathname is library/index.html, which specifies a file named index.html stored in a folder named library.

Not all URLs include a pathname. If you don't specify a pathname or filename in a URL, most Web browsers open a file named index.htm or index.html, which is the default name for a Web site's main page.

Opening a Web Page Using a URL

One way to open a Web page in Internet Explorer is to provide a URL, which you can often find in advertisements, informational materials, and on the Web. When you have the URL for a Web page you want to view, you can enter it in the Address bar of Internet Explorer.

In most cases, URLs are not case sensitive, so you can enter a URL using all lowercase or all uppercase text. However, if the Web server storing a Web page uses the UNIX operating system, the URL might be case sensitive. For mixed case URLs, it's safer to enter them using the mixed case exactly as printed.

Opening a Web Page Using a URL	Reference Window

- Click the Address box on the Address bar.
- Type the URL of the Web page you want to open, and then press the Enter key.

The first Web page you want to open for David is for the Colorado State tourism office. You'll open the page by entering a URL for the New Perspectives Online Companion Web page, and then click a link on that page to go to the Colorado State tourism Web page.

To open a page on the Web using a URL:

▶ **1.** Click the **Address** box on the Address bar. The contents of the Address box, which should be the URL for your home page, are selected. Anything you now type replaces the selected URL.

  Trouble? If the contents of the Address box are not selected, drag to select the entire address.

▶ **2.** Type **www.course.com/np/vista** in the Address box, and then press the **Enter** key. Internet Explorer adds the *http://* protocol for you, and then opens the Web page for the New Perspectives on Windows Vista Online Companion.

  Trouble? If you receive a Not Found error message, you might have typed the URL incorrectly. Repeat Steps 1 and 2, making sure that the URL in the Address box matches the URL in Step 2. If you still receive an error message, ask your instructor or technical support person for help.

▶ **3.** In the list of Online Companion links, click the **Tutorial** link.

▶ **4.** Click the link for **Colorado State Tourism** to open the main page for the Colorado State tourism Web site. See Figure 4-5. This page plays a slide show of images to promote Colorado. The images you see might be different from those in the figures.

Figure 4-5 | **Opening the Colorado State tourism Web page**

Internet Explorer confirms that you are viewing the Colorado State tourism Web page by displaying the name of the Web page in the title bar and on the page tab.

Because Web content changes frequently, the Web pages you open might differ from the figures in this tutorial.

InSight | **Home Page or Main Page?**

The term *home page* has at least two definitions. The definition already introduced in this tutorial is the Web page a browser is set to open by default. The main page for a Web site is also called a home page, though this tutorial uses *main page* to avoid confusion. On a Web site, pages link to and are organized in relation to the main page.

You can show David how to explore the information the Colorado Web site provides by navigating links on its main page.

Navigating with Links

The main page for a typical Web site includes plenty of links to help you navigate to its Web pages, and those pages also include links you can click to navigate from one page to another. Recall that links can be text, images, or a combination of both. Text links are usually colored and underlined, though the exact style can vary from one Web site to another. To determine whether something on a Web page is a link, point to it. If the pointer changes to 🖑 and a URL appears in the status bar of your Web browser, the text or image is a link you can click to open a Web page. For some graphic links, a ScreenTip also appears next to your pointer.

You'll show David how to navigate the Colorado Web site by clicking links to find information about travel destinations in Colorado that are accessible to low-mobility travelers.

To navigate a Web site using links:

► **1.** Point to **Vacation Ideas** on the Colorado main page. The pointer changes to 🖑 and the URL for that link appears in the status bar. On this page, pointing to the Vacation Ideas link also displays a menu. See Figure 4-6.

Pointing to a link ◄ **Figure 4-6**

Trouble? If the Colorado main page does not include a Vacation Ideas link, point to any other similar link and substitute that link when you perform Step 2.

► **2.** Click **Vacation Ideas** to open the Vacation Ideas Web page. See Figure 4-7. The Web page you open might look different.

Figure 4-7   Vacation Ideas Web page

> **3.** Click **Accessible Colorado** to open the Accessible Colorado Web page, which describes activities, transportation, and resources for low-mobility travelers.
>
> **Trouble?** If the Accessible Colorado link does not appear on the current Web page, click any other link on the page.

Besides clicking links to navigate from one Web page to another, you can use tools that Internet Explorer provides.

Navigating with Internet Explorer Tools

Recall that when you use Windows Explorer and Computer, you can click the Back and Forward buttons to navigate the devices and folders on your computer. Internet Explorer includes similar buttons. As you navigate from one Web page to another, Internet Explorer keeps track of the pages you visited. To return to the previous page, you can click the Back button. To retrace even earlier pages, continue clicking the Back button. After you click the Back button, you can click the Forward button to continue to the next page in the sequence.

You can also use the Recent Pages menu to revisit a Web page in the sequence. Click the arrow next to the Forward button, and then select a page in the list.

To return to previously viewed Web pages:

> **1.** Click the **Back** button ⬅ to return to the Vacation Ideas Web page.
>
> **2.** Click the **Forward** button ➡ to return to the Accessible Colorado page.

Trouble? If you opened different Web pages in the previous set of steps, substitute the names of the pages as appropriate in Steps 1 and 2.

▶ **3.** Click the **Recent Pages** button ▾ to open the Recent Pages menu, and then click **Colorado.com | Plan Your Colorado Weekend** to return to the Colorado main page.

▶ **4.** Close Internet Explorer.

One limitation of the Back, Forward, and Recent Pages buttons is that they apply only to your current session in the browser. If you close and then restart Internet Explorer, it starts keeping track of a fresh sequence of pages. To revisit Web pages you opened in previous sessions, you can use the History list.

Using the History List

To open any Web page you've visited in the last 20 days, you can use the History list, which is available in the Internet Explorer Favorites Center. The Favorites Center organizes Web page links and other information, including the History list. (You'll explore the Favorites Center shortly.) The History list includes the Web sites you visited today, last week, two weeks ago, and three weeks ago. You can also change the setup in the History list to view pages by date, by site, by the number of times visited, and in the order visited today. You can also search the pages in the History list to locate a specific Web site you've recently visited.

David wants to open the Web page on the Colorado Web site that provides accessibility information. Because you already closed Internet Explorer, you can't use the Back button to return to that page. You'll use the History list to revisit the Accessible Colorado Web page.

To use the History list:

▶ **1.** Start Internet Explorer.

▶ **2.** Click the **Favorites Center** button ☆ on the toolbar to open the Favorites Center.

▶ **3.** Click the **Pin the Favorites Center** button on the Favorites Center toolbar to keep the Favorites Center open.

Trouble? If your Pin the Favorites Center button does not appear on your Favorites Center toolbar, the Favorites Center is already pinned to the Internet Explorer window. Skip Step 3.

▶ **4.** If the History button in the Favorites Center is not currently selected, click the **History** button to display the History list. See Figure 4-8.

Tip

To display feeds you subscribe to, click the Feeds button on the Favorites Center toolbar.

Displaying the History list | Figure 4-8

click a calendar icon to expand the list of Web sites visited

selected History button

your History list might include additional dates

Trouble? If your History list is not organized by date as shown in Figure 4-8, click the History button arrow and then click By Date.

▶ **5.** Click **Today** in the History list. The list expands to show the Web sites you visited today.

▶ **6.** Click **colorado (www.colorado.com)** to expand the list to show the pages you visited on that Web site.

▶ **7.** Click **Colorado.com | Colorado Vacation Ideas and Travel Tips for Accessible Colorado Vacations**. The corresponding Web page opens in Internet Explorer. See Figure 4-9.

Figure 4-9 **Revisiting a Web page**

Next, you want to show David how to open other Web pages without closing the Accessible Colorado Vacations Web page.

Managing Multiple Web Pages

If you want to open a new Web page without closing the one you're currently viewing, you can use **tabbed browsing**, a feature in Internet Explorer that lets you open more than one Web page in the single browser window. To use tabbed browsing, you open a tab for each new page you want to view. On the new tab, you open a Web page as you usually do. You can also open a new tab by pressing the Ctrl key as you click a link on a Web page or by right-clicking the link and then clicking Open in New Tab on the shortcut menu. You can then switch from one Web page to another by clicking their tabs. If you have two or more tabs open, you can use the Quick Tabs button to display a thumbnail of each Web page so you can see all of your open pages at once. You click a thumbnail to switch to the corresponding page. To close a tab, you click its Close button.

Now that you've explored a few pages on the Colorado tourism site, you want to compare that information to the state of Colorado Web page, which provides instructions for applying for hunting and fishing licenses, buying state park passes, reserving campsites in state parks, and other information David's clients often want to know. You'll show David how to open a new tab in Internet Explorer, and then use it to open the state of Colorado Web page.

To open a second Web page on a new tab:

1. Click the **New Tab** button on the toolbar. (This button changes to when you point to it.) A blank page opens on the new tab. See Figure 4-10.

Opening a new tab | Figure 4-10

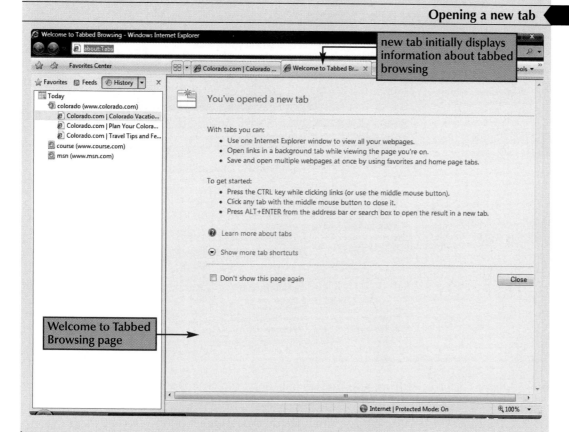

2. In the History list, click the **course (www.course.com)** folder.

3. Click the link to the **Microsoft Windows Vista Online Companion**. The Microsoft Windows Vista Online Companion Web page opens on the new tab.

4. Click the **Tutorial** link.

5. Click the **State of Colorado** link. The main page for the state of Colorado appears on the new tab. See Figure 4-11. Your Web page might differ.

Figure 4-11   State of Colorado Web page on the new tab

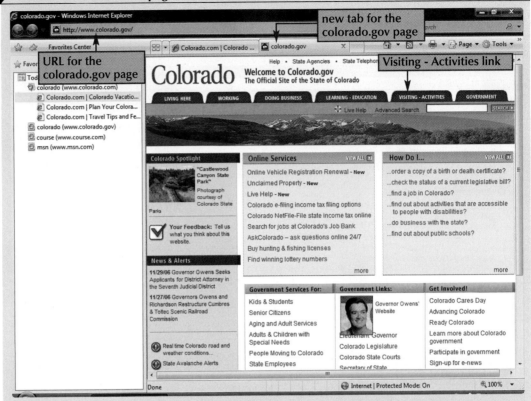

▶ **6.** Right-click the **Visiting – Activities** link, and then click **Open Link in New Tab** on the shortcut menu. The Visiting – Activities Web page opens in a new tab.

   Trouble? If the Visiting – Activities link does not appear on the current Web page, right-click a different link on the page.

▶ **7.** Click the **Quick Tabs** button on the toolbar. Thumbnails appear showing a miniature version of each open Web page. See Figure 4-12.

Tip

You can also switch to a different Web page by clicking the Tab List button and then clicking the name of a Web page.

Thumbnails of the open Web pages ◄ Figure 4-12

8. Click the first **colorado.gov** thumbnail to display the main state of Colorado Web page.

Although tabbed browsing helps you manage open Web pages, the Favorites Center helps you organize Web pages you open often. You'll show David how to use the Favorites Center next.

Using the Favorites List

As you explore the Web, you'll find pages that are your favorites, those you visit frequently. You can save the location of your favorite Web pages in the **Favorites list**, a collection of links to the Web pages that you visit often. To display the Favorites list, you open the Favorites Center, where you can manage the Favorites list, feeds, and the History list. The Favorites list initially includes a few Web sites that Microsoft provides, such as a link to MSN.com. Your computer manufacturer might also include a few links in the Favorites list. If you find a Web page you want to visit often, you can add it to your Favorites list. When you want to retrieve one of your favorite Web pages, you can click its link in the Favorites list and display the page in your browser. As your list of favorite pages grows, you can organize the links into folders. For example, you could create a Favorites folder for travel Web sites and another for news Web sites.

To display the Favorites list:

▶ **1.** Click the **Favorites** button in the Favorites Center. Internet Explorer displays the Favorites list. See Figure 4-13. Your Favorites list might be different.

| Figure 4-13 | Displaying the Favorites list |

You'll use the Microsoft Windows Vista Online Companion Web page later in this tutorial, so you can add it to your Favorites list. The Accessible Colorado Web page also provides the kind of information you often need when organizing trips for Entrée Tours. You'll also add that page to the Favorites list.

Adding an Item to the Favorites List

To add a Web page to the Favorites list, you access the page in Internet Explorer, and then you use the Add to Favorites command. By default, Windows Vista adds the new page to the end of the Favorites list. If you organize the Web pages into folders, you can add a Web page to one of the folders. You can store the page using the title of the Web page as its name, or you can change the name if you like.

| Reference Window | **Adding a Web Page to the Favorites List** |

- Open the Web page in Internet Explorer.
- Click the Add to Favorites button on the toolbar, and then click Add to Favorites.
- Enter a new name for the Web page and select a folder, if necessary.
- Click the OK button.

If you are working on a network, you might not be able to change the content of the Favorites list. In that case, read through the following steps and examine the figures, but do not perform the steps.

To add Web pages to your Favorites list:

▶ **1.** In the Address box, start typing the address for the Online Companion page for this book: **www.course.com/np/vista**. After you type the first few characters, Internet Explorer displays the complete address below the Address box. Click the complete address to return to the Online Companion page.

▶ **2.** Click the **Add to Favorites** button 🖈 on the Favorites Center toolbar, and then click **Add to Favorites**. The Add a Favorite dialog box opens, displaying the name of the Web page in the Name text box.

▶ **3.** Type **Online Companion** in the Name text box, and then click the **Add** button. A link for the Windows Vista Online Companion appears in the Favorites list.

▶ **4.** Click the **Colorado.com** tab to open that Web page.

▶ **5.** Click the **Add to Favorites button** 🌟 **and then click Add to Favorites.**

▶ **6.** Type **Accessible Colorado** in the Name text box, and then click the **Add** button to add the Web page to the Favorites list.

Next, you can organize your favorite Web pages into folders.

Organizing the Favorites List

As you add more items to the Favorites list, you can organize its links by deleting some and moving others to new folders. Using folders is an excellent way to organize your favorite files and pages.

Organizing the Favorites List | Reference Window

- Click the Add to Favorites button on the Favorites Center toolbar, and then click Organize Favorites to open the Organize Favorites dialog box.
- To create a new folder, click the New Folder button.
- To move a link into a Favorites folder, drag the link to the folder or select the item, click the Move to Folder button, select the new folder for the item, and then click the OK button.
- To remove an item from the Favorites list, select the item, and then click the Delete button.
- Click the Close button to close the Organize Favorites dialog box.

To organize your Favorites list:

▶ **1.** Click the **Add to Favorites** button 🌟 on the Favorites Center toolbar, and then click **Organize Favorites**. The Organize Favorites dialog box opens.

▶ **2.** Click the **New Folder** button, type **Windows Vista** for the new folder name, and then press the **Enter** key.

▶ **3.** Click the **New Folder** button, type **Colorado Travel** for the new folder name, and then press the **Enter** key.

▶ **4.** In the Organize Favorites dialog box, drag the **Online Companion** link to the **Windows Vista** folder.

▶ **5.** Drag the **Accessible Colorado** link to the **Colorado Travel** folder.

▶ **6.** Click the **Close** button to close the Organize Folders dialog box. The two new links you added are now stored in the Windows Vista and Colorado Travel folders in the Favorites list. See Figure 4-14.

Tip

If the number of items in the Favorites list makes it difficult to drag links to folders, you can use the Move to Folder button in the Organize Favorites dialog box instead of dragging.

Figure 4-14 ▶ New folders in the Favorites list

Favorites list now includes two new folders →

← your Favorites list might contain different links

Before you finish showing David how to use Internet Explorer, he asks you to print the Visiting and Activities Web page on the state of Colorado Web site so he can use it for reference when he's away from the computer.

Printing a Web Page

If you want to refer to the information you find on the Web when you don't have computer access, you can print a Web page. Although Web pages can be any size, printers usually use 8.5 × 11-inch sheets of paper. Sometimes, Web pages include a link for printing a Web page, such as "Printer Friendly Format," indicating that the Web site formats the page for a standard size sheet of paper before printing. However, not all Web pages provide such an option. You should therefore preview the page before you print it so see how it will look when printed. In the Print dialog box, you can change the page orientation from portrait (8.5 × 11 inches) to landscape (11 × 8.5 inches) if necessary to print all the information, and specify that you want to print some or all of the document.

Before printing the Visiting and Activities Web page, you'll show David how to preview the page. You can then determine whether to print the information in portrait or landscape orientation and whether to print the entire document or only some pages.

To preview and then print a Web page:

▶ **1.** Click the second **colorado.gov** tab to display the Visiting and Activities Web page in Internet Explorer.

▶ **2.** Click the **Print button arrow** 🖨 ▾ and then click **Print Preview** to open the Print Preview window. See Figure 4-15.

Previewing a Web page before printing ◀ Figure 4-15

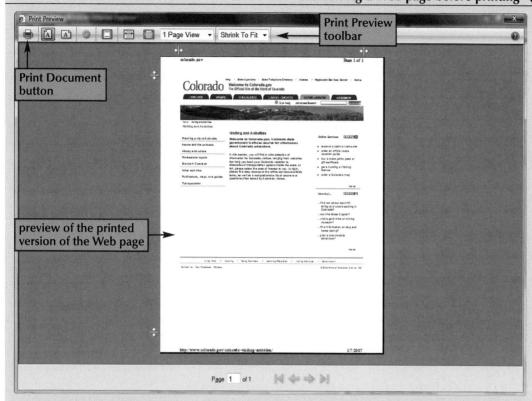

3. Click the **Print Document** 🖨 button to open the Print dialog box.

4. In the Page Range section, click the **Pages** option button, and make sure the Pages text box shows "1".

   Trouble? If a value other than "1" appears in the Pages text box, select the text in the text box, and then type 1.

5. Click the **Print** button to print the first page of the Visiting and Activities Web page.

Some printers are set up to print headers and footers in addition to the Web page itself, so when you retrieve the page from your printer, you might find the page's title, its URL, the date, and other similar information at the top and bottom of the page.

Saving Web Pages

Although a Web page appears in your browser window and you can add the page to your Favorites list or find it in your History list, the page itself is still stored on a remote computer (a computer located elsewhere on the Internet). You can save the Web page and store it on your computer by clicking the Page button on the Internet Explorer toolbar, and then clicking Save As. You can also save a graphic image displayed on a Web page. However, doing so is not always legal or ethical. Many of the images displayed on Web pages are the intellectual property of someone else, usually the person who took the photograph, commissioned the logo, or created the drawing. Just as owners have rights to physical property, creators of intellectual property (original works including art and photographs) have rights to their work. You need to be aware of these **intellectual property rights** because Web content such as software, video, music, and images are easy to copy in their digital form. However, if this material is protected by copyright, you usually cannot copy or share it unless you receive permission from the owner. The term **copyright** applies to the originator's exclusive legal right to reproduce, publish, or sell intellectual property. Copyright laws protect intellectual property—if you copy someone else's work without giving that person credit, you are committing plagiarism.

Before you copy or save the graphics, images, sounds, videos, or other information on Web sites that you visit, you need to find out if and how you can use the materials. If you want to use material you find on a Web site, first get permission from the owner of the site. Often, Web sites include their copyright and permission-request information on their main pages. Some Web sites indicate that the material is free, but almost everything on the Internet is copyrighted. Even if you think that information or material you found is not copyrighted, you should always request permission to use it. You might be able to copy a photo to your computer, for example, but you don't have the right to reproduce it in your own work.

As you examine the permission information on Web sites, you might encounter the term **fair use**. This term applies to material that can be used for educational or nonprofit purposes, as opposed to commercial profit. Information that is considered factual or materials that are so old that copyright protection no longer applies fall under the category of fair use. You should still give credit to any Web site that you use in your research.

Because you printed the information David needs, you don't need to save the Visiting and Activities Web page or any of its content. You can also access this page later by using your Favorites list. You're ready to close Internet Explorer. If you only have one tab open, you close Internet Explorer the way you do any other program: click the Close button on the title bar. If more than one tab is open, however, you can choose to close a tab to leave a Web page instead of closing the entire program. To close the tab for the current Web page, you click the Close Tab button. If you have more than one tab open and exit Internet Explorer, it asks if you want to close all tabs before exiting the program.

To close tabs and exit Internet Explorer:

▶ **1.** Point to the tab for the Visiting and Activities Web page, and then click the **Close Tab** button ☒ . The Visiting and Activities Web page closes.

▶ **2.** Click the **Close** button ☒ on the Internet Explorer title bar. A dialog box opens and asks if you want to close all tabs.

▶ **3.** Click the **Close Tabs** button to close the remaining two tabs and exit Internet Explorer.

So far, you have learned about the structure of the Internet and the Web and how to use Internet Explorer to open, navigate, and organize Web pages. In the next session, you'll use another service the Internet provides—e-mail.

| Review | **Session 4.1 Quick Check**

1. Explain the relationship of the Internet and the Web.
2. A _____ _____ is a collection of Web pages that have a common theme or focus.
3. True or False. A browser is a program that lets you create and publish Web pages.
4. When you start Internet Explorer, what does it display by default?
5. The address of a Web page is called a(n) _____ .
6. Name two ways to open a Web page in Internet Explorer.
7. Describe three ways you can open a Web page you visited recently.
8. True or False. The Favorites list includes only those links that Microsoft or your computer manufacturer initially provided.

Session 4.2

Getting Started with Windows Mail

Windows Mail, one of the tools that comes with Windows Vista, allows you to send, receive, and manage **electronic mail** or **e-mail**—electronic messages transferred between users on a network such as the Internet. You can send e-mail to and receive e-mail from anyone in the world who has an e-mail address, regardless of the operating system or type of computer the person is using.

Examining How E-Mail Works

An **e-mail message** is a simple text document that you can compose and send using an **e-mail program**, such as Windows Mail. When you send a message, it travels from your computer, through the network, and arrives at a computer called an **e-mail server**. Typically, the system administrator of your network or ISP manages the e-mail server.

The e-mail server stores the e-mail messages until the recipients request them. Then the server forwards the messages to the appropriate computers. Because e-mail uses this **store-and-forward technology**, you can send messages to anyone on the network, even if they don't have their computers turned on. When it's convenient, your recipients log on to the network and use their e-mail programs to receive and read their messages. Figure 4-16 illustrates sending and receiving e-mail messages.

Sending and receiving e-mail ◄ Figure 4-16

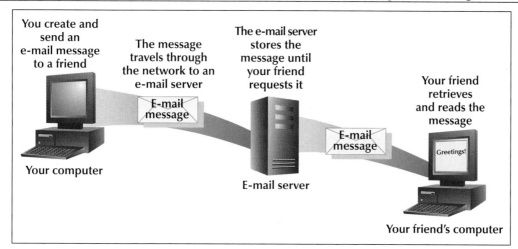

As Figure 4-16 shows, to send and receive e-mail, you must be able to access an e-mail server on the network. If your computer is part of a network at a college or university, for example, you log on to the network to access its services. An e-mail server provides mail services to faculty, staff, and students who have access to the network. When someone sends you a message, it is stored on your e-mail server until you log on to the network and use an e-mail program to check your mail. The e-mail server then transfers new messages to your electronic mailbox. You use an e-mail program to open, read, print, delete, reply to, forward, and save the mail.

If your computer is not part of a network, you can access an e-mail server on the Internet. To do so, you open an **e-mail account** with a service that provides Internet access. For example, e-mail accounts are included as part of the subscription fee for most ISPs. E-mail accounts are also provided free of charge by advertiser-supported Web sites, such as Yahoo! and Google. After you establish an e-mail account, you can connect to the Internet to send and receive your e-mail messages.

Addressing E-Mail

Just as you must address a piece of ordinary mail, you need to supply an address for an e-mail message. The e-mail address you enter directs the message to its destination. Your e-mail address is included in the message as the return address, so your recipients can easily respond to your message. Anyone who has an e-mail address can send and receive electronic mail. If you work for a company or attend a school that provides e-mail, a system administrator probably assigns an e-mail address for you. Other times, you create your own e-mail address, though it must follow a particular format. See Figure 4-17.

Figure 4-17 ▶ **Typical format of an e-mail address**

The **user name**, or **user ID**, is the name entered when your e-mail account is set up. The @ symbol signifies that the e-mail server name is provided next. In Figure 4-17, *DavidSanchez* is the user name and *entree.net* is the e-mail server.

The easiest way to learn a person's e-mail address is to ask the person. You can also look up an e-mail address in a network or Internet directory. Most businesses and schools publish a directory listing e-mail addresses of those who have e-mail accounts on their network. Many Web sites also provide e-mail directories for people with e-mail accounts on the Internet, such as *www.worldemail.com* and *www.people.yahoo.com*.

When you sign up for an e-mail account, you can send your new e-mail address to friends, colleagues, and clients. If your e-mail address changes, such as when you change e-mail services, you can subscribe to an e-mail forwarding service so you don't miss any mail sent to your old address.

Observing E-Mail Etiquette

Because e-mail is a widespread form of communication, you should follow standard guidelines when using e-mail. Most of these guidelines are commonsense practices, such as using appropriate language. Others might be new to you. For example, you should understand that e-mail is not private. When you correspond with others using e-mail, the information you send can be read by other users, especially if you work for a corporation or private institution. Your correspondents can easily forward your message to others, deliberately or inadvertently revealing information you consider confidential. It's a good idea to be professional and courteous about what you say to and about others.

Another guideline is to provide meaningful information in the subject line. Most e-mail programs show the subject line, date, and sender address for incoming mail. Let your correspondents know the purpose of your message by including information in the subject line that concisely and accurately describes the message contents. For example, a subject such as "Staff meeting rescheduled" is more informative than "Meeting."

Keep the following guidelines in mind when you are composing e-mail messages so that you use e-mail to communicate effectively, without offending or annoying your correspondents.

- **Reply only as necessary**. When you want to respond to an e-mail message, you can click the Reply button to reply to the original sender or you can click the Reply All button to respond to everyone who received the original message. When you use the Reply All button, make sure that everyone listed as recipients really needs to receive the message so that you are not flooding electronic inboxes with unnecessary e-mails.
- **Include your response first**. When you reply to an e-mail, you can include text from the original message. If you do, make sure that your response is at the top of the message so your recipients can find it easily.
- **State your subject clearly**. As mentioned earlier, include a brief summary of your message in the subject line so your recipients know what it's about.
- **Don't e-mail sensitive or confidential information**. Keep in mind that e-mail is not private, and your recipients can forward your message to others, either intentionally or accidentally.
- **Be concise and direct**. People often read e-mail messages while they are doing something else. As a courtesy to your correspondents and to make sure your message is read, get right to the point and keep your messages short.
- **Avoid abbreviations**. Although you should strive to be brief, don't overcompensate by using nonstandard abbreviations. Stick to the abbreviations that are common in business writing, such as FYI and ASAP.
- **Don't use all capital letters**. Using all capital letters as in "SEND ME THE REPORT TODAY" makes it look like you're shouting and can be difficult to read.
- **Pause and reread before sending**. Be sure to read the e-mails you write before you send them, and consider how they could be received. A message that you intend to be funny could be misinterpreted as rude. If you wrote an e-mail in anger, calm down and revise your message before sending it. After you send an e-mail message, you can't retrieve or stop it.

Setting Up Windows Mail

To use e-mail, you need an Internet connection, an e-mail program such as Windows Mail, and an e-mail address. Make sure you have an Internet connection and e-mail address before performing the steps in this section. Windows Vista provides Windows Mail, so you don't need to install that e-mail program separately.

After you set up an account with an e-mail service provider (usually this is your ISP), you add your account to Windows Mail so you can use it to exchange e-mail. If you are in a university or other institution, this has probably been done for you, but if you are using your own computer, you probably have to add it yourself. At a minimum, Windows Mail needs to know your e-mail address, password, and the names of your incoming and outgoing e-mail servers. The type of server you specify corresponds to the type of account you have with your service provider. Windows Mail supports the following types of e-mail accounts:

- **Post Office Protocol 3 (POP3)**: These servers hold incoming e-mail messages until you check your e-mail; then they deliver it to your computer. After delivering messages, e-mail servers usually delete them. POP3 is the most common account type for personal e-mail.

- **Internet Message Access Protocol (IMAP)**: With this type of account, your e-mail is stored on an e-mail server, not on your computer. You can access your e-mail directly on the server, and then preview, delete, and organize messages. IMAP is usually used for business e-mail accounts.
- **Simple Mail Transfer Protocol (SMTP)**: These accounts are for outgoing e-mail. You use them with a POP3 or IMAP account for incoming e-mail.

The first time you start Windows Mail, a series of dialog boxes guides you through the process of setting up an account. The following steps show you how to set up a Windows Mail account. If you already have an e-mail account, read but do not perform the following steps.

David Sanchez has an e-mail account with Entrée Tours, but he hasn't set up Windows Mail to use that account. Because this is the first time you're starting Windows Mail on his Windows Vista computer, you'll show him how to set up Windows Mail to use his Entrée Tours account.

To set up Windows Mail:

Tip

If Windows Mail is your default e-mail program, you can start it by clicking the Start button and then clicking E-mail.

1. Click the **Start** button 🔵 on the taskbar, point to **All Programs**, and then click **Windows Mail**. The Windows Mail program starts. If this is the first time you started Windows Mail, the Your Name dialog box opens, requesting your display name.

   Trouble? If you have already set up Windows Mail, the main Windows Mail window opens instead of the Your Name dialog box. Read but do not perform the rest of the steps.

   Trouble? If the main Windows Mail window opens instead of the Your Name dialog box and you have not set up an e-mail account yet, click Tools on the menu bar, click Accounts, click the Add button, click E-mail Account, and then click the Next button to open the Your Name dialog box.

   Trouble? If a dialog box opens asking if you want Windows Mail to be your default mail program, click the Yes button only if you are using your own computer and want to use Windows Mail as your mail program. If you are using a school or institutional computer, click the No button or ask your technical support person for assistance.

2. Enter the name you want to appear as the sender of the e-mails you send, such as **David Sanchez**. Click the **Next** button. The Internet E-mail Address dialog box opens.

3. Enter your e-mail address, such as **DavidSanchez@entree.net**, and then click the **Next** button. The Set up e-mail servers dialog box opens.

4. Click the **Incoming e-mail server type arrow**, if necessary, to select the type of incoming e-mail server you use. (Your ISP typically provides this information.) Enter the name of your incoming e-mail server, such as **pop.entree.net**, and your outgoing e-mail server, such as **smtp.entree.net**. If your server requires a user name and password when sending mail in addition to when receiving it, click the **Outgoing server requires authentication** check box.

5. Click the **Next** button. The Internet Mail Logon dialog box opens.

6. Enter your e-mail user name and password. (Your ISP might provide this information initially, though you can often change it.) Click the **Next** button.

7. The Congratulations dialog box opens. If you do not want to download your e-mail now, click the **Do not download my e-mail at this time** check box. Click the **Finish** button.

   Trouble? If a dialog box opens asking if you want to import mail from another e-mail program, do not import the e-mail unless your instructor indicates that you should do so.

Now you can show David how to send and receive e-mail.

Sending and Receiving E-Mail Using Windows Mail

The Windows Mail program installs with Windows Vista so you can compose, send, and receive e-mail messages. After you set up an e-mail account, you're ready to start using Windows Mail to manage your e-mail.

To start Windows Mail:

▶ 1. Start Windows Mail, if necessary. (Click the **Start** button 🔵 on the taskbar, point to **All Programs**, and then click **Windows Mail**.) The main Windows Mail program window opens. See Figure 4-18. The e-mail account shown in the figures in this tutorial belongs to David Sanchez. Your screens will therefore look different from the figures.

Windows Mail window | Figure 4-18

Trouble? If the Folders list does not appear in the Windows Mail window, click View on the menu bar, click Layout, click the Folder List check box, and then click the OK button.

Trouble? If this is the first time you started Windows Mail, your Inbox contains a Welcome message from Microsoft Windows Mail. You do not need to do anything with this message now.

In addition to the standard Windows components, such as the title bar, Close button, and scroll bars, the Windows Mail window includes the following elements:

- **Menu bar**: Provides menus of commands for working with e-mail, accounts, and Windows Mail
- **Search box**: Lets you find e-mail messages by searching for text contained in any part of the message
- **Toolbar**: Provides buttons for frequently performed commands, such as creating, replying to, and forwarding e-mail
- **Folders list**: Displays the default Windows Mail folders, including the Inbox, Outbox, Sent Items, Deleted Items, Drafts, and Junk E-mail folders. Windows Mail organizes your e-mail into these folders automatically. You can create additional folders for the messages you create and receive.
- **Message list:** When you start Windows Mail, it displays a list of the messages in your Inbox by default. These are the messages you've received. If you select a different folder, Windows Mail displays those messages in the list.
- **Preview pane**: Displays the contents of the selected message

Now that you've identified the parts of the Windows Mail window, you're ready to show David how to create and send a message.

Creating and Sending E-Mail Messages

An e-mail message uses a format similar to a standard memo: it typically includes Date, To, and Subject lines, followed by the content of the message. The To line indicates who will receive the message. Windows Mail automatically supplies the date you send the message in the Date line (as set in your computer's clock). If more than one account is set up in Windows Mail, a From line might appear so you can select the account you want to use for sending the message. The Subject line, although optional, alerts the recipient to the topic of the message. Finally, the message area contains the content of your message. You can also include additional information, such as a Cc line, which indicates who will receive a copy of the message, or a Priority setting, which indicates the importance of the message.

InSight	**Using the Cc and Bcc Lines**

In the To line, restrict the e-mail addresses to those of your primary recipients. Use the Cc (courtesy copy) line for secondary recipients who should receive a copy of the message. If you are sending an e-mail message to a large group of people, use the Bcc (blind courtesy copy) line. (Click the Cc button to specify that you want to use an additional Bcc line.) Windows Mail sends an individual message to each person listed in the Bcc line, and the only other e-mail address that appears is the sender's.

To send an e-mail message, you first compose the message and then click the Send button on the message window. Windows Mail sends the message from your computer to your e-mail server, which routes it to the recipient.

| Creating and Sending an E-Mail Message | Reference Window |

- Click the Create Mail button on the toolbar.
- Enter the e-mail address of the recipient in the To box.
- Click the Subject box and then type the subject of the message.
- Click the message area and then type the content of the message.
- Click the Send button.

To create and send an e-mail message:

▶ 1. Click the **Create Mail** button on the Windows Mail toolbar. The New Message window opens. See Figure 4-19.

New Message window | Figure 4-19

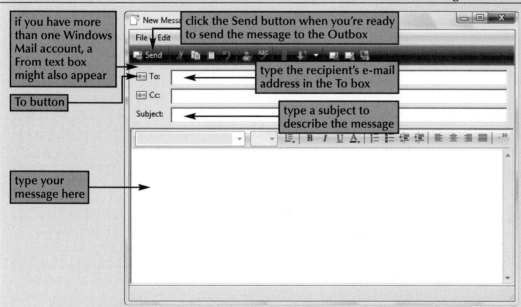

if you have more than one Windows Mail account, a From text box might also appear

click the Send button when you're ready to send the message to the Outbox

To button

type the recipient's e-mail address in the To box

type a subject to describe the message

type your message here

▶ 2. Type your e-mail address in the To text box.

Trouble? If you're not sure what e-mail address you should enter, check with your instructor or technical support person.

▶ 3. Click the **Subject** text box, and then type **Test e-mail**.

▶ 4. Click in the message area, type **This is just a practice test message**, press the **Enter** key, and then type your name.

▶ 5. Click the **Send** button on the toolbar. Windows Mail places the message in the Outbox. After a few moments, Windows Mail removes the message from the Outbox, sends the message to your e-mail server, and then places a copy of the sent message in the Sent Items folder.

To make sure your message has been sent, you can open the Sent Items folder to see all the messages you have sent.

Trouble? If, after several seconds have passed, Windows Mail still displays "(1)" to the right of the Outbox folder in the Folders list, indicating that there is one unsent message, then Windows Mail is not configured to send messages immediately. In that case, click the Send/Receive button on the toolbar to send your message.

> **6.** Click the **Sent Items** folder in the Folders list. Your message appears in the right pane of the Windows Mail window. See Figure 4-20.

Figure 4-20   **Sent Items folder**

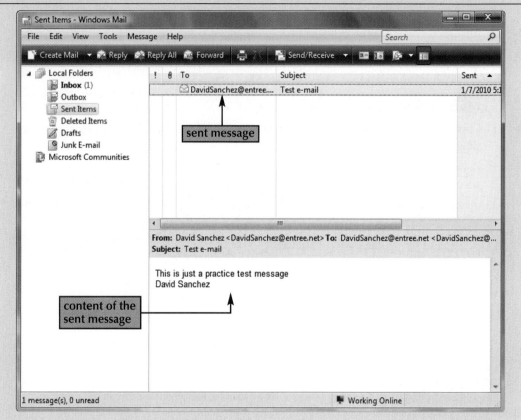

If you had wanted to send this message to many people, you could have typed more than one e-mail address in the To or Cc text boxes. You must separate each address with a comma or semicolon. You can also add the e-mail addresses of people (your contacts) to Windows Contacts, which you'll do shortly.

Receiving and Reading E-Mail Messages

Windows Mail automatically checks to see if you've received e-mail whenever you start the program and periodically after that. (Every 30 minutes is the default.) Windows Mail also checks for received e-mail when you click the Send/Receive button. E-mail you receive appears in your Inbox. By default, the Inbox shows only the name of the sender, the subject, and the date you received the message. Mail you have received but have not read yet appears in bold. To preview a message, you click the message in the list to display its contents in the Preview pane, or you can double-click the message to open it in a separate window. In either case, you can print the messages you receive.

To receive, read, and print the Test e-mail message:

> **1.** Click **Inbox** in the Folder list to display the contents of the Inbox folder in the right pane.

▶ **2.** Click the **Send/Receive** button on the toolbar. Windows Mail retrieves your messages from your e-mail server, routes them to your Inbox, and displays the number of unread messages to the right of the Inbox folder. The content of the selected message appears in the Preview pane. See Figure 4-21. Your Inbox folder might contain additional e-mail messages from other people.

Inbox folder   **Figure 4-21**

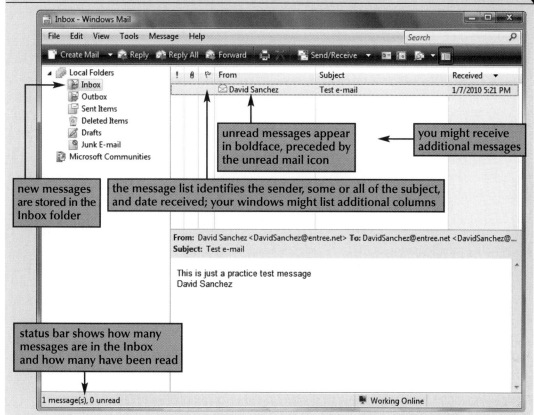

Trouble? If a dialog box opens requesting your user name and password, enter the information and continue with Step 3. See your instructor or technical support person if you need help entering the correct user name or password.

Trouble? If the message you sent doesn't appear in the Inbox, wait a few minutes, and then click the Send/Receive button again.

Trouble? If you received more than one message, click Test e-mail in the message list to display the message in the Preview pane.

▶ **3.** Double-click **Test e-mail** in the message list. The Test e-mail message window opens. See Figure 4-22.

| Figure 4-22 | Reading a message |

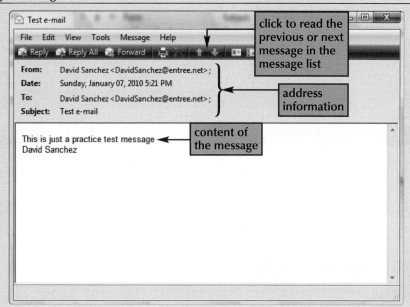

4. Read the message, and then click the **Close** button 🪟 to close the Test e-mail window.

When you are working with e-mail in your Inbox, you can change the width of the columns in the message list by dragging the dividing line between column headers. You can also click a column button to sort columns. For example, if you click the From column button, Windows Mail sorts messages in the current folder alphabetically by name. The default sort order is by date and time received, with newest messages at the beginning of the list.

Next, you'll show David how to perform another common e-mail task—replying to the messages you receive.

Replying to E-Mail Messages

Some of the e-mail you receive asks you to provide information, answer questions, or confirm decisions. Instead of creating a new e-mail message, you can reply directly to a message that you receive. When you reply to a message, Windows Mail inserts the e-mail address of the sender and the subject into the proper lines in the message window, and includes the text of the original message.

| InSight | **Using Reply and Reply All** |

You can reply to messages by clicking the Reply or Reply All button. If the original message was sent to more than one person, click the Reply button to respond to only the original sender. Use the Reply All button to respond to all the other recipients as well. Keep in mind the e-mail etiquette guideline about using the Reply All button carefully so that the only messages people receive from you are those they need to read.

You can reply to an open message or to one selected in your message list.

To reply to the Test e-mail message:

▶ **1.** With the Test e-mail message selected in the message list, click the **Reply** button on the toolbar. The Re: Test e-mail window opens. See Figure 4-23.

Replying to a message   **Figure 4-23**

recipient's user name or nickname automatically appears

subject automatically appears, preceded by Re:

space for the new message

original message is quoted, indicated by vertical line or other symbol

▶ **2.** In the message area, type **This test was successful**.

▶ **3.** Click the **Send** button on the toolbar. If necessary, click the **Send/Receive** button on the toolbar to send the message.

Depending on his preferences, David might want to delete the e-mail messages he's read. You'll show him how to delete e-mail messages next.

Deleting E-Mail Messages

After you read and respond to your messages, you can delete any message you no longer need. When you delete a message, it moves to the Deleted Items folder. Messages remain in the Deleted Items folder until you empty, or permanently delete, the folder contents. This folder might be set up to permanently delete its contents when you close Windows Mail. If not, you should do so periodically by right-clicking the Deleted Items folder in the Folders list, clicking Empty 'Deleted Items' Folder on the shortcut menu, and then clicking the Yes button to confirm the deletion.

To delete the Test e-mail message:

▶ **1.** Click **Test e-mail** in the message list, and then click the **Delete** button 🗙 on the toolbar. The Inbox message list no longer displays the Test message.

InSight | **Dealing with Junk E-Mail**

Junk e-mail, or spam, is unsolicited e-mail, often containing advertisements, fraudulent schemes, or legitimate offers. Windows Mail includes a junk e-mail filter that analyzes the content of the e-mail messages you receive and moves suspicious messages to the Junk E-mail folder, where you can examine and manage them as necessary. To reduce the amount of junk e-mail you receive, avoid posting your e-mail address on Web sites or other public areas of the Internet. If a Web site requests your e-mail address, read its privacy statement to make sure it doesn't disclose your e-mail address to others. Finally, never respond to junk e-mail—you're likely to receive even more spam.

David mentions that clients often request itineraries of upcoming trips, which he stores in separate documents. You'll show him how to attach a file to an e-mail message so he can reply to clients and provide the documents they request.

Attaching a File to a Message

Besides sending e-mail to others, you can also transfer files by attaching the files to messages. You can send any kind of file, including documents, pictures, music, or videos.

You'll show David how to send and open an e-mail message that includes an attachment. As before, you'll create a test message and send it to yourself.

To create and send a message with an attachment:

▶ 1. Click the **Create Mail** button on the toolbar.

▶ 2. Type your e-mail address in the To box.

▶ 3. Click the **Subject** box, and then type **Itinerary you requested**.

▶ 4. Click the **Attach File To Message** button 📎 on the toolbar. The Open dialog box opens.

▶ 5. Navigate to the **Tutorial.04\Tutorial** folder provided with your Data Files, and then double-click **Colorado Itinerary**. Windows Mail attaches the file to the message. See Figure 4-24.

Attaching a file to a message ◀ **Figure 4-24**

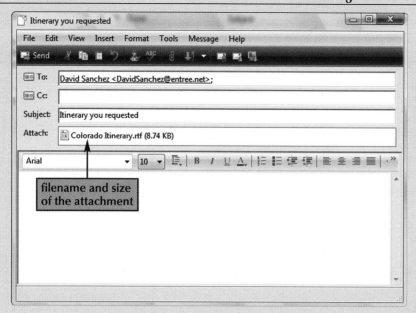

filename and size of the attachment

▶ **6.** In the message area, type **This is a test e-mail message with a file attachment.**

▶ **7.** Click the **Send** button on the toolbar.

Trouble? If a Spelling dialog box opens indicating that a word you typed is not in the dictionary, click the Ignore button.

▶ **8.** If necessary, click the **Send/Receive** button on the toolbar to send the message.

When you receive a message that contains an attachment, you can choose to save or open the attached file. You should open files only from people you know and trust—some people spread harmful software, called **viruses**, in e-mail attachments. To open the file, you need to make sure the program used to create the attachment is installed on your computer. If it's not, you can sometimes use a text editor, such as Word-Pad or Notepad, to open and read the attached file.

The Colorado Itinerary document you attached to the test message is a text file, so you can open it on your computer.

To receive and open a message with an attachment:

▶ **1.** When the Itinerary you requested message appears in your Inbox, click the message in the message list so the contents appear in the Preview pane.

Trouble? If the message you sent doesn't appear in the Inbox, wait a few minutes, and then click the Send/Receive button.

▶ **2.** Click the **paper clip** 📎 icon in the Preview pane to display a list of attachments and options, including those for saving or opening the attachment. See Figure 4-25.

Figure 4-25 ▷ **Message with a file attachment**

3. Click **Colorado Itinerary.rtf (6.86 KB)**. The file opens in a word-processing program, such as Word or WordPad. You could save the document now if necessary.

   Trouble? If a message box appears and asks if you want to open the file, click the Open button.

4. Close the word-processing program.

InSight | **Avoiding E-Mail Viruses**

Windows Mail blocks certain types of file attachments that are commonly used to spread e-mail viruses, including files with the following filename extensions: .exe, .pif, and .scr. If Windows Mail blocks an attachment in an e-mail message, an Information bar appears below the toolbar and displays a message letting you know that it has blocked an attachment. If you need to send a file to someone, check to see if it has a blocked filename extension. If it does, compress the file in a zip folder—Windows Mail does not block attachments with a .zip extension by default.

Another bit of e-mail etiquette applies to attachments. If you attach a large file to an e-mail message, it might take a long time for your recipient to download your message. Most e-mail servers limit the size of the files you can attach; some allow files no larger than 1 MB. Check with your correspondents before sending large file attachments to find out about size restrictions and set up a convenient time to send the attachment.

Adding Information to Windows Contacts

You can use Windows Contacts to keep track of all your e-mail correspondents—it works like an address book for Windows Mail. You can also use Windows Contacts on its own to save information about people and organizations. In addition to storing e-mail addresses, you can store related information such as street addresses, home phone numbers, and personal information such as anniversaries and birthdays. When you create an e-mail message, you can click the To button to open a dialog box listing your contacts. Click the name you want, and then click the To button to indicate that you want to send a message to this contact.

You can add contact information to Windows Contacts by creating a new contact, and then entering as much information as you want about that contact in the contact's Properties dialog box. When you send an e-mail message to someone, you can add their information to Windows Contacts by right-clicking their e-mail address and then clicking Add Sender to Contacts.

To retrieve a contact's information and address for an e-mail message quickly, you can give the contact a nickname. When you enter the nickname as the recipient of an e-mail message, Windows Mail enters the correct e-mail address. You can also add pictures to contacts, making it easier to identify and remember people.

> **Tip**
>
> To use Windows Contacts on its own, click the Start button, point to All Programs, and then click Windows Contacts.

Adding a Contact in Windows Mail | Reference Window

- Click Tools on the menu bar, and then click Windows Contacts.
- Click the New Contact button on the toolbar.
- Enter contact information in the Properties dialog box for the new contact.
- Click OK.

or

- Click an e-mail message in the message list.
- Click Tools on the menu bar, and then click Add Sender to Contacts.
- Enter contact information in the Properties dialog box for the new contact.
- Click OK.

You'll show David how to use Windows Contacts in Windows Mail to add a new contact.

To add a contact:

1. Click the **Contacts** button ▣ on the Windows Mail toolbar. The Contacts window opens, listing your contacts. Because you sent an e-mail to yourself, you are already listed in the Contacts window.

2. Click the **New Contact** button on the toolbar. The Properties dialog box opens to the Name and E-mail tab. See Figure 4-26.

Figure 4-26 | **Entering contact information**

enter an e-mail
address, and then
click the Add button

▶ 3. Type **David** in the First text box, press the **Tab** key twice, and then type **Sanchez** in the Last text box.

▶ 4. Click the **Nickname** text box, and then type **David Sanchez**.

▶ 5. Click the **E-mail** text box, type **DavidSanchez@entree.net**, click the **Add** button, and then click the **OK** button.

▶ 6. Click **David Sanchez** in the list to view his detailed contact information. See Figure 4-27.

Tip

If you often send e-mail to a standard group of people, create a contact group by clicking the New Contact Group button on the Windows Contacts toolbar.

▶ **7.** Click the **Close** button [X] to close the Contacts window.

You're finished showing David how to use Windows Mail to exchange e-mail. Next, you want to help him manage his schedule with the Windows Calendar.

Managing Your Schedule with Windows Calendar

Windows Calendar is another tool available in Windows Mail and on its own. You use it to schedule appointments, track tasks, and stay on top of deadlines. Windows Calendar also lets you schedule recurring events, such as weekly staff meetings, and set reminders so you don't miss an important appointment. When you schedule an event, Windows Calendar blocks out the time in your schedule, helping you avoid scheduling conflicts.

You can also use Windows Calendar to subscribe to Web calendars, which you can share with others who have Web access. Windows Calendar works with calendars in the iCalendar format (.ics). Many major sports teams, television and radio shows, and academic institutions offer calendars in this format on the Internet that include events such as games, shows, lectures, and other special events. When you subscribe to one of these calendars, you can set how often you want to update your personal calendar with the subscription calendar's event dates.

In Windows Calendar, you can enter either appointments or tasks. Appointments take place at a specified time and place and have a duration, such as one hour or all day. Tasks are activities you want to complete within a particular period of time. Tasks have start and end dates, but don't have to be performed at a certain time.

Because David works so often at his computer, he is ready to use an electronic calendar full time. You'll show him how to start Windows Calendar, schedule an appointment, add a task to his task list, and then personalize the view of his calendar.

Starting Windows Calendar

Tip

To use Windows Calendar on its own, click the Start button, point to All Programs, and then click Windows Calendar.

As with Windows Contacts, you can start Windows Calendar on its own from the Start menu or when you're working in Windows Mail.

To start Windows Calendar:

▶ **1.** Click the **Windows Calendar** button 🗓 on the Windows Mail toolbar. The Windows Calendar window opens, showing your schedule for the day. See Figure 4-28.

Figure 4-28 ▶ **Windows Calendar**

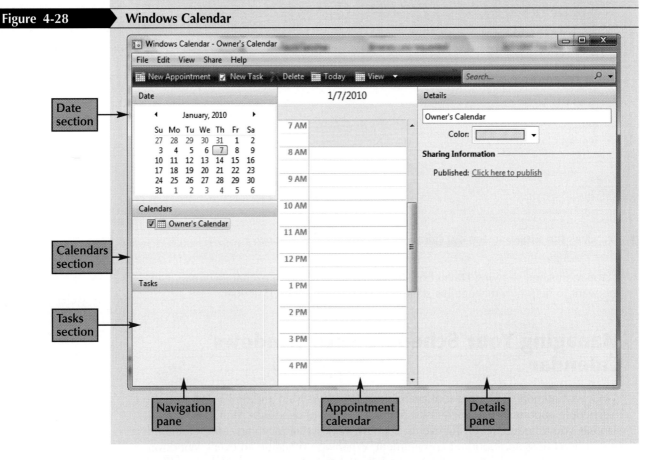

Figure 4-29 describes the parts of the Windows Calendar window.

Parts of the Windows Calendar window ◄ **Figure 4-29**

Calendar section	Description
Navigation pane	The Navigation pane includes a monthly calendar showing today's date, a list of calendars you are using (including Web calendars you subscribe to), and a list of tasks.
Date section	This part of the Navigation pane displays a calendar for the current month, with today's date highlighted. You can select another date in the month by clicking it. You can also use the left or right arrow keys to open calendar pages for other months.
Calendars section	This part of the Navigation pane shows the calendars in use on your computer. You can keep calendars for each user or only for yourself. You can also maintain calendars for different purposes, such as a professional and a social calendar.
Tasks section	This part of the Navigation pane shows your task list, including completed and pending tasks.
Appointment calendar	The middle pane shows a calendar in a daily, weekly, or monthly format. Click the View button arrow on the toolbar to change the view of the appointment calendar.
Details pane	The Details pane shows details about the selected calendar, appointment, or task.

Now that you've started Windows Calendar, you can use it to schedule appointments and track tasks.

Scheduling Appointments and Creating Tasks

When you schedule appointments, you can specify that they are recurring, such as training that takes place once a week, sales meetings scheduled once a month, or birthdays and other annual events. You can also set a reminder message to appear minutes, hours, days, or weeks before the scheduled appointment.

Scheduling an Appointment in Windows Calendar | Reference Window

- Click the New Appointment button on the Windows Calendar toolbar.
- Type a description of the appointment, and then press the Enter key.
- In the Location box, enter the location of the appointment.
- If you have more than one calendar, click the Calendar arrow, and then select the calendar you want to use to schedule the appointment.
- If you are scheduling an all-day appointment, click the All-day appointment check box.
- In the Start and End date boxes, click the arrow, and then click a date on the calendar.
- In the Start and End time boxes, click the arrows to change the times, or click to select the times and then enter the times you want.
- To specify a recurring appointment, click the Recurrence arrow, and then click how often the appointment recurs.
- To set a reminder, click the Reminder arrow, and then click an amount of time.
- To invite someone to the event, click an e-mail address in the Invite box, and then click the Invite button. If the e-mail address does not appear in the list, type an e-mail address in the Attendees box and press the Enter key, or click the Attendees button to select an address from your Contacts list.

The first appointment David wants to schedule is the weekly Wednesday morning staff meeting, which is usually an hour long. He also wants to receive a reminder message 15 minutes before a meeting.

To schedule an appointment:

▶ **1.** Click the **New Appointment** button on the toolbar. An appointment block is highlighted in the appointment calendar, and the Details pane shows the details you can enter for the new appointment. See Figure 4-30.

Figure 4-30	Scheduling an appointment

▶ **2.** Type **Weekly staff meeting** as the appointment description, and then press the **Enter** key. The new Weekly staff meeting entry appears in the Appointments calendar.

▶ **3.** In the Details pane, click in the **Location** box, and then type **West conference room**.

▶ **4.** Click the **Start** arrow, and then click the date for this coming Wednesday on the calendar.

▶ **5.** Click the **hour** value in the Start time text box, and then type **9** so the time appears as 9:00 AM.

   Trouble? If the minutes display a value other than 00, click the minutes and type 00. If the time is followed by PM, click PM and then type A to change this to AM.

▶ **6.** Click the **Recurrence** arrow, and then click **Weekly** to specify that this is a recurring appointment.

▶ **7.** Click the **Reminder** arrow, and then click **15 minutes** to set a reminder to appear 15 minutes before each staff meeting. A dialog box opens asking if you want to change the entire series. This means you will receive a reminder before every staff meeting.

▶ **8.** Click the **Change the series** button.

You've created an appointment for David's weekly staff meeting, and specified that Windows Calendar display a reminder message 15 minutes before the meeting. When David receives the reminder, he can dismiss it or have Windows Calendar remind him again in five minutes. (Dismissing a reminder means you won't be reminded again until the next occurrence of the appointment.)

Creating a task is similar to creating an appointment. When you create a task, you can assign it a priority and also set a reminder message to appear on a specified date.

To prepare for the next weekly staff meeting, David wants to present a new slate of tours to the Canadian Rockies. He's running out of time to finish it, so this task has a high priority. He also wants to be reminded about this task on its due date. You'll show him how to add this task to the Tasks list.

To create a task:

▶ **1.** Click the **New Task** button on the toolbar. A new task appears in the Task list and the Details pane shows the details you can enter for the new task. See Figure 4-31.

Creating a task ◀ **Figure 4-31**

▶ **2.** Type **Prepare list of new Canadian tours**, and then press the **Enter** key. The new task is listed in the Tasks section of the Navigation pane.

▶ **3.** In the Details pane, click the **Priority** arrow, and then click **High** to assign this task a high priority.

▶ **4.** Click the **Due date** button, and then click this coming Wednesday in the calendar.

▶ **5.** Click the **Reminder** arrow, and then click **On date**. Windows Calendar will send you a reminder on Wednesday indicating that the list of Canadian tours is due. See Figure 4-32.

Figure 4-32 ▶ **Completed task**

Besides maintaining calendars on your own computer, you can subscribe to Web calendars. If you want to share your appointments with others, you can publish your calendar.

Sharing a Calendar

Recall that many organizations, including sports teams and television shows, offer Web calendars that include special events. You can subscribe to one of these calendars and then update your personal calendar with the subscription calendar's event dates. To see a list of calendars you can subscribe to online, click Share on the Windows Calendar toolbar, click Subscribe, and then click the Windows Calendar Web site link.

You can also publish your own calendar on the Web so that others can see and share it. If you want, you can publish your personal schedule with password protection, so that you can choose who can access and view it. You can also share your calendar by printing it in a daily, weekly, or monthly format.

Reference Window | **Subscribing to a Web Calendar**

- Click the Subscribe button on the Windows Calendar toolbar.
- In the first wizard dialog box, enter the address of the Web calendar you want to use, and then click the Next button.
- The next steps vary depending on the calendar you choose. Follow the instructions in the wizard, and then click the Finish button to subscribe to the calendar.

Publishing a Web Calendar

- Click Share on the Windows Calendar menu bar, and then click Publish.
- In the Calendar name text box, type the name of the calendar you want to share.
- In the Location to publish calendar text box, enter the URL of the Web site or other location where you want to publish the calendar, or click the Browse button to navigate to the location.
- Click the Automatically publish changes made to this calendar check box if you want new appointments and other changes to appear on the published calendar.
- Click the Notes, Reminders, or Tasks check boxes to include those details on the published calendar.
- Click the Publish button.

Another way to share a calendar is to print it. You can print the calendar using one of many formats: Day, Work Week, Week, or Month. The Work Week option prints only Monday through Friday, while the Week option includes weekends. David wants to print his calendar using the Work Week format.

To print a calendar:

▶ 1. Click **File** on the menu bar, and then click **Print**. The Print dialog box opens. See Figure 4-33.

Printing a calendar ◀ Figure 4-33

▶ 2. In the Print Style box, click **Work Week**.

▶ 3. In the Print Range section, click the **End** arrow, and then use the calendar to select the date one week from today.

▶ 4. Click the **OK** button to print the calendar.

▶ 5. Close all open windows.

Now that you've finished exploring the Internet and e-mail on David's computer, you should restore the computer to its original settings.

Restoring Your Settings

If you are working in a computer lab or a computer other than your own, complete the steps in this section to restore the original settings on your computer.

To restore your settings:

▶ **1.** Start Internet Explorer, click the **Tools** button, click **Delete Browsing History**, click the **Delete all** button, and then click the **Yes** button.

▶ **2.** Click the **Add to Favorites** button ⭐ on the Favorites Center toolbar, and then click **Organize Favorites**.

▶ **3.** Click the **Windows Vista** folder, click the **Delete** button, and then click the **Yes** button. Click the **Colorado Travel** folder, click the **Delete** button, and then click the **Yes** button. Click the **Close** button to close the Organize Folders dialog box.

▶ **4.** Click the **Close** button ✖ to close the Favorites Center.

▶ **5.** Close Internet Explorer.

▶ **6.** Start Windows Mail, click the **Itinerary you requested** message in the Inbox, and then click the **Delete** button ✖ on the Windows Mail toolbar. Do the same to delete the **Re: Test e-mail** message.

▶ **7.** Click the **Sent Items** folder in the Folders list, select the **Test e-mail**, **Re: Test e-mail**, and **Itinerary you requested** messages, and then click the **Delete** button ✖ .

▶ **8.** Right-click the **Deleted Items** folder in the Folders list, click **Empty 'Deleted Items' folder**, and then click the **Yes** button.

▶ **9.** Click the **Contacts** button 🔳 on the Windows Mail toolbar. Select **your name** and **David Sanchez** in the list of contacts, right-click the selection, click **Delete** on the shortcut menu, and then click the **Yes** button. Close the Windows Contacts window.

▶ **10.** Click the **Windows Calendar** button 📅 on the Windows Mail toolbar. Right-click the appointment you added to the calendar, click **Delete** on the shortcut menu, and then click the **Delete the series** button. Right-click the task you added to the Tasks list, and then click **Delete** on the shortcut menu.

▶ **11.** Close all open windows.

Review | **Session 4.2 Quick Check**

1. A(n) _____ is a simple text document that you can compose and send using Windows Mail.
2. Identify the user name and the e-mail server name in the following e-mail address: HalWilson@chambers.net.
3. True or False. You can send messages to anyone on the Internet or network, even if they don't have their computers turned on.
4. Explain the purpose of the Sent Items folder in Windows Mail.
5. Why should you open e-mail file attachments only from people you know and trust?
6. True or False. You can open Windows Contacts when you are working in Windows Mail or you can open it from the Start menu.
7. In Windows Calendar, you can enter appointments or _____ .

Tutorial Summary | Review

In this tutorial, you explored the structure of the Internet and the role of the Web. You learned how to use Internet Explorer to access Web pages and navigate with links and other tools. You used the Internet Explorer Favorites list to maintain a list of Web pages you visit often, and you learned how to print and save Web pages. You also explored e-mail technology to learn how e-mail works. You sent and received e-mail messages, replied to messages, and sent an e-mail message with a file attachment. Finally, you used Windows Contacts and Windows Calendar to manage your contacts, appointments, and tasks.

Key Terms

broadband connection
browser
copyright
dial-up connection
digital cable
digital subscriber
    line (DSL)
domain name
electronic mail (e-mail)
e-mail account
e-mail address
e-mail message
e-mail program
e-mail server
fair use
Favorites list

home page
hyperlink
Hypertext Transfer
    Protocol (HTTP)
intellectual property rights
Internet
Internet Protocol (IP)
    address
Internet service
    provider (ISP)
link
network
protocol
search engine
store-and-forward
    technology

tabbed browsing
uniform resource
    locator (URL)
user ID
user name
virus
Web
Web directory
Web page
Web server
Web site
wireless connection
World Wide Web

Practice the skills you learned in the tutorial.

For a list of Data Files in the Review folder, see page 157.

You already showed David how to conduct research on tours in Colorado for low-mobility travelers. He also needs information about accessible travel in the state of Washington. Some of his clients want to use wheelchairs or scooters on hiking trails, and then fish on a lake or stream. You'll use Internet Explorer to research this information. Complete the following steps:

1. Start Internet Explorer, and go to the Windows Vista Online Companion Web page (*www.course.com/np/vista*).
2. Click the Review link.
3. Open the Washington State Accessible Outdoor Recreation Guide Web page on a new tab by pressing the Ctrl key and clicking the Washington State Parks link on the Online Companion Web page.
4. Click a link on this page to find more information about accessible hiking trails in coastal Washington. Find at least one location that provides accessible fishing for low-mobility people.
5. Return to the Online Companion Web page, press Ctrl, and then click the Accessible Trails link to open that Web page on a new tab.
6. In the Washington State Accessible Trails section, click a few links to learn about trails in various parts of Washington State that are accessible to wheelchairs and scooters. Do the same in the Other Links on Accessibility section. Find at least two pages that provide information that people in wheelchairs and scooters can use to access wilderness fishing spots.
7. Use the History list or other Internet Explorer tools to navigate to a Web page you think will be especially useful to Entrée Tours, and then add it your Favorites list.
8. Print the first page of a Web page you added to your Favorites list.
9. Start Windows Mail and create an e-mail message. Enter your e-mail address in the To box, your instructor's e-mail address in the Cc box, and the following text in the Subject box: **Best spots for Entrée Tours in Washington State**.
10. In the message area, write a message describing the best places in Washington State for disabled and low-mobility travelers, based on your research.
11. Attach the **Washington Itinerary** file to the message. (This file is stored in the Tutorial.04\Review folder provided with your Data Files.)
12. Send the message, and then add your e-mail address and your instructor's e-mail address to the Contacts list.
13. Add an appointment to Windows Calendar to meet with David at Entrée Tours today for 30 minutes. Set a reminder to appear five minutes before the appointment. Add yourself and your instructor as invitees. Then print the calendar using the Day view.
14. Restore your computer by clearing the History list in Internet Explorer, deleting the Web pages you added to the Favorites list, deleting the e-mails you sent and received, emptying the Deleted Items folder, deleting yourself and your instructor from the Contacts list, and deleting the appointment you created on the Windows Calendar.
15. Close Internet Explorer and Windows Mail.
16. Submit the results of the preceding steps to your instructor, either in printed or electronic form, as requested.

| Apply | | Case Problem 1 |

Use the skills you learned in the tutorial to conduct research for an organization promoting astronomy for kids.

There are no Data Files needed for this Case Problem.

Supernova Center Gordon Bernhardt is the director of the Supernova Center, a non-profit organization in Santa Fe, New Mexico, that promotes astronomy and planetary science for kids from kindergarten through eighth grade. Gordon wants to take advantage of the astronomy information posted on the Web by national science organizations and compile it for science teachers. Recently, Gordon hired you to help provide outreach to educators. To prepare for an upcoming presentation at an educators conference, you want to pull together some innovative ideas for teaching astronomy in the classroom. Complete the following steps:

1. Start Internet Explorer, and go to the Windows Vista Online Companion Web page (*www.course.com/np/vista*).
2. Click the Case1 link. Maximize the Internet Explorer window.
3. On new tabs, open the four astronomy Web pages by clicking the links for Astronomy for Kids – 1, Astronomy for Kids – 2, Starchild Learning Center, and Windows to the Universe.
4. Click links and use the Internet Explorer tools to find three Web pages that provide ideas for teaching astronomy in the classroom.
5. Save the three Web pages you found in Step 4 in your Favorites list in a folder named Astronomy.
6. Pin the Favorites Center to the Internet Explorer window, if necessary, so that the Favorites list stays open. Open the Astronomy folder in the Favorites list to display the Web pages you found.
7. With the Internet Explorer window displaying the contents of the Astronomy folder and at least four tabs containing Astronomy Web pages suitable for school-age children, press the Alt+Print Screen keys to capture an image of the Internet Explorer window. Start Paint, paste the screen image in a new Paint file, and then save the file as **Astronomy Web pages** in the Tutorial.04\Case1 folder provided with your Data Files.
8. Start Windows Mail and create an e-mail message addressed to you and your instructor. Enter the following text in the Subject box: **Ideas for astronomy lessons**.
9. In the message area, write a message describing one of the ideas you found for teaching astronomy to students in grades kindergarten through eighth grade.
10. Attach the **Astronomy Web pages** file to the message, and then send it.
11. Add an appointment to Windows Calendar to make a presentation to the educators conference one month from today. Set a reminder to appear two days before the conference. Add yourself and your instructor as invitees. Then print the calendar showing the presentation appointment using the Week view.
12. Restore your computer by clearing the History list in Internet Explorer, deleting the folder you added to the Favorites list, deleting the e-mails you sent and received, emptying the Deleted Items folder, and deleting the appointment you created on the Windows Calendar.
13. Close Internet Explorer and Windows Mail.
14. Submit the results of the preceding steps to your instructor, either in printed or electronic form, as requested.

| Apply | | Case Problem 2 |

Use the skills you learned in the tutorial to research museum services for an art restoration company.

There are no Data Files needed for this Case Problem.

Leroux Fine Art Restoration Evelyn Leroux is the owner of Leroux Fine Art Restoration, a company in Philadelphia, Pennsylvania, that provides expert restoration services to authenticate, conserve, and scientifically study paintings. Her specialty is early American portrait painting. Evelyn often works with the conservation departments of Philadelphia museums to restore paintings and is interested in expanding her company to work with museums around the United States. As her marketing and sales assistant, you offer to research the restoration services provided by museums outside of Philadelphia. Complete the following steps:

1. Start Internet Explorer, and go to the Windows Vista Companion Web page (*www. course.com/np/vista*).

2. Click the Case2 link. Maximize the Internet Explorer window.

3. On additional tabs, open the three museum Web pages by clicking the links for the Metropolitan Museum of Art, the Minneapolis Institute of Arts, and Smithsonian Museums.

4. Click links and use the Internet Explorer tools to find at least one Web page for each museum that describes its restoration or conservation services. For the Metropolitan Museum of Art, you can access the Objects Conservation page from the Features page in the Works of Art category. For the Minneapolis Institute of Arts, restoration is considered a online educational resource. (*Hint*: Look for a "Restoring a Master-work" link.) For the Smithsonian, look for links to the Museum Conservation Institute, which is part of Smithsonian Research.

5. Save the Web pages you found in Step 4 in your Favorites list in a folder named Restoration.

✛**EXPLORE** 6. On the Web site for the Metropolitan Museum of Art, find a page that provides the terms and conditions and frequently asked questions (FAQ) about copying images. (*Hint*: Look for an FAQs link at the bottom of the main page, and then click a link describing Web site terms and conditions.) Save this page as a single HTML file named **Met FAQ** in the Tutorial.04\Case2 folder provided with your Data Files. (*Hint*: Click the Page button on the Internet Explorer toolbar, click Save As, click the Save as type arrow, click Webpage, HTML only (*.htm; *.html), enter the filename, and then click the Save button.)

✛**EXPLORE** 7. On the Metropolitan Museum of Art Web site, find a portrait of George Washington. (*Hint*: On the main page, click the Permanent Collection link.) Right-click the image, click Save Picture As on the shortcut menu, and then save the image as a file named **Washington** and store it in the Tutorial.04\Case2 folder provided with your Data Files.

8. Start Windows Mail and create an e-mail message addressed to you and your instructor. Enter the following text in the Subject box: **American portraits**.

9. In the message area, write a message listing examples of the types of art objects the Metropolitan Museum, the Minneapolis Institute of Arts, or the Smithsonian restores.

10. Attach the **Met FAQ** and **Washington** files to the message, and then send it.

11. Add two tasks to Windows Calendar to research restoration services at museums and to write a report on your findings. Set the priority for both tasks to Medium. Set the Start and Due date for the research task to today. Set the Start date for the report task to today and the Due date to one week from today. Set a reminder for the report task to the day before the due date.

12. Mark the research task as completed, and then print the calendar showing both tasks using Month view.

13. Restore your computer by clearing the History list in Internet Explorer, deleting the folder you added to the Favorites list, deleting the e-mails you sent and received, emptying the Deleted Items folder, and deleting the tasks you created on the Windows Calendar.

14. Close Internet Explorer and Windows Mail.

15. Submit the results of the preceding steps to your instructor, either in printed or electronic form, as requested.

Challenge	Case Problem 3

Go beyond what you've learned to help a start-up magazine find information about gardening in the upper Midwest.

There are no Data Files needed for this Case Problem.

Northern Gardening Magazine The Northern Gardening Magazine is a new monthly periodical published in St. Paul, Minnesota, for gardeners in the upper midwestern states of Michigan, Wisconsin, Minnesota, North Dakota, and South Dakota. Michael Nilsson is the publisher and a master gardener. He hired you as his director of communications, and asked you to find Web sites providing basic information for the readers of Northern Gardening Magazine. Complete the following steps:

1. Start Internet Explorer, and go to the Windows Vista Online Companion Web page (*www.course.com/np/vista*).

2. Click the Case3 link. Maximize the Internet Explorer window.

3. On additional tabs, open the gardening Web pages by clicking the links for the UM Extension, the UW Extension, and the Minnesota Department of Natural Resources.

4. Click links and use the Internet Explorer tools to find at least one Web page for each site that recommends gardening techniques or plants for residents of the upper Midwest. (*Hint*: If the Web site provides a Search tool, type **gardening** in the Search box.)

⊕ EXPLORE 5. Save the group of open tabs in your Favorites list as a tab group named Gardening. (*Hint*: Click the Add to Favorites button, click Add Tab Group to Favorites, name the group Gardening, and then click the Add button.)

⊕ EXPLORE 6. On the Web site for the Minnesota Department of Natural Resources, find a page explaining how to landscape with native plants. Save this page as a single HTML file named **Native Plants** in the Tutorial.04\Case3 folder provided with your Data Files. (*Hint*: Click the Page button on the Internet Explorer toolbar, click Save As, click the Save as type arrow, click Webpage, HTML only (*.htm; *.html), enter the filename, and then click the Save button.)

⊕ EXPLORE 7. On the main Web page for the UW Extension agriculture topics, click the Urban Horticulture link, and then click a link for Wisconsin Garden Facts. On the Wisconsin Garden Facts page, look for files you can download. For example, look for a WORD or PDF link next to the name of an article. (PDFs, or Portable Document Files, are files containing text and images that you can often download from a Web site and read with a program called Adobe Reader. DOC files are Microsoft Word documents, which you can also open in WordPad.) Right-click the link to the file, click Save Target As, and then save the file as **Wisconsin Horticulture** in the Tutorial.04\Case3 folder provided with your Data Files.

8. Start Windows Mail and create an e-mail message addressed to you and your instructor. Enter the following text in the Subject box: **Midwestern gardening**.

9. In the message area, write a message listing a few types of plants that can be grown in the upper Midwest.

10. Attach the **Native Plants** and **Wisconsin Horticulture** files to the message, and then send the message.

11. Add one task to Windows Calendar to research gardening in Michigan tomorrow. Add an appointment to meet with Michael to discuss next month's issue of Northern Gardening Magazine two days from today at 1:00 in the afternoon. Set a reminder to appear the same day as the task. Set another reminder to appear 30 minutes before the meeting. Print the calendar showing the task and appointment using the Work Week view.

12. Restore your computer by clearing the History list in Internet Explorer, deleting the folder you added to the Favorites list, deleting the e-mails you sent and received, emptying the Deleted Items folder, and deleting the appointment and task you created on the Windows Calendar.

13. Close Internet Explorer and Windows Mail.

14. Submit the results of the preceding steps to your instructor, either in printed or electronic form, as requested.

| Challenge | **Case Problem 4** |

Go beyond what you've learned to help a booster club promote women's college volleyball.

There are no Data Files needed for this Case Problem.

Volleyball Boosters   Volleyball Boosters is a club in Kalamazoo, Michigan, that supports and promotes women's college volleyball teams at small American colleges. Felicia Andrade, the club president, recently hired you as a part-time assistant. You help Felicia write the club newsletter and organize promotional events. Felicia wants you to visit college Web sites periodically to make sure they are promoting their women's volleyball teams. Complete the following steps:

1. Start Internet Explorer, and go to the Windows Vista Online Companion Web page (*www.course.com/np/vista*).

2. Click the Case4 link. Maximize the Internet Explorer window.

3. On additional tabs, open the college Web pages by clicking the links for Hiram College, Kalamazoo College, Mount Holyoke College, and Northland College.

4. Click links and use the Internet Explorer tools to find at least one Web page for each college that describes or reports on the women's volleyball team.

⊕ **EXPLORE**   5. Save the group of open tabs in your Favorites list as a tab group named Volleyball. (*Hint*: Click the Add to Favorites button, click Add Tab Group to Favorites, name the group Volleyball, and then click the Add button.)

⊕ **EXPLORE**   6. On the Web site for any of the four colleges, find a schedule for the current or upcoming volleyball season. Click the Print button arrow, click Print Preview, and examine the schedule image. Using the buttons on the Print Preview toolbar, adjust the image of the schedule so that it will print on one page. Then click the Print Document button on the Print Preview toolbar to print the schedule.

⊕ EXPLORE

7. Close the Print Preview window, click the Page button on the Internet Explorer tool-bar, and then click Send Page by E-mail. Address the message to you and your instructor. Enter the following text in the Subject box: **Volleyball Schedule**. Then send the e-mail message.

⊕ EXPLORE

8. Start Windows Mail and click the Send/Receive button to receive the e-mail. Click the Volleyball Schedule message in the message list, click File on the menu bar, and then click Save As. Save the e-mail message as **Volleyball Schedule** in the Tutorial. 04\Case4 folder provided with your Data Files.

⊕ EXPLORE

9. Start Windows Calendar, open the Subscribe to a Calendar dialog box, and then visit the Windows Calendar Web site to find a volleyball calendar. With the appropriate Web page open in Internet Explorer, press the Alt+Print Screen keys to capture an image of the Internet Explorer window. Start Paint, paste the screen image in a new Paint file, and then save the file as **Volleyball Calendar** in the Tutorial.04\Case4 folder provided with your Data Files.

10. Restore your computer by clearing the History list in Internet Explorer, deleting the folder you added to the Favorites list, and deleting the e-mails you sent and received.

11. Close Internet Explorer and Windows Mail.

12. Submit the results of the preceding steps to your instructor, either in printed or electronic form, as requested.

Review | **Quick Check Answers**

Session 4.1

1. The Web is a service that the Internet provides. Whereas the Internet is a collection of networks connected by communication media such as fiber-optic cables and wireless connections, the Web is a collection of documents connected by links.
2. Web site
3. False
4. its home page
5. URL, or uniform resource locator
6. Type the URL in the Address bar or click a link on a Web page.
7. Using the Back button, Forward button, Recent Pages list, or History list
8. False

Session 4.2

1. e-mail message
2. HalWilson is the user name and chambers.net is the server name.
3. True
4. It contains copies of the e-mail messages you sent.
5. Some people spread viruses in e-mail attachments.
6. True
7. tasks

Ending Data Files

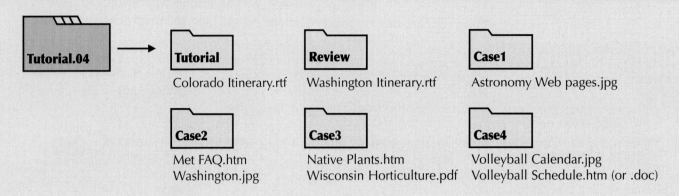

Tutorial.04 →

Tutorial
Colorado Itinerary.rtf

Review
Washington Itinerary.rtf

Case1
Astronomy Web pages.jpg

Case2
Met FAQ.htm
Washington.jpg

Case3
Native Plants.htm
Wisconsin Horticulture.pdf

Case4
Volleyball Calendar.jpg
Volleyball Schedule.htm (or .doc)

Objectives

Session 5.1
- Set up Windows Firewall and Windows Update
- Protect your computer from viruses and other malicious software
- Use Windows Defender to protect against spyware
- Manage Windows Mail security

Session 5.2
- Manage Microsoft Internet Explorer security
- Set up user accounts
- Control access to your computer
- Secure and share folders

Protecting Your Computer

Managing Computer Security

Case | Presto Global Translators

A few years ago, Curt Mickelson founded Presto Global Translators in Ithaca, New York. Presto translates written material to and from English and dozens of other languages for corporate clients around the world. Curt has hired and trained experienced translators, proofreaders, and quality assurance managers in the United States. His staff works with native speakers in other countries who specialize in technology, law, finance, and other fields so that Presto can offer top-notch translation teams of language, writing, and subject matter experts.

Presto's challenge is to keep pace with the changing terminology in these fields. Curt regularly evaluates new dictionaries and glossaries, both print and online, and maintains lists of terms that have special meaning in particular industries. A recent concern is the security of Presto's computers. Many of Curt's translators work at their client's offices, using notebook computers running Windows Vista. Although these translators can access the Internet with their computers, they can't usually connect to the Presto network, where an administrator oversees security. Instead, they must take advantage of the security tools in Windows Vista to prevent problems stemming from viruses, spyware, and other types of harmful software. Curt recently hired you to support the Presro Global translation staff. One of your first duties is to investigate the security features in Windows Vista and show Curt how to use them to address security threats.

In this tutorial, you explore the tools provided in the Windows Security Center, including Windows Firewall and Windows Update. You also learn how to set up Windows Vista to work with antivirus software. In addition, you learn how to use other security practices, including setting up user accounts, and securing and sharing folders. You also examine Microsoft Internet Explorer security settings so that you can use the Internet safely.

Starting Data Files

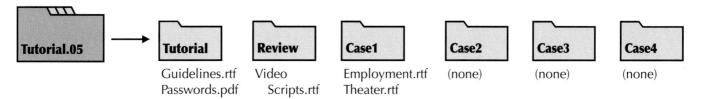

Tutorial.05 → Tutorial | Review | Case1 | Case2 | Case3 | Case4

Tutorial
Guidelines.rtf
Passwords.pdf

Review
Video
Scripts.rtf

Case1
Employment.rtf
Theater.rtf

Case2
(none)

Case3
(none)

Case4
(none)

Session 5.1

Using the Windows Vista Security Center

Many of the most improved features in Windows Vista focus on security—keeping your computer safe from threats such as harmful software, unsolicited e-mail, and invasions of your privacy. When you connect to the Internet, send and receive e-mail, or share your computer or files with others, your computer is vulnerable to harm from others who might attempt to steal your personal information, damage your files, or interrupt your work. You need to use the Windows Vista security tools and other techniques to defend against these threats and protect your computer effectively.

Harmful software (also called malicious software, or malware) includes **viruses**, which are programs that are attached to a file and run when you open the file. A virus can harm your computer by changing your desktop settings, for example, displaying an annoying image, or deleting files on your hard disk. Viruses are often spread by e-mail and run when you open an e-mail attachment or the e-mail message itself. In contrast, another type of malware called a **worm** does not have to be attached to a file—it can spread and run by itself. Worms are also usually distributed by e-mail. People who create and send malware are called **hackers**, a generic term that refers to anyone who intends to access a computer system without permission. (Hackers with criminal intent are sometimes called **crackers**.) Hackers can also invade your privacy by accessing your computer via the Internet to find information such as passwords and financial account numbers. Hackers sometimes access your computer using **spyware**, software that secretly gathers information about you and your computer actions, including sensitive information, and passes it to advertisers and others.

If you are working on a computer that is connected to a network, a network administrator probably defends the network against security threats such as viruses, worms, spyware, and hackers. Otherwise, if you are working on a home computer, for example, you should take advantage of the security features that Windows Vista provides. Windows Vista offers the following programs and options that help you keep your computer secure:

- **Security Center**: Use this Control Panel tool to manage your firewall, antivirus software, and Windows updates. All of these topics are covered in this session.
- **Windows Defender**: Use this program to prevent some types of malware from infecting your computer. You'll use Windows Defender later in this session.
- **User Account Control**: This service displays a dialog box requesting your permission to install software or open programs that could harm your computer or make it vulnerable to security breaches. You'll examine User Account Control later in this tutorial.
- **Back Up and Restore**: Use these tools to back up your files and settings regularly so that you can recover your files if they are damaged by malware or hardware problems.

The first place to go to secure your computer is the Security Center, a Control Panel tool that helps you manage security from a single window. You can manage the security settings of the features listed in Figure 5-1 when you work with the Security Center.

Security Center features | Figure 5-1

Security Feature	Description
Windows Firewall	Windows Firewall monitors and restricts communication with the Internet, which helps protect your computer from viruses and hackers. Before a program can send or receive information via the Internet, Windows Firewall must allow it to do so.
Windows Update	This feature checks for the latest Windows updates on the Microsoft Web site, and then downloads and installs the updates for you. Because Windows updates often include security enhancements, using this feature helps to make sure that your computer is secure against most current threats.
Malware protection	Antivirus software is your best protection against viruses, worms, and other types of harmful software. If you have antivirus software, Windows reminds you to use it regularly to scan your computer for virus infections and to monitor e-mail. If you do not have antivirus software, Windows lists vendors that provide it.
Other security settings	Security Center also checks that your Web browser is using appropriate security settings and whether the User Account Control is turned on to help prevent malware from damaging your system.

The features listed in Figure 5-1 are considered essential—you should turn on these features to keep your computer secure. If Windows detects a problem with any of these security essentials, such as when your firewall is turned off, a Security Center icon, such as 🛡 appears in the notification area of your taskbar along with a message. You can click the message or double-click the icon to open the Security Center and find out how to address the problem. Otherwise, you can open the Security Center from the Control Panel.

You'll start showing Curt how to use the security features in Windows Vista by opening the Security Center.

To open the Security Center:

▶ **1.** Click the **Start** button 🪟 on the taskbar, and then click **Control Panel**. The Control Panel window opens.

▶ **2.** If the Control Panel opens in Classic view, double-click **Security Center** to open the Windows Security Center window. If the Control Panel opens in Category view, click **Security**, and then click **Security Center**.

▶ **3.** If necessary, maximize the Windows Security Center window and then click each heading to expand the sections. See Figure 5-2.

Figure 5-2   Windows Security Center window

Leave the Windows Security Center window open to perform the tasks described in the following sections.

Managing Windows Firewall

Windows Firewall is software that serves as a barrier between your computer and a network or the Internet. As shown in Figure 5-3, it checks information coming from the Internet and either blocks it from your computer or allows it to pass, depending on your settings. In this way, Windows Firewall prevents unauthorized users from accessing your computer and is the first line of defense against malware.

How Windows Firewall protects your computer ◄ Figure 5-3

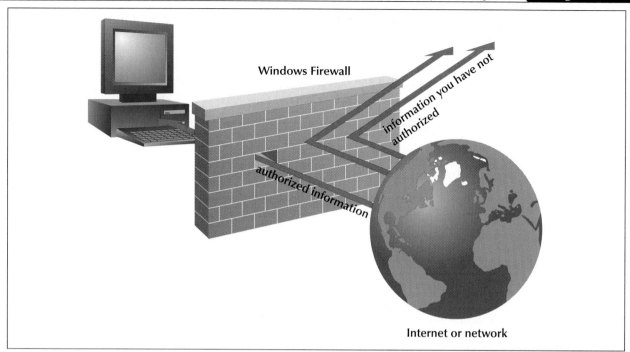

Windows Firewall

information you have not authorized

authorized information

Internet or network

Understanding What a Firewall Can Do | InSight

A firewall defends against malware trying to gain access to your computer by monitoring your network and Internet connections. However, a firewall does not scan e-mail, so it cannot detect viruses sent in e-mail messages (a common way to spread viruses). Furthermore, a firewall can't protect you from e-mail scams, called phishing, that deceive you into revealing private information, such as passwords. To protect against e-mail viruses, use antivirus software. To minimize phishing attempts, use the Internet Explorer phishing filter. (Both topics are covered later in this tutorial.)

Windows Firewall is turned on by default, so it doesn't allow communications with most programs via the Internet or a network. (One exception is Core Networking, which helps you connect to the Internet.) When someone tries to connect to your computer from the Internet, Windows Firewall blocks the connection. For example, suppose that you are running an instant-messaging program and exchanging digital photos with a friend. When your friend sends you the first photo file, Windows Firewall detects the communication and opens a dialog box asking if you want to block or allow the connection by the instant-messaging program. If you know that your friend is using the instant-messaging program to send you a file, you can allow, or unblock, the connection. Windows Firewall then adds an **exception** to its list of programs, meaning that it will allow the instant-messaging program to communicate with your computer now and in the future. Instead of turning off Windows Firewall, you can customize it by adding exceptions to its list of programs so that it maintains a level of security that's right for you. You can add a program to the Windows Firewall exception list manually, without waiting for that program to communicate with you.

Adding a Program to the Windows Firewall Exception List

- Click the Start button, click Control Panel, click Security, and then click Windows Firewall.
- In the left pane, click Allow a program through Windows Firewall, and then click the Continue button, if necessary.
- In the Program or port list, click to select a program check box. If a program does not appear in this list, click the Add program button, click a program in the Add a Program dialog box, or click the Browse button to locate and select a program.
- Click the OK button.

You select most of the Windows Firewall settings using the Windows Firewall dialog box. On the General tab of this dialog box, you can select one of three settings:

- **On (recommended)**: This setting is selected by default, meaning that most programs are blocked from communicating through the firewall.
- **Block all incoming connections**: When you connect to a public network, such as in a hotel or airport, you might want to use the Block all incoming connections settings. Windows blocks all programs, informing you when it does, and allows the programs on the exception list.
- **Off (not recommended)**: The only time you should select this setting is when another firewall is running on your computer.

The Windows Firewall dialog box also includes an Exceptions tab, where you specify which programs to allow through the firewall, and the Advanced tab, where you can specify which network connections Windows Firewall should monitor. The recommended setting is to turn on Windows Firewall for all network connections.

Curt often uses Windows Meeting Place, a Windows Vista program that lets you collaborate on documents with others on the Internet or a local network. Before remote meeting attendees can communicate with Curt's computer to let him know they are ready for the meeting, Windows Firewall must allow incoming connections from Windows Meeting Place. First, you'll make sure Windows Firewall is running on Curt's computer, and then you'll show Curt how to add Windows Meeting Place to the exception list so he can meet online without interruption.

If you are performing the following steps in a computer lab, you might not be allowed to change exceptions. Check with your instructor or technical support person to determine whether you can specify Windows Meeting Place as an exception to the Windows Firewall. If you cannot, read but do not perform the following steps.

Tip

Windows Firewall might restrict features in programs that depend on low security settings. If you are having trouble running a program, add it to the exception list to see if that solves your problem.

To verify Windows Firewall is running and add a program to the exception list:

▶ 1. In the left pane of the Windows Security Center window, click **Windows Firewall**. The Windows Firewall window opens. See Figure 5-4. Your settings might differ.

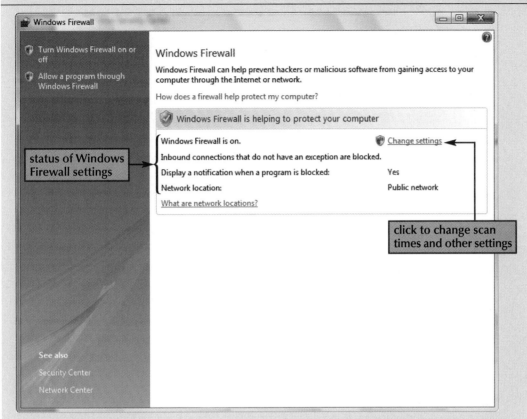

Trouble? If Windows Firewall is turned off or a firewall other than Windows Firewall is running on your computer, this window displays a warning. If the Firewall section of the Windows Security Center window (see Figure 5-2) reports that a firewall is turned on, you can ignore the warning in the Windows Firewall window. Otherwise, turn on Windows Firewall by clicking Use recommended settings, or turn on another firewall according to the manufacturer's instructions.

▶ 2. In the left pane, click **Allow a program through Windows Firewall** to open the Windows Firewall Settings dialog box to the Exceptions tab. See Figure 5-5.

Trouble? If a dialog box opens requesting an administrator password or your permission to continue, make sure you have permission to change Windows Firewall settings (check with your instructor, if necessary), and then enter the password or click the Continue button.

Figure 5-5	Windows Firewall Settings dialog box

Tip

If the program you want to add as an exception does not appear in the Program or port list, click the Add program button and then add any program installed on your computer to the exception list.

▶ **3.** Scroll to the end of the Program or port list, and then click the **Windows Meeting Space** check box, if necessary, to select it.

    Trouble? If you are not allowed to change the exceptions for Windows Firewall, click the Cancel button in the Windows Firewall Settings dialog box and then skip Step 4.

▶ **4.** Click the **OK** button to add Windows Meeting Space to the exception list.

▶ **5.** Close the Windows Firewall window.

Keep in mind that when you add a program to the Windows Firewall exception list, you are making your computer easier to access, and therefore more vulnerable to malware infection. If you add too many programs to the exception list, you minimize the security that Windows Firewall can provide. You should therefore allow an exception only when you really need it, and never make an exception for a program that you don't recognize—it could be a virus or a worm. Finally, be sure to remove an exception when you no longer need it.

Recall that if Windows does not detect a firewall on your computer, it displays a red Security Center icon and a periodic message in the notification area of the taskbar. If you are sure a firewall is running on your computer, click Show me my available options on the Windows Security Center window. (This option is only available if Windows does not detect that a firewall is turned on.) When the Windows Security Center dialog box opens, click I have a firewall solution that I'll monitor myself to stop receiving notifications.

Setting Up Windows Update

An **update** is a change to software that can prevent or repair problems, enhance the security of the computer, or improve the computer's performance. Microsoft Corporation occasionally releases updates to Windows Vista and provides them for download on its Web site. You can look for, download, and install these updates any time you visit the

Microsoft Web site. However, because updates often include critical security repairs and enhancements, Microsoft also makes them available to you through the Windows Update feature.

When you use the Update feature, Windows periodically checks for updates to the operating system from Microsoft, including security updates, critical updates, and service packs. If an update is available, Windows Update can download the software and install it for you. Windows downloads the updates in the background according to a schedule you set, as long as you're connected to the Internet. If you disconnect from the Internet before Windows finishes downloading, Windows continues downloading the next time you connect to the Internet.

You can specify whether Windows automatically downloads only important updates, both important and recommended updates, or does not download automatically at all. Important updates are those you should install to maintain the security and reliability of Windows. Recommended updates usually enhance your computing experience and repair problems that are not considered critical. Microsoft also provides optional updates, which don't apply to all Windows users. For example, if you use a particular piece of hardware, such as a digital music player, Windows might provide an optional update for the player's driver.

In addition to the types of updates you want Windows to download, you can also specify when Windows should install the updates. To notify you that updates are available or that Windows is ready to download or install updates, an icon appears in the notification area of the taskbar. The icon depends on the updating options you select. Figure 5-6 summarizes the download and installation options for Windows Update and the action you can take to download and install the updates.

> **Tip**
>
> To visit the Windows Update Web site and download any type of update, click the Start button, point to All Programs, and then click Windows Update.

Options for downloading and installing updates   Figure 5-6

Option	Notification Icon	Action
Download and install updates automatically	Update icon	Windows performs all the actions. You can point to the Update icon to see a ScreenTip displaying the progress of the download and installation.
Download updates automatically, but install them yourself	Update icon	Click the Update icon to install the updates.
Check for updates, but download and install them yourself	Security Warning icon	Click the Security Warning icon to download the updates, and then click the Update icon to install them.

To view your current update status and settings for Windows Update, you open the Windows Update window from the Security category of the Control Panel. You can also use this window to review your update history by clicking the View update history link.

You recommend that Curt turn on automatic updating for important and recommended updates so he doesn't miss any for Windows Vista. He wants to check for updates every morning at 8:00 while he is typically meeting with his staff. Although he is not using his computer then, it is turned on and connected to the Internet.

As you perform the following steps, note your original settings so you can restore them later.

To set up Windows Updates:

▶ 1. In the left pane of the Windows Security Center window, click **Windows Update**. The Windows Update window opens. See Figure 5-7. Your settings might differ.

Figure 5-7   Windows Update window

2. In the left pane, click **Change settings**. The Change settings dialog box opens. See Figure 5-8.

Figure 5-8   Changing Windows Update settings

▶ **3.** Click the **Install updates automatically (recommended)** option button, if necessary. Selecting this option means that Windows checks for updates according to schedule, and then downloads and installs them for you when they are available.

▶ **4.** In the Install new updates section, click the time button (which appears as 3:00 AM by default), and then click **8:00 AM**.

▶ **5.** If necessary, click the **Include recommended updates when downloading, installing, or notifying me about updates** check box to select it.

▶ **6.** Click the **OK** button.

Trouble? If a dialog box opens requesting an administrator password or your permission to continue, enter the password or click the Continue button.

▶ **7.** Close the Windows Update window.

Now that you know Curt's copy of Windows Vista is up to date, you can turn to protecting his computer from viruses and other types of malware.

Protecting Your Computer from Malware

A virus is a program that replicates itself and attaches to files or programs, usually affects your computer's performance and stability, and sometimes damages or removes files. Viruses are often transmitted through e-mail attachments or downloaded files, but don't spread until you open the attachment or file. In contrast, a worm is harmful computer code that spreads without your interaction. A worm slips from one network connection to another, replicating itself on network computers. As it does, a worm consumes network resources, overwhelming computers until they become slow or unresponsive. Another type of malware related to viruses and worms is a Trojan horse, which is malware that hides inside other programs. These programs are usually legitimate, such as a photo viewing program you download from the Web. When you install the program, however, the Trojan horse infects the operating system, allowing a hacker to access your computer and your personal information. Trojan horses can't spread on their own; they depend on programs, including viruses and worms, to proliferate. Common symptoms of malware are when your computer runs much slower than normal, messages appear unexpectedly, programs start or close on their own, or Windows shuts down suddenly.

Your best protection against harmful software is to use current versions of antivirus software, which scans e-mail messages, attachments, and other files on your computer for viruses, worms, and other types of malware. Antivirus software locates a virus by comparing identifying characteristics of the files on your computer to a list of known viruses. When it finds a virus, or any type of malware, antivirus software notifies you about the virus and then quarantines it by moving it to an isolated place on your computer or deletes the harmful file before it damages your computer.

Most vendors of antivirus software offer a subscription service that provides regular updates for current viruses. Like Windows, antivirus programs often use an automatic update feature that downloads and installs updates to the software and adds new viruses to your virus list. Keeping the virus list current helps to protect your computer from new attacks. If your list of viruses is out of date, your computer is vulnerable to new threats.

Windows Vista does not provide antivirus software, so you should make sure that you have an antivirus program installed and running on your computer. (Your computer manufacturer probably installed antivirus software for you—look on the All Programs submenu of the Start menu and then point to the icons in the notification area of the taskbar to make sure antivirus software is installed and running on your computer.) Be sure to select the options in the antivirus software to scan incoming e-mail automatically and to scan your entire system for malware periodically (usually once a week). Windows does detect most types of antivirus software and displays their status in the Windows Security Center window.

Tip

If antivirus software is not installed and running on your computer, visit the Microsoft Web site (*www.microsoft.com*) and search for "antivirus partners" to find software publishers who provide antivirus software for Windows Vista.

Also make sure that the antivirus software uses the most current virus definitions list. If your virus list is out of date, your computer is vulnerable to new threats. Refer to the antivirus software's help system to learn how to run the software and receive regular updates. In most cases, you can also use the Security Center to determine whether your antivirus software needs to be updated.

Curt is certain that antivirus software is installed on his computer, but asks you to check to make sure it is up to date and that virus scanning is turned on.

To check for malware protection on your computer:

1. In the Windows Security Center window, examine the settings in the **Malware protection** section, which should report that virus protection and spyware protection are both turned on.

   Trouble? If the Windows Security Center window reports that your virus protection is up to date and virus scanning is on, read but do not perform the remaining steps. If virus protection is turned on but not up to date, skip Steps 2 and 3.

   Trouble? If the Windows Security Center window reports that antivirus software is not installed on your computer, read but do not perform the remaining steps.

2. If necessary, click the **Turn on now** button.

3. When a dialog box opens requesting your permission to run the antivirus program, click the **Yes** button. The Windows Security Center window reports that virus scanning is on, but the antivirus program is not up to date. See Figure 5-9.

Figure 5-9	Antivirus software needs to be updated

Trouble? If your Windows Security Center window reports that virus scanning is on and up to date, read but do not perform Step 4.

▶ **4.** Click the **Update now** button. Your antivirus software starts and checks for updates on its manufacturer's Web site. When it is finished updating, close the antivirus software window.

Avoiding Viruses | InSight

You can defend against viruses in the following ways:

- Do not open unexpected e-mail attachments. If the message containing the attachment is from a trusted source, send an e-mail to that person asking about the file and what it contains.
- Regularly scan your hard drive with an antivirus program. Most antivirus software includes an option to schedule a complete system scan. You only need to make sure your computer is turned on to perform the scan.
- Set your antivirus program to scan all incoming e-mail.
- Keep your antivirus software up to date. New viruses are introduced frequently, and your antivirus software needs to use the latest virus definitions to protect your computer.
- Back up your work files periodically. Viruses can corrupt or destroy data files, which are the most valuable files on your computer.

Another security concern is spyware, which can also affect your computing experience.

Defending Against Spyware

Spyware is software that can install itself or run on your computer without your consent or control. It's called *spyware* because it monitors your computing actions, usually while you are online, to collect information about you. When spyware installs itself on your computer, it can change system settings, interrupt programs, and slow your computer's performance. Spyware often infects your computer when you visit certain Web sites or download a free program, such as a screen saver or search toolbar. Less frequently, spyware is distributed along with other programs on a CD, DVD, or other type of removable media. Sometimes, spyware passes information about your Web browsing habits to advertisers, who use it to improve their products or Web sites. Other times, a special type of spyware called **adware** changes your browser settings to open **pop-up ads**, which are windows that appear while you are viewing a Web page and advertise a product or service. Pop-up ads interrupt your online activities and can be difficult to close; they can also be vehicles for additional spyware or other types of malware. At the least, spyware is annoying; at worst, it can invade your privacy and harm your computer.

Because spyware can download, install, and run on your computer without your knowledge or consent, it's often difficult to know if spyware is infecting your computer. If you are experiencing any of the following symptoms, they are most likely due to spyware; you should scan your computer with a program that detects and removes spyware.

- New toolbars, links, or favorites appear in your Web browser unexpectedly.
- Your home page, mouse pointer, or search program changes without your consent.
- When you enter a URL for a Web site, such as a search engine, you go to a different Web site without notice.
- Pop-up ads interrupt you, even when you're not on the Internet.
- Your computer suddenly starts or runs slowly.

Scanning Your Computer with Windows Defender

Tip

Read the license agreements before installing software you download. Look for text explaining that you must accept ads and pop-ups or that the software collects and transmits data to the software publisher.

To protect your computer against spyware, you can run up-to-date antispyware software. Some antivirus programs include antispyware components. Windows Vista also provides Windows Defender, which helps prevent spyware from installing itself and running on your computer and which periodically scans your computer to detect and remove spyware. Besides monitoring and scanning your computer, Windows Defender also provides access to the Microsoft SpyNet community, where you can learn how others respond to software that hasn't been classified as spyware. When you are considering whether to download a free screen saver, for example, you can check the SpyNet Web site first to see if that program includes spyware or other types of malware.

Reference Window | **Performing a Quick Scan with Windows Defender**

- Click the Start button, click Control Panel, click Security, and then click Windows Defender.
- Click the Scan button arrow on the toolbar, and then click Quick Scan.

As with antivirus software, you need to keep the spyware definitions in Windows Defender up to date. The definitions are files that list the characteristics of known spyware; Windows Defender refers to the definitions to determine if software it detects is spyware or another type of malware. When you update your computer, Windows Update installs any new spyware definitions. You can also set Windows Defender to check for updated definitions before scanning your computer.

To protect Curt's computer, you'll show him how to start Windows Defender and scan for spyware. You can run a quick scan or a full system scan. A quick scan checks the locations on your computer that spyware is most likely to infect. A full scan checks all your files and programs, but takes longer than a quick scan and can make your computer run slowly. You recommend that Curt run a quick scan every day and run a full system scan only if he suspects spyware is infecting his computer.

To start Windows Defender and perform a quick scan:

1. In the left pane of the Windows Security Center window, click **Windows Defender**. The Windows Defender window opens. See Figure 5-10. Your settings might differ.

Windows Defender ◀ Figure 5-10

Trouble? If a dialog box opens indicating that Windows Defender is turned off, click the Turn on Windows Defender link, and then close the dialog box. When a dialog box opens requesting an administrator password or your permission to continue, enter the password or click the Continue button.

▶ 2. Click the **Scan button arrow** on the toolbar, and then click **Quick Scan**. Windows Defender scans your computer, displaying first its progress and then the results of the scan. Depending on the number of programs on your computer, your scan might take a few minutes. Wait for the scan to finish and for the results window to open before continuing. Figure 5-11 shows the results of a scan. Your results might differ.

Figure 5-11 Results of a quick scan

If Windows Defender finds files that might be spyware, it **quarantines** the files, which means it moves them to another location on your computer where it prevents them from running until you remove or restore the files. You can open the Quarantined items page to review the quarantined files. Windows Defender lists the quarantined files by their name, alert level, and date of quarantine. Figure 5-12 summarizes the alert levels and their recommended actions.

Figure 5-12 Windows Defender alert levels

Alert Level	Description	Recommended Action
Severe	Malicious spyware that can damage your computer	Remove
High	Spyware that invades your privacy, often by collecting information or changing settings without your knowledge or consent	Remove
Medium	Software that might affect your privacy or change your settings	If you do not recognize and trust the software publisher, remove
Low	Software that might collect information about you or change settings, but is running according to its license agreement	If you do not recognize and trust the software publisher, remove
Not yet classified	Software that is usually not harmful unless it was installed without your knowledge	If you're a SpyNet community member, check the member ratings to see if other users trust the software

The Quarantined items page also provides alert details to help you determine your best course of action. For example, it might indicate that a file is an adware program that has potentially unwanted behavior. The alert details sometimes include a link to a Web page on the Microsoft Web site, separate from the SpyNet community, that provides an up-to-date description of the program and identifies whether it is a known threat.

If Windows Defender quarantined any items, you should review the quarantined files and then remove or restore them.

To remove a quarantined file:

▶ **1.** In the Windows Defender window, click the **Tools** button on the toolbar to open the Tools and Settings page, and then click **Quarantined items**. The Quarantined items page opens. See Figure 5-13.

Quarantined items in Windows Defender   ◀ **Figure 5-13**

Trouble? If Windows Defender did not quarantine any items after its quick scan or you do not have permission to work with quarantined items, read but do not perform Step 2.

The item shown in Figure 5-13, WhenU.SaveNow, has a Medium alert level, and its details indicate this is adware that can behave in an unwanted manner. Curt does not recognize the publisher of this program, so you should remove it.

▶ **2.** In the Quarantined items list, click **WhenU.SaveNow** (or other item with a Severe, High, or Medium alert level and a publisher you do not recognize), and then click the **Remove** button.

Trouble? If a dialog box opens requesting an administrator password or your permission to continue, enter the password or click the Continue button.

Now that you've scanned Curt's computer and handled the items Windows Defender found, you can set options to make sure Windows Defender runs effectively.

Setting Windows Defender Options

The Options page in Windows Defender lets you set five categories of options: automatic scanning, default actions, real-time protection, advanced, and administrator options. When you select automatic scanning options, you choose whether you want Windows Defender to scan your computer according to a schedule, and then set the frequency, approximate time, and type of scan (quick scan or full system scan). You can also indicate whether Windows Defender should check for updated definitions before scanning, which is the recommended setting for keeping the spyware definitions up to date.

Default actions are those you want Windows Defender to perform when it detects potentially unsafe software installed or trying to install itself on your computer. You can specify default actions according to alert level. For example, if Windows Defender detects a program with a Low alert level, you can automatically ignore the program.

By default, Windows Defender is set to constantly monitor your computer for spyware activity. Windows Defender then alerts you when suspicious software attempts to install itself or to run on your computer, and notifies you when programs try to change important Windows settings. Real-time protection options let you turn this constant monitoring on and off, specify which Windows programs and settings it should monitor, select the type of activity Windows Defender should notify you about, and choose when a Windows Defender icon appears in the notification area: only when it detects activity or always.

The Advanced options on the Windows Defender Options page let you specify four additional options when scanning your computer for spyware. You can scan the contents of archived files and folders, which increases the scan time but might find spyware and other unwanted software concealed in these locations. Windows Defender can also use heuristics, or problem solving by trial and error, in addition to definition files to detect potentially harmful software. Scanning archived files and using heuristics is a good idea if you suspect spyware is infecting your computer but Windows Defender does not find the program during a quick or full system scan. Before applying actions to detected items, you can create a restore point, a collection of system file settings that your computer can return to if it becomes unstable. Finally, you can list any files or folders that you don't want Windows Defender to scan.

You use the two Administrator options to specify whether you want to turn Windows Defender on or off and who should use it. Windows Defender is turned on by default so it can monitor your computer for suspicious software activity, check for new definitions, scan your computer according to schedule, and automatically remove harmful software it detects during a scan. In addition, all users on your computer are set to use Windows Defender by default. If you turn off this option, only the administrator can use Windows Defender.

Curt wants to follow your recommendation of performing a quick scan every day. You'll show him how to schedule the daily spyware scan for 5:00 p.m., just before he leaves the office.

As you perform the following steps, note your settings so you can restore them later.

To schedule a spyware scan:

▶ 1. In the Windows Defender window, click the **Tools** button on the toolbar to open the Tools and Settings page, and then click **Options**. The Options page opens. See Figure 5-14.

2. Click the **Approximate time** button, and then click **5:00 PM**.

3. Except for the Approximate time setting, make sure the other Automatic scanning options match those in Figure 5-14. If they do not, click the appropriate check box or value to change the setting.

Trouble? If a dialog box opens requesting an administrator password or your permission to continue, enter the password or click the Continue button.

Besides scanning your computer regularly, you should keep Windows Defender turned on whenever you are using your computer. When Windows Defender is on, it alerts all users if it detects spyware or other unwanted software trying to run or install itself on your computer. In addition, you can use a feature called real-time protection to monitor certain Windows programs and settings that spyware often attempts to change, such as Internet Explorer options that prevent programs from switching your home page or installing a toolbar without your consent. As with quarantined items, when Windows Defender detects suspicious software, it assigns an alert level to the software. Then it displays a dialog box where you can choose one of the following actions:

• **Ignore**: Install or run the software on your computer. If the software is still running during the next scan, or if the software tries to change security-related settings on your computer, Windows Defender alerts you about this software again.
• **Quarantine**: Quarantine the program. Windows Defender prevents the software from running and allows you to restore it or remove it from your computer.

- **Remove**: Permanently delete the software from your computer.
- **Always Allow**: Add the software to the Windows Defender Allowed items list and run it on your computer. Windows Defender does not alert you to risks that the software might pose to your privacy or your computer unless you remove the program from the Allowed items list.

Windows Defender also alerts you if software already running on your computer attempts to change important Windows settings. In this case, you can either permit or deny the software to make the change.

If you set Windows Defender to scan your computer unattended (such as in the middle of the night) or you want Windows Defender to always take a certain action when it detects potential spyware, you can set default actions for the items it detects. By default, Windows Defender checks its definition list, and then acts accordingly by quarantining items with a High alert level, for example. You can specify whether you want Windows Defender to ignore or remove items with High, Medium, and Low alert levels. You don't need to specify an action for Severe items because Windows Defender automatically removes them or alerts you to do so. If an item is not yet classified, you must review information about the software and then choose an action.

You'll show Curt how to make sure Windows Defender is turned on and using real-time protection, and then you'll set it to remove any items it detects with a High alert level. You perform all of these tasks on the Windows Defender Options page.

To verify and set Windows Defender options:

▶ 1. Scroll to the bottom of the Options page in the Windows Defender window to view the Administrator options. Make sure the Use Windows Defender check box is selected. This means Windows Defender is turned on.

▶ 2. Scroll the Options page as necessary to view the Default actions and Real-time protection options sections. See Figure 5-15.

3. Click the **High alert** button and then click **Remove**.

4. Make sure the Use real-time protection (recommended) check box is selected, and then click the **Save** button.

Trouble? If a dialog box opens requesting an administrator password or your permission to continue, enter the password or click the Continue button.

5. Close the Windows Defender, Windows Security Center, and Control Panel windows.

Windows Defender monitors the programs and settings listed in the Real-time protection options section of the Options page. (See Figure 5-15.) For example, it monitors the programs that are allowed to run automatically when you start your computer and tracks the security settings in Internet Explorer. It issues an alert if it detects changes to these programs and settings.

Defending Against E-mail Viruses with Windows Mail

An annoying and potentially dangerous type of privacy invasion is **spam**, or junk e-mail. Spam is a form of electronic direct mail, offering products and services that are sometimes fake or misleading. Some users receive thousands of spam messages a day; the volume alone makes spam a nuisance. In addition, spam can be a vehicle for malware. Although sending and reading e-mail messages is one of the most popular activities on the Internet, e-mail is the most common way for computer viruses to spread. Because viruses and other security threats are often contained in e-mail attachments, the security settings in Windows Mail block e-mail attachments that might be harmful. Files with names that end in .exe, .bat, and .js can contain malware, and are blocked by default. When Windows Mail blocks an attachment, it displays an Information bar below the toolbar that includes a message explaining that it blocked an attachment.

To help prevent spam and potentially offensive material, Windows Mail does not download graphics with messages sent in HTML format. People sending spam (called spammers) often use graphics to access your e-mail address. Viewing a picture in a junk e-mail message might notify the sender that you have read or previewed the message. This validates your e-mail address and often results in more junk e-mail. Using plain text for e-mail messages is therefore more secure than using the HTML format. Windows Mail also displays an Information bar when it blocks graphics. If you trust the sender, you can click an option on the Information bar to download and display the pictures in an open message.

Spammers can also take advantage of vulnerabilities in your computer to use it to send spam to other computers without your permission, a practice known as an **e-mail relay**. This lets spammers work without being detected and can seriously downgrade the performance of your computer. By default, Windows Mail helps prevent spammers from using your computer for e-mail relays.

Selecting Windows Mail Security Settings

You select your e-mail security settings using the Security tab of the Windows Mail Options dialog box. This dialog box provides the following categories of settings for securing your e-mail:

- **Virus Protection**: To help protect your computer from e-mail viruses, Windows Mail uses a restricted security zone by default, which prevents some types of malware from running on your computer. It also warns you when other applications try to send mail using your identity and does not allow you to save or open attachments that could be viruses.
- **Download Images**: By default, Windows Mail blocks images and other external content in HTML mail.
- **Secure Mail**: If you're concerned about the security of your outgoing mail, you can include a digital ID with your e-mail. Digital IDs are special documents that prove your identity in electronic transactions. You can also **encrypt**, or code, the contents and attachments of your outgoing mail.

| InSight | | **Encrypting E-Mail Messages** |

When you exchange unencrypted e-mail messages, they are sent across the Internet in a plain text format. On their way to their recipients, hackers or automated programs can intercept, read, and even change the messages. In contrast, encrypted messages have a digital ID and are sent in a scrambled format that only your recipient can read. The encryption hides the e-mail contents, and the digital ID indicates whether a message has been altered in transit. You should therefore encrypt important e-mail messages. However, to send and read encrypted messages, both the sender and receiver must have copies of one another's digital ID. If you need a digital ID for your recipient, ask your recipient to send you a digitally signed message. Whenever you receive a digitally signed email message, Windows Mail automatically adds the sender's digital ID to the appropriate record in Windows Contacts.

You'll show Curt how to examine the security settings in Windows Mail. If he is using the default settings, you don't need to change them.

To examine security settings in Windows Mail:

▶ 1. Click the **Start** button 🔵 on the taskbar, click All Programs, and then click **Windows Mail** to start Windows Mail.

▶ 2. Click **Tools** on the menu bar, and then click **Options**. The Options dialog box opens.

▶ 3. Click the **Security** tab to examine the enhanced security settings. See Figure 5-16.

Security settings for Windows Mail **Figure 5-16**

▶ 4. Three check boxes are for enhanced security features in Windows Mail: Warn me when other applications try to send mail as me, Do not allow attachments to be saved or opened that could potentially be a virus, and Block images and other external content in HTML e-mail. Make sure that each box is checked, and then click the **OK** button.

In addition to selecting security settings in Windows Mail, some of the security settings you select for Internet Explorer apply to Windows Mail. You'll work with Internet Explorer security settings in the next session.

Blocking Spam and Other Junk Mail

Windows Mail includes a junk e-mail filter that catches obvious spam messages and moves them to a built-in Junk E-mail folder. You can then examine the messages in the Junk E-mail folder and delete them, open them, or move them back to your Inbox, if necessary. Windows Mail also maintains two lists of senders. The Safe Senders list contains addresses of messages you never want to treat as junk mail. The Blocked Senders list contains addresses of messages you always want to treat as junk mail. You can add e-mail addresses to these lists to customize the kind of security Windows Mail provides.

Usually, you add an address to the Safe Senders or Blocked Senders list when you receive a junk e-mail message. You can block further messages from that same sender by adding that sender to the Block Senders List. Alternatively, you can add the sender's domain to the Blocked Senders list. For example, if you receive spam from *JSmith@domain.net*, you can block all future e-mail from either that specific address or from any address in domain.net. Any further e-mail from that sender or domain will then be stored in the Junk E-mail folder automatically. Adding people to the Safe Senders list works the same way—you can add either an address or a domain to the Safe Senders list. If you haven't received any e-mail from someone you want to add to your Safe or Blocked Senders list, you can do so manually by using the Junk E-mail Options dialog box. If you somehow include the same person on both lists, you'll receive e-mail from that person in your Inbox because the Safe Senders list has priority over the Blocked Senders list.

By default, Windows Mail includes your Windows Contacts in the Safe Senders list. You can also automatically add people to whom you send e-mail to the Safe Senders list.

Reference Window | **Adding a Sender to the Blocked Senders or Safe Senders List**

- To block a sender in Windows Mail, right-click a message whose sender you want to add to the Blocked Senders list, point to Junk E-mail, and then click Add Sender to Blocked Senders List on the shortcut menu.
- To always allow a sender, right-click a message whose sender you want to add to the Safe Senders list, point to Junk E-mail, and then click Add Sender to Safe Senders List on the shortcut menu.
- Click the OK button.

In addition, you can set the level of junk e-mail protection you want in Windows Mail. By default, Windows Mail uses a low level of junk e-mail protection; you can change this based on how much junk e-mail you receive. You can use any of the following protection levels:

- **No Automatic Filtering**: This setting does not block any junk e-mail messages except for those from senders on your Blocked Senders list.
- **Low**: This setting blocks only the most obvious spam. Choose this level if you don't receive many junk e-mail messages.
- **High**: This setting blocks as much potential spam as possible. Choose this level if you receive a large volume of junk e-mail messages. However, be sure to review the messages in your Junk E-mail folder frequently to make sure it doesn't contain legitimate e-mail messages.
- **Safe List Only**: This setting blocks all e-mail messages except for those from senders on your Safe Senders list. Also review the messages in your Junk E-mail folder frequently for legitimate e-mail.

You'll check the level of junk e-mail protection that Curt is using, and then show him how to add people to the Safe and Blocked senders list.

To set junk e-mail options:

▶ 1. Click **Tools** on the Windows Mail menu bar, and then click **Junk E-mail Options**. The Junk E-mail Options dialog box opens. See Figure 5-17.

Junk E-mail Options dialog box | **Figure 5-17**

Curt doesn't receive much junk e-mail, so the Low setting is appropriate for him.

▶ 2. Click the **Safe Senders** tab to view your Safe Senders list. You can add your e-mail address to this list.

▶ 3. Click the **Add** button to open the Add address or domain dialog box.

▶ 4. Type your e-mail address, and then click the **OK** button.

▶ 5. Click the **Blocked Senders** tab to view your Blocked Senders list. Adding a sender to this list works the same way as the Safe Senders list—you click the Add button and enter an e-mail address.

Before closing the Junk E-mail Options dialog box, you want to show Curt one more way to protect his computer from harmful e-mail.

Defending Against Phishing Messages

Phishing (pronounced *fishing*) is an attempt to deceive you into revealing personal or financial information when you respond to an e-mail message or visit a Web site. A typical phishing scam starts with an e-mail message that looks like an official notice from a trusted person or business, such as a bank, credit card company, or reputable online merchant. The e-mail message asks you to reply with sensitive information, such as an account number or password, or directs you to a fraudulent Web site that requests this information. Phishers usually use the information for identity theft.

By default, if Windows Mail detects links to Web sites in the e-mail messages you receive, and the links seem fraudulent, Windows Mail blocks access to the links in that message and displays a message on the Information bar explaining its actions. If you are certain the message contains legitimate links, you can click an option on the Information bar to turn on the links in the message. You can also specify that when Windows Mail-suspects a message is a phishing e-mail, it moves the message to the Junk E-mail folder. You'll show Curt how to select this setting.

To set phishing e-mail options:

▶ **1.** In the Junk E-mail Options dialog box, click the **Phishing** tab.

▶ **2.** Make sure the **Protect my Inbox from messages with potential Phishing links** check box is selected.

▶ **3.** Click the **Move phishing E-mail to the Junk Mail folder** check box, if necessary, to select that option.

▶ **4.** Click the **OK** button to close the Junk E-mail Options dialog box.

▶ **5.** Close Windows Mail.

In the next session, you'll also work with Internet Explorer settings to protect against phishing attempts.

| Review | **| Session 5.1 Quick Check** |

1. What is malware?

2. The _____ _____ is a Control Panel tool that helps you manage security from a single window.

3. True or False. Windows Firewall checks communication coming from the Internet and either blocks it from your computer or allows it to pass.

4. Why might you add a program to the Windows Firewall exception list?

5. A(n) _____ is a change to software that can prevent or repair problems, enhance the security of the computer, or improve the computer's performance.

6. True or False. Windows Vista does not provide any type of malware protection.

7. What is the purpose of spyware?

8. _____ is a form of electronic direct mail, and can be a vehicle for malware.

Session 5.2

Managing Microsoft Internet Explorer Security

Your computer is most vulnerable to security threats when you are connected to the Internet. You should therefore take advantage of the security settings in Internet Explorer to help to protect your computer by identifying viruses and other security threats that are circulated over the Internet and to guard your privacy, making your computer and personal information more secure. Internet Explorer offers the following security and privacy features:

- **Phishing filter**: This feature helps detect online scams, such as Web sites that trick you into revealing financial account information.
- **Protected mode**: This feature guards against Web sites that try to save files or install malware on your computer.
- **Digital signatures**: Internet Explorer can detect and display digital signatures, which are electronic security marks added to files to verify their authenticity.
- **Pop-up Blocker**: Use this tool to limit or block most pop-up windows.
- **Add-on Manager**: Use this tool to disable or allow programs or controls that extend your browser's features.
- **Privacy settings and alerts**: These settings specify how to handle identifying information when you're online and alert you when a Web site you're visiting doesn't meet your criteria.
- **Secure connections**: Internet Explorer informs you when it is using a secure connection to communicate with Web sites that handle sensitive personal information.

> **Tip**
>
> To make sure you have a secure connection with a Web site, look for a padlock icon in the Internet Explorer status bar and "https" (rather than "http") at the beginning of the Web address.

Using the Phishing Filter

Recall that phishing is an attempt to deceive you into revealing personal or financial information when you respond to an e-mail message or visit a Web site. Internet Explorer can help protect you from phishing scams by detecting possible phishing Web sites. The Phishing Filter compares the addresses of Web sites you visit to a list of reportedly legitimate Web sites. The first time you navigate to a Web site that is not on the legitimate list, Internet Explorer asks whether you want to automatically check this Web site and others you visit for phishing history or characteristics. If you do, Internet Explorer sends the address of any potentially fraudulent Web site you visit to Microsoft, who checks it against an updated list of reported phishing sites and then alerts you. When you check Web sites automatically, the Phishing Filter also analyzes the Web pages you open to check for characteristics common to phishing sites. If they share these characteristics, Internet Explorer submits them to Microsoft for verification.

If you do not choose to check Web sites automatically, Internet Explorer displays a Phishing Filter security icon in the status bar when you visit a Web site that might be fraudulent. See Figure 5-18.

Phishing Filter security icon ◄ **Figure 5-18**

click to find out whether this Web site has been reported as a phishing Web site

You can check the Web site manually by clicking the Phishing Filter security icon, and then clicking Check This Website. If the security icon does not appear in the status bar, you can manually check a Web site by clicking the Tools button on the Internet Explorer toolbar, clicking Phishing Filter, and then clicking Check This Website. Internet Explorer then sends the Web site address to Microsoft to check it against a list of reported phishing sites.

After checking a Web site, Internet Explorer lets you know if it is a reported phishing site or is suspicious. A suspicious site shares some characteristics of typical phishing sites, but is not listed as a reported site nor as a legitimate site. You should not submit personal or financial information to a suspicious site unless you are sure it is trustworthy. If you're not sure whether to trust a Web site with your sensitive information, look for the Web site's privacy policy. Most Web sites that collect personal information provide a link to their privacy statement, which you should read carefully. Conditions that allow the Web site to share your information with others or require you to accept e-mail or advertising might indicate that the site will misuse your information.

| InSight | **Protecting Yourself from Phishing Attempts** |

In addition to using the Internet Explorer Phishing Filter, use the following guidelines to protect yourself from online phishing:
- Never provide personal information in an e-mail, instant message, or pop-up window.
- Do not click links in e-mail and instant messages from senders you do not know or trust. Even messages from friends and family can be faked, so check with the sender to make sure they actually sent the message.
- Only use Web sites that provide privacy statements or indicate how they use your personal information.

You'll show Curt how to check a Web site to make sure it is not a phishing site, and then turn on the Phishing Filter so Internet Explorer does this automatically.

To turn on the Phishing Filter and check a Web site:

▶ **1.** Click the **Start** button 🌀 on the taskbar, and then click **Internet Explorer** to start Internet Explorer. Your home page opens.

Tip

You can also click the Phishing Filter Security icon and then click Phishing Filter Settings to open the Microsoft Phishing Filter dialog box.

▶ **2.** Click the **Tools** button on the toolbar, point to **Phishing Filter**, and then click **Check This Website**. Internet Explorer sends the URL of your home page to Microsoft for verification.

Trouble? If a dialog box opens explaining how the Phishing Filter works, click the OK button.

Trouble? If you are not connected to the Internet, skip Steps 2 and 3.

▶ **3.** When the Phishing Filter dialog box opens to indicate this is not a phishing Web site, click the **OK** button.

▶ **4.** Click the **Tools** button on the toolbar, point to **Phishing Filter**, and then click **Turn On Automatic Website Checking**. The Microsoft Phishing Filter dialog box opens. See Figure 5-19. Internet Explorer selects the Turn on automatic Phishing Filter option button for you.

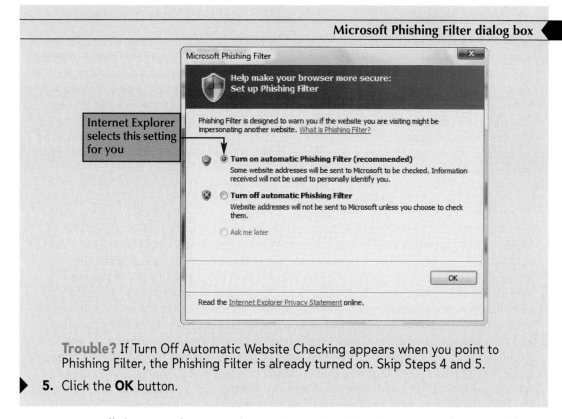

Internet Explorer selects this setting for you

Trouble? If Turn Off Automatic Website Checking appears when you point to Phishing Filter, the Phishing Filter is already turned on. Skip Steps 4 and 5.

▶ 5. Click the **OK** button.

Next, you'll show Curt how to make sure Internet Explorer is using protected mode, which helps to keep your computer free of harmful software.

Blocking Malware with Protected Mode and Security Zones

To install or run programs on your computer, hackers often take advantage of Web programming tools, such as scripts and ActiveX controls that are designed to enhance your online experience. A **script** is programming code that performs a series of commands, and can be embedded in a Web page. For example, a Web site designer might use a script to verify that you've completed all the necessary fields in an online form. In contrast, hackers use scripts on a Web page to automatically download programs that can collect and transmit information about you without your knowledge or authorization. A common way for hackers to distribute adware and spyware is to download **ActiveX controls**, which are small, self-contained programs, from a Web page to your computer. Some ActiveX controls make it easier to perform tasks, such as submit information to a Web site. Other ActiveX controls can harm your computer and files, especially those controls that lack **digital signatures**, meaning they are unverified. Internet Explorer offers a few ways to protect against malicious scripts and ActiveX controls, including protected mode and security zones.

InSight | **Digital Signatures**

Internet Explorer (and other programs, including Windows Vista) detects whether a file has a digital signature, which is an electronic security mark that identifies the publisher of a file and verifies that the file has not changed since it was signed. A file without a valid digital signature might not be from the stated source or might have been tampered with (possibly by a virus) since it was published. Avoid opening an unsigned file unless you know for certain who created it and whether the contents are safe to open. However, even a valid digital signature does not guarantee that the contents of the file are harmless. When you download a file, determine whether to trust its contents based on the identity of the publisher and the site providing the file.

Internet Explorer runs in protected mode by default, making it difficult for hackers to install malware on your computer. When protected mode is turned on, a notification appears in the Internet Explorer status bar. If a Web page tries to install any type of software or run a script, Internet Explorer displays a dialog box warning you about the attempt. If you trust the program, you can allow it to run once or always. If you are not familiar with the program or don't want to run it, you can deny it once or always.

In addition to protected mode, Internet Explorer uses security zones so you can tailor your security needs to the kind of online computing you do. Internet Explorer classifies all Web sites in one of four security zones: Internet, Local intranet, Trusted sites, and Restricted sites. Each zone uses a certain level of security settings ranging from Low to High. You can also select custom settings, which mix levels. For example, Web sites in the Trusted sites zone use Medium-level security settings. If a Web site you've assigned to the Trusted sites zone tries to download files onto your computer, Internet Explorer asks your permission only if the files are potentially unsafe. When you visit a Web site that has been assigned to a security zone, the appropriate icon appears in the Internet Explorer status bar. Figure 5-20 summarizes the four security zones. Note that the security zones you set in Internet Explorer also apply to Windows Mail.

Figure 5-20 | **Internet Explorer security zones**

Security Zone	Description	Protected Mode Default
Internet	Internet Explorer assigns all Internet Web sites to this zone by default, and applies a Medium-high security level, which is appropriate for most sites. You can change the level to Medium or High.	On
Local intranet	Internet Explorer assigns Web sites on your intranet (a corporate or business network) to this zone and applies a Medium-low security level. You can change this to any other level.	On
Trusted sites	To this zone you assign Web sites you trust not to damage your computer or files. This zone has a Medium level of security by default, but you can change it to any other level.	Off
Restricted sites	To this zone you assign Web sites that might damage your computer or files. Adding sites to this zone does not block them, but does prevent them from using scripts or active content. This zone has a High level of security by default and cannot be changed.	On

You'll show Curt how to check the security level of his home page.

To check the security level of your home page:

▶ **1.** With Internet Explorer open to your home page, double-click the **Protected Mode** notification in the status bar. The Internet Security dialog box opens. See Figure 5-21.

Curt's home page is assigned to the Internet zone, which uses a Medium-high security level and protected mode by default. At this level, Internet Explorer does not download unsigned ActiveX controls and requests permission before downloading content that might be unsafe.

▶ **2.** Click the **OK** button to close the dialog box.

Next, you'll show Curt how to use the pop-up blocker to limit or block most pop-up windows when he visits Web sites.

Blocking Pop-up Ads

A pop-up ad is a small Web browser window that appears when you visit a Web site and that advertises a product or service. Many legitimate advertisers use pop-up ads because they effectively get your attention while you are online and provide information or services that might interest you. However, some pop-up ads are annoying because they repeatedly interrupt your online activities, can be difficult to close, and display objectionable content. Other pop-up ads are dangerous; they can download spyware or **hijack** your browser, opening many more new windows each time you close one pop-up window until you have to close your browser or restart your computer.

To avoid the nuisance and danger of pop-up ads, Internet Explorer includes a pop-up blocker, which enables Internet Explorer to warn you about or block pop-up ads. The pop-up blocker in Internet Explorer is turned on by default, meaning that Internet Explorer blocks most pop-up ads. However, if you click a link or button to open a pop-up window, Internet Explorer does not block that window unless you change a setting. You can select settings in Internet Explorer to block all pop-up ads, allow more pop-up ads, or specify which Web sites can display pop-up ads in your browser.

Reference Window | **Blocking Pop-up Ads**

- Click Tools on the Internet Explorer toolbar, point to Pop-up Blocker, and then click Pop-up Blocker Settings.
- Click the current Filter level setting, and then click a setting ranging from High to Low.
- Click the Close button.

When you visit a Web site with pop-up ads and the pop-up blocker is turned on, an Information bar opens below the Internet Explorer toolbar and displays a message informing you that it blocked a pop-up ad. You can click the Information bar to display a menu of settings, such as to temporarily allow pop-up ads on the Web site.

Internet Explorer displays the Information bar in many situations, including when a Web site tries to install or run an ActiveX control, open a pop-up window, or download a file; when your security settings are below recommended levels; and when you need to install an updated ActiveX control or add-on program.

Curt has had problems with pop-up ads before, so he wants to block all pop-ups in Internet Explorer. You'll show him how to change the pop-up blocker settings to do so.

As you perform the following steps, note your original settings so you can restore them later.

To change the pop-up blocker settings in Internet Explorer:

▶ 1. Click the **Tools** button on the Internet Explorer toolbar, point to **Pop-up Blocker**, and then click **Pop-up Blocker Settings**. The Pop-up Blocker Settings dialog box opens. See Figure 5-22.

Figure 5-22 | Pop-up Blocker Settings dialog box

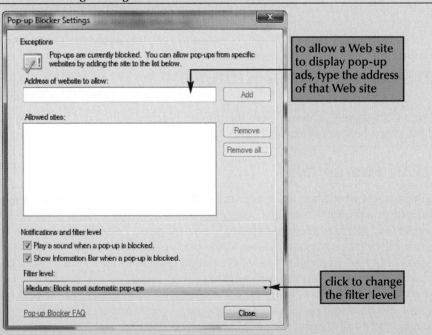

to allow a Web site to display pop-up ads, type the address of that Web site

click to change the filter level

▶ 2. Click the **Filter level** button, and then click **High: Block all pop-ups (Ctrl+Alt to override)**.

Trouble? If you are working in a computer lab, you might not have permission to change the pop-up blocker settings. In that case, skip Step 2.

▶ **3.** Click the **Close** button.

Managing Add-on Programs

A browser **add-on** is a program offered by any software vendor that provides enhancements such as a toolbar or improved search feature. Some add-ons are safe and make your browser more effective; other add-ons, especially those that are installed without your permission, can affect the performance of Internet Explorer and even make it stop working. Internet Explorer provides an add-on manager so you can review, disable, update, or report add-ons to Microsoft. Other security features, such as protected mode, security levels, and the Information bar, warn you when a Web site is trying to download add-on software to your computer.

You can usually install and use browser add-ons without any problems, but some cause Internet Explorer to shut down unexpectedly. If this happens, you can update the add-on to make sure that it is compatible with your version of Internet Explorer. If the add-on continues to cause problems, you can disable it. In this case, you should also report the problem to Microsoft. Reporting is anonymous and only provides information to Microsoft about what caused the add-on problem.

Internet Explorer usually asks permission before running an add-on for the first time. If you don't recognize the program or its publisher, you can deny permission. Internet Explorer also maintains a list of preapproved add-ons that have been checked and digitally signed. It runs add-ons in this list without requesting your permission. You can view the list of preapproved add-ons in the Manage Add-ons dialog box.

Curt isn't aware of any add-ons his browser uses, so he wants to view the preapproved add-ons and any others Internet Explorer is running.

To examine and manage add-ons:

▶ **1.** Click the **Tools** button on the Internet Explorer toolbar, point to **Manage Add-ons**, and then click **Enable or Disable Add-ons**. The Manage Add-ons dialog box opens. By default, this dialog box displays the add-ons that Internet Explorer is currently using.

▶ **2.** Click the **Show** button, and then click **Add-ons that run without requiring permission**. The preapproved add-ons appear in the list. See Figure 5-23.

Figure 5-23   Manage Add-ons dialog box

3. Click the **OK** button to close the Manage Add-ons dialog box.

If you are having problems with an add-on, such as Internet Explorer closing unexpectedly when you use an add-on, you can first try to update the add-on by clicking its name in the Manage Add-ons dialog box, and then clicking the Update ActiveX button. (If the Update ActiveX button is not available, that means you cannot update the add-on.) If problems persist, you can disable the add-on by clicking it in the Manage Add-ons dialog box and then clicking the Disable option button. In some cases, you might be prompted to report a problem with an add-on to Microsoft. If you are connected to the Internet, you can follow the steps in the reporting dialog box to report the problem.

Selecting Privacy Settings

In addition to security protection, Internet Explorer also includes tools to protect your privacy. One privacy concern is cookies, which many Web sites store on your computer when you visit the site. A **cookie** is a small file that records information about you, such as the type of browser you are using, your e-mail address, and your preferences for using a Web site. Like other Web tools, cookies can enhance your online experience by helping trusted Web sites customize their service to you, but they can also pose a security risk—hackers can retrieve cookies to search for private information such as passwords or use cookies to track the Web sites you visit. In Internet Explorer, you can specify privacy settings that allow Web sites to or prevent them from saving cookies on your computer.

One way to protect your privacy with Internet Explorer is to block cookies on some or all of the Web sites you visit. You should be selective about which Web sites can store cookies on your computer. Blocking all cookies keeps your Web site visits private, but might also limit your experience or prove annoying. Allowing all cookies might compromise your privacy. Most users find that the default medium-high privacy setting provides a good balance, because it allows most **first-party cookies**, which are generated from the Web sites you visit and contain information the Web site reuses when you return. For example, to keep track of products you add to an electronic shopping cart or wish list, a Web site saves a first-party cookie on your computer. In contrast, the medium-high privacy setting blocks most **third-party cookies**, which are generated from Web site advertisers, who might use them to track your Web use for marketing purposes.

Selecting Privacy Settings | Reference Window

- Click Tools on the Internet Explorer toolbar, and then click Internet Options.
- Click the Privacy tab in the Internet Options dialog box.
- Drag the slider to select a privacy setting ranging from Block All Cookies to Accept All Cookies.
- Click the OK button.

Curt often visits his clients' Web sites for research as he prepares or performs translation projects. He wants to protect the privacy of Presto Global Translators and his clients by blocking all cookies and then allowing only those issued by sites he trusts.

As you perform the following steps, note your original settings so you can restore them later.

To change privacy settings for saving cookies:

▶ 1. Click the **Tools** button on the Internet Explorer toolbar, and then click **Internet Options**. The Internet Options dialog box opens.

▶ 2. Click the **Privacy** tab to view privacy settings. See Figure 5-24.

Privacy tab in the Internet Options dialog box ◀ Figure 5-24

Trouble? If you are working in a computer lab, you might not have permission to change the privacy settings. In that case, read but do not perform Steps 3–6.

3. Drag the slider up to the **Block All Cookies** setting. Internet Explorer will not let a Web site store any cookies on your computer unless you explicitly allow it to do so.

4. Drag the slider back to **Medium**. This setting blocks cookies except for those created by Web sites you identify.

5. Click the **Sites** button to open the Per Site Privacy Actions dialog box. See Figure 5-25. You use this dialog box to specify the Web sites you want to allow to store cookies on your computer. (If you had selected a lower privacy setting, you could also use this dialog box to block certain Web sites from storing cookies.)

| Figure 5-25 | Per Site Privacy Actions dialog box |

6. Click the **OK** button to close the Per Site Privacy Actions dialog box.

7. Click the **OK** button to close the Internet Options dialog box.

Tip

To view temporary files before deleting them, click the Tools button on the Internet Explorer toolbar, click Internet Options, click the General tab, click the Settings button in the Browsing history section, and then click View files.

Internet Explorer will block most cookies on Curt's computer from now on, but if Web sites stored cookies on his computer before you changed the privacy setting, they remain there until you delete them. You can delete cookies by clearing Web page history. In addition to cookies, Internet Explorer stores temporary Internet files, a history of the Web sites you've visited, information you've entered in the Address bar, and Web passwords you've saved. Usually, maintaining this history information improves your Web browsing because it can fill in information that you would otherwise have to retype. If you have particular privacy concerns, however, such as when you are using a public computer, you can clear some or all of your browsing history to delete this information. Curt wants to delete all of the cookies and the list of Web sites he has visited.

To clear your browsing history:

1. Click the **Tools** button on the Internet Explorer toolbar, and then click **Delete Browsing History**. The Delete Browsing History dialog box opens. See Figure 5-26.

Delete Browsing History dialog box ◄ **Figure 5-26**

Trouble? If you are working in a computer lab, you might not have permission to clear your browsing history. In that case, read but do not perform Steps 2–5.

► **2.** Click the **Delete cookies** button to delete all the cookies stored on your computer.

► **3.** When asked if you are sure you want to delete cookies, click the **Yes** button.

► **4.** Click the **Delete history** button to delete the list of Web sites you have visited.

► **5.** When asked if you are sure you want to delete your browsing history, click the **Yes** button.

► **6.** Click the **Close** button.

Tip

When you delete all of your browsing history, you do not delete your list of favorites or subscribed feeds.

Finally, you want to examine the advanced Internet Explorer settings to make sure they are protecting Curt's computer.

Verifying Internet Explorer Advanced Settings

In addition to using the Phishing Filter, security zones, pop-up blocker, add-on programs, and privacy settings, you can manage advanced Internet Explorer settings to enhance the security of your computer. You select these settings on the Advanced tab of the Internet Options dialog box, which organizes them into categories of options you turn on or off. By default, Internet Explorer turns on settings to achieve a balance between security and performance. If you suspect your Internet activity is causing problems on your computer, you can check these settings to see if any have changed, or you can click the Restore Advanced Settings button to return the Internet Explorer settings to their original state. Some malware can gain access to your computer by changing the Advanced settings, so you should monitor the settings from time to time. If Internet Explorer becomes corrupted and unusable, you can click the Reset button on the Advanced tab to delete all of your temporary files, disable add-ons, and reset all of your changed settings.

In addition to the default settings, you can change the following Advanced settings to enhance your security when browsing:

• **Enable third-party browser extensions**: A third-party extension is a program that extends the features of Internet Explorer, such as an additional toolbars. Like add-ons, browser extensions can be benign or malicious. If you turn this setting off, browser extensions are installed only with your consent.

- **Do not save encrypted pages to disk**: A secure Web site usually sends sensitive information in an encrypted, or coded, form that prevents others from seeing the information. Browsers save Web pages, including encrypted ones, on your hard disk. To prevent a hacker from accessing your computer and these encrypted pages, you can turn this setting on.
- **Empty Temporary Internet Files folder when browser is closed**: Because a temporary file could contain information a hacker might use, you can empty the Temporary Internet Files folder (also called the **cache**) whenever you close Internet Explorer.
- **Warn if changing between secure and not secure mode**: When you are viewing a secure Web site, a padlock icon appears in the status bar and the URL starts with "https" instead of "http." When you are visiting a regular site that is not secure, the padlock icon does not appear and the URL starts with "http." You can have Internet Explorer display a Security Alert dialog box to inform you that you are switching from one kind of Web site to another.

You'll show Curt which Advanced settings to change in Internet Explorer. Note your original settings so you can restore them later.

To change Internet Explorer Advanced settings:

▶ 1. Click the **Tools** button on the Internet Explorer toolbar, and then click **Internet Options**. The Internet Options dialog box opens.

▶ 2. Click the **Advanced** tab, and then scroll the list to view most of the Browsing category. See Figure 5-27.

Figure 5-27 ▶ **Internet Explorer Advanced settings**

Trouble? If you are working in a computer lab, you might not have permission to change the Advanced settings. In that case, read but do not perform Steps 3–6.

▶ **3.** Click the **Enable third-party browser extensions** check box, if necessary, to remove the check mark.

▶ **4.** Scroll down to the Security category, and click the **Do not save encrypted pages to disk** check box to select it.

▶ **5.** Click the **Empty Temporary Internet Files folder when browser is closed** check box to select it.

▶ **6.** Click the **Warn if changing between secure and not secure mode** check box to select it.

▶ **7.** Click the **OK** button to close the Internet Options dialog box.

▶ **8.** Close Internet Explorer.

Now that you have thoroughly explored the security settings in Internet Explorer, you can review another way to protect your computer—by using user accounts.

Setting Up User Accounts

In Windows Vista, a **user account** is a collection of information that indicates the files and folders you can access, the types of changes you can make to the computer, and your preferred appearance settings (such as your desktop background or color scheme). If you have a user account on a computer that you share with other people, you can maintain your own files and settings separate from other users. When you start Windows Vista, the Welcome screen appears and displays the accounts that are available on the computer. To access your user account, you select your user name. For security purposes, you can also set Windows to request your password.

Windows Vista provides the following three types of user accounts, and each type gives the user a different level of control over the computer.

- **Standard**: This type of account is designed for everyday computing, and can protect your computer and data by preventing users from changing settings that affect all users. To make this type of change, such as installing software or changing security settings, Windows requests permission or a password for an Administrator account. Microsoft recommends that every regular user on a computer have a Standard account.
- **Administrator**: This type of account is created when Windows Vista is installed, and provides full access to the computer. The Administrator can access the files of any user, install software, and change any settings. The intention is that when you install Windows Vista, you first log on to the computer as the Administrator and then create a Standard user account for yourself and for each person who will use the computer.
- **Guest**: This type of account is primarily for people who need temporary access to the computer and is not used often.

To create an account, you provide a user name and select an account type. You are not required to protect every account with a password, but Microsoft strongly recommends that you do so. Using a password is one of the most effective ways you can keep your computer secure. When your computer is protected with a password, only someone who knows the password can log on to it.

Reference Window | Creating a Password-Protected User Account

- Open the Control Panel in Category view, click User Accounts and Family Safety, and then click User Accounts.
- Click Manage another account.
- Click Create a new account.
- Type the new account name, click the Standard user option button or the Administrator option button, and then click the Create Account button.
- Click Create a Password.
- Click in the New password text box, and then type your password.
- Click in the Confirm new password text box, and then type your password again.
- Click in the Type a password hint text box, and then type a hint to help you remember your password.
- Click the Create password button.

Curt is concerned that he and his staff at Presto Global Translators are all using the Administrator accounts that Windows created when it was installed. He wants to make sure that everyone creates a Standard user account with a password. Some part-time employees share a single computer, and Curt wants those employees to create separate Standard accounts on the same computer.

Creating a Password-Protected Standard User Account

When you create a user account, you provide a name for the account, which is usually your name, and then select the account type. You can then change the picture for the account and create a password. In Windows Vista, a password is a series of letters, numbers, spaces, and symbols that you provide to access your files, programs, and other resources on the computer. Windows passwords are case sensitive, so CuBote18 is different from cubote18. Passwords strengthen computer security because they help to make sure that no one can access the computer unless they are authorized to do so. You should therefore not give your passwords to others or write it in a place where others can see it.

When creating a password, make sure you devise a **strong password**, one that is difficult to guess but easy for you to remember. Strong passwords have the following characteristics:

- Contain at least eight characters
- Do not include your user name, real name, or company name
- Are not words you can find in the dictionary
- Are significantly different from your previous passwords
- Contain characters from each of the following categories: uppercase letters, lowercase letters, numbers, and symbols (including spaces)

Creating Strong Passwords | InSight

Microsoft provides the following guidelines for creating strong passwords:

- Create an acronym that's easy for you to remember. For example, select a phrase that is meaningful to you, such as "My birthday is February 12." From that phrase, you could create Mbdi02/12 as your password.
- Use numbers, symbols, and misspellings in place of letters or words in an easy-to-remember phrase. For example, you could change "My birthday is February 12" to MiBD I$ Two12.
- Relate your password to something that interests you, such as a hobby, sport, pet, or goal. For example, *Travel to Central America* could become Trvl 2 Cntrl@mrca.

Curt wants to start by creating a Standard user account on his computer with a strong password to protect it. If you can use an Administrator account to perform the following steps, log on to Windows using that Administrator account. If you do not have access to an Administrator account, read but do not perform the following steps.

To create a Standard user account:

▶ **1.** Click the **Start** button 🔵 on the taskbar, and then click **Control Panel** to open the Control Panel.

▶ **2.** In Category view, click **User Accounts and Family Safety**. The User Accounts and Family Safety window opens.

   Trouble? If the Control Panel opens in Classic view, click Category View in the left pane, and then repeat Step 2.

▶ **3.** Click **User Accounts** to open the User Accounts window. See Figure 5-28. Your window will differ.

User Accounts window ◀ Figure 5-28

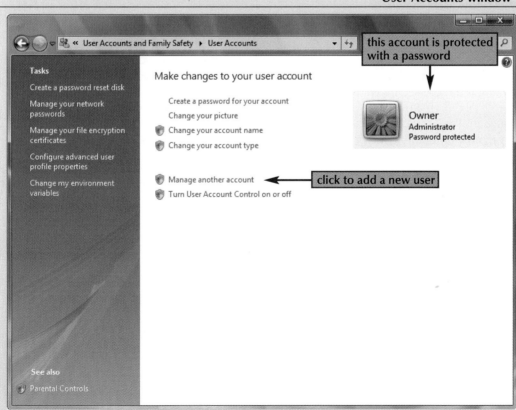

▶ **4.** Click **Manage another account** to open the Manage Accounts window.

Trouble? If a dialog box opens requesting an Administrator password or confirmation, enter the password or click the Continue button.

▶ **5.** Click **Create a new account**. The Create New Account window opens. See Figure 5-29.

Figure 5-29 ▶ Create New Account window

▶ **6.** Type **Curt** as the new account name, and then click the **Standard user** option button, if necessary.

▶ **7.** Click the **Create Account** button. The Manage Accounts window opens, listing the new account.

After you create a user account, you can change its properties, such as the user picture, account type, or account name, and you can create a password for the account. When you create a password, you can also create a hint to help you remember it. Using a hint is a more secure way to remember a password than writing it where others might see it. You'll create a password for Curt's account. For security, he can log on to his account later and change the password. For now, you'll use Prsto! 08 as the password, a combination of the name of Curt's company and the year it was founded.

To create a password:

▶ **1.** In the Manage Accounts window, click the **icon** for Curt's account, and then click **Create a password**. The Create Password window opens. See Figure 5-30.

2. In the New password text box, type **Prsto! 08**. Be sure to include a space after the exclamation point. You must type the password again to confirm it.

3. Click in the Confirm new password text box, and then type **Prsto! 08**.

4. Click in the Type a password hint text box, and then type **Company and first year**.

5. Click the **Create password** button. The Change an Account window opens, displaying the new account and indicating that it is password protected.

6. Click **User Accounts** in the Address bar to return to the User Accounts window.

Now you and Curt can show all of the Presto Global employees how to create accounts and passwords on their computers.

Controlling Access to Your Computer

One way to manage access to your computer is to take advantage of User Account Control (UAC), a feature that is turned on by default and can help prevent unauthorized changes to your computer. As you performed the previous steps, you might have seen UAC at work, asking for permission or an Administrator password before performing actions that could affect your computer's settings. A UAC dialog box usually opens when a program or action is about to start. The dialog box requests an Administrator password or your permission to start the program. By notifying you, UAC can help prevent malware from installing itself on or changing your computer without permission. When a UAC dialog box opens, make sure the name of the action or program it mentions is one that you intended to start. The dialog box indicates whether the program or action is part of Windows, is not part of Windows, is unidentified, or is blocked by the Administrator. The dialog box also indicates whether the program has a digital signature. If you are working on your own computer on which you've set up an Administrator account and one or more Standard accounts, the UAC dialog box helps to protect your computer by asking for an Administrator password so that software can't be installed without your knowledge or permission.

The UAC feature is turned on by default, and should not be turned off. You'll show Curt how to make sure UAC is turned on for all the Presto Global computers.

To verify User Account Control is turned on:

► **1.** In the User Accounts window, click **Turn User Account Control on or off**. The Turn User Account Control On or Off window opens.

   Trouble? If a User Account Control dialog box opens requesting an Administrator password or confirmation, enter the password or click the Continue button.

► **2.** Make sure the **Use User Account Control (UAC) to help protect your computer** check box is selected, and then click the **OK** button.

► **3.** Close the User Accounts window.

Locking Your Computer

Another way to protect your privacy and reduce power consumption is to let your computer go to sleep after a specified amount of idle time, which it does by default. Before going to sleep, Windows saves your files, settings, and the current state of your desktop in temporary memory, so you can return to work easily, and then plays a screen saver or blanks the screen. To wake the computer, you might move the mouse, press a key, or press the Power button, depending on your settings. Windows then displays your user account icon, and indicates the account is locked. If you use a password to log on to Windows, you must click your user icon and enter your password. Take this extra precaution of locking your account to protect the confidential information you store on your computer. To manually lock your computer, click the Start button, and then click the Lock button.

Besides controlling access to your computer with passwords and User Account Control, you can secure folders that contain files you share with other users.

Securing and Sharing Folders

If more than one person uses your computer, you can share files and folders with them in two ways: by explicitly allowing another user to share a folder or by storing files in the Public folder. The Public folder is designed for files any user can access. To share files from the Public folder, you copy or move your files to your Public folder so that other users can access them. Be aware, however, that any user on your computer can view all the files in the Public folder. You cannot restrict users from viewing only some of the files in the Public folder, though you can restrict them from changing the files or creating new ones. Use the Public folder for sharing if you prefer sharing your files from a single location on your computer, you want to monitor your shared files by opening a single folder, you want to keep your shared files separate from your other personal files, or you don't need to set sharing permissions for individual users.

When you explicitly share files, you set sharing permissions that determine who can change your files and what kinds of changes they can make. In this way, you can allow only some users on your computer to view, change, or create files in your folders. Set permissions to share any folder if you prefer to share folders directly from their original location (such as when you store many large photos in your Pictures folder), or when you want to allow only some users to access the folder.

Curt has a document named Guidelines that contains some general guidelines for translating documents. He wants to create a Translation folder in the Public folder on his computer and add other documents to it so that any user can access the documents. You'll show him how to do so.

To share a document in the Public folder:

▶ **1.** If necessary, insert the USB flash drive containing your Data Files into a USB port on your computer.

Trouble? If you do not have a USB flash drive, insert a different type of removable disk, such as a Zip disk, but not a CD, into the appropriate drive.

▶ **2.** In a folder window, open the **Tutorial.05** and then the **Tutorial** folder in your Data Files.

▶ **3.** Right-click the **Guidelines** document, and then click **Copy** on the shortcut menu.

▶ **4.** If necessary, click the **Folders** button in the Navigation pane to display the Folders list.

▶ **5.** In the Folders list, right-click the **Public** folder, point to **New**, and then click **Folder.**

Trouble? If User Account Control dialog boxes open requesting your permission, an Administrator password or confirmation, enter the password or click the Continue button.

▶ **6.** Type **Translation** as the name of the new folder, and then press the **Enter** key.

Trouble? If User Account Control dialog boxes open requesting your permission, an Administrator password or confirmation, enter the password or click the Continue button.

▶ **7.** Right-click the **Translation** folder, and then click **Paste** on the shortcut menu.

Now any user logged on to Curt's computer can access the Translation folder and its files.

Assigning Permissions to Folders

To specify which users can access a folder you want to share, you click the folder in a folder window, click Share on the toolbar, and then enter the account name of another user on the computer. Then you indicate whether that user is a Reader (can only read the files in the shared folder), Contributor (can read all files in the shared folder and can add, change, or delete their own files in the folder), or Co-owner (can read, change, add, or delete any file in the shared folder).

Curt has a sample password policy that he wants you to review before he revises it and distributes it to his employees. He wants to store it in a shared folder that only you can access and contribute to. First, you'll create a folder for the policy document. You also need to create a user account for yourself on Curt's computer, which you can do just before you assign permissions to the new folder.

To create a folder and a new account:

▶ **1.** Click the **Documents** folder in the Favorite Links list in your Navigation pane.

▶ **2.** Create a folder named **Policies** in the Documents folder.

▶ **3.** Copy the **Password Policy** file in the Tutorial.05\Tutorial folder in your Data Files to the Policies folder.

▶ **4.** Click the **Policies** folder, and then click the **Share** button on the toolbar. The File Sharing dialog box opens. See Figure 5-31.

Figure 5-31 ▶ **File Sharing dialog box**

▶ **5.** Click the **arrow button** to the right of the first list box (see Figure 5-31), and then click **Create a new user**. The User Accounts window opens.

▶ **6.** Click **Manage another account**, and then click **Create a new account**.

   Trouble? If a dialog box opens requesting an Administrator password or confirmation, enter the password or click the Continue button.

▶ **7.** Type **your first name** as the new account name, click the **Standard user** option button, if necessary, and then click the **Create Account** button.

▶ **8.** Click the icon for the new account, and then click **Create a password**.

▶ **9.** In the New password text box, type **T5 Pw-2010**. (Be sure to type the hyphen before 2010).

▶ **10.** Click in the Confirm new password text box, and then type **T5 Pw-2010**.

▶ **11.** Click the **Create password** button.

▶ **12.** Close the Change an Account window.

Now you can share the folder Policies folder so that only you and Curt can access it.

To share a folder:

▶ **1.** In the folder window, click the **Policies** folder, and then click the **Share** button on the toolbar. The File Sharing dialog box opens.

▶ **2.** Click the **arrow** button to the right of the top (empty) list box, and then click your user name.

▶ **3.** Click the **Add** button to add your user name to the list.

▶ **4.** Click the **permission level** (such as Reader) for your user name. See Figure 5-32.

Setting a permission level ◀ **Figure 5-32**

▶ **5.** Click **Contributor** so that you can view, add, and change your own files.

▶ **6.** Click the **Share** button. Windows displays the progress of the sharing process, and then confirms your folder is shared.

    Trouble? If a dialog box opens requesting an Administrator password or confirmation, enter the password or click the Continue button.

▶ **7.** Click the **Done** button.

▶ **8.** Close all open windows.

After you receive confirmation that your folder is shared, you can send a link to your shared files to the people with whom you are sharing the files. That way, the other users will know the files are shared and how to access them. You can click "e-mail these links" in the File Sharing confirmation window to open a Windows Mail e-mail message with the link to your shared files.

Restoring Your Settings

If you are working in a computer lab or a computer other than your own, complete the steps in this section to restore the original settings on your computer. If a User Account Control dialog box opens requesting an Administrator password or confirmation after you perform any of the following steps, enter the password or click the Continue button.

To restore your settings:

▶ **1.** Open the Control Panel in Category view, click **Security**, and then click **Security Center**.

▶ **2.** In the left pane of the Windows Security Center window, click **Windows Firewall**, and then click **Change settings** to open the Windows Firewall Settings dialog box. Click the **Exceptions** tab to view the exception list.

▶ **3.** Click the **Windows Meeting Space** check box, and the **OK** button to close the Windows Firewall dialog box, and then close the Windows Firewall window.

▶ **4.** In the Windows Security Center window, click **Windows Update**, and then click **Change settings** in the left pane. In the Install new updates section, click the update time, click the original time set for installing updates, and then click the **OK** button. Close the Windows Update window.

▶ **5.** In the Windows Security Center window, click **Windows Defender** in the left pane. Click the **Tools** button on the toolbar, and then click **Options**. Click the **Approximate time** button, click the original time set for scanning, and then click the **Save** button. Close all open windows.

▶ **6.** Start Windows Mail, click **Tools** on the menu bar, and then click **Junk E-mail Options**. Click the **Safe Senders** tab, click **your e-mail address** in the list, and then click the **Remove** button.

▶ **7.** Click the **Phishing** tab, click the **Move phishing E-mail to the Junk Mail folder** check box to remove the check mark, click the **OK** button to close the Junk E-mail Options dialog box, and then close Windows Mail.

▶ **8.** Start Internet Explorer, click the **Tools** button on the Internet Explorer toolbar, point to **Pop-up Blocker**, and then click **Pop-up Blocker Settings**. Click the **Filter level** button, and then click your original setting. Click the **Close** button to close the Pop-up Blocker Settings dialog box.

▶ **9.** Click the **Tools** button on the Internet Explorer toolbar, click **Internet Options**, click the **Privacy** tab, and then drag the slider to its original setting. Click the **OK** button to close the Internet Options dialog box.

▶ **10.** Click the **Tools** button on the Internet Explorer toolbar, click **Internet Options**, click the **Advanced** tab, and then restore your original settings for the **Enable third-party browser extensions**, **Do not save encrypted pages to disk**, **Empty Temporary Internet Files folder when browser is closed**, and **Warn if changing between secure and not secure mode** check boxes. Click the **OK** button to close the Internet Options dialog box, and then close Internet Explorer.

▶ **11.** Open the Control Panel in Category view, click **User Accounts and Family Safety**, click **User Accounts**, and then click **Manage another account**. Click the **Curt** account icon, click **Delete the account**, click the **Delete Files** button, and then click the **Delete Account** button.

▶ **12.** Click the account icon for your account, click **Delete the account**, click the **Delete Files** button, and then click the **Delete Account** button.

▶ **13.** Navigate to the **Public** folder on your hard disk, and then move the **Translation** folder to the Tutorial.05\Tutorial folder provided with your Data Files.

▶ **14.** Navigate to the **Documents** folder on your hard disk, and then move the **Policies** folder to the Tutorial.05\Tutorial folder provided with your Data Files. Delete the files in the Tutorial.05\Tutorial folder so that the folder contains only subfolders.

▶ **15.** Close all open windows.

Session 5.2 Quick Check

1. How can Internet Explorer help protect you from phishing scams?
2. True or False. When you visit a Web site with pop-up ads and the pop-up blocker is turned on, you can use the Information bar to open the pop-up window.
3. A browser _____ program provides enhancements such as a toolbar or improved search feature.
4. True or False. All cookies pose some type of security risk.
5. What type of user account does Microsoft recommend for every regular user on a computer?
6. Name three characteristics of a strong password.
7. When does a User Account Control (UAC) dialog box usually open?
8. If more than one person uses your computer, you can share files and folders with them in two ways: by explicitly allowing another user to share a folder or by storing files in the _____ folder.

Tutorial Summary

In this tutorial, you used the Windows Vista Security Center to manage Windows Firewall, Windows Update, and your antivirus software. You used Windows Defender to guard against spyware, and you selected options in Windows Mail to protect your computer from e-mail viruses and junk e-mail. You also used the security features in Internet Explorer to browse safely, including using the Phishing Filter, protected mode, security zones, and privacy settings. You also learned how to block pop-up ads and manage add-on programs. To enhance security, you set up a password-protected user account and learned how to share your folders.

Key Terms

ActiveX control	exception	spyware
add-on	first-party cookie	strong password
adware	hacker	third-party cookie
cache	hijack	update
cookie	phishing	user account
cracker	pop-up ad	virus
digital signature	quarantine	worm
e-mail relay	script	
encrypt	spam	

| Practice | **Review Assignments** |

Practice the skills you learned in the tutorial.

For a list of Data Files in the Review folder, see page 211.

Curt Mickelson, owner of Presto Global Translators, recently bought a new Windows Vista computer for you to share with Donna Cordoza, one of his project managers who specializes in translating videos that she plays on Windows Media Player. You'll show Donna how to keep the new computer secure and set up accounts for the two of you. Complete the following steps, noting your original settings so you can restore them later:

1. Open Windows Firewall, choose to allow a program through Windows Firewall, and then add Windows Media Player to the exception list.
2. Change the settings in Windows Update to automatically check for and install updates every day at 7:00 a.m.
3. Maximize the Windows Security Center window, expand the Firewall and Automatic updating sections, and then press the Alt+Print Screen keys to capture an image of the window. Open Paint, and then press Ctrl+V to paste the image in a Paint file. Save the file as **SecurityCenterXY**, where *XY* are your initials, in the Tutorial.05\ Review folder provided with your Data Files.
4. Use Windows Defender to perform a quick scan on your computer.
5. Change the Windows Defender settings to scan every day at 10:00 p.m.
6. With the Windows Defender home page window open on your desktop, press the Alt+Print Screen keys to capture an image of the window. Open Paint, and then press Ctrl+V to paste the image in a Paint file. Save the file as **DefenderXY**, where *XY* are your initials, in the Tutorial.05\Review folder provided with your Data Files. Close all open windows.
7. In Windows Mail, add the following e-mail address to your Safe Senders list: **DonnaCordoza@presto.net**.
8. In Internet Explorer, open a Web page in your Favorites list or go to the home page of a popular search engine, such as Google (www.google.com) or Yahoo! (www.yahoo.com). Use the Phishing Filter to verify this Web site is not a phishing Web site.
9. Make sure the pop-up blocker in Internet Explorer is turned on, and then visit a popular news Web site, such as www.cnn.com, until you find one that includes pop-up windows. With the Information bar displayed in the Internet Explorer window, press the Alt+Print Screen keys to capture an image of the window. Open Paint, and then press Ctrl+V to paste the image in a Paint file. Save the file as **PopUpXY**, where *XY* are your initials, in the Tutorial.05\Review folder provided with your Data Files. Close all open windows.
10. Create Standard user accounts for you and for Donna Cordoza. Use a name and password you prefer for your user account, making sure these are different from any other account on the computer. Use **Donna** as the name and **iLuv MVs98** as the password for Donna's account.
11. With the User Accounts window open on the desktop, press the Alt+Print Screen keys to capture an image of the window. Open Paint, and then press Ctrl+V to paste the image in a Paint file. Save the file as **UsersXY**, where *XY* are your initials, in the Tutorial.05\Review folder provided with your Data Files.
12. Move the **Video Scripts** document from the Tutorial.05\Review folder provided with your Data Files to a new folder named **Marketing** created in your Documents folder.

13. Share the **Marketing** folder with Donna as a Contributor. With the final Sharing Files window open on your desktop, press the Alt+Print Screen keys to capture an image of the window. Open Paint, and then press Ctrl+V to paste the image in a Paint file. Save the file as **SharingXY**, where *XY* are your initials, in the Tutorial.05\Review folder provided with your Data Files.

14. Restore the settings on your computer. Remove Windows Media Player from the Windows Firewall exception list. Restore the settings in Windows Update and Windows Defender to install updates and scan at their original times. Remove Donna Cordoza's e-mail address from the Windows Mail Safe Senders list. Move the **Marketing** folder to the Tutorial.05\Review folder provided with your Data Files. Delete the user accounts you created for yourself and Donna Cordoza.

15. Close all open windows.

16. Submit the results of the preceding steps to your instructor, either in printed or electronic form, as requested.

| Apply | | **Case Problem 1** |

Use the skills you learned in the tutorial to select security settings for a theater restoration company.

For a list of Data Files in the Case1 folder, see page 211.

Trang Restoration   Alice and Lou Trang run a small business in Portland, Oregon, named Trang Restoration, which restores old theaters, many from the vaudeville era. Their most successful efforts are multiuse theaters that host live productions, independent films, and training classes for actors, directors, and others in the acting and film fields. Alice conducts most of her marketing work on a laptop computer running Windows Vista, and is concerned about maintaining security as she communicates with clients and researches restoration materials on the Internet. She has experienced problems with spam and wants to know how to block senders in Windows Mail. You'll help her use the Windows Vista security settings to protect her computer. Complete the following steps, noting your original settings so you can restore them later:

1. Add Wireless Portable Devices to the Windows Firewall exception list.

2. Change the settings in Windows Update to automatically check for and install updates every day at 5:00 a.m.

3. Change the Windows Defender settings to scan every day at 11:00 p.m.

4. Arrange both windows so both status summaries are visible, and then press the Print Screen key to capture an image of the desktop. Open Paint, and then press Ctrl+V to paste the image in a Paint file. Save the file as **SecurityXY**, where *XY* are your initials, in the Tutorial.05\Case1 folder provided with your Data Files. Close all open windows.

5. In Windows Mail, add your e-mail address to the Blocked Senders list. Send an e-mail to yourself. When Windows Mail receives and blocks this message, press the Alt+Print Screen keys to capture an image of the dialog box. Open Paint, and then press Ctrl+V to paste the image in a Paint file. Save the file as **BlockedMailXY**, where *XY* are your initials, in the Tutorial.05\Case1 folder provided with your Data Files. Close Windows Mail.

6. In Internet Explorer, change the security level for the Trusted sites zone to Low. Press the Alt+Print Screen keys to capture an image of the window. Open Paint, and then press Ctrl+V to paste the image in a Paint file. Save the file as **SecurityZoneXY**, where *XY* are your initials, in the Tutorial.05\Case1 folder provided with your Data Files.

7. In the Manage Add-ons dialog box, display a list of downloaded ActiveX controls. Press the Alt+Print Screen keys to capture an image of the window. Open Paint, and then press Ctrl+V to paste the image in a Paint file. Save the file as **AddOnsXY**, where XY are your initials, in the Tutorial.05\Case1 folder provided with your Data Files. Close all open windows.

8. Create Standard user accounts for Alice and Lou Trang. For Alice's account, use **Alice** as the name and **MiBd I$ 05/14** as her password. For Lou's account, use **Lou** as the name and **ILuv*The8tr** as his password.

9. With the User Accounts window open on the desktop, press the Alt+Print Screen keys to capture an image of the window. Open Paint, and then press Ctrl+V to paste the image in a Paint file. Save the file as **AccountsXY**, where XY are your initials, in the Tutorial.05\Case1 folder provided with your Data Files.

10. Move the **Pioneer Trail Theater** document from the Tutorial.05\Case1 folder provided with your Data Files to a new folder named **Projects** in the Public folder on your computer.

11. Move the **Employment** document from the Tutorial.05\Case1 folder provided with your Data Files to a new folder named **Jobs** in your Documents folder.

12. Share the **Jobs** folder with Alice and Lou as Co-owners. Open three windows on your desktop: the Public folder window, the Documents folder window, and the final Sharing Files window. Resize and arrange all as necessary to see their contents. Press the Print Screen key to capture an image of the desktop. Open Paint, and then press Ctrl+V to paste the image in a Paint file. Save the file as **SharedFoldersXY**, where XY are your initials, in the Tutorial.05\Case1 folder provided with your Data Files.

13. Restore the settings on your computer. Remove Wireless Portable Devices from the Windows Firewall exception list. Restore the settings in Windows Update and Windows Defender to install updates and scan at their original times. Remove your e-mail address from the Windows Mail Blocked Senders list. Restore the security level for the Trusted sites zone to its original setting. Move the **Projects** and **Jobs** folders to the Tutorial.05\Review folder provided with your Data Files. Delete the user accounts you created for Alice and Lou Trang.

14. Close all open windows.

15. Submit the results of the preceding steps to your instructor, either in printed or electronic form, as requested.

Apply | **Case Problem 2**

Use the skills you learned in the tutorial to select security settings for a day spa.

There are no Data Files needed for this Case Problem.

Revive Day Spa Rita Patel owns the Revive Day Spa in Charleston, West Virginia, which is part of the Charleston Golf Resort. Revive offers spa services ranging from massage therapy to facial treatments for day or weeklong packages. Guests of the Charleston Golf Resort can use a spa menu to select services such as hydrotherapy and yoga for golfers. Rita uses Windows Meeting Space to meet with managers of the Charleston Golf Resort and regularly uses Windows Mail and Internet Explorer to run her business. She has experienced problems with spyware and viruses, and wants to know when to trust e-mail she receives and Web sites she visits. You'll help her use the Windows Vista security settings to protect her computer. Complete the following steps, noting your original settings so you can restore them later:

1. Add Windows Meeting Space to the Windows Firewall exception list. Capture an image of the Exceptions tab in the Windows Firewall Settings dialog box, and save it in a Paint file named **FirewallXY**, where *XY* are your initials, in the Tutorial.05\Case2 folder provided with your Data Files.

⊕ EXPLORE
2. In Windows Update, view your update history, and then check for updates. (*Hint*: In the Windows Update window, click View update history and then click Check for updates in the left pane.) When Windows Update finishes checking for updates, capture an image of the Review your update history window, and save it as a Paint file named **UpdatesXY**, where *XY* are your initials, in the Tutorial.05\Case2 folder provided with your Data Files.

3. In Windows Mail, find out how to get a digital ID. (*Hint*: Click the Get Digital ID button on the Security tab of the Options dialog box.) Find the Web page explaining how to find services that issue or use a digital ID, and then save the page as a Web Archive, single file named **Digital IDXY**, where *XY* are your initials, in the Tutorial.05\Case2 folder provided with your Data Files. Close Windows Mail.

4. In Internet Explorer, open a Web page in your Favorites list or go to the home page of a popular search engine, such as Google (www.google.com) or Yahoo! (www.yahoo.com). Use the Phishing Filter to verify this Web site is not a phishing Web site. Capture an image of the Internet Explorer window and Phishing Filter dialog box, and save it in a Paint file named **PhishingXY**, where *XY* are your initials, in the Tutorial.05\Case2 folder provided with your Data Files.

5. In Internet Explorer, change the security level for the Internet sites zone to High. Capture an image of the dialog box, and save it in a Paint file named **HighSecurityXY**, where *XY* are your initials, in the Tutorial.05\Case2 folder provided with your Data Files.

6. Create a Standard user account for Rita Patel. Use **Rita** as the name and **Re:VeyeV10** as her password.

⊕ EXPLORE
7. Create a guest account on the computer. (*Hint*: In the Manage Accounts window, click the Guest account, and then click the Turn On button.)

8. With the User Accounts window open on the desktop, capture an image of the dialog box, and save it in a Paint file named **AccountsXY**, where *XY* are your initials, in the Tutorial.05\Case2 folder provided with your Data Files.

9. Restore the settings on your computer. Remove Windows Meeting Space from the Windows Firewall exception list. Restore the security level for the Internet sites zone to its original setting. Delete the user account you created for Rita Patel and turn off the Guest account.

10. Close all open windows.

11. Submit the results of the preceding steps to your instructor, either in printed or electronic form, as requested.

Challenge | **Case Problem 3**

Go beyond what you've learned to protect a computer at a sports center.

There are no Data Files needed for this Case Problem.

Urban Sports Urban Sports is a sports center in Bloomington, Indiana, that organizes leagues in soccer, football, basketball, softball, and other sports for children and adults.

Henry Lange manages the center and provides computers with Internet connections to members who want to use them. Henry is particularly concerned about the security of these computers. You'll help him use the Windows Vista security settings to protect a public computer. Complete the following steps, noting your original settings so you can restore them later:

⊕ EXPLORE
1. In Windows Firewall, block all incoming connections. (*Hint*: Select an option on the General tab of the Windows Firewall Settings dialog box.)

⊕ EXPLORE
2. Set Windows Defender to perform a full scan of your computer every day at 11:00 p.m. Also set default actions for High and Medium alert items so that Windows Defender removes these items.

3. Arrange the Windows Defender Options window and the Windows Firewall window to display the settings you changed, and then capture an image of the desktop. Save the image as a Paint file named **FullScan*XY***, where *XY* are your initials, in the Tutorial.05\Case3 folder provided with your Data Files. Close all open windows.

4. In Windows Mail, set the Junk E-mail protection level to High. Also specify that you want to move phishing e-mail to the Junk Mail folder. Close Windows Mail.

5. In Internet Explorer, change the privacy level for the Internet sites zone to High. Capture an image of the dialog box, and save it in a Paint file named **HighPrivacyXY**, where *XY* are your initials, in the Tutorial.05\Case3 folder provided with your Data Files.

6. Delete all temporary files and cookies in Internet Explorer.

⊕ EXPLORE
7. Set Internet Explorer so that it does not store a list of browsing history. (*Hint*: On the General tab of the Internet Options dialog box, click the Settings button in the Browsing history section, and then change the Days to keep pages in history setting.) Capture an image of the dialog box, and save it in a Paint file named **NoHistoryXY**, where *XY* are your initials, in the Tutorial.05\Case3 folder provided with your Data Files.

⊕ EXPLORE
8. Create a password for your account on your computer, if necessary, and then create a guest account. (*Hint*: In the Manage Accounts window, click the Guest account, and then click the Turn On button.)

9. With the User Accounts window open on the desktop, capture an image of the window, and save it in a Paint file named **GuestAccountXY**, where *XY* are your initials, in the Tutorial.05\Case3 folder provided with your Data Files.

10. Restore the settings on your computer. Restore the original general setting in Windows Firewall. Restore the settings for a Windows Defender scan to their original settings, including the default actions. Restore the Junk E-mail options in Windows Mail to their original settings. In Internet Explorer, restore the privacy level for the Internet sites zone to its original setting, and restore the number of days Internet Explorer keeps your browsing history to its original setting. Turn off the Guest account.

11. Close all open windows.

12. Submit the results of the preceding steps to your instructor, either in printed or electronic form, as requested.

Research | Case Problem 4

Work with the skills you've learned and use the Internet to research computer security for a group of soil scientists.

There are no Data Files needed for this Case Problem.

Osborne & Associates   Tyler Osborne is the head scientist for Osborne & Associates, a firm providing soil science services in Columbia, Missouri. Osborne & Associates maps and classifies soils for land planners and managers and conducts research on soil degradation or erosion. Tyler wants to protect the computers his scientists use against security threats. To do so, he first wants to understand who typically attacks computers and their data. He also wants to learn more about the types of attacks people use to access computers, and how much damage attacks have caused. He asks you to research these topics and report your findings. Complete the following steps:

1. Use your favorite search engine to find information about the types of people behind attacks on desktop computers. (Attacks on networks are in a separate category.) Try searching for information about the following types of attackers:
   - Hackers
   - Crackers
   - Computer spies
   - Social engineers

2. Use your favorite search engine to find information about the types of attacks that can affect a desktop computer. Try searching for information about the following types of attacks:
   - Malicious software, or malware
   - Viruses
   - Worms
   - Logic bombs
   - Password guessing

3. Use your favorite search engine to find information about the costs to businesses and individual computer users to recover from an attack, such as a virus infestation.

4. Use a word processor to summarize your findings in one or two pages. Be sure to define any new terms and cite the Web sites where you found your information. Save your document as Attacks.docx in the Tutorial.05\Case4 folder provided with your Data Files. (The filename extension of your document might differ.)

5. Submit the results of the preceding steps to your instructor, either in printed or electronic form, as requested.

Review | Quick Check Answers

Session 5.1

1. malicious or harmful software
2. Security Center
3. True
4. to allow that program to communicate with your computer now and in the future
5. update
6. False
7. Spyware monitors your computing actions to collect information about you, change settings on your computer, or interrupt programs and slow your computer's performance.
8. Spam

Session 5.2

1. The Phishing Filter detects possible phishing Web sites.
2. True
3. add-on
4. False
5. Standard account

6. Strong passwords contain at least eight characters; do not include your user name, real name, or company name; are not words you can find in the dictionary; are significantly different from your previous passwords; and contain characters from each of the following categories: uppercase letters, lowercase letters, numbers, and symbols (including spaces)
7. when a program or action is about to start
8. Public

Ending Data Files

Tutorial.05 →

Tutorial

None

Review

DefenderXY.jpg
PopUpXY.jpg
SecurityCenterXY.jpg
SharingXY.jpg
UsersXY.jpg

Case1

AccountsXY.jpg
AddOnsXY.jpg
BlockedMailXY.jpg
SecurityXY.jpg
SecurityZoneXY.jpg
SharedFoldersXY.jpg

Case2

AccountsXY.jpg
Digital IDXY.mht
FirewallXY.jpg
HighSecurityXY.jpg
PhishingXY.jpg
UpdatesXY.jpg

Case3

FullScanXY.jpg
GuestAccountXY.jpg
HighPrivacyXY.jpg
NoHistoryXY.jpg

Case4

Attacks.docx

Objectives

Session 6.1
- Develop search strategies
- Find files by name, type, and category
- Examine search results and save a search
- Add tags and other details to files
- Use Boolean filters in advanced searches

Session 6.2
- Speed searches by indexing
- Search the Internet
- Narrow searches using advanced search features
- Select search providers in Internet Explorer
- Collaborate with others using Windows Meeting Space

Searching for Information and Collaborating with Others

Finding and Sharing Information

Case | TrendSpot Magazine

TrendSpot is an online magazine for marketing professionals that features articles, profiles, and commentary about consumer trends. Kendra Cho, the founder of *TrendSpot*, works out of offices in Roswell, Georgia, though she collaborates with *TrendSpot* editors around the country. As Kendra's editorial assistant, your duties include organizing the information submitted with articles and finding supporting material, such as photos and quotations.

In this tutorial, you'll learn how to develop search strategies for finding information, and then use the Windows Vista search tools to find files. You'll refine your searches by using advanced techniques such as Boolean filters and multiple criteria, and then index your computer to speed searches. You'll also learn how to apply these search strategies when using Internet Explorer to find information on the Web. To share this information, you'll use Windows Meeting Space to collaborate and distribute the information to others.

Starting Data Files

Session 6.1

Developing Search Strategies

As you install programs and store data on your computer, the number of files and folders you have grows, and it becomes harder to locate a particular item. Using an effective organization scheme helps you find files and folders when you need them. However, if pinpointing an item means browsing dozens or hundreds of files and folders or if you don't know where to look, you can use a Windows Vista search tool. You have already used the Search box in a folder window to find files by name and file contents. Windows Vista provides three other tools for finding files and folders: the Search pane in a folder window, the Start Search box on the Start menu, and the Search folder. Figure 6-1 recommends when to choose one search tool over another.

| Figure 6-1 | Choosing a search tool |

Search Tool	When to Use	Notes
Search box in a folder window	When you know where to start looking for a file or folder and want to search by file-name or contents	Windows searches in the current folder and all of its subfolders.
Search pane in a folder window	When you want to use criteria other than text in the filename or contents or you want to combine search criteria	Windows can search any single folder and its subfolders.
Search box on the Start menu	When you want to find a program, a Web site included in your browser's history, or a file or folder stored in your personal folder	Your personal folder includes Documents, Pictures, Music, Desktop, and other common locations.
Search folder	When you don't know where a file or folder is located or are looking for files from several folders	Windows can search one, some, or all of the folders on your computer.

When you use any of the Windows Vista search tools, you provide **search criteria**, which are conditions that the file or folder must meet to have Windows find it. These conditions help you define and narrow your search so you can quickly find the item you want. For example, if you provide a filename such as Budget as the search criterion, Windows locates and displays every file that matches that criterion—in other words, all files whose filename contains a word starting with *Budget*.

If you use text in the filename or the file contents as search criteria, you are conducting a basic search. If you use other properties such as tags or authors as search criteria, you are conducting an advanced search. A **tag** is a word or phrase you add to photos and other types of files to describe them. The other properties you can use as search criteria include any detail you can display as a column in a folder window. (Recall that you can display columns in a folder window by right-clicking a column heading, and then clicking a detail on the shortcut menu. If the detail you want to display does not appear on the shortcut menu, you can click More to open the Choose Details dialog box.) Figure 6-2 describes common criteria you can use when you conduct basic and advanced searches to find a file.

Typical search criteria ◀ Figure 6-2

File Property	Description	Example
Basic Searches		
Filename	All or part of the filename	To find a file named April sales.xlsx, enter *Apr* or *sales* as the criterion.
File type	Filename extension	To find all of your photos, enter *JPG*.
Contents	Text the file contains	To find a file that uses "Trends for June" as a heading, start typing *Trends for June*.
Advanced Searches		
Date	Date the file was modified, created, or accessed	To find a document edited on May 2, 2010, enter *5/2/10* as the criterion.
Size	Size of the file in kilobytes (KB)	To find files larger than 1 MB, enter *1000* as the criterion.
Tag	Word or phrase added to the file	To find a photo with "winter, vacation, ski" as tags, enter *winter* as the criterion.
Author	Name of the person who created the file	To find a document that Kendra created, enter *Kendra* as the criterion.

When you combine criteria, such as to find a file named Agenda that you created last Monday, you are also conducting an advanced search. You'll learn how to combine search criteria later in the tutorial.

Before you start looking for a file or folder on your computer, determine what you already know about the item; this helps you develop a search strategy. Choose the search tool that best fits your needs, and use search criteria that are most likely to find the item. For example, suppose you want to find a photo that you took last New Year's Eve and stored somewhere in the Pictures folder. Because you know the location of the photo, you can use the Search box in the Pictures folder window. You also know when you took the photo, so you can conduct an advanced search using *12/31/09* as the search criterion.

Kendra asks you to help her prepare a column on travel trends for the upcoming issue of *TrendSpot*. She has received photos and text files from contributors and asks you to help find the right content for the travel column. You'll use the Windows Vista search tools to assist Kendra and complete this task.

Searching in a Folder Window

You have already used the Search box in a folder window to find files based on their filenames and contents. To conduct these kinds of basic searches, you type text in the Search box. Windows then displays only those files in the current folder or its subfolders that match the criterion: files whose contents or filename includes a word starting with the text you typed. In addition to text in the filename or file contents, you can enter a filename extension as the search criterion to find files by type, such as JPG to find files with a .jpg extension (usually photo files). When you search for files by type, you can enter the filename extension on its own (JPG or jpg) or using an asterisk and a dot before the filename extension (*. JPG or *.jpg). In this case, the asterisk is a **wildcard**, a symbol that stands for one or more unspecified characters in the search criterion.

Using a wildcard is a good idea if you want to search for certain types of files, such as those with a DOC filename extension, but some of your filenames include words that start with the extension text, such as Doctor Visit, June Docket, or Kendra Docs. In this case, using a wildcard makes it clear that you are searching by filename extension only, and produces more accurate search results.

You can also conduct advanced searches from a folder window. To search only certain types of files, such as e-mail messages, documents, or pictures, you can display the **Search pane**. You use the Search pane to narrow a search to a specified category of files. For example, if you click the Document button on the Search pane and then type text in the Search box, Windows displays only the text files, spreadsheets, presentations, and other documents that meet your criteria.

Reference Window | **Searching for a File by Type**

- Open the folder you want to search.
- Click in the Search box, and then type the filename extension on its own, such as JPG, or using a wildcard character, as in *.jpg.

Kendra is writing her travel column about two places that are emerging as hot spots for budget travelers: Australia and Egypt. First, she wants to know how many photos her contributors submitted featuring these two locations. Because all of these photos are stored in two subfolders, you can provide the information Kendra wants by conducting a basic search in a folder window using the filename extension JPG as the search criterion.

To search for files by type:

▶ **1.** If necessary, insert the USB flash drive containing your Data Files into a USB port on your computer.

   Trouble? If you do not have a USB flash drive, make sure you can access your Data Files from your computer.

▶ **2.** In a folder window, open the **Tutorial.06** folder and then the **Tutorial** folder in your Data Files.

▶ **3.** Click in the Search box, and then type **JPG**. Windows displays only the files with a .jpg extension in the folder window.

▶ **4.** If necessary, click the **Views** button arrow, and then click **Large Icons** to see the contents of the files clearly. See Figure 6-3.

Searching for files with a JPG filename extension ◀ **Figure 6-3**

Note that the Details pane at the bottom of the folder window indicates that the subfolders in the Tutorial folder contain 19 JPG files.

Searching Versus Sorting, Filtering, Grouping, and Stacking | InSight

Recall that instead of using the Search box, you can find files by sorting, filtering, grouping, or stacking files using the column headings in a folder window. The method you choose depends on the number of files you want to search, the location of the files, and their names. For example, suppose you need to find JPG files. If you want to search the current folder *and* its subfolders, use the Search box—the other options find files only in the current folder. If you're searching a single folder, the Search box is also preferable if the folder contains similar filenames (because sorting would list together many files that start with the same text) or many different types of files (because grouping or stacking would produce many groups or stacks). If you want to find a particular file in a very large folder, it is often easier to use the Search box rather than deal with a long file list; however, if the folder doesn't contain too many files, then sorting, grouping, stacking, or filtering is usually a quicker method.

The 19 JPG files you found all have filenames starting with *Photo* followed by a number, such as Photo01 and Photo02. Kendra asked the contributors to name the files this way to streamline the layout and publication of the magazine. As Kendra prepares the column on Egypt, for example, she'll indicate where to insert photos in sequence. For the first photo, she'll include a note such as *Insert Egypt Photo01 here*, for the second photo,

Insert Egypt Photo02 here, and so on. That way, when the page designers compose the column on travel in Egypt, they don't have to find files with long or cryptic names. They can also tell from the filenames the number of files to include and the sequence in which they should appear. Although this file-naming scheme works well for editing and producing the magazine, it poses challenges for your research because the filenames do not reveal anything about the content except that they are photos.

Finding Files by Category with the Search Pane

For searching purposes, Windows classifies files into five general categories. By default, the folder window shows all categories of files. You can open the Search pane in any folder window to narrow your search to a general category of files by clicking a button on the Search pane: E-mail (e-mail messages stored in the folder or its subfolder), Document (text files, spreadsheets, and presentations), Picture (graphic files such as photos and drawings), or Music (audio files such as music and speech). If you click the Other button on the Search pane, you narrow the search to all kinds of files except for e-mail, documents, pictures, and music. You can select an option on the Search pane with or without entering a search criterion in the Search box. If you enter a criterion in the Search box and select an option on the Search pane, Windows displays only those files that meet both criteria—they contain the specified text and are e-mail messages, for example.

Reference Window | Searching for a File by Category

- Open the folder you want to search.
- Enter a filename or file contents search criterion in the Search box.
- Click the Organize button on the toolbar, point to Layout, and then click Search Pane. If you are working in a Search Results window, click the Search Tools button, and then click Search Pane.
- Click a button on the Search Pane to select a category.

Kendra now wants to find a text file that Sam Moriarity, a novice contributor, submitted. As Kendra requested, Sam created a short document describing the type of photograph that would best illustrate a sidebar he wrote listing travel tips for budget travelers. He does not recall where he saved the file or its filename, though it's likely the word *photo* appears in the filename or contents. If you conduct a basic search by entering *photo* in the Search box, you will find the 19 JPG files as well as any other files containing the word *photo* in their filenames or contents. To narrow the search to documents only, you'll use the Search pane.

To narrow a search using the Search pane:

1. Click the **Back** button ⟵ to return to the Tutorial folder window, click the Search box, and then type **pho** to begin entering *photo*. Windows displays all the files in the Tutorial subfolders with a filename that contains a word beginning with *pho*.

2. Click the **Search Tools** button on the toolbar, and then click **Search Pane** to open the Search pane. See Figure 6-4.

Tip

The Search Tools button appears on a folder window toolbar only after you've used the Search box to search for files or folders.

Search pane in a folder window ◀ Figure 6-4

3. Click the **Document** button on the Search pane. Windows reduces the search results to files that meet both criteria—only documents whose filenames contain a word beginning with *pho*.

Examining the Search Results

After you enter search criteria using the Search box or the Search pane, Windows filters the view of the folder window to display files that meet your criteria. These are your search results. Figure 6-5 shows the results of the search performed in the preceding set of steps: documents whose filenames contain a word beginning with *photo*. When a folder window displays search results, it provides extra tools to help you work with the files you found. For example, the toolbar contains a Save Search button for saving the criteria you used to perform a search. If you often look for a certain group of files, you can save the search so you don't have to reconstruct the criteria each time you want to find the files. The toolbar still contains a Search Tools button, which provides additional search options. (You'll use the Search Tools button later in this tutorial.)

| Figure 6-5 | Search results |

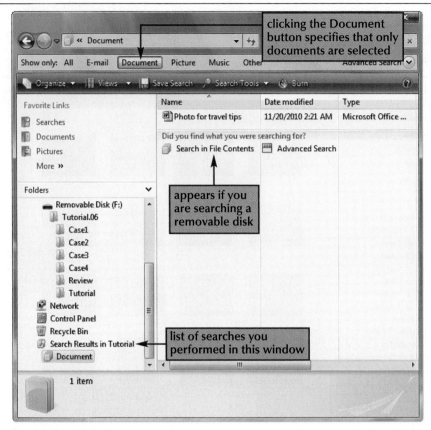

At the bottom of the Folders list in a Search Results window, Windows includes the searches you performed in that window, and stores them there until you close the window. If you want to redisplay the results of a previous search, you can click the appropriate search results in the Folders list. In the right pane of a search results window, Windows asks, "Did you find what you were searching for?" and provides links to perform an advanced search. (If you are searching files on a removable disk, you can also choose to search in the file contents.)

In addition to the extra tools provided in a search window, you can use the standard folder window tools to open, move, copy, rename, or delete a file. You can also verify that a file you found is one you want without opening the file. First, you can select the file in the folder window and then review the information in the Details pane. If you're not sure this is the right file, you can open the Preview pane, which displays the contents of the selected file. You'll verify the Photo for travel tips file you found is the document Sam sent describing the type of photograph that would best illustrate his list of travel tips.

To verify you found the right file:

▶ 1. In the folder window, click the **Photo for travel tips** file. Information about the file appears in the Details pane, including the file type, size, and the date it was modified. (Your window might show additional information.)

▶ 2. Click the **Organize** button on the toolbar, point to **Layout**, and then click **Preview Pane**. The Preview pane opens in the folder window, displaying the contents of the Photo for travel tips file. See Figure 6-6.

Verifying a found file ◄ Figure 6-6

Trouble? If the Preview pane doesn't seem to open, widen the folder window to display the Preview pane.

The Photo for travel tips file appears to be the file that Kendra needs. Now she needs to find the most recent photos she has of Australia and Egypt. To do that, you can conduct an advanced search in the Search pane.

Conducting Advanced Searches with the Search Pane

The Search box and the default Search pane make it easy to use multiple criteria, as long as you want to find files by specifying text and a file category. To use other types of criteria, such as date modified, size, or tags, you conduct an advanced search using the expanded Search pane. When you expand the Search pane, you can conduct an advanced search by specifying one or more of the criteria shown in Figure 6-7.

Figure 6-7 ▸ **Advanced search criteria**

Expanded Search Pane Option	When to Use	How to Refine the Option
All Files		
Location	To search locations other than the current folder	Specify any drive or folder on your computer, including indexed locations.
Date	To search for files by date created, date modified, or date accessed	Specify a particular date or dates before or after a particular date.
Size	To search for files by size	Specify any size or one equal to, less than, or greater than a particular size.
Filename	To search for files by filename	Specify all of the filename or only the first few characters.
Tags	To search for files by their tags	Specify one or more tags.
Authors	To search for files by their authors	Specify one or more authors.
Additional Options for E-mail		
Date	To search for e-mail by date received, sent, modified, created, or accessed	Specify a particular date or dates before or after a particular date.
Subject	To search for e-mail by subject	Specify all or part of the text in the Subject line.
From names	To search for e-mail by sender	Specify one or more sender names.
To names	To search for e-mail by recipient	Specify one or more recipient names.
Additional Options for Pictures		
Date	To search for pictures by date taken, modified, created, or accessed	Specify a particular date or dates before or after a particular date.
Title	To search for pictures by title	Specify all or part of the picture title.
Additional Options for Music		
Title	To search for music by title	Specify all or part of the picture title.
Artists	To search for music by artist	Specify contributing artist.
Album	To search for music by album	Specify album name.

One of the locations you can search is your **indexed locations**, a group of folders including all of the folders in your personal folder (Documents, Pictures, Music, Desktop, and other common locations), e-mail, and offline files. (You'll work with these indexed locations later in the tutorial.) Windows indexes these folders so it can search them quickly. By default, Windows searches *both* filenames and contents when you are searching in an indexed location. Searching filenames and contents can take a long time in large folders that are not indexed. Because removable disks are not included in the indexed locations, Windows searches only the names of the files on a removable disk by default, and then offers to search in file contents, as shown in Figure 6-6.

You can expand the Search pane in two ways: by clicking the Advanced Search button on the Search pane or by clicking the Advanced Search link in a search results window. For example, when you entered JPG as the search criterion earlier, Windows displayed 19 .jpg files and asked, "Did you find what you were searching for?" If the JPG search criterion did not produce the results you needed, you could have clicked the Advanced Search link in the folder window to expand the Search pane.

Selecting Criteria in the Expanded Search Pane

When you set criteria in the expanded Search pane, you select or enter details about the properties of the files you want to find. For example, for the size property, you can specify that you are looking for files that are equal to, smaller than, or larger than the size you enter. You can combine the size criterion with another property, such as date created or filename, to narrow your search. The more criteria you specify, the more you narrow the search. You need to select the properties you use carefully, however, so you don't use criteria that inadvertently eliminate a file that you want. For example, if you want to find only documents you created last week, make sure you select the Date created property, not the default Date property, which finds files created, modified, or accessed on the date you specify.

Searching for a File Using Multiple Criteria | Reference Window

- Open the folder you want to search.
- Enter filename or file contents search criteria in the Search box.
- If Windows does not find the files you want, click Advanced Search in the Search Results window or click the Search Tools button, click Search Pane, and then click the Advanced Search button.
- Select additional criteria using the options in the expanded Search pane.
- Click the Search button.

In her travel trends column, Kendra wants to use recent photos of Egypt and Australia, which are those taken after September 30, 2010. To find these files, you can start with the same criterion you used to find JPG files, using a wildcard this time, and combine it with additional date criteria in the expanded Search pane.

To find JPG files taken after September 30, 2010:

▶ **1.** In the folder window, click the **Tutorial** folder in the Folders list to return to the Tutorial window. Maximize the window. If the Preview pane is open click the **Organize** button on the toolbar, point to **Layout**, and then click **Preview Pane** to close the Preview pane.

▶ **2.** Click the **Search** box, and then type ***.jpg**. Windows displays the 19 .jpg files in the search results. Next, you'll enter additional criteria to narrow the results to JPG files taken after September 30, 2010.

▶ **3.** Click the **Advanced Search** link to open the expanded Search pane. See Figure 6-8.

Expanded Search pane ◀ Figure 6-8

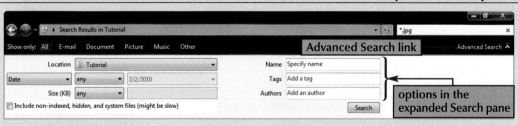

▶ **4.** In the Search pane, click the **Date** button, and then click **Date modified**.

▶ **5.** Click the **any** button next to Date modified, and then click **is after**.

> **6.** Click the button displaying today's date to open a calendar.

> **7.** Use the calendar controls to select **September 30, 2010**. To change the month, click the **left arrow** ◄ and **right arrow** ► buttons. When the calendar page for September 2010 appears, click **30**. See Figure 6-9.

Figure 6-9 ▶ **Setting date criteria**

> **8.** Click the button displaying **9/30/2010** to close the calendar.

> **9.** Click the **Search** button. Windows finds the files that meet your criteria and displays them in the window.

This search worked well, and Kendra anticipates that she'll want to conduct this search again. You'll save the search so you can use it later.

Saving a Search

If you conduct a successful search, especially one that uses two or more criteria, you can save the search. Saving a search preserves your original criteria and folder location so you can perform the search again without reconstructing the criteria. By default, Windows saves the search in the Searches folder, which you can open from the Navigation pane. The Searches folder lists your searches by name so you can easily find the one you want. Because a saved search includes folder and file location information, you can conduct a saved search only on the same computer where you conducted the original search or on one that mirrors the folder and file location of the original search. For this reason, the contents of the Searches folder are called **virtual folders**, which means they don't contain actual files, only criteria to find files. To search using a virtual folder, you open the Searches folder and then double-click a virtual folder.

To save a search and perform it again:

> **1.** In the search results window, click the **Save Search** button on the toolbar. The Save As dialog box opens, providing .jpg modified9-30-2010 as the filename. See Figure 6-10.

Figure 6-10 ▶ **Saving a search**

▶ **2.** Change the filename to **JPG Oct**, and then click the **Save** button to save the search in the Searches folder.

▶ **3.** To view the saved search, click the **Searches** folder in the Navigation pane. The JPG Oct search appears in the folder.

▶ **4.** To perform the search again, double-click **JPG Oct** in the Searches folder. Windows conducts the search again, and finds the JPG files modified after September 30, 2010. See Figure 6-11.

Performing saved search | Figure 6-11

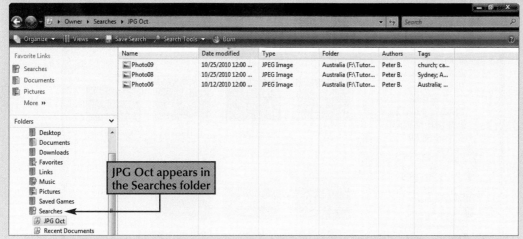

As you've been performing searches, Kendra has noticed the Tags property and wonders if using tags would help to find and identify files. In fact, one of the most useful properties you can use when searching for files is a file tag, which is one or more descriptive words you store with a file to help define its purpose or contents. You are sure that adding tags to the photo files would save you and Kendra a lot of time when searching for photos. You'll show her how to do so next.

Using Tags and Other Properties

As you know, properties are characteristics of files, such as their name and size, that provide detailed information about a file. You set some file properties when you create or modify a file, including the filename, location, and date created or modified. You can add other properties later, including tags, ratings, titles, authors, and comments. Tags are often the most useful because they make files easier to find.

To add properties to a file, you can use the Details pane or the file's Properties dialog box. To use the Details pane, you select a file, click a property text box in the Details pane, and then enter the appropriate information, such as the author's name or comments about the file. Figure 6-12 shows the Details pane when the Winter Leaves photo in the Sample Pictures folder is selected.

Figure 6-12 ▶ **File properties in the Details pane**

details, including tags, in the Details pane (yours might differ)

Tip

You can add or modify the properties of only some types of files. For example, you can add properties to Microsoft Office documents, but not to TXT or RTF files.

Most of the other properties you can add using the Details pane work the same way, and vary by file type. For photos, you can specify tags, authors, comments, title, and subject by using the appropriate text box in the Details pane. You can also rate photos by clicking a star in a series of five stars. If you click the first star, you apply a one-star rating. If you click the fourth star, you apply a four-star rating.

If you want to specify file properties other than the ones that appear in the Details pane by default, you can open the Properties dialog box for a file. To do so, you right-click a file, and then click Properties on the shortcut menu. On the Details tab, you can add or modify dozens of properties. Figure 6-13 shows the Properties dialog box for the Winter Leaves photo file. (The details for this file might differ on your computer.)

File details in the Properties dialog box **Figure 6-13**

Adding Tags to Files

You can add a tag to a file by using the Save As dialog box when you save the file or by using the Details pane or the file's Properties dialog box after you save the file. To use the Details pane, you select the file, click the Tags text box in the Details pane, and then type a word or phrase that will help you find the file later. To add more than one tag, separate each word or phrase with a semicolon. For example, if you have a photo of yourself on the peak of the Blackrock Mountain in Virginia, you could use *Blackrock; mountain; Virginia* as tags.

Adding Tags to Files | Reference Window

- In a folder window, click the file to which you want to add a tag.
- Click the Tags text box in the Details pane, and then type a tag. To enter another tag, type a semicolon (;) followed by the next tag.
- Click the Save button on the Details pane.

Much of the research you do for Kendra involves finding photos suitable for the columns and articles published in *TrendSpot Magazine*. Some photographers already add details to files, including tags, to help identify their photos. To facilitate your research, you'll review the files photographers recently submitted for Kendra's column on budget travel in Australia and Egypt and add tags to the files that need them.

To add tags to files:

▶ **1.** Open the **Australia** folder in the Tutorial.06\Tutorial folder, and then switch to Details view, if necessary.

2. Display the Tags column, if necessary, by right-clicking any column heading and clicking **Tags** on the shortcut menu. Note that Photo02 and Photo04 do not have any tags.

3. Click **Photo02** and then point to the **Title** text box in the Details pane. The photographer has provided "Middleton Beach, Western Australia" as the title.

   Trouble? If the Title text box does not appear in the Details pane, maximize the folder window and then drag the top border of the Details pane to increase its height, if necessary.

4. Click the **Tags** text box in the Details pane, and type **Australia** as the first tag. Type **;** and then type **L** to begin to enter "Landscape." Windows might suggest typical or already used tags that start with the letter L. See Figure 6-14. The suggestions on your computer might differ.

| Figure 6-14 | Adding tags to a file |

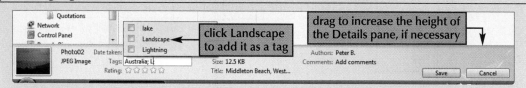

5. Click the **Landscape** check box or type **Landscape**, if necessary, and then click the **Save** button in the Details pane. Windows saves the tags you added.

6. Add the following tags to the Photo04 file: **Beach; Landscape; Australia**, and then click the **Save** button. Note that after you add a tag to one file, that tag appears in the list of suggested tags for other files.

7. Resize the **Tags** column in the folder window to display all of the tag text.

| InSight | | **Selecting Tags for Files** |

To create tags that will help you find files later, keep the following guidelines in mind:
- **Include the obvious**: Use words or phrases that describe the overall purpose or content of the file. For photo files, use tags that list the people in the picture, the location of the photo, and the occasion. For documents, describe the type of document, such as a proposal or report, and its subject.
- **Consider the sample tags**: You can find typical tags for files by typing a letter in the Tags text box in the Details pane. For example, type *p* to find sample tags that start with *p*, such as People, Pet Owners, Pets, and Photography.
- **Use complete words and phrases**: Avoid abbreviations and codes because you might not remember them later. Assign complete words or use phrases to be as clear as possible. Feel free to use text that appears in the filename; doing so might help you find other related files with the same tag but different filename.

Adding Other Details to Files

You can add dozens of details to files to help you identify or find the files later. The Details pane provides the most common ones, and a file's Properties dialog box includes those and many others. Kendra wants to add details to the Photo for travel tips document that Sam sent earlier. In particular, she wants to add a subject, tags, and the name of Sam's manager in California, who is Taylor Baldwin. To do so, you'll use the Properties dialog box.

To add details using a file's Properties dialog box:

▶ 1. Open the **Egypt** folder in the Tutorial.06\Tutorial folder.

▶ 2. Right-click **Photo for travel tips** and then click **Properties** on the shortcut menu. The Photo for travel tips Properties dialog box opens.

▶ 3. Click the **Details** tab to work with the details for this file. See Figure 6-15. Windows scanned the first line of this file, which is *Kendra:*, and provided that text as the title.

Photo for travel tips Properties dialog box ◀ **Figure 6-15**

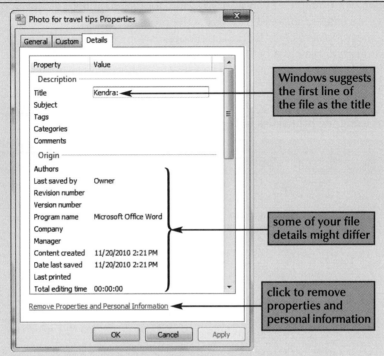

Windows suggests the first line of the file as the title

some of your file details might differ

click to remove properties and personal information

▶ 4. In the Title text box, delete **Kendra:**, type **Travel Tips**, and then press the **Enter** key.

▶ 5. Point to the right of Subject, and then click in the **Subject** text box. Type **General photo suggestions**, and then press the **Enter** key.

▶ 6. Click the **Tags** text box, type **Sam; sidebar; travel tips; photo suggestions**, and then press the **Enter** key.

▶ 7. Click the **Manager** text box, and then type **Taylor Baldwin**.

▶ 8. Click the **OK** button to save the details with the file and close the dialog box.

Tip

Before sending a file to others, you can remove properties by opening the file's Properties dialog box, clicking the Details tab, and then clicking Remove Properties and Personal Information. The Remove Properties dialog box opens, listing the properties you can remove.

Now that you've entered tags and other properties for files, you're ready to use this information to build advanced criteria for smarter searching.

Using Advanced Criteria in the Search Box

As you know, when you enter text in a folder window's Search box, Windows looks in the name of the folders and files in the folder window. If you enter *photo*, for example, Windows finds files named Photo01, Photo for travel tips, and Understanding photons. If you are searching an indexed location, such as in the Documents folder on your hard disk, Windows also looks in the file contents. For example, using *photo* as the criterion also finds files containing words and phrases such as *art photography, photorealism* and *twenty-four hour photos.* You can use the Search box to find files in two other ways: searching for files by property, and searching for files that meet multiple criteria.

Searching for Files by Property

If you don't want to search for a file by name or contents, you can use the Search box to search for other properties, including date, size, and tags. To use any property as criteria in the Search box, you specify the property using the following shorthand notation: *property name:criterion.* For example, if you want to search for files modified on November 1, 2010, you could enter *Modified:11/1/2010.* (The properties are not case sensitive, so you could also enter *modified:11/1/2010.*) The properties you can use as search criteria include any detail you can display as a column in a folder window. Figure 6-16 provides examples of the shorthand notation you can use to specify file properties as search criteria in the Search box.

Figure 6-16 ▶ **Examples of using file properties in the Search box**

Property	Example	Finds
Name	Name:City	Files and folders with names that contain a word beginning with *city*
Date modified	Modified:10/28/2010	Files and folders modified on October 28, 2010
	Modified:<10/28/2010	Files and folders modified before October 28, 2010
Date created	Created:>10/28/2010	Files and folders created after October 28, 2010
	Created:2010	Files and folders created during the year of 2010
Size	Size:200KB	Files with a size of 200 KB
	Size:>1MB	Files larger than 1 MB
Type	Filename:doc	Files with a .doc filename extension
Tags	Tag:(Egypt)	Files that include *Egypt* as a tag
Authors	Author:Peter	Files that specify Peter as the author
Artists	Artist:Elvis	Files that specify artists with *Elvis* in their names, such as Elvis Presley and Elvis Costello

Although the expanded Search pane guides you to select properties and specify criteria, you are restricted to the properties the Search pane contains: date (created or modified), size, filename, tags, and authors. When you use the shorthand notation in the Search box, however, you can use any file detail; this is especially useful when you are working with photos, music, and videos, because they have file properties that don't appear in the Search pane, such as Artists, Album, Rating, and Length.

As Kendra plans her travel trends column, she wants to include at least two photos of Sydney, Australia's largest city. Besides showing the Sydney Opera House, she'd like to show a contrasting work of architecture. You recall that some photographers provided titles for their photos. You'll use the Title property in the Search box to find photographs of Sydney.

To find files by specifying a property in the Search box:

▶ **1.** Open the **Australia** folder in the Tutorial.06\Tutorial folder. Restore the folder window to its original size.

> **2.** Click the **Search** box, and then type **title:Sydney**. As you type, Windows filters the view of the files in the folder window, and finally displays two files that contain the word *Sydney* in their Title property: Photo08 and Photo09.

> **3.** Click **Photo08** and look for the title in the Details pane. (Resize the Details pane, if necessary.) This is a photo of the Sydney Opera House.

> **4.** Click **Photo09**. Point to the Title text box in the Details pane to display the title in a ScreenTip. See Figure 6-17.

Title property in the Details pane   **Figure 6-17**

By searching for text in the Title property, you found two photos for Kendra—one showing the Sydney Opera House and the other showing St. Andrews Cathedral in Sydney.

Combining Criteria When Searching File Contents

To perform a precise search, you can combine criteria in the Search box. For example, suppose you store your financial documents on your computer and need to find a list of charitable donations you made in 2010. You don't recall where you've stored this information and scanning the filenames in your Financial folder doesn't reveal the file. If you search the content of the files using *donation* as the search criteria, you'll find lists of donations for many years as well as other documents, including e-mail messages with text such as "Thanks for your support! Every donation helps." If you search the contents of files using *2010* as the search criteria, you'll find dozens of documents that mention that year. If you search for *donations 2010*, you won't find files that include the text *donations for 2010* or *donations in 2010*. To pinpoint your search, you can combine the criteria to find files that contain the word *donations* and the date *2010*. When you search file contents, you can use **Boolean filters**, which let you search for specific information using the words AND, OR, and NOT to combine search criteria. You can use quotation marks and parentheses to refine the search conditions further. Figure 6-18 describes how to use AND, OR, and NOT along with quotation marks and parentheses when combining search criteria.

Combining search criteria   **Figure 6-18**

Word or Punctuation	Example	When to Use
AND	donations AND 2010	To narrow the search to files that contain *donations* and *2010* even if the words are not next to each other
OR	donations OR 2010	To broaden the search to files that contain *donations* or *2010*
NOT	donations NOT 2010	To restrict the search to files that contain *donations* but not *2010*
" " (quotation marks)	"donations 2010"	To pinpoint the search to files that contain the exact phrase *donations 2010*
( ) (parentheses)	(donations 2010)	To open the search to files that contain both items next to each other, but in any order

Note that when you use the words AND, OR, and NOT, you must enter them using all uppercase letters.

One of your ongoing projects for *TrendSpot Magazine* is maintaining an archive of quotations on wide-ranging subjects. Kendra started the archive years ago, and now she and the *TrendSpot* editors use these quotations in columns and articles, and often request a quotation from a particular author or on a particular topic just before publishing an issue of the magazine. You have therefore created a Quotations folder with two subfolders: an Authors folder that contains documents of quotations listed alphabetically by author, and a Topics folder that contains documents of quotations listed by general topic. Because authors and editors use a variety of word-processing programs, you've stored collections of quotations in TXT documents to make sure anyone at *TrendSpot* can use the documents. However, this means that you cannot add tags or other properties to the files—you can add these details only to Microsoft Office documents. To find quotations that Kendra and others want, you can use Boolean logic to combine search criteria in a folder window's Search box.

In one part of her column, Kendra plans to highlight a few contemporary Australian writers, and wants to start that section with a quotation about Australian writers. You can combine search criteria to search the contents of the Quotations folder to find suitable quotations. Before you do, first select the text you will use in your search criteria. Then determine whether you should use AND, OR, or NOT to combine the criteria and whether you need quotation marks or parentheses to find the files you want. Using AND is the most common way to combine search criteria, followed by OR, and then NOT. Using quotation marks is more common than using parentheses. To determine the best criteria, test each method in order starting with AND.

Although you want to find quotations about Australian writers, using *Australian* and *writers* as search criteria won't find quotations that include *Australia* or *writer* or even *write*, which might be appropriate quotations. A good rule of thumb when selecting search text is to use the root of the word, such as *writ* to find documents containing *writer*, *writers*, *writes*, and *writing*. For your purposes, you should use *Australia* and *writ* as search criteria.

Next, determine the best way to combine the criteria, as shown in the following list.

- Australia AND writ finds documents that include both words.
- Australia OR writ finds documents that include at least one of the words.
- Australia NOT writ finds documents that include *Australia*, but not those that include *writ*.
- "Australia writ" finds documents that include the exact phrase *Australia writ*.
- (Australia writ) finds documents that include the exact words *Australia* and *writ* consecutively in either order.

Because *Australia* AND *writ* produces the results you want, you'll use that as your search criteria to find quotations about Australian writers.

To find files using AND criteria:

1. Open the **Quotations** folder in the Tutorial.06\Tutorial folder.

2. Click the **Search** box, and then type **Australia AND writ**. As you type, Windows searches filenames that meet your criteria.

3. If necessary, click **Search in File Contents** to search the file contents instead of filenames. Windows finds one file that meets your criteria. See Figure 6-19.

Finding files that contain *Australia* AND *writ*   Figure 6-19

> **4.** To verify this file contains a quotation you can use, double-click **Comedy** to open it in a text-editing program such as Notepad.

> **5.** Page through the file until you find a quotation by Geoffrey Cottrell (*In America only the successful writer is important, in France all writers are important, in England no writer is important, and in Australia you have to explain what a writer is*), and then close the text-editing program.

Kendra mentions that she could use quotations that either mention Australia or mention writers—she can work either type into her column. You can try your search again, this time using the Boolean filter OR to find files that contain either *Australia* or *writ*.

To find files using OR criteria:

> **1.** Display the contents of the **Quotations** folder again.

> **2.** Click the **Search** box, and then type **Australia OR writ**.

> **3.** If necessary, click **Search in File Contents** to search the file contents instead of filenames. Now Windows finds three files that contain the word *Australia* or the text *writ*. See Figure 6-20.

Finding files that contain *Australia* OR *writ*   Figure 6-20

To really pinpoint what you want to find and refine your search criteria, you can combine Boolean filters and file properties.

Combining Boolean Filters and File Properties

When you search files by file property, you can use Boolean filters to combine criteria. For example, suppose you want to find files where Kendra or Sam is specified as the author. You can use *author: Kendra OR Sam* as the search criteria. This search finds files where Kendra is the author or where *Sam* is included in any file property, including author or filename. To restrict the search to files authored by Kendra or Sam, use parentheses, as in *author: (Kendra OR Sam)*. You can also use quotation marks to search literally for more than one word. For example, *author: "Sam Moriarity"* finds files only where Sam's full name is provided as the author.

Kendra is working on the Egypt section of her travel column, and requests a photo of an Egyptian pyramid. You can search the tags of the photo files to find those that contain this text. To search efficiently, you can use the Boolean filter AND to combine the criteria and search for photos that include the tags *Egypt* and *pyramid*. (If you used the Boolean filter OR, you would find photos of Egypt, but not necessarily of a pyramid, and also photos of pyramids that are not in Egypt.) If you use *tag: Egypt AND pyramid*, Windows searches for files that include *Egypt* as a tag and *pyramid* in any property, including filename and contents. To restrict the search to tags only, enclose the criteria in parentheses.

To find files by combining file property criteria:

▶ **1.** Display the contents of the **Tutorial** folder.

▶ **2.** Click the **Search** box, and then type **tag: (Egypt AND pyramid)**. Windows finds five files that meet your criteria. See Figure 6-21.

Figure 6-21 ▷ **Combining Boolean filters with file properties**

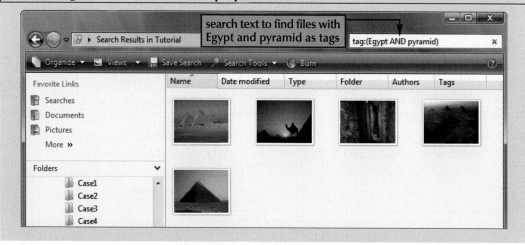

When you tell Kendra that you found a number of photos of Egyptian pyramids, she mentions that Denyce, one of the photographers, said she took a terrific shot of Giza, one of the major Egyptian pyramids. Kendra asks you to find the photo of an Egyptian pyramid that Denyce took. You can search for this file by adding criteria to your search text, which could become complicated. Another way to search for files is to use a natural language search, which is especially helpful when you want to use many criteria.

Finding Files with Natural Language Criteria

Besides using Boolean filters to combine search criteria, you can turn on the Windows natural language search and perform searches in a simpler way, without using colons and Boolean filters such as AND and OR. For example, instead of using *tag: (Egypt AND pyramid)* as the search criteria, you could use either *Egypt pyramid* or *photos Egypt pyramid*. As you'll see when you search the Internet in the next section, natural language criteria let you search your files using the same kind of casual search text you use when you search the Internet.

To use natural language search, you turn it on in the Folder Options dialog box. After you turn it on, you can search files using natural language criteria or the stricter short-hand notation (specifying properties and using colons, quotation marks, and parentheses) and Boolean filters. Natural language search also examines the same file properties as default searching, including filenames, contents, tags, and dates.

To find the photo of an Egyptian pyramid taken by Denyce, you can first turn on natural language searching and then enter search text using natural language criteria.

To turn on natural language searching and use it to find files:

▶ **1.** Display the contents of the **Tutorial** folder, click the **Organize** button on the toolbar, and then click **Folder and Search Options**. The Folder Options dialog box opens.

▶ **2.** Click the **Search** tab, and then click the **Use natural language search** check box to turn on natural language searching. Click the **OK** button.

▶ **3.** Click the **Search** box, and then type **photo Egypt pyramid**. If necessary, click **Search in file contents**. Windows finds the same five files shown earlier in Figure 6-21. These are photos that contain *Egypt* and *pyramid* as tags.

▶ **4.** Type **Denyce** to add that to the search text to find photos of Egyptian pyramids taken by Denyce. See Figure 6-22. Now you can give that photo to Kendra so she can use it in her column.

Conducting a natural language search **Figure 6-22**

▶ **5.** Close the folder window.

You've already explored many ways to search for files on your computer. Besides searching filenames and contents, you've learned how to use the Search pane to conduct advanced searches, how to use shorthand notation to specify tags and other file properties in search criteria, and how to combine criteria using Boolean filters. You've also learned how to simplify the search text by using natural language searching. In the next session, you'll apply these techniques to search for programs and for files that could be stored anywhere on your computer. You'll also examine the Windows index, develop techniques for searching the Internet, and collaborate with other people.

1. What are search criteria?
2. True or False. When you develop a search strategy, you choose the search tool that best fits your needs and select search criteria that are most likely to find the item.
3. You can narrow your search to a general category of files by clicking a button on the _____ _____ .
4. Name two ways you can verify that a file you found is one you want without opening the file.
5. Your _____ _____ include your personal folder (Documents, Pictures, Music, Desktop, and other common locations), e-mail, and offline files.
6. True or False. Saving a search saves the results in a folder you specify.
7. Name three types of properties you can add to photo files.
8. If you use *tag: landscape OR beach*, what files would you find?

Session 6.2

Searching for Programs from the Start Menu

As you've learned, you can use the Search box or the Search pane to find any file or folder on your computer. But if you're looking for a program, a Web page stored in your browser's History list, or a file or folder saved in your personal folder, you can use the Start Search box on the Start menu. (Recall that your personal folder contains your most frequently used folders, such as Documents, Pictures, Music, and Favorites, and other folders specific to your user account. Your personal folder is labeled with the name you use to log on to your computer and is the first folder listed on the right side of the Start menu, by default.)

When you use the Start Search box on the Start menu, you enter text just as you do when you use the Search box in a folder window. As you type, Windows displays the programs and files that meet your criteria, filtering the list with every character you type. Windows lists the search results on the left side of the Start menu. At the top of the list are programs that meet your criteria, followed by files. First are files with filenames that match your criteria and then are the files with tags that match your criteria. Windows also displays two links at the bottom of the search results—See all results and Search the Internet. You can click the See all results link to display the files in a search results window that identifies the path and other details about the file. You can click the Search the Internet link to perform the same search in your browser. You'll search the Internet later in this session.

- Click the Start button, and then click the Start Search text box.
- Type your search criteria.

Now that you have found a few photos and quotations for Kendra's travel column, she wants to find programs on her computer that let her view and edit photos. Usually, she just views the files in a folder window using a large icons view so she can see the content of the photos. She has heard that Windows Vista provides at least one program she can use to crop and recolor photos. You'll show her how to search for programs from the Start menu.

To search for programs from the Start menu:

▶ **1.** Click the **Start** button , and then click in the **Start Search** text box.

▶ **2.** Type **pho** to start entering *photo* as the search text. The Start menu lists programs for working with photos at the top of the Start menu. It also lists files whose filenames contain a word starting with *photo*, and files with tags that start with *photo*. See Figure 6-23.

Searching for programs　**Figure 6-23**

Windows includes programs at the top of the list

your results might vary

click to see all the results in a Search Results window

▶ **3.** Click **Windows Photo Gallery** to open that program. See Figure 6-24.

Figure 6-24 Windows Photo Gallery

▶ **4.** Click the **first photo** in the window. (The images displayed with a filmstrip icon are videos, not photos.) By default, the first photo in the window is one of the sample photos provided in your Pictures folder.

▶ **5.** Click the **Fix** button on the toolbar. The photo opens in a window where you can adjust the image, including its color, and crop it if necessary.

▶ **6.** Close Windows Photo Gallery.

Now that you've found a program Kendra can use to edit photos, you want to explore one more way to search for files on her computer. Before you do, you can set search options, including those for indexing, to speed up your searches.

Setting Search Options

You can set search options to improve the efficiency of your searches. When Windows Vista searches for a file in a folder window, it checks every file in the folder and its subfolders to see if the file meets your search criteria. When you are searching your personal folder or your entire computer, searching this way takes too much time. Instead of looking through your entire hard disk for a filename or property, Windows scans the **index**, which keeps track of the files on your computer similar to the way an index in a book keeps track of its contents. Using an index allows Windows to find most results in a fraction of the time that a search without the index would take.

Another way to set search options is to use the Search tab in the Folder Options dialog box to fine-tune what Windows searches and how it searches. By default, it searches filenames and contents only in indexed locations, which include any files in your personal folder and its subfolders. If necessary, you can set Windows to always search filenames and contents outside of your personal folder. Be aware, however, that setting this option can slow the search considerably. You can also set Windows to search only filenames and not contents, which can speed searches.

As you know, when you type a search criterion in the Search box, Windows searches the current folder and its subfolders by default. It also finds files that match your criterion even if you haven't finished entering the complete criterion. You can change this searching behavior on the Search tab of the Folder Options dialog box.

Verifying Search Options

You rarely need to change the Windows search options unless your searches take a long time. If you don't want to search file contents, you can set Windows to search filenames only when you enter text in the Search box. If you often start searching in a folder that is likely to contain the file you want, you can speed searches by not including subfolders when you use the Search box.

You want to make sure that the Windows Search options are set to their defaults, so you'll open the Search tab on the Folder Options dialog box.

Tip

You can also open the Search tab in the Folder Options dialog box from a folder window displaying search results. Click the Search Tools button on the toolbar, and then click Search options.

To verify search options:

▶ **1.** Open the **Tutorial** folder provided with your Data Files.

▶ **2.** Click the **Organize** button on the toolbar, and then click **Folder and Search Options**. The Folder Options dialog box opens.

▶ **3.** Click the **Search** tab. Figure 6-25 shows the Search tab and the default indexing options and the natural language search option selected.

Search tab in the Folder Options dialog box ◀ **Figure 6-25**

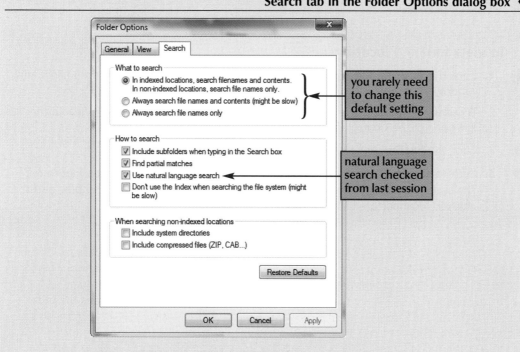

▶ **4.** Click the **OK** button to close the dialog box.

Another way to make sure Windows is performing searches efficiently is to check its indexing options.

Setting Index Options

The Windows index stores information about files, including the filename, date modified, and other properties such as tags, authors, and rating. By default, Windows indexes the files most people use often, including those in your personal folder, your e-mail, and offline files. (Offline files are those usually stored on a network resource, but saved in a location you can access when you're not connected to the network.) Windows does not index program files and system files because you rarely need to search the contents of those files.

Although you can't access the index, you can see a complete list of the locations that are indexed on your computer. To do so, you open the Indexing Options dialog box, which also reports the status of the indexing service. If you regularly search a different location, such as a Public folder, you can add that folder to the list of indexed locations. (Only users with Administrator accounts can change indexed locations.) To do so, you click the Modify button in the Indexing Options dialog box, and then select the folders on your computer you want to include. You can also exclude folders you rarely search in the same way.

InSight	**Selecting Index Locations**

Make sure you don't index too many locations for searching, or index a very large location, such as your entire computer. Doing so increases the size of the index, which hampers the efficiency of your searches. For best results, Microsoft recommends that you only add folders to the index that contain your personal files.

You want to make sure Windows is indexing your files efficiently, so you'll open the Indexing Options dialog box to view the list of indexed locations and check the status of the indexing service.

Tip

You can also open the Indexing Options dialog box from a folder window displaying search results. Click the Search Tools button on the toolbar, and then click Modify Index Locations.

To view indexed locations:

▶ 1. Click the **Start** button ⊕, and then click **Control Panel** to open the Control Panel window in Category view.

 Trouble? If your Control Panel opens in Classic view, click Category View in the left pane of the Control Panel window.

▶ 2. Click the **System and Maintenance** category.

▶ 3. Click **Indexing Options**. The Indexing Options dialog box opens. See Figure 6-26. The status of the indexing service is indicated at the top of the dialog box, and the indexed locations are listed in the Included Locations list.

4. Click the **Close** button to close the dialog box.

5. Close all open windows.

By default, Windows uses the index when it searches in the Search folder, which you'll do next.

Using the Search Folder

Besides using the Search box or Search pane in a folder window, or the Start Search box on the Start menu, you can find files using the Windows Search folder. Use the Search folder if the file you want to find could be located anywhere on your computer. The Search folder is also a good choice if you want to include files from more than one folder, especially if these folders are two or more of your common folders, such as Pictures and Music. Because the Search folder uses the same Search pane that you can open in a folder window, you can easily conduct searches using more than one criterion.

Selecting a Search Location

When you use the Search folder, by default Windows searches your indexed locations, which you examined in the previous set of steps. If you want to search additional locations or a different location, you can specify the locations before conducting the search. The locations you specify in this way override the defaults, so if you want to search a particular folder plus the usual indexed locations, you must specify both.

TrendSpot contributors often send articles, photos, and other material to Kendra via e-mail. Some of this material includes files that you need to work with. If Kendra receives only a few small files, she usually forwards them to you as attachments to an e-mail message. However, when she receives many files or a few large files, she saves them on a USB flash drive and gives that to you. Windows does not include the drives for removable media in its index. Because it's efficient for you to include your USB flash drive in your searches, you can include this drive in the list of search locations.

Kendra wants to use a quotation about Cleopatra for her travel column, and thinks one from Shakespeare's *Antony* and *Cleopatra* would be appropriate. She knows she gave you a file of Shakespeare quotations, but you're not sure where you stored it. It might be in a

Tip

You can specify multiple search locations using the expanded Search pane in any window.

folder on your USB flash drive or somewhere in your personal folder on the hard disk. To speed your search, you'll modify the list of search locations to include a folder on the USB flash drive and your indexed locations so that Windows searches both.

The following steps assume that your Data Files are stored on a removable disk on drive F. If you are using Data Files stored in a different location, substitute that location in these steps.

To search multiple locations using the Search folder:

▶ **1.** Click the **Start** button 🌐 , and then click **Search**. A Search Results window opens displaying the Search pane and Search box.

▶ **2.** Click the **Advanced Search** button on the Search pane. The Search pane expands in the Search Results window.

▶ **3.** Click the **Indexed Locations** button, and then click **Choose search locations** to open the Choose Search Locations dialog box. See Figure 6-27. Your locations might differ.

Figure 6-27 ▶ **Choose Search Locations dialog box**

select locations to index from this list; your list might differ

Tip

You can select Everywhere in the Choose Search Locations dialog box to search your entire computer.

▶ **4.** In the list of locations, expand the **Computer** icon, expand **Removable Disk (F:)**, and then click the **Tutorial** folder in the Tutorial.06 folder provided with your Data Files.

The Tutorial folder is now the only location for this search. You need to add the indexed locations to the list.

▶ **5.** Scroll to the end of the locations list, and then expand **Search Folders**. A list of saved searches, including Indexed Locations, appears in the list.

▶ **6.** Click the **Indexed Locations** check box to select it. Two locations appear in the Summary of selected locations. See Figure 6-28.

Setting two search locations ◀ **Figure 6-28**

▶ **7.** Click the **OK** button to accept the settings and close the dialog box. Your expanded Search pane should look similar to the one in Figure 6-29.

Expanded Search pane with two locations ◀ **Figure 6-29**

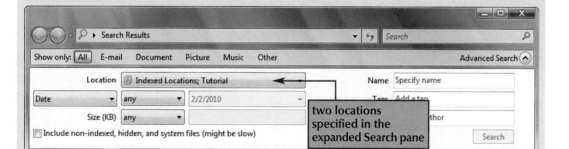

Now you can search indexed locations and the Tutorial folder on your removable disk for Shakespeare quotations to find one about Cleopatra.

To search specified locations using the Search folder:

▶ **1.** Click in the **Search** box, and then type **Shakespeare**. Windows finds one file named Shakespeare in the Tutorial folder on the removable disk. See Figure 6-30.

Figure 6-30 **Searching specified locations**

2. Click **Shakespeare** in the file list, click the **Organize** button on the toolbar, point to **Layout**, and then click **Preview Pane** to open the Preview pane and view the contents of the Shakespeare file. Quotations from *Antony and Cleopatra* appear at the beginning of the document.

3. Close all open windows.

Now that you found the file of Shakespeare quotations, you can send the quotations from *Antony and Cleopatra* to Kendra. She wants you to continue researching information for her column on budget travel in Australia and Egypt. However, the information she now wants you to find is not available in any of the files on your computer. Instead, you can use Internet Explorer to search the Internet for the information. Most of the searching techniques you've learned for searching files apply to searching for information in the millions of Web sites on the Internet.

Searching the Internet

The Internet provides access to a wealth of information; the challenge is to find the information you need or want. You have already learned how to develop search strategies and specific criteria to find files on your computer. You can use many of the same search strategies to find information on the Internet. Instead of using tools provided in a folder window, such as the Search box and Search pane, you use the search tools provided in Internet Explorer. Figure 6-31 summarizes the search tools you can use in Internet Explorer.

Figure 6-31 **Internet Explorer search tools**

Search Tool	Description
Live Search box	Type a word or phrase to find Web pages associated with that topic.
Address bar	Type Find, Go, or ? followed by a word or phrase to find Web pages associated with that topic. If the word or phrase you enter is the name of a Web site, its main page opens in Internet Explorer.
Search provider	Click the Live Search button arrow, and then select a search provider to use their tools to search the Internet.

The terminology that you use when searching the Internet is slightly different from the terminology you use to search for files on your computer. The word or phrase on which you search is typically called a **search expression**. Each word in the search expression is usually called a **keyword**. After you enter a search expression using one of Internet Explorer's search tools, Internet Explorer displays the results, which are links to Web pages that meet your criteria. You can click these links, or **hits**, to access Web pages that contain the keywords in your search expression.

When you provide a search expression to Internet Explorer, it uses a search provider, which is a Web site that specializes in searching the Internet. Popular search providers include Google and Windows Live Search. Because searching all of the Web pages on the Internet to find those that contain your search expression would take a prohibitive amount of time, search providers typically search a database of indexed Web pages. These databases are updated periodically, though not often enough to keep all of the indexed Web pages up to date. This is why a page of search results might include inactive or broken links.

Web site designers and owners can make their Web pages easier for search providers to find by **optimizing** the site. In its Web page headings, an optimized site lists keywords and phrases that you and other Web users are likely to use to find the information on the Web page. Conversely, you are more likely to find the Web pages you want if you are aware of the types of keywords Web designers often use.

Searching the Internet Effectively | InSight

Keep the following guidelines in mind to search the Internet efficiently.

- **Be specific**: If you search for general categories, you'll find an overwhelming number of pages. Searching for specific terms or details is more likely to provide results you can use. For example, instead of searching for *desserts*, search for *pear cake recipe*.
- **Form a question**: Think of your search expression as a question you want answered, such as *Are there restaurants in the Denver area that serve vegetarian food?* Eliminate the articles and common words to form a workable search expression, such as *restaurants Denver vegetarian*.
- **Search the results**: Most search providers let you reduce the number of pages to search by searching your results. For example, suppose you search for *pear cake recipe* and find many thousands of results. Because you want a recipe similar to the one your Swedish grandmother made, you can search the results using *Swedish* as your search expression.

Kendra is now working on a section of her column that describes the popular restaurants in the capital cities of Australia and Egypt. So far, she has plenty of information on the restaurants in Sydney, but she wants to know more about the restaurants in Cairo. As her editorial assistant, you offer to search the Internet to find the information. You'll start by using *Cairo Egypt restaurants* as the search expression to find Web pages describing restaurants in Cairo.

Because Web pages and search indexes change frequently, the search results you find when you perform the steps in this section will differ from those shown in the figures.

To search using a search expression:

▶ **1.** Start Internet Explorer.

▶ **2.** Click in the Live Search box, type **Cairo Egypt restaurants**, and press the **Enter** key. The Live Search provider looks for Web pages containing the search expression you entered, and then displays the results. See Figure 6-32.

Figure 6-32 Search results for the search expression *Egypt restaurants*

Using *Cairo Egypt restaurants* as the search expression produced thousands of results, which is typical. Although the first few Web pages listed might provide the information you seek, to find more useful Web pages, you need to narrow your search.

Narrowing Your Search

You can narrow your Internet search by modifying your search expression or by limiting the kinds of Web pages you want in your results. One way to modify your search expression is to use quotation marks to search for specific phrases. If you enclose a phrase in quotation marks, you restrict the results to Web pages that contain that exact phrase. For example, using a search expression such as *Radcliffe College Library* finds Web pages that include those three words anywhere on the page. If you enclose the search expression in quotation marks, as in *"Radcliffe College Library"*, you find only Web pages that include the exact text in the specified order.

Another way to modify your search expression is to use the advanced search features that search providers typically offer. Figure 6-33 shows the Advanced Search page from Google, a popular search provider.

Google Advanced Search page   Figure 6-33

Similar to the expanded Search pane for searching files, an advanced search page lets you specify and combine search conditions. Most advanced search pages provide the following types of options:

- Find pages that include all of the words. This is the default for most search providers.
- Limit the results to pages that match the exact phrase. This is the same as using quotation marks to enclose an expression.
- Find pages that include at least one of the words in the search expression.
- Specify keywords that you do not want included in the Web page.
- Search only pages written in a particular language.
- Find pages of a certain type, such as Microsoft Word or Adobe Acrobat PDF.
- Search pages that have been updated within a specified period of time.
- Limit results to pages in a specified Web site or domain.

Besides providing an advanced search page for narrowing your search expression, most search providers include tabs or links that specify the kind of results you want. For example, the Live Search results page shown in Figure 6-32 includes six tabs: Web, Images, News, Maps, Classifieds, and More. By default, Live Search displays Web pages in the results. If you are searching for images, such as photos and drawings, you can click the Images tab before or after you enter a search expression to restrict the results to pages including images that meet your criteria.

Some of the Web pages you found when you used *Cairo Egypt restaurants* as a search expression described Cairo, Egypt, but didn't necessarily focus on restaurants. You can try narrowing your search by enclosing the expression in quotation marks to see if the results are more useful.

To narrow a search to an exact match:

▶ **1.** On the search results page, click in the search text box at the top of the page.

▶ **2.** Edit the text so it appears as **"Cairo Egypt restaurants"** and press the **Enter** key. This time, you find many fewer results because the search is restricted to only those Web pages that include the exact phrase you entered. See Figure 6-34.

Figure 6-34 ▶ **Search results for an exact phrase search expression**

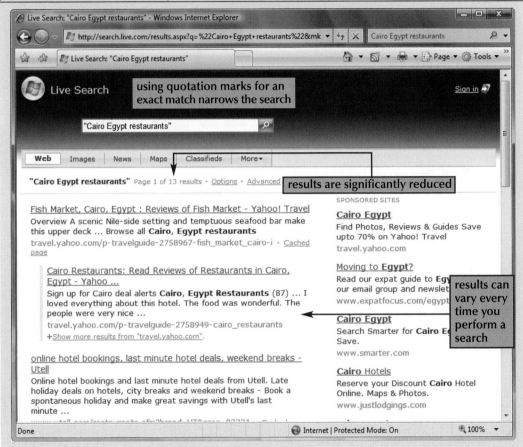

Using an exact phrase produced a list of restaurants in Cairo, Egypt, that is useful to you and Kendra. Now Kendra wants to briefly mention quality restaurants in other parts of Egypt that budget travelers might want to visit. These are any budget restaurants that are not located in Cairo. To specify this kind of search condition, you can use a search provider's advanced search page. You have used Google in the past, so you can try this search using Google instead of Live Search. You'll specify that you want to search for budget restaurants in Egypt, but not those in Cairo.

To narrow a search by excluding keywords:

▶ **1.** Click the Address bar, type **www.google.com**, and then press the **Enter** key to open the main page on the Google Web site. See Figure 6-35.

Main page on the Google Web site ◄ Figure 6-35

▶ **2.** Click the **Advanced Search** link to open the Advanced Search page.

▶ **3.** In the Find results section, click the **with all of the words** text box, and then type **Egypt budget restaurants**.

▶ **4.** Click the **without the words** text box, type **Cairo**, and then press the **Enter** key. The search results list more than a million Web pages, including many for hotels. You'll exclude the keyword *hotel* from the search.

▶ **5.** Click the **Advanced Search** link, click the **without the words** text box, and then type **hotel** so that "Cairo" and "hotel" both appear in the text box.

▶ **6.** Click the **Google Search** button. The search results page includes fewer hits, with the best matches on the first page, which will help you find a few restaurants for Kendra's column.

Evaluating Web Pages in the Search Results | InSight

Although a Web page might be listed at the top of the search results, that doesn't guarantee the page provides reliable and up-to-date information that meets your needs. Before using a Web page or citing it as a source, review the content with a critical eye. At the bottom of the Web page, look for the author and evidence of the author's credentials. Look for links to the original source of quoted information, which tends to validate the information on a Web page. Also look for signs of bias, such as unsubstantiated claims or extreme points of view.

Kendra also wonders if you can find any photos of Egyptian restaurants that she can include in her column. She'd prefer those that show restaurant interiors. To fulfill her request, you can use the Images tab in Google. Recall that Live Search and other search providers include a similar tool.

To limit the results to Web pages with images:

▶ **1.** In the Google search results page, click the **Images** link near the top of the page. Google looks for Web pages containing images that meet your search criteria—those of budget restaurants not in Cairo. See Figure 6-36.

Figure 6-36 | **Searching for images**

These are not promising results. However, Kendra said the photos could be of any Egyptian restaurant, so you can change the search expression.

Tip

The -*Cairo* in the search expression is a shorthand way of excluding *Cairo* from the search.

▶ **2.** Click the **search** text box near the top of the Images page, and edit the search expression to be **Egypt restaurants**.

▶ **3.** Click the **Search** button. Google displays images that meet your criteria, including many that show restaurant interiors.

Choosing Search Providers

In Internet Explorer, you can choose which provider you want to use when you search for information on the Internet. You can change the search provider for a specific search, and you can specify which search provider you prefer to use by default. When you first install Internet Explorer, only one provider might be available. You can add search providers to increase your searching options.

Reference Window | **Selecting a Search Provider**

- Click the Live Search button arrow next to the Address bar, and then click Find More Providers.
- Click a provider in the list, and then click Add Provider.

Your installation of Internet Explorer includes Windows Live Search as a search provider, but not Google, which you and Kendra use often. You'll add this search provider to the provider list, which you can access by clicking the Live Search button arrow. You can also choose to make a new search provider the default one to use when you search from the Address bar or Search box.

To add a search provider to the provider list:

▶ **1.** Click the **Live Search button arrow**, and then click **Find More Providers**. A list of possible search providers appears. See Figure 6-37.

▶ **2.** Click **Google** in the list to open the Add Search Provider dialog box.

▶ **3.** Click the **Add Provider** button.

▶ **4.** Click the **Live Search** button arrow to verify that Internet Explorer added Google to the list of search providers.

▶ **5.** Close Internet Explorer.

Now Internet Explorer makes Google and Live Search available as search providers. To set the default search provider to use, you can click the Live Search button arrow, click Change Search Defaults, and then select the provider you want to use regularly.

Collaborating with Other People

Because people often work together from separate locations, they occasionally need a way to meet online to exchange information or collaborate on projects without physically traveling to convene in the same place. You can use Windows Meeting Space to meet and collaborate with others who are not in your same location. Using Windows Meeting Space, you can share documents, programs, and your desktop with other meeting participants. Similar to meeting in a physical location, you can distribute and collaborate on documents, pass notes to other participants, and connect to a network project to give a presentation. To do so, you start a meeting and invite other people to join it, or you join an existing meeting.

Setting Up Windows Meeting Space

Before you can use Windows Meeting Space for the first time, you need to set it up by turning on some services and signing onto People Near Me, a feature that identifies people using computers near you so you can use Windows Meeting Space. If you are working on a network, Windows Meeting Space uses that network to connect meeting participants. Otherwise, Windows Meeting Space sets up an **ad hoc network**, which is a temporary network used for sharing files or an Internet connection. In an ad hoc network, computers and devices are connected directly to each other instead of to a central device, such as a hub or router. By setting up an ad hoc network, Windows Meeting Space lets you meet in a conference room, outside the office, or anyplace else.

To set up Windows Meeting Space:

▶ 1. Click the **Start** button 🔵, point to **All Programs**, and then click **Windows Meeting Space**. Because this is the first time you are using Windows Meeting Space, the Windows Meeting Space Setup window opens.

   Trouble? If a message appears indicating that Windows cannot start Windows Meeting Space because of a Windows Firewall setting, click the OK button, open the Windows Firewall Settings dialog box, and then click the Block all incoming connections check box to remove the check mark. Repeat Step 1.

▶ 2. Click **Yes, continue setting up Windows Meeting Space**. The People Near Me dialog box opens. See Figure 6-38.

Figure 6-38 ▶ **People Near Me dialog box**

   Trouble? If this is not the first time you are using Windows Meeting Space, the Windows Meeting Space window opens. Skip Steps 2–4.

   Trouble? If a User Account Control dialog box opens, provide a password, if necessary, and then click the Continue button.

▶ 3. In the Your display name text box, type **Kendra**.

▶ 4. Click the **OK** button. The Windows Meeting Space window opens so you can start or join a meeting. A People Near Me icon 👤 also appears in the notification area of the taskbar.

Now you can start a new meeting, and invite Bev to attend.

Starting a New Meeting

After you set up Windows Meeting Space, you can use it to start new meetings or join existing ones. In either case, you need to provide a name and password for the meeting. If you are starting a meeting, Windows assigns your display name and the current time as the meeting name. You can set your own password, though the password must be at least eight characters long and should be a strong password. (Recall that strong passwords are easy for you to remember but difficult for others to guess. Furthermore, strong passwords do not contain your name in any form or a complete word, and include one or more uppercase letters, lowercase letters, numbers, and keyboard symbols.)

Starting a Meeting and Inviting Participants | Reference Window

- Start Windows Meeting Space, and then click Start a new meeting.
- Provide a meeting name, if necessary, and a password.
- Click the Create a meeting button.
- Click Invite people.
- Click the check boxes for the people you want to invite, and then click the Send Invitations button.

Kendra is nearly finished with her column, and wants to meed online with Bev Parkinson, a *TrendSpot* page designer, to discuss the layout and illustrations for the column. You'll start the meeting by entering a password and then inviting Bev to join.

If you are not connected to a network, read but do not perform the following steps.

To start a meeting and invite a participant:

▶ **1.** In the Windows Meeting Space window, click **Start a new meeting**. The window displays text boxes for providing a meeting name and password. See Figure 6-39.

Starting a new meeting   **Figure 6-39**

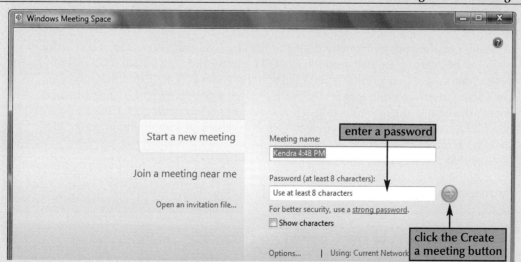

▶ **2.** In the Password text box, type **tSpot 24#**, and then click the **Create a meeting** button ⊚. Windows opens a window for the new meeting. See Figure 6-40.

Figure 6-40 Windows Meeting Space window

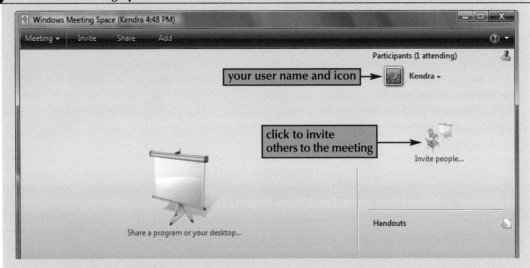

▶ **3.** Click **Invite people** to open the Invite People dialog box.

Trouble? If you are working on an ad hoc network, contact the people you want to invite, and ask them to start Windows Meeting Space and click Join a meeting near me. After they select the name of your meeting and enter a password, they appear as participants in the Windows Meeting Space window.

▶ **4.** Click the **Bev** check box to invite her to the meeting, and then click the **Send invitations** button. After a few minutes, Bev receives the invitation and joins the meeting.

Trouble? If the Invite People dialog box does not include a participant named Bev, click the check box for another person you know to invite him or her to the meeting.

Trouble? If the Invite People dialog box does not include any participants, contact the people you want to invite, and ask them to start Windows Meeting Space and click Join a meeting near me. If they are not connected to the same network and using Windows Vista, they cannot join the meeting. Read but do not perform the remaining steps in the Windows Meeting Space section, and then close Windows Meeting Space.

Besides inviting people directly during a meeting, you can also invite people using e-mail or by creating an invitation file. To send an invitation via e-mail, click Invite people during a meeting, click Invite others in the Invite People dialog box, and then click Send an invitation in e-mail. To create an invitation file, you also open the Invite People dialog box during a meeting. Click Invite others and then click Create an invitation file. After you save the file, you can give it to others as you would any other file, such as on removable media.

Now that you've started a meeting and invited Bev to join, Kendra wants to share some of the photos for the travel trends column. You do so by distributing handouts to the meeting participants.

To distribute files to the meeting participants:

▶ **1.** In the Windows Meeting Space window, click **Add a handout**. A dialog box opens, notifying you that the handouts, or files, will be copied to each participant's computer.

2. Click the **OK** button. The Select files to add dialog box opens.

3. Navigate to the **Tutorial** folder in the Tutorial.06 folder provided with your Data Files, and then open the **Australia** folder.

4. Click **Photo08**, hold down the **Ctrl** key, and then click **Photo09** to select the two photos.

5. Click the **Open** button. Windows displays the two handouts in the Windows Meeting Space window and distributes them to the meeting participants.

Bev could modify the files, if necessary, and then return them to you. Before you end the meeting, Kendra wants to show Bev the photos you found of Egyptian restaurants. To do so, you'll share your desktop with Bev.

To share your desktop:

1. In the Windows Meeting Space window, click **Share a program or your desktop**.

2. When asked if you want other people to see your desktop, click the **OK** button. The Start a shared session window opens.

3. Click **Desktop**, and then click the **Share** button. The desktop colors might briefly change as Windows shows your desktop to the meeting participants. The meeting participants can now see all the activity on your desktop. See Figure 6-41.

Sharing your desktop in Windows Meeting Space Figure 6-41

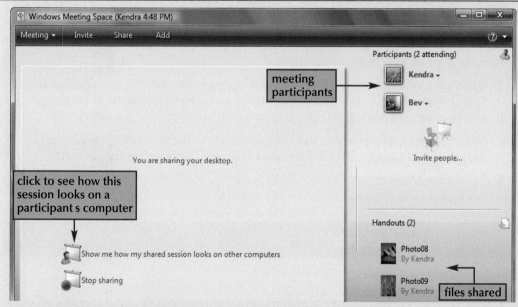

Trouble? If a message appears indicating that Windows changed your color scheme, click the OK button. You can verify your color scheme settings when you restore your computer.

4. Start Internet Explorer.

5. In the Address box, type **www.google.com**, and then press the **Enter** key.

6. In the Google text box, type **Egypt restaurants**, click the **Images** link near the top of the page, and then click the **Search Images** button. Photos of Egyptian restaurants again appear in the search results. This time, however, your meeting participants can see the results. Windows Meeting Space lets you verify what participants can see.

> **7.** In the Windows Meeting Space window, click **Show me how my shared session looks on other computers**. Windows displays an image of your desktop as it appears on a participant's desktop; it might appear with a telescoping effect, which is normal.

Now that Kendra has provided two photo resources to Bev, you can end the meeting. Bev will examine the photos she received, return to the Web page listing photos of Egyptian restaurants, and use all the photos as she begins to work on the layout of the magazine.

To end the meeting:

> **1.** Close Internet Explorer.

> **2.** Click the **Meeting** button on the toolbar, and then click **Leave Meeting**. A dialog box opens asking if you want to save handouts.

> **3.** Click the **No** button. The original Windows Meeting Space window opens.

> **4.** Close the Windows Meeting Space window.

> **5.** Right-click the **People Near Me** icon in the notification area of the taskbar, and then click **Exit**.

Restoring Your Settings

If you are working in a computer lab or a computer other than your own, complete the steps in this section to restore the original settings on your computer.

To restore your settings:

> **1.** Open a folder window, click the **Organize** button on the toolbar, click **Folder and Search Options**, click the **Search** tab, and then click the **Use natural language search** check box to turn off natural language searching. Click the **OK** button.

> **2.** Start Internet Explorer, click the **Live Search** arrow button, click **Change search defaults**, click **Google**, click the **Remove** button, and then click the **OK** button.

> **3.** Close all open windows.

Review | Session 6.2 Quick Check

1. What is a search provider?
2. True or False. When you enter a search expression, a search provider searches all of the Web pages on the Internet to find those that match your criteria.
3. One way to modify a search expression is to use _____ _____ to search for specific phrases.
4. True or False. Search providers let you limit the search results to pages of a certain type.
5. Name three guidelines for searching the Internet efficiently.
6. You can use Windows Meeting Space on an _____ _____ network, which is a temporary network used for sharing files or an Internet connection.

Tutorial Summary | Review

In this tutorial, you developed search strategies for finding files on your computer and information on the Internet. You used the Search box in a folder window to find files by type, and used the Search pane to find files by category. You also conducted advanced searches using the expanded Search pane and saved a search so you could use it again. After adding tags and other properties to a file, you searched for these details in files. You also learned how to set search options, including those for indexing, and performed searches on the Search menu and in the Search folder. Finally, you used Internet Explorer and its search providers to find information on the Internet and collaborated with others using Windows Meeting Space.

Key Terms

ad hoc network	keyword	Search pane
Boolean filter	optimize	tag
hit	search criteria	wildcard
index	search expression	virtual folder
indexed locations		

Review Assignments | Practice

Practice the skills you learned in the tutorial.

For a list of Data Files in the Review folder, see page 265.

You are now working with Kendra Cho on an article for *TrendSpot Magazine* on a disturbing trend: the incidents of extreme or destructive weather have increased in recent years. Kendra is editing an article on weather and needs your help to research the photos she'll use in the upcoming issue of the magazine. As an online publication, the magazine often includes multimedia files so that readers can play sound, music, and videos as they read articles. Kendra also wants you to help her search for audio and video files and find a program that can play them. Complete the following:

1. In a folder window, open the **Review** folder in the Tutorial.06 folder provided with your Data Files.
2. Use the Search box to search for WAV files. Move the WAV files to a new subfolder named **Sounds** in the Review folder.
3. Display the **Review** folder again, and then use the Search box and the Search pane to find documents whose filenames start with the text **pho**. Verify that the file you found lists credits for the photos in the Review folder. If it does, move the file you found to a new subfolder named **Documents** in the Review folder. Otherwise, do not move the file you found.
4. Add the following tags to Photo32: **Island; Ocean**.
5. Add the following tags to Photo41: **Lightning; Night; Sky; Thunderstorm**.
6. In the folder window, verify that the new tags are now assigned to Photo32 and Photo41. If necessary, maximize the folder window, switch to Details view, right-click a column heading, and then click Tags to display the Tags column.
7. In the Review folder, search for photos that have *tornado* as a tag. Move the files you found to a new subfolder named **Tornado** in the Review folder.
8. In the Review folder window, find a photo that has *snow* and *winter* as tags. Change the name of this file to **Winter**.

9. Search for a program on your computer that lets you play media files. Start the program, and then explore its toolbars. (If you need to set up the program, choose the Express Setup option.) Press Alt+Print Screen to capture an image of the program window, and then paste the image in a new Paint file. Save the file as **Media Program** in the Tutorial.06\Review folder provided with your Data Files. Close the media program.

10. Use the Search folder to find video files in the indexed locations on your computer. (*Hint*: Use *video* in your search criteria.) Press Alt+Print Screen to capture an image of the Search Results window, and then paste the image in a new Paint file. Save the file as **Videos** in the Tutorial.06\Review folder provided with your Data Files.

11. Start Internet Explorer, and use Windows Live Search to find Web pages providing information about extreme weather in the current year. Narrow the search by finding only images of extreme weather in the current year. Press Alt+Print Screen to capture an image of the first screen of search results, and then paste the image in a new Paint file. Save the file as **Weather Images** in the Tutorial.06\Review folder provided with your Data Files.

12. Switch to Google as your search provider, and display the results of the search for Web pages providing information about extreme weather in the current year. Perform an advanced search to find Web pages that contain the exact text *extreme weather* but not for the current year. Press Alt+Print Screen to capture an image of the first screen of search results, and then paste the image in a new Paint file. Save the file as **Weather** in the Tutorial.06\Review folder provided with your Data Files. Close Internet Explorer.

13. Start Windows Meeting Space and start a meeting. If possible, invite someone you know to the meeting. Share your desktop with the meeting participants, and open Internet Explorer. Use the default search provider to find news stories about recent extreme weather. Resize the windows so that both are mostly visible. Press Print Screen to capture an image of the desktop, and then paste the image in a new Paint file. Save the file as **Weather Meeting** in the Tutorial.06\Review folder provided with your Data Files.

14. Close Paint and Internet Explorer, leave the meeting, close Windows Meeting Space, and then exit from People Near Me.

15. Submit the results of the preceding steps to your instructor, either in printed or electronic form, as requested.

| Apply | **Case Problem 1** |

Use the skills you learned in the tutorial to research images for a graphic arts firm.

For a list of Data Files in the Case1 folder, see page 265.

G & K Graphic Arts Marco Garcia and Joel Knightly own G & K Graphic Arts, a small firm in Nashville, Tennessee, that provides graphic design services to local businesses. They are currently working on a project for a recording studio to design a Web page and a CD insert for a CD featuring the work of studio musicians, tentatively called Bluegrass Studio. Marco and Joel ask you to help them find images they can use for the Web page and CD. They also want to back up their files on a DVD later, and ask you to find information about programs they can use to do so. Complete the following steps:

1. Open the **Case1** folder in the Tutorial.06 folder provided with your Data Files.
2. Review the tags and other properties already assigned to the files in the Case1 folder. Then add the tag **fiddle** or **bluegrass** to files as appropriate.
3. Using a file's Properties dialog box, add **Marco** as the author of the following photos: P01, P05, and P12.

4. Use the expanded Search pane and the Search box to find photos that include the tag *guitar* and have Marco as the author. Move the file(s) you found to a new sub-folder named **Marco Guitar** in the Case1 folder.

5. In any of the indexed locations on your computer, search for WMA music files. Save the search as **WMA** in the Case1 folder.

6. Remove all the properties and personal information from the **P09** file in the Case1 folder. (*Hint*: Click the appropriate link in the P09 Properties dialog box, click the option button to Remove the following properties from this file, click the Select All button, and then click the OK button.)

7. Search for a program on your computer that lets you store files on a DVD. Start the program, and then press Alt+Print Screen to capture an image of the program window. Paste the image in a new Paint file. Save the file as **DVD Program** in the Tutorial.06\Case1 folder provided with your Data Files. Close the DVD program.

8. Search for a program on your computer that lets you back up and restore files. Start the program, and then press Alt+Print Screen to capture an image of the program window. Paste the image in a new Paint file. Save the file as **Backup Program** in the Tutorial.06\Case1 folder provided with your Data Files. Close the backup program.

9. Start Internet Explorer, and use Windows Live Search to find Web pages providing information on bluegrass music in Nashville. Narrow the search to find only images of bluegrass music in Nashville. Press Alt+Print Screen to capture an image of the first screen of search results, and then paste the image in a new Paint file. Save the file as **Nashville Images** in the Tutorial.06\Case1 folder provided with your Data Files.

10. Switch to any other search provider, and display the results of the original search for information about bluegrass music in Nashville. Modify the search to show information about bluegrass music not in Nashville. Press Alt+Print Screen to capture an image of the first screen of search results, and then paste the image in a new Paint file. Save the file as **Not Nashville** in the Tutorial.06\Case1 folder provided with your Data Files.

11. Close all open windows.

12. Submit the results of the preceding steps to your instructor, either in printed or electronic form, as requested.

| Apply | **Case Problem 2** |

Use the skills you learned in the tutorial to search for files and information for a pet adoption organization.

For a list of Data Files in the Case2 folder, see page 265.

Amherst Pet Adoption   Michelle Rangely is the director of the Amherst Pet Adoption agency in Amherst, Massachusetts. She is developing a presentation to give to local groups such as parent-teacher organizations, neighborhood associations, and senior centers about the pets available at the agency and the value they provide to people and families. She asks you to help her organize the pictures she has of pets and research information about the benefits of keeping a pet. She also wants to find photographs of wildlife for part of her presentation. Because she will eventually distribute the presentation via e-mail, she wants to be aware of file size so that she can select small image files. Complete the following steps:

1. Open the **Case2** folder in the Tutorial.06 folder provided with your Data Files.

2. Add a tag to each file in the Case2 folder to identify the type of animal shown in the photo. Use **cat**, **dog**, **duck**, **rabbit**, or **parrot** as a tag. (*Hint*: Use a Large Icons or Extra Large Icons view to see the images clearly.)

3. Using a file's Properties dialog box, add **Available for adoption** as the comment in the following photos: Pic01, Pic04, Pic06, and Pic09.

✦ EXPLORE

4. Search for photos of cats that are available for adoption. (*Hint*: Start your search using **comment** as the property name in the Search box.) Move the files you found to a new subfolder named **Cats to Adopt** in the Case2 folder.

✦ EXPLORE

5. Using **Dimensions** as the property name in the search box, find files that are 120 pixels wide. Press Alt+Print Screen to capture an image of the search results window showing the files you found. Paste the image in a new Paint file, and save the file as **Dim 120** in the Tutorial.06\Case2 folder provided with your Data Files.

6. In any of the indexed locations on your computer and in the Tutorial.06\Case2 folder, search for files that are exactly 16 KB in size. Press Alt+Print Screen to capture an image of the search results window showing the files you found. Paste the image in a new Paint file, and save the file as **16 KB** in the Tutorial.06\Case2 folder provided with your Data Files.

7. In any of the indexed locations on your computer, search for picture files that have *wildlife* as a tag. Press Alt+Print Screen to capture an image of the search results window showing the files you found. Paste the image in a new Paint file, and save the file as **Wildlife** in the Tutorial.06\Case2 folder provided with your Data Files.

8. In any of the indexed locations on your computer, search for picture files that have *wildlife* as a tag and a file size less than 200 KB. Press Alt+Print Screen to capture an image of the search results window showing the files you found. Paste the image in a new Paint file, and save the file as **Small Pix** in the Tutorial.06\Case2 folder provided with your Data Files.

9. Search for a program on your computer that lets you connect to a network projector to play presentations. Start the program, and then press Alt+Print Screen to capture an image of the opening window. Paste the image in a new Paint file. Save the file as **Projector Program** in the Tutorial.06\Case2 folder provided with your Data Files. Close the projector program.

10. Start Internet Explorer, and use Windows Live Search to find Web pages providing information on the benefits of adopting pets. Narrow the search to Web pages that provide this information only about Amherst, Massachusetts. Press Alt+Print Screen to capture an image of the first screen of search results, and then paste the image in a new Paint file. Save the file as **Amherst Pets** in the Tutorial.06\Case2 folder provided with your Data Files.

11. Switch to any other search provider, and use it to conduct the original search for information about providing information on the benefits of adopting pets. Modify the search to show only news items in the search results. Press Alt+Print Screen to capture an image of the first screen of search results, and then paste the image in a new Paint file. Save the file as **Pet News** in the Tutorial.06\Case2 folder provided with your Data Files. Close Paint and Internet Explorer.

12. Submit the results of the preceding steps to your instructor, either in printed or electronic form, as requested.

| Create | **Case Problem 3** |

Using the figures as guides, find files and information for a small antiques shop.

For a list of Data Files in the Case3 folder, see page 265.

Vandemain Antiques   Harold Dougal recently bought an antiques shop named Vandemain Antiques in Asheville, North Carolina. Harold wants to promote his most unusual objects in the local visitor's magazine. He asks you to help him find appropriate images and to research information about his competitors in Asheville. Complete the following steps:

1. Open the **Case3** folder in the Tutorial.06 folder provided with your Data Files.
2. Conduct a search to produce the results shown in Figure 6-42.

Figure 6-42

3. Press Alt+Print Screen to capture an image of the search results, and then paste the image in a new Paint file. Save the file as **Search1** in the Tutorial.06\Case3 folder provided with your Data Files.
4. Conduct another search to produce the results shown in Figure 6-43.

Figure 6-43

5. Press Alt+Print Screen to capture an image of the search results, and then paste the image in a new Paint file. Save the file as **Search2** in the Tutorial.06\Case3 folder provided with your Data Files.
6. Conduct another search to produce the results shown in Figure 6-44.

Figure 6-44

7. Press Alt+Print Screen to capture an image of the first screen of search results, and then paste the image in a new Paint file. Save the file as **Search3** in the Tutorial.06\ Case3 folder provided with your Data Files.

8. Start Internet Explorer, and conduct a search to produce the results shown in Figure 6-45.

Figure 6-45

9. Press Alt+Print Screen to capture an image of the first screen of search results, and then paste the image in a new Paint file. Save the file as **Search4** in the Tutorial.06\Case3 folder provided with your Data Files. Close Paint and Internet Explorer.

10. Submit the results of the preceding steps to your instructor, either in printed or electronic form, as requested.

Research | **Case Problem 4**

Work with the skills you've learned, and use the Internet, to learn about other ways to search for information.

There are no Data Files needed for this Case Problem.

Ask Me Anything   Diana and Paul Seefert are former librarians who recently started a company called Ask Me Anything in San Antonio, Texas. They provide a wide range of research services, including finding marketing and demographic information for businesses, answering questions about trivia, and uncovering local history stories. When they were trained as librarians, they learned to use mostly print documents as source materials. They hired you as an intern to help them learn how to take full advantage of the Internet. Complete the following steps:

1. Start Internet Explorer and use any search provider to research the difference between search engines, metasearch engines, and subject directories.

2. Find an example of each type of search tool and capture an image of its main page. Save the search engine image in a file named **Search Engine** in the Case4 folder. Save the metasearch engine image in a file named **Metasearch** in the Case4 folder. Save the subject directory image in a file named **Subject Directory** in the Case4 folder.

3. Use any search provider to find information about Boolean logic or Boolean operators. Narrow the results to find pages that explain how to use Boolean logic or operators to find information on the Web. Create a document using WordPad or another word-processing program with four column headings: **Operator**, **Alternate Operator**, **Description**, and **Example**. Enter information in each column to describe at least four Boolean operators you can use to search the Web. Complete the columns according to the following descriptions.

Operator	Alternate Operator	Description	Examples
List text terms for Boolean operators.	List symbols used for Boolean operators, if any.	Provide a brief description of the operator or its purpose.	Give examples of how to use the operator, one using the text operator, and one using the symbol (if possible).

4. Save the document as **Boolean** in the Case4 folder provided with your Data Files.

5. Submit the results of the preceding steps to your instructor, either in printed or electronic form, as requested.

Review | **Quick Check Answers**

Session 6.1

1. one or more conditions that a file or folder must meet to have Windows find it
2. True
3. Search pane
4. Select the file and then review the information in the Details pane, or select the file and then view its contents in the Preview pane.
5. indexed locations
6. False
7. tags, ratings, titles, authors, and comments
8. You would find files that contain *landscape* as a tag or *beach* in any file property.

Session 6.2

1. a Web site that specializes in searching the Internet
2. False
3. quotation marks
4. True
5. use specific words instead of generic ones, form a question, and search the results
6. ad hoc

Ending Data Files

Tutorial.06 → **Tutorial**

Review

Media Program.jpg
Videos.jpg
Weather.jpg
Weather Images.jpg
Weather Meeting.jpg

Case1

Backup Program.jpg
DVD Program.jpg
Nashville Images.jpg
Not Nashville.jpg
WMA.search-ms

Case2

16 KB.jpg
Amherst Pets.jpg
Dim 120.jpg
Pet News.jpg
Projector Program.jpg
Small Pix.jpg
Wildlife.jpg

Case3

Search1.jpg
Search2.jpg
Search3.jpg
Search4.jpg

Case4

Boolean.rtf
Metasearch.jpg
Search Engine.jpg
Subject Directory.jpg

Reality Check

Now that you are familiar with the Windows Vista tools that can help you personalize your computer, make it more secure, and communicate with others, set up your computer to suit your style of work. As you select settings, capture and save images of your computer so you can document what you've done. Complete the following tasks:

1. Start Windows Vista and log on, if necessary.
2. Set up shortcuts on your desktop to the folders, devices, and documents you use often.
3. Change the desktop image, screen saver, Quick Launch toolbar, and Start menu to suit your preferences.
4. Use Internet Explorer to research themes you can use on your computer. If you find a theme you like, download and install it on your computer.
5. Open the dialog box showing your screen saver, and then capture an image of the desktop.
6. In Internet Explorer, add the Web pages that you visit often to your Favorites list. Open the Favorites Center, and then capture an image of the Internet Explorer window.
7. Using Windows Contacts, create contacts for your correspondents. Capture an image of the main Windows Contacts window.
8. Using Windows Calendar, set up your appointments and tasks for the upcoming week. Capture an image of the appointment calendar.
9. Open the Windows Vista Security Center and make sure you are using all of the recommended security settings. Capture an image of the Security Center window. Do the same for Windows Mail and Internet Explorer.
10. Submit the images you captured to your instructor, either in printed or electronic form, as requested.

Objectives

- Prepare to connect to the Internet
- Set up a broadband connection
- Set up a wireless connection
- Set up a dial-up connection
- Troubleshoot your Internet connection

Connecting Computers to the Internet

Setting Up an Internet Connection

Appendix A

Windows Vista makes it easy to connect to the Internet, whether your computer uses a DSL modem, cable modem, or dial-up connection. This appendix is designed for you if you are working with your own computer and want to connect to the Internet. It discusses the most popular types of technologies for connecting to the Internet, and explains what you need to prepare for connecting. It also discusses the pros and cons of the various connection methods. This appendix provides step-by-step instructions for setting up a broadband Internet connection in Windows Vista, a wireless Internet connection, and a dial-up Internet connection. Finally, the appendix lists suggestions for troubleshooting these types of connections if you have trouble accessing the Internet.

Starting Data Files

There are no Student Data Files needed for this appendix.

Preparing to Connect to the Internet

Windows Vista makes communicating with computers easier than ever because it provides tools that allow you to connect your computer to other computers and to the Internet. If you are using a computer on a university or institutional network or any other type of local area network (LAN), you are probably already connected to the Internet, and you can skip this appendix. This appendix is useful for people who are not connected to the Internet but who have their own computer and devices designed for accessing the Internet, including a modem and phone line or cable connections. Figure A-1 describes what you need to set up an Internet connection.

Figure A-1 ▶ **What you need to set up an Internet connection**

Device or Service	Type	Description
Internet service provider (ISP)	National or local	An ISP provides access to the Internet. You sign up for an account with an ISP as you do for telephone service or utilities. Some ISPs, such as America Online (AOL), serve a broad area, while others are more limited.
Hardware	Broadband	A high-capacity, high-speed device that is usually included as part of the start-up hardware from your ISP when you sign up for a broadband account
	Dial-up	A device that usually comes installed in your computer and lets you connect to an ISP via telephone lines
	Cables	Cables that connect your modem to your computer or phone jack

To access the Internet, you need to connect your computer to an Internet service provider (ISP), which is a company that provides Internet access. ISPs maintain servers that are directly connected to the Internet 24 hours a day. You use hardware attached to your computer—either broadband or dial-up devices—to contact your ISP's server and use its Internet connection. You pay a fee for this service, most often a flat monthly rate.

After you set up a computer with the appropriate hardware and establish an account with an ISP, you can use Windows Vista to manage the connection to the Internet. This appendix explains how to use the tools in Windows Vista to set up a broadband or a dial-up connection to the Internet.

Using a Broadband Connection

As the popularity of the Internet has increased, the technologies for connecting to the Internet have improved, providing faster and more reliable connections. If you want to use the Internet to listen to Web radio stations, download music and videos to your computer, send digital photographs to family and friends, play online games, or browse animated Web sites, you need an Internet connection that lets you transfer data quickly. The most popular technology that provides a fast Internet connection is called a **broadband connection**, which is a high-capacity, high-speed medium for transmitting voice, video, and data at the same time. The two most common and practical broadband connections for home and small office users are digital subscriber lines (DSL) and digital cable connections. DSL and digital cable connections are fast because they have a lot of **bandwidth**, which is the amount of data that can be transmitted per second through a connection. The bandwidth for digital cable allows speeds from 64 kilobits per second (Kbps) to 20 megabits per second (Mbps), and DSL allows between 128 Kbps and 7.5 Mbps.

A DSL connection uses telephone lines to connect your computer to your ISP. See Figure A-2. Your ISP usually provides and installs a DSL modem with your computer and a DSL splitter at your home or office. The modem is plugged into your computer on one end and a telephone jack on the other. When you connect to the Internet, the DSL splitter separates the computer data signals from your voice telephone signals, so a DSL connection does not interrupt your phone service. The DSL splitter connects to the public phone lines and uses them to exchange computer data with your ISP, which provides Internet access to you.

DSL connection ◀ **Figure A-2**

One advantage of a DSL connection is that it is always on, maintaining a constant high-speed, high-bandwidth connection to the Internet. The speed and bandwidth varies, however, depending on the distance between your DSL modem and the DSL access multiplexer (DSLAM). The greater the distance, the lower the bandwidth and speed of your connection. The maximum distance is about three miles.

A digital cable connection is also a fast and popular way to connect to the Internet. This broadband technology uses a cable modem attached to cable television lines to connect your computer to your ISP. See Figure A-3. As with DSL connections, digital cable connections are always on. One consideration for digital cable is that users within a geographic location, such as an apartment or neighborhood, share bandwidth. When only a few people in that location are online, the digital cable connection can be very fast. When many people in that location are online, the connection often slows. Because the performance of digital cable can vary, people who are seeking broadband connections and live within range of a DSLAM often opt for DSL over digital cable.

Figure A-3 ▷ Digital cable connection

As mentioned earlier, before you can use a broadband service to connect to the Internet, you need to find an ISP that works with DSL or digital cable. The ISP often provides the special equipment you need, such as a cable modem, and establishes an account you use to connect to their server. The ISP also provides account information, including a user name and password, to identify you to the ISP's server. You need this information to set up an Internet connection in Windows Vista.

Using a Wireless Connection

Many personal computers, especially laptops and other mobile computers, use a wireless connection to access the Internet. A **wireless connection** uses infrared light or radio-frequency signals, rather than cables, to transmit data from your computer to a broadband device that connects you to the Internet. To establish a wireless Internet connection in your home, for example, you typically need the following equipment:

- **Broadband Internet connection**: Establish at least one physical connection to the Internet through a broadband connection, such as a DSL or cable modem.
- **Wireless router**: A **router** is a computer device that converts the signals from your Internet connection into a wireless broadcast.

- **Computer with wireless capabilities**: Your computer needs a wireless network adapter or a built-in wireless network card to communicate with the router. This wireless device detects and interprets the wireless broadcast signals transmitted by your wireless router. Most recent computers provide built-in wireless capabilities, especially portable computers. If your computer does not have built-in wireless capabilities, you can use a wireless network adapter, which typically plugs into a USB port on a desktop computer or a card slot on a laptop.

After you acquire the equipment you need for a wireless connection, you need to set up a **wireless network**, which is a way to share Internet access, files, and printers among a group of computers. If you are setting up a wireless network at the same time that you establish a broadband connection to the Internet, your ISP often configures the network for you. Even if your ISP does not provide this service, you can establish a wireless network by connecting your wireless router to your DSL or cable modem, as shown in Figure A-4.

Setting up a wireless Internet connection   **Figure A-4**

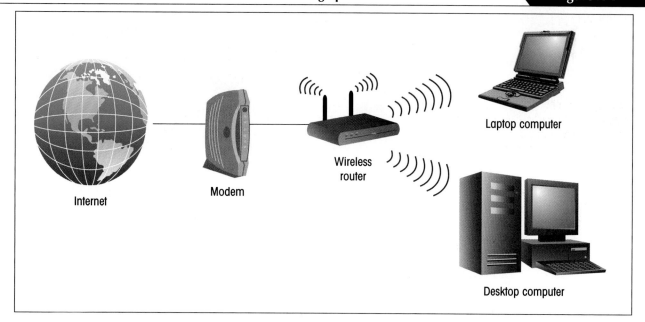

Internet — Modem — Wireless router — Laptop computer — Desktop computer

After you set up a wireless network at home, the wireless card or adapter on your computer detects the network so you can use it to connect to the Internet.

If you are away from your wireless home nework, you can connect to the Internet without cables by using a **hotspot**, a public space equipped with wireless Internet access, such as a hotel, airport, convention center, or restaurant. To connect to a hotspot, you need a computer, typically a laptop, with wireless capabilities. As mentioned earlier, most new laptops come equipped with wireless technology. Older laptops require a wireless access card. When you are in range of a hotspot, you can turn on your computer and check to see if you're receiving a network signal. You might need to sign in with information such as user name, password, and method of payment. After you do so, you are connected to the Internet.

Using a Dial-Up Connection

If affordable broadband service is not available in your area, you can connect to the Internet using a **dial-up connection**, which uses a modem in your computer connected to public telephone lines to transmit your signal to a server at your ISP. See Figure A-5.

Figure A-5 ▶ **Phone line connection to the Internet**

To establish a dial-up connection, you attach the modem in your computer to a phone jack and set the modem to dial the ISP's server, which is directly connected to the Internet. Although regular phone lines are often the only practical choice for some home and small business users, using a dial-up connection has a few drawbacks. Unlike a broadband connection, which is always on, you maintain a dial-up connection only as long as you need to access the Internet because it uses the same telephone lines that you use to make phone calls—if you want to talk on the phone while you are online, you need a second phone line. Phone connections are also less reliable than broadband connections. If there are any problems with the phone connection, you can lose data. Furthermore, the bandwidth of a dial-up connection is much lower than broadband connections. Although it is adequate for reading textual information and transferring small files, a dial-up connection can be inefficient when you want to work with multimedia files online. In some areas, **Integrated Services Digital Network (ISDN) lines**, which are telephone wires that provide a completely digital path from one computer to another, are dropping in price so that small businesses and homeowners can afford them. ISDN lines offer much more bandwidth and speed than regular phone lines, though you must still establish dial-up connections to use them to access the Internet.

Setting Up a Broadband Connection

After you set up an account with an ISP and configure the hardware you need to make a broadband connection to the Internet, you're ready to use Windows Vista to access the Internet. If your ISP sends a service person to your home or office to set up a broadband Internet connection, you do not need to set it up yourself. Your broadband connection is configured by the service person and ready to use.

If you need to set up a broadband connection yourself, you can do so by using the Connect to the Internet wizard. This wizard guides you through the steps of connecting to the Internet using a broadband, wireless, or dial-up connection. You choose the broadband method if your computer is connected directly to a broadband modem (a DSL or cable modem), and you have a Point-to-Point Protocol or Ethernet (PPPoE) Internet account. With this type of account, you must provide a user name and password to connect. (Your ISP indicates what type of account it is providing when you sign up for the account.)

To set up a broadband connection:

1. Click the **Start** button 🌐, and then click **Control Panel**. Control Panel opens in Category view.

   Trouble? If Control Panel opens in Classic view, click the Control Panel Home link in the left pane to open Control Panel in Category view.

2. In the Network and Internet category, click **Connect to the Internet**. The Connect to the Internet wizard starts and asks how you want to connect to the Internet. See Figure A-6.

   Trouble? If the Connect to the Internet link does not appear in the Network and Internet category, your computer might already be connected to the Internet. If you still want to set up a broadband connection, disconnect from the Internet first by clicking the network icon in the notification area of the taskbar, clicking Connect or disconnect, and then clicking the Disconnect button. Repeat Step 2.

   Trouble? If the Connect to the Internet link does not appear in the Network and Internet category and you are not connected to the Internet, click Network and Internet in Control Panel, click Network and Sharing Center, click Set up a connection or network, and then click Connect to the Internet.

Connect to the Internet wizard **Figure A-6**

3. Click **Broadband (PPPoE)**. The next dialog box in the wizard opens, requesting your user name and password. See Figure A-7.

| Figure A-7 | Providing your user name and password |

information provided by your ISP

click this check box if you want Windows to remember this password so you don't need to enter it again

you can provide a descriptive name for this connection to remember it easily

4. In the User name text box, type the user name your ISP gave you. This is often your first and last name combined without any spaces.

5. In the Password text box, type the password your ISP gave you.

6. Click the **Connect** button. Windows Vista sets up a broadband connection to the Internet, and then displays a dialog box indicating the connection was successful.

   Trouble? If the connection is not successful, Windows might identify the reason it cannot connect to the Internet. Follow the instructions or suggestions in the dialog box to solve the problem.

7. Click the **Next** button. Windows tests your Internet connection and lets you know you are connected to the Internet. Click the **Close** button.

To verify the connection, start a program that uses the Internet, such as Internet Explorer. A network icon also appears in the notification area of the taskbar to indicate your computer is connected to the Internet.

Troubleshooting a Broadband Connection

After you set up a broadband Internet connection, you can access the Internet with programs such as Internet Explorer and Windows Mail. Even if you shut down and restart your computer, you can access the Internet simply by starting Internet Explorer, for example—you don't need to contact your ISP to make a connection to their server first.

If your broadband connection is interrupted, make sure all the cables and wires are connected properly. If that doesn't solve the problem, you can perform the following steps to repair the connection.

To troubleshoot a broadband connection:

1. Right-click the **network** icon 🖳 in the notification area of the taskbar, and then click **Diagnose and repair**. Windows communicates with your network device and repairs the connection if possible. If Windows requires you to take action or it cannot solve the problem, the Windows Network Diagnostics window opens, listing possible problems. See Figure A-8. Your problems might differ.

Diagnosing broadband connection problems | **Figure A-8**

your list of problems will differ

if your computer has a wireless card or adapter, one suggestion is to connect to a wireless network

2. Read the possible problems to find the one that seems the most likely for your computer. Take the suggested action, and then click the option, if necessary.

3. If you still cannot connect to the Internet after attempting to repair the connection, perform the following troubleshooting tasks:

   • Check the status indicator lights on the DSL or cable modem to make sure that it is connected to your ISP.

   • Put the DSL or cable modem on standby (most modems have a Standby button or one with a similar name), and then make the modem active again. Wait a few minutes, and then test your Internet connection.

   • Note the actions you have already performed, and then contact your ISP.

Setting Up a Wireless Connection

You set up a wireless Internet connection using the Connect to the Internet wizard. When you do, you choose the wireless method if you are using a wireless router or network or if you're connecting to a hotspot (even if you also have a broadband connection).

To set up a wireless connection:

▶ 1. Open **Control Panel** in Category view, and then click **Connect to the Internet** in the Network and Internet category. The Connect to the Internet wizard starts and asks how you want to connect to the Internet.

   Trouble? If the Connect to the Internet link does not appear in the Network and Internet category, your computer might already be connected to the Internet. If you still want to set up a wireless connection, disconnect from the Internet first by clicking the network icon in the notification area of the taskbar, clicking Connect or disconnect, and then clicking the Disconnect button. Repeat Step 1.

   Trouble? If the Connect to the Internet link does not appear in the Network and Internet category and you are not connected to the Internet, click Network and Internet in Control Panel, click Network and Sharing Center, click Set up a connection or network, and then click Connect to the Internet.

▶ 2. Click **Wireless**. The next dialog box in the wizard opens, listing the wireless networks nearby. See Figure A-9. Your list of wireless networks will differ.

Figure A-9 ▶ **Selecting a wireless network**

click to refresh the list of wireless networks nearby

security icon indicates an unsecured network

signal icon indicates the strength of the wireless signal

▶ 3. Click the wireless network to which you want to connect, and then click the **Connect** button.

▶ **4.** If you are connecting to a secured network, type the network security key or passphrase you need to connect to this network. (Usually, the person who set up the network gives you this security information.) Then click the **Connect** button.

If you are connecting to an unsecured network, a dialog box opens indicating this network is unsecured. Click **Connect Anyway** to connect to the unsecured network.

Trouble? If you do not want to connect to the unsecured network, click **Connect to a different network** to return to the dialog box shown in Figure A-9, and then repeat Step 3.

Windows attempts to connect to the network, and then displays a dialog box indicating the connection was successful.

▶ **5.** Click the **Next** button. Windows tests your Internet connection and lets you know you are connected to the Internet. Click the **Close** button.

To troubleshoot a wireless connection, follow the steps in the "Troubleshooting a Broadband Connection" section.

Setting Up a Dial-Up Connection

You set up a dial-up Internet connection using the Connect to the Internet wizard. When you do, you choose the dial-up method if you are using a dial-up modem (not a DSL or cable modem) or an ISDN line to connect your computer to the Internet.

To set up a dial-up connection:

1. Open **Control Panel** in Category view, and then click **Connect to the Internet** in the Network and Internet category. The Connect to the Internet wizard starts and asks how you want to connect to the Internet.

   Trouble? If the Connect to the Internet link does not appear in the Network and Internet category, your computer might already be connected to the Internet. If you still want to set up a dial-up connection, disconnect from the Internet first by clicking the network icon in the notification area of the taskbar, clicking Connect or disconnect, and then clicking the Disconnect button. Repeat Step 1.

   Trouble? If the Connect to the Internet link does not appear in the Network and Internet category and you are not connected to the Internet, click Network and Internet in Control Panel, click Network and Sharing Center, click Set up a connection or network, and then click Connect to the Internet.

2. Click **Dial-up**. The next dialog box in the wizard opens, requesting information about your ISP account. See Figure A-10.

Figure A-10 Setting up a dial-up connection

Trouble? If Dial-up does not appear as an option, click Show connection options that this computer is not set up to use.

▶ **3.** In the Dial-up phone number text box, type the phone number your ISP gave you. This is the number your modem dials to contact your ISP.

▶ **4.** In the User name text box, type the user name or account name your ISP gave you.

▶ **5.** In the Password text box, type the password your ISP gave you.

▶ **6.** Click the **Connect** button. Windows Vista sets up a dial-up connection to the Internet, and then displays a dialog box indicating the connection was successful.

Trouble? If a Create button appears instead of a Connect button, click the Create button.

▶ **7.** Click the **Next** button. Windows tests your Internet connection and lets you know you are connected to the Internet. Click the **Close** button.

Your dial-up account remains connected until you disconnect from your account. In some cases, your ISP might disconnect you automatically if your computer is idle for several minutes.

To disconnect a dial-up connection:

▶ **1.** Right-click the **network** icon ▦ in the notification area of the taskbar, and then click **Disconnect**.

Troubleshooting a Dial-Up Connection

If your dial-up connection is interrupted, refer first to the "Troubleshooting a Broadband Connection" section for steps to solve the problem. If you are still having trouble making and maintaining a dial-up connection to the Internet, try performing the following steps:

- Make sure that you are dialing the correct number, including any required access numbers (such as 9), and that the number is not busy.
- Make sure that the phone jack is working by plugging in a working phone and checking for a dial tone. Similarly, make sure that the phone cable is working properly by plugging a working phone into the telephone jack of your modem and verifying you receive a dial tone.
- Make sure that the phone cable is plugged into the line jack on your modem, not the telephone jack.
- If you have call waiting, try disabling it, and then try the connection again.
- If someone picked up the phone while you were online, you might have been automatically disconnected. Try connecting again.
- Make sure that your modem is working properly. For more information, check the information that came with your modem or go to the manufacturer's Web site.
- Contact your telephone company to verify the quality of your line.

Tutorial Summary | Review

In this tutorial, you learned how to prepare to connect to the Internet if you need to set up an Internet connection on your own. You explored the hardware and technologies you need to use a broadband, wireless, or dial-up connection, and then you learned how to set up each type of connection. You also examined ways to troubleshoot your Internet connection if it is interrupted or experiences other problems.

Key Terms

bandwidth	hotspot	router
broadband connection	Integrated Services Digital	wireless connection
dial-up connection	Network (ISDN) line	wireless network

Ending Data Files

There are no ending Data Files for this tutorial.

Glossary/Index

Note: Boldface entries include definitions.

Special Characters

() (parentheses), WIN 285

"" (quotation marks), WIN 285

A

active program The program you are currently using. WIN 13

ActiveX control One of a set of technologies from Microsoft that enables interactive content on a Web page. WIN 239

ad hoc network A temporary network created for sharing files or an Internet connection. WIN 206

Additional Options category, WIN 119

add-on A product designed to complement another product; specifically, a program offered by any software vendor that provides enhancement features. WIN 243

Address bar
Internet Explorer, WIN 298
Windows Explorer, WIN 54, WIN 59–60

Address toolbar, WIN 136

Administrator user account, WIN 249

Advanced Appearance dialog box, WIN 125

adware A type of spyware that collects information about a computer user's browsing patterns in order to display advertisements in the user's Web browser. WIN 223

Aero The user interface in Windows Vista. WIN 4, WIN 13

AND, combining search criteria, WIN 285–287

antivirus software, updating, WIN 222–223

Appearance and Personalization category, WIN 119

application Software that a computer uses to complete tasks; also called program. WIN 2. *See also* program

appointment, scheduling in Windows Calendar, WIN 197–200

Appointment calendar, Windows Calendar window, WIN 197

B

Back button, Windows Explorer, WIN 54

Back Up and Restore, WIN 212

background, desktop, WIN 121–123

backup A duplicate copy of important files that you need. WIN 51

bandwidth The amount of data that can be transmitted per second. WIN A–2

Bcc line, e-mail messages, WIN 184

Block Senders list, WIN 234, WIN 235
adding senders, WIN 234

Boolean filter Any of the Boolean operators AND, OR, and NOT, which can be used to combine multiple search criteria into a single search expression. WIN 285–289
combining with file properties, WIN 287–288

broadband connection A connection that uses a high-capacity, high-speed medium capable of transmitting voice, video, and data simultaneously. The two most common and practical broadband connections for home and small office users are digital subscriber lines (DSL) and digital cable connections. WIN 162, WIN A–2—A4
setting up, WIN A6–A8
troubleshooting, WIN A8–A9

browser A program that locates, retrieves, and displays Web pages. Internet Explorer is the Microsoft browser. WIN 161–162

browsing history, clearing, WIN 246–247

C

cache The Temporary Internet Files folder on a computer. WIN 248

calendar
printing, WIN 201
sharing, WIN 200–201
Web, subscribing to, WIN 200

Calendar gadget, WIN 104

Calendars section, Windows Calendar window, WIN 197

categories, Control Panel, WIN 119–120

Cc line, e-mail messages, WIN 184

CD. *See* compact disc

Change Icon dialog box, WIN 103

Choose Search Options dialog box, WIN 296

click To press a mouse button and immediately release it. WIN 5

Clipboard A temporary storage area for files and information that you have copied or moved from one place and plan to use somewhere else. WIN 65–66

Clock, Language, and Region category, WIN 119

Clock dialog box, WIN 106

Clock gadget, WIN 104

collaborating with others. *See* Windows Meeting Space

collapse icon, WIN 53

color
desktop, WIN 123
display setting, WIN 130–131

color scheme A set of colors that can be applied to Windows elements. WIN 124
desktop elements, WIN 124–126

compact disc (CD) A removable optical disc that typically can store up to 680 MB of data. WIN 48

compressed (zipped) folder A folder that reduces the size of the files it contains. WIN 85–87

computer
controlling access, WIN 253
locking, WIN 254

Computer command, WIN 146

Computer window A tool that you use to view, organize, and access the programs, files, and drives on your computer. WIN 10
copying files and folders, WIN 67–68
panes, WIN 52

Connect To command, WIN 146

Connect to the Internet wizard, WIN A7

contact
adding in Windows Mail, WIN 193–195
groups, WIN 195

Contacts gadget, WIN 104

Microsoft Windows Vista Task Reference

TASK	PAGE #	RECOMMENDED METHOD
Colors setting, change	WIN 131	Right-click the desktop, click Personalize, click Display Settings, click Colors button arrow, click a color setting, click OK
Compressed folder, create	WIN 85	In a folder window, select the files and folders to be compressed, right-click the selection, point to Send to on the shortcut menu, click Compressed (zipped) Folder, type a folder name, press Enter
Compressed folder, extract all files and folders from	WIN 86	Right-click the compressed folder, click Extract All on the shortcut menu
Connection, set up broadband	WIN A7	Click 🟦, click Control Panel, click Connect to the Internet, click Broadband (PPPoE), type user name and password, click Connect, click Next, click Close
Connection, set up dial-up	WIN A12	Click 🟦, click Control Panel, click Connect to the Internet, click Dial-up, type telephone number, user name and password, click Connect, click Next, click Close
Connection, set up wireless	WIN A10	Click 🟦, click Control Panel, click Connect to the Internet, click Wireless, select network, click Connect, type network pass phrase, click Connect, click Next, click Close
Control Panel, open	WIN 118	Click 🟦, click Control Panel
Desktop background, change	WIN 121	See Reference Window: Changing the Desktop Background
Desktop colors, change	WIN 124	Right-click the desktop, click Personalize, click Window Color and Appearance, click a color, click OK
Desktop icon, change image for	WIN 103	Right-click the desktop, click Personalize, click Change desktop icons, click an icon, click Change Icon, select an image, click OK, click OK
Desktop icons, change location of	WIN 101	Right-click the desktop, point to View, click Auto Arrange to deselect that option, right-click the desktop, point to View, click Align to Grid to deselect that option, drag desktop icons to new location
Desktop icons, change size of	WIN 101	Right-click the desktop, point to View, click a size
Desktop icons, display standard	WIN 100	See Reference Window: Displaying Standard Desktop Icons
Desktop icons, hide	WIN 102	Right-click the desktop, point to View, click Show Desktop Icons to deselect that option
Desktop icons, sort	WIN 115	Right-click the desktop, click Sort By, select sort criterion
Desktop image, position	WIN 123	Right-click the desktop, click Personalize, click Desktop Background, click position option button, click OK
Desktop shortcut, create to drive	WIN 109	Drag the drive icon from a folder window to desktop
Desktop shortcut, create to file, folder, or program	WIN 111	Right-drag the file, folder, or program icon to desktop, click Create Shortcuts Here
Desktop shortcut, create to printer	WIN 114	Right-click the printer, click Create Shortcut
Desktop shortcut, delete	WIN 116	Click the shortcut, press Delete key
Desktop theme, change	WIN 126	Right-click the desktop, click Personalize, click Theme, click Theme button, click a theme, click OK
Desktop theme, save new	WIN 126	Right-click the desktop, click Personalize, click Theme, click Theme button, click My Current Theme, click Save As, type a name, click Save, click OK

TASK	PAGE #	RECOMMENDED METHOD
E-mail message, attach file to	WIN 190	Click 📎, double-click file
E-mail message, create	WIN 185	*See* Reference Window: Creating and Sending an E-mail Message
E-mail message, delete	WIN 189	Click message, click ✕
E-mail message, reply to	WIN 189	Click message, click Reply
Favorites Links list, add file or folder to	WIN 84	Drag a file or folder to the list
Favorites list, add Web page to	WIN 174	*See* Reference Window: Adding a Web Page to the Favorites List
Favorites list, open	WIN 174	Click ☆
Favorites, list, organize	WIN 175	*See* Reference Window: Organizing the Favorites List
File, copy	WIN 67	*See* Reference Window: Copying a File or Folder in Windows Explorer or Computer
File, create	WIN 71	Start program and enter data
File, delete	WIN 70	Right-click the file, click Delete on shortcut menu, click Yes
File, move	WIN 65	*See* Reference Window: Moving a File or Folder in a Folder Window
File, open from folder window	WIN 73	Navigate to the file, double-click the file
File, rename	WIN 69	Right-click the file, click Rename on shortcut menu, type new filename, press Enter
File, save	WIN 72	Click File, click Save As, navigate to a location, type filename, and then click Save
File, search for within folder	WIN 61	Click in the Search box, type word or phrase to be found in file or filename
Filename extension, show	WIN 82	Click Organize in folder window, click Folder and Search Options, click View, click Hide extensions for known file types to clear the check box
Files, select multiple	WIN 67	Hold down the Ctrl key and click files
Flip-3D, use	WIN 16	Click 🗗, press the Tab key to cycle through programs, click a program window
Folder list, expand	WIN 55	Click ▷
Folder window, return to a previously visited location	WIN 60	Click ▾, click a location in the list
Folder window, return to previous location	WIN 60	Click ⬅
Folder, copy	WIN 67	*See* Reference Window: Copying a File or Folder in Windows Explorer or Computer
Folder, create in Windows Explorer	WIN 63	*See* Reference Window: Creating a Folder Using Windows Explorer
Folder, delete	WIN 70	Right-click the folder, click Delete on shortcut menu, click Yes
Folder, filter files in	WIN 77	In a folder window, click a column heading arrow button, click a filter option
Folder, group files in	WIN 78–79	In a folder window, click a column heading arrow button, click Group
Folder, move	WIN 65	*See* Reference Window: Moving a File or Folder in a Folder Window
Folder, sort files in	WIN 75	In a folder window, click a column heading
Folder, stack files in	WIN 78	In a folder window, click a column heading arrow button, click a stacking option
Folders list, open or close	WIN 84	Click the Folders button
Gadget, customize	WIN 106	Click 🔧 on gadget

TASK	PAGE #	RECOMMENDED METHOD
Graphic file, use as desktop background	WIN 122	Right-click the desktop, click Personalize, click Desktop Background, click Browse, double-click graphic file, click OK
Help, find topic	WIN 38	In Help, click in the Search Help box, type word or phrase, click 🔍
Help, start	WIN 35	Click 🪟, click Help and Support
Internet Explorer, block pop-up ads in	WIN 242	See Reference Window: Blocking Pop-up Ads
Internet Explorer, delete browsing history in	WIN 246	Start Internet Explorer, click Tools, click Delete Browsing History, click Delete cookies, click Yes, click Delete history, click Yes, click Close
Internet Explorer, manage add-ons	WIN 243	Start Internet Explorer, click Tools, point to Manage Add-ons, click Enable or Disable Add-ons
Internet Explorer, select security settings in	WIN 245	See Reference Window: Selecting Privacy Settings
Internet Explorer, set Phishing Filter	WIN 238	Click 🪟, click Internet Explorer, click Tools, point to Phishing Filter, click Turn On Automatic Website Checking, click OK
Internet Explorer, start	WIN 162	Click 🪟, click Internet Explorer
Link, open in new tab	WIN 171	Right-click the link, click Open Link in New Tab
List box, scroll	WIN 24	Click the scroll down or up arrow button, or drag the scroll box
Meeting, start	WIN 307	See Reference Window: Starting a Meeting and Inviting Participants
Menu option, select	WIN 22	Click the option on the menu
New tab, open	WIN 171	Click 📄
Password, create for user account	WIN 252	Click 🪟, click user icon, click Create a password
Permission, assign to folder	WIN 255	Click the folder, click Share, click arrow to right of first text box, click a user name, click Add, click Permission Level, click a permission level, click Share, click Done
Program, close	WIN 12	Click ❌
Program, close inactive	WIN 16	Right-click the program button on the taskbar, click Close
Program, start	WIN 10	See Reference Window: Starting a Program
Program, switch to another open	WIN 14	Click the program button on the taskbar
Property, add to file	WIN 281	Right-click the file, click Properties, click Details, type property, click OK
Quick Launch toolbar, add program icon to	WIN 136	Drag the program icon to the Quick Launch toolbar
Recycle Bin, open	WIN 7	Double-click 🗑
Screen resolution, change	WIN 130	Right-click the desktop, click Personalize, click Display Settings, drag the Resolution slider, click OK
Screen saver delay time, change	WIN 128	Right-click the desktop, click Personalize, click Screen Saver, click Wait arrow buttons, click OK
Screen Saver, change	WIN 128	Right-click the desktop, click Personalize, click Screen Saver, click Screen Saver button, click a screen saver, click OK
ScreenTip, view	WIN 5	Position pointer over an item
Search, locate file by category	WIN 272	See Reference Window: Searching for a File by Category
Search, locate file by type	WIN 270	See Reference Window: Searching for a File by Type
Search, locate file using multiple criteria	WIN 277	See Reference Window: Searching for a File Using Multiple Criteria
Search, locate program	WIN 290	See Reference Window: Searching for Programs on the Start Menu
Search, save	WIN 278	Click Save Search, click Save

TASK	PAGE #	RECOMMENDED METHOD
Search, select Internet search provider	WIN 304	*See* Reference Window: Selecting a Search Provider
Security Center, open	WIN 213	Click 🪟, click Control Panel, click Security, click Security Center
Sidebar, add gadget to	WIN 104	Click ➕, double-click a gadget
Sidebar, keep on top of other windows	WIN 107	Right-click the sidebar, click Properties, click Sidebar is always on top of other windows, click OK
Sidebar, remove gadget from	WIN 108	Point to the gadget, click ❌
Start menu icons, change size	WIN 141	Right-click 🪟, click Properties, click Customize, click Use large icons, click OK
Start menu, add command to	WIN 145	Right-click 🪟, click Properties, click Customize, select command, click OK
Start Menu, open	WIN 6	Click 🪟
Start menu, pin a program to	WIN 143	Right-click the program name in the Start menu, click Pin to Start Menu
Tag, add to file	WIN 281	*See* Reference Window: Adding Tags to Files
Taskbar, add Desktop toolbar to	WIN 138	Right-click the taskbar, point to Toolbars, click Desktop
Taskbar, create Custom toolbar for	WIN 139	*See* Reference Window: Creating a Custom Taskbar Toolbar
Taskbar, hide	WIN 135	Right-click the taskbar, click Properties, click Auto-hide the taskbar, click OK
Taskbar, move	WIN 133	*See* Reference Window: Moving and Resizing the Taskbar
Taskbar, resize	WIN 133	*See* Reference Window: Moving and Resizing the Taskbar
User account, create new	WIN 250	*See* Reference Window: Creating a Password-Protected User Account
User picture, change	WIN 140	Click 🪟, click user picture, click Change your picture, click picture, click Change Picture
View, change in a folder window	WIN 32	*See* Reference Window: Changing the Icon View
Web calendar, publish	WIN 201	*See* Reference Window: Publishing a Web Calendar
Web calendar, subscribe to	WIN 200	*See* Reference Window: Subscribing to a Web Calendar
Web page, open using URL	WIN 165	*See* Reference Window: Opening a Web Page Using a URL
Web page, print	WIN 176	Click 🖨 ▾, click Print
Web page, return to next	WIN 168	Click ➡
Web page, return to previous	WIN 168	Click ⬅
Web page, return to recent	WIN 169	Click ▾, click a page
Web page, return to using History List	WIN 169	Click ⭐, click History, click a date, click a Web page
Window colors, change	WIN 124	Right-click the desktop, click Personalize, click Window Color and Appearance, click color, click OK (Aero only)
Window, maximize	WIN 20	Click ◻
Window, minimize	WIN 19	Click ▬
Window, move	WIN 20	Drag the title bar
Window, resize	WIN 21	Drag an edge or corner
Window, restore	WIN 20	Click ◲
Windows Calendar, schedule an appointment	WIN 197	*See* Reference Window: Scheduling an Appointment in Windows Calendar

TASK	PAGE #	RECOMMENDED METHOD
Windows Defender, perform a quick scan with	WIN 222	*See* Reference Window: Performing a Quick Scan with Windows Defender
Windows Defender, schedule scan	WIN 226	Start Windows Defender, click Tools, click Options, click Approximate time
Windows Defender, start	WIN 222	Click 🟦, click Control Panel, click Security, click Windows Defender
Windows Explorer, start	WIN 33	Click 🟦, point to All Programs, click Accessories, click Windows Explorer
Windows Firewall, add an exception	WIN 214	*See* Reference Window: Adding a Program to the Windows Firewall Exception List
Windows Mail, add a contact	WIN 191	*See* Reference Window: Adding a Contact in Windows Mail
Windows Mail, add a sender to the Blocked Senders or Safe Senders list	WIN 232	*See* Reference Window: Adding a Sender to the Blocked Senders or Safe Senders List
Windows Mail, set junk e-mail options	WIN 232	Start Windows Mail, click Tools, click Junk E-mail Options
Windows Mail, start	WIN 181	Click 🟦, point to All Programs, click Windows Mail
Windows Update, set up	WIN 217	Click 🟦, click Control Panel, click Security, click Security Center, click Windows Update, click Change settings
Windows Vista, log off	WIN 39	Click 🟦, point to ▶, click Log Off
Windows Vista, start	WIN 2	Turn on the computer
Windows Vista, turn off	WIN 39	Click 🟦, point to ▶, click Shut Down
Windows, arrange on desktop	WIN 132	Right-click the taskbar, click Cascade Windows, Show Windows Stacked, or Show Windows Side by Side